ELITE WOMEN IN ASCENDANCY IRELAND 1690–1745

Irish Historical Monograph Series

ISSN 1740-1097

Previous titles in this series

I. Ruling Ireland 1685–1742: Politics, Politicians and Parties, *D. W. Hayton*, 2004

II. Lord Broghill and the Cromwellian Union with Ireland and Scotland, *Patrick Little*, 2004

III. Irish Migrants in New Zealand, 1840–1937: 'The Desired Haven', *Angela McCarthy*, 2005

IV. The Fenian Ideal and Irish Nationalism, 1882–1916, *M. J. Kelly*, 2006

V. Loyalism in Ireland, 1789–1829, *Allan Blackstock*, 2007

VI. Constructing the Past: Writing Irish History, 1600–1800, *edited by Mark Williams and Stephen Forrest*, 2010

VII. The Making of the Irish Protestant Ascendancy: The Life of William Conolly, 1662–1729, *Patrick Walsh*, 2010

VIII. The Militia in Eighteenth-Century Ireland: In Defence of the Protestant Interest, *Neal Garnham*, 2012

IX. The Anglo-Irish Experience, 1680–1730: Religion, Identity and Patriotism, *D. W. Hayton*, 2012

X. The Presbyterians of Ulster, 1680–1730, *Robert Whan*, 2013

XI. The Welsh and the Shaping of Early Modern Ireland, 1558–1641, *Rhys Morgan*, 2014

XII. The Irish in the Spanish Armies in the Seventeenth Century, *Eduardo de Mesa*, 2014

XIII. Consumption and Culture in Sixteenth-Century Ireland: Saffron, Stockings and Silk, *Susan Flavin*, 2014

ELITE WOMEN IN ASCENDANCY IRELAND 1690–1745

Imitation and Innovation

Rachel Wilson

THE BOYDELL PRESS

First published 2015
The Boydell Press, Woodbridge

ISBN 978-1-78327-039-2

The Boydell Press is an imprint of Boydell & Brewer Ltd
PO Box 9, Woodbridge, Suffolk IP12 3DF, UK
and of Boydell & Brewer Inc.
668 Mt Hope Avenue, Rochester, NY 14620–2731, USA
website: www.boydellandbrewer.com

A CIP catalogue record for this title is available from the British Library

The publisher has no responsibility for the continued existence or accuracy of URLs for external or third-party internet websites referred to in this book, and does not guarantee that any content on such websites is, or will remain, accurate or appropriate

This publication is printed on acid-free paper

Typeset by Fakenham Prepress Solutions, Fakenham, Norfolk NR21 8NN

Printed and bound in Great Britain by
TJ International Ltd, Padstow, Cornwall

FSC www.fsc.org MIX Paper from responsible sources FSC® C013056

Dedicated to my parents,

Adair and Elizabeth,

with love

Contents

Acknowledgements

I would like to express my gratitude towards the staff of the Public Record Office of Northern Ireland, the National Library of Ireland, the National Archives of Scotland, Trinity College Dublin, the Irish Architectural Archive, the British Library, the Chatsworth House Archives and the McClay Library at Queen's University Belfast, for the assistance they gave me during my research for this book. I would also like to thank Michael Page of the Surrey History Centre for the use of his transcripts of the Brodrick papers.

Many friends and colleagues have been invaluable to me during the research and writing process. I particularly wish to thank Professor David Hayton for all his advice and help over the past few years, for giving me the benefit of his expertise on early modern Ireland on many occasions, and for looking over earlier drafts of this book. I would also like to thank Georgina Larkin for proofreading the manuscript, and Erica Doherty, Michael Houston, Katie Houston and Louise Nash for all their moral support, for keeping me company on the occasional research trip, and in Louise's case, for putting me up (and putting up with me) when I was visiting the archives in Edinburgh.

Last, but by no means least, I wish to thank my parents. Not only have they encouraged my love of history since I was little, they have also shown me unending support and unstinting generosity, both in the completion of this book and in everything else I have ever done. Although I am sure I haven't said it as often as I should have, I am forever grateful for this help, for the holidays they surrendered to my research trips and for the times they put up with my grumpiness – verging on a caveperson persona really – when I was in the midst of a bad day. In addition, my Dad has always solved any and all computer problems which have come my way, while drilling into me the mantra 'back-up, back-up, back-up' so that my work is probably better insured against loss than the house! My Mum meanwhile, has always been on hand to proofread sections of text for me when I was too tired to even spell my own name correctly any more, while making sure that I didn't slip into a lifestyle consisting of junk food eaten at the computer and no natural light. My book would not be here without them and so it is to them that I dedicate it.

Abbreviations

The following abbreviations are used throughout:

Archives

BL	British Library
IAA	Irish Architectural Archive
NLI	National Library of Ireland
NRS	National Records of Scotland
PRONI	Public Record Office of Northern Ireland
SHC	Surrey History Centre
TCD	Trinity College Dublin
TNA	The National Archives [of the United Kingdom]

Collections

Add. MS	Additional Manuscript

Other

Cal. Treas. bks.	*Calendar of Treasury books and papers*, ed. William Shaw (5 vols, London, 1897–1903)
D.I.B.	*Dictionary of Irish Biography*, accessed online at www.dib.cambridge.org
H.C. 1690–1715	Eveline Cruickshanks, Stuart Handley and D.W. Hayton (eds), *The history of parliament: the House of Commons 1690–1715* (Cambridge, 2002)
H.M.C.	*Historical Manuscripts Commission*
Oxford D.N.B.	*Oxford Dictionary of National Biography*, accessed online at www.oxforddnb.com

Please note that all contemporary printed sources have been consulted through 'Early English Books Online' or 'Eighteenth Century Collections Online'. These resources were accessed online at (http://eebo.chadwyck.com.queens.ezp1.qub.ac.uk/home) and (http://gale.cengage.co.uk/product-highlights/history/eighteenth-century-collections-online.aspx).

For pamphlets and other contemporary works with particularly long titles, shortened versions have been employed throughout the text, while the full citation is given in the Bibliography.

Unless otherwise stated, information on the legislation of the Irish parliament is taken from the Irish Legislation Database (www.qub.ac.uk/ild).

A note on the presentation of material in the text

All dates have been given in Old Style, but with the year taken to begin on 1 January. Dates have been presented as they were found in the manuscripts, though if only the Old Style year was provided, the New Style has been given in square brackets. If it was unclear to which year a letter belonged dated between 1 January and 24 March, question marks have been employed within the brackets. Estimated dates are preceded by c. and are presented in brackets.

All spellings and capital letters have been modernised and abbreviations silently expanded unless otherwise indicated. Punctuation has been unaltered, with occasional exceptions where the meaning of the original is clear. Again, these changes have been made silently. Words which were unclear in the original text have been supplied in square brackets within question marks. Those which were completely illegible or absent due to damage to the manuscript are denoted by an ellipsis and a question mark, also within square brackets. My own interpolations are presented in italics within square brackets.

Introduction

Over the past twenty-five years, a mountain of material has been written (and continues to be written) on the English elite of the late seventeenth and eighteenth centuries and, increasingly, on its female members. Some of this material has taken the form of biographies of the more famous (or infamous) ladies of the age, including queens, royal mistresses, royal favourites like Sarah, duchess of Marlborough, and politicians and socialites like Georgiana, duchess of Devonshire.[1] Other scholars have concentrated on the lives of the female elite as a whole, producing numerous survey-style books which chart their group history at court and around the country.[2] For a more detailed analysis of their education, legal position, domestic, political, social or cultural roles, one need only look to the impressive array of case studies in the form of chapters and articles on particular women, families or topics, which have strengthened the literature as a whole and helped to make it a nuanced and thorough body of work. Looking beyond England, the Welsh experience has attracted less independent attention, but this has been offset somewhat by the fact that England and Wales are often taken as a single unit.[3] The scholarship on early

1 Frances Harris, *A passion for government: the life of Sarah, duchess of Marlborough* (Oxford, 1991); Amanda Foreman, *Georgiana, duchess of Devonshire* (London, 1988); Molly McClain, *Beaufort: the duke and his duchess, 1657–1715* (London, 2001); L.C. Davidson, *Catherine of Bragança: infanta of Portugal* (London, 1908); Janet Southorn, *Mary of Modena, queen consort of James II and VII* (Royal Stuart Society, 1992); Hester Chapmen, *Mary II, queen of England* (Bath, 1972); Edward Gregg, *Queen Anne* (London, 1984); R.L. Arkell, *Caroline of Ansbach: George the second's queen* (London, 1939); Sonya Wynne, *The mistresses of Charles II and Restoration court politics, 1660–1685* (Cambridge, 1997).

2 Anne Laurence, *Women in England 1500–1760: a social history* (New York, 1994); Ingrid Tague, *Women of quality: accepting and contesting ideals of femininity in England, 1690–1760* (Woodbridge, 2002); Amanda Vickery, *The gentleman's daughter: women's lives in Georgian England* (London, 1998); eadem, *Behind closed doors: at home in Georgian England* (London, 2009); Jacqueline Eales, *Women in early modern England 1500–1700* (London, 1998); Felicity Heal and Clive Holmes, *The gentry in England and Wales, 1500–1700* (London, 1994); Anthony Fletcher, *Gender, sex and subordination in England 1500–1800* (London, 1995); Robert Shoemaker, *Gender in English society, 1650–1850: the emergence of separate spheres?* (London, 1998).

3 This historiography will be covered in more detail in the ensuing chapters, however, for a sample, see Bridget Hill, 'The marriage age of women and the demographers', *History Workshop Journal*, xxviii (1989), pp 129–47; Janelle Greenberg, 'The legal status of the English woman in early eighteenth century common law and equity', *Studies in Eighteenth-Century Culture*, iv (1975), pp 171–81; Susan Staves, *Married women's separate property in England, 1660–1833* (London, 1990); Eileen Spring, *Law, land, and family: aristocratic inheritance in England, 1300–1800* (London, 1993); Judith Lewis, '"'Tis a misfortune to be a great ladie": maternal mortality in the British aristocracy, 1558–1959', *Journal of British Studies*, xxxvii (1998), pp 26–53; eadem, *Sacred to female patriotism: gender, class, and politics in late Georgian Britain* (London, 2003); Elaine Chalus, '"My Minerva at my elbow": the political roles of women in eighteenth-century England' in Stephen Taylor, Richard Connors and Clyve Jones (eds), *Hanoverian Britain and empire: essays in memory of Philip Lawson* (Woodbridge, 1998), pp 210–28; Rachel Weil, *Political passions: gender, the family and political argument in England, 1680–1714* (Manchester, 2009). For an example of some independent Welsh historiography, see Philip Jenkins, *The making of a ruling class: the Glamorgan gentry 1640–1790* (Cambridge, 1983).

modern Scotland, however, is fast gathering pace as its historians, led by the likes of Katie Barclay, Katharine Glover and Stana Nenadic, begin to ask more and more where its female elite fitted into the country's past and how elite women interacted with their southern neighbours before and after the 1707 Act of Union.[4] Taken together, this body of work has gone far to recapturing knowledge long forgotten or ignored by historians and reintegrating women into an overwhelmingly male historical record. It has also sparked equally important historiographical discussions as to how women's history should be approached from a methodological point of view.

Of particular interest to historians studying early modern women's and gender history has been the question of where the boundaries, or perceived boundaries, of public and private life lay for contemporaries and how these lines affected their choices, options and experiences.[5] The general consensus within the most recent literature is that there were no clear differences between the two. Instead, ideas of public and private were malleable and transient, not just for women, but for men too. For Amanda Vickery, 'privacy for eighteenth-century historians is a moveable feast', and she has pointed out the multiple definitions given by historians to the terms public and private, which, aside from differing from each other, may also not have fitted the meanings assigned to the words by women at any given point in the past.[6] John Brewer agrees, concluding that there is a 'remarkable interpenetration of public and private in this period' and that 'the one is represented in and by

4 Rosalind Marshall, *Virgins and viragos: a history of women in Scotland from 1080 to 1980* (London, 1983); Stana Nenadic, 'Experience and expectations in the transformation of the Highland gentlewoman, 1680 to 1820', *Scottish Historical Review*, lxxx (2001), pp 201–20; Lynn Abrams, Eleanor Gordon, Deborah Simonton and Eileen Yeo (eds), *Gender in Scottish history since 1700* (Edinburgh, 2006); Stana Nenadic, *Lairds and luxury: the Highland gentry in eighteenth-century Scotland* (Edinburgh, 2007); Katharine Glover, '"Polite London Children": educating the daughters of the Scottish elite in mid-eighteenth-century London' in Stana Nenadic (ed.), *Scots in London in the eighteenth-century* (Cranbury, 2010), pp 253–71; Katie Barclay, *Love, intimacy and power: marriage and patriarchy in Scotland, 1650–1850* (Manchester, 2011); Katharine Glover, *Elite women and polite society in eighteenth-century Scotland* (Woodbridge, 2011); Rosalind Carr, 'Female correspondence and early modern Scottish political history: a case study of the Anglo-Scottish Union', *Historical Reflections*, xxxvii (2011), pp 39–75; Katie Barclay, 'Love and courtship in eighteenth-century Scotland' in eadem and Deborah Simonton (eds), *Women in eighteenth-century Scotland: intimate, intellectual and public lives* (Farnham, 2013), pp 37–54.

5 For a sample of this extensive historiography, see Jürgen Habermas, *The structural transformation of the public sphere: an inquiry into a category of bourgeois society* (Darmstadt, 1962); Joan Landes, 'The public and the private sphere: a feminist reconsideration' in Johanna Meehan (ed.), *Feminists read Habermas: gendering the subject of discourse* (New York, 1995), pp 91–116; eadem, *Women and the public sphere in the age of the French Revolution* (London, 1988); John Brewer, 'This, that and the other: public, social and private in the seventeenth and eighteenth centuries' in Dario Castiglione and Lesley Sharpe (eds), *Shifting the boundaries: transformations of the languages of public and private in the eighteenth century* (Exeter, 1995), pp 1–21; Mary Ryan, 'Gender and public access: women's politics in nineteenth-century America' in Craig Calhoun (ed.), *Habermas and the public sphere* (London, 1992), pp 259–88; Markman Ellis, 'Coffee-women, *The Spectator* and the public in the early eighteenth century' in Elizabeth Eger, Charlotte Grant, Clíona Ó Gallchoir and Penny Warburton (eds), *Women, writing and the public sphere, 1700–1830* (Cambridge, 2001), pp 27–52.

6 Quote from Vickery, *Behind closed doors*, p. 27. See also Vickery, 'Golden age to separate spheres?', p. 412.

the other'.[7] Others have shown how gendered ideas of public and private became confused when they interacted with politics, domesticity, the place of servants in a household, sociability and even education.[8] Sarah Richardson has noted that 'much of élite women's political activity took place in semi-public areas', while Judith Lewis dismisses the whole notion of politics as a public activity and the home as a private space, stating that 'it is not merely that women refused to stay home, but also that politics refused to stay "in public"'.[9] Thus, there is no single, accepted definition of either concept, for each was customised to fit the person, place, circumstances and time period in question.

This debate has overlapped to a large extent with that concerning the validity of the 'separate spheres' model as a way of examining gender history. It holds that early modern men and women had different functions in life, designating the domestic 'sphere' as being private and feminine and the world outside the home, in which politics and paid employment were included, as public and male. Like rigid definitions of public and private, however, the idea of 'separate spheres' is now largely discredited. Linda Colley has described it as 'more didactic than descriptive', and several scholars have cited the problems raised by trying to separate the authority of men from women, whether within the home, where the mistress of the house would have dominion over her male servants, or beyond, where men of the lower orders were expected to show deference and respect to their social superiors, including those who were female.[10] Linda Kerber has concluded that 'to continue to use the language of separate spheres is to deny the reciprocity between gender and society, and to impose a static model on dynamic relationships'.[11] She has even questioned the need to 'speak of worlds, of spheres, or of realms at all'. Amanda Vickery meanwhile, feels that 'the metaphor of separate spheres fails to capture the texture of female subordination and the complex interplay of emotion and power in family life'.[12]

7 Brewer, 'This, that and the other', pp 10, 17. See also Sarah Richardson, '"Well-neighboured houses": the political networks of elite women, 1780–1860' in eadem and Kathryn Gleadle (eds), *Women in British politics, 1760–1860: the power of the petticoat* (London, 2000), pp 59–60; Glover, *Elite women and polite society*, pp 18, 116.

8 Judith Lewis, '1784 and all that: aristocratic women and electoral politics' in Amanda Vickery (ed.), *Women, privilege, and power: British politics, 1750 to the present* (Stanford, 2001), pp 89–122; Ingrid Tague, 'Aristocratic women and ideas of family in the eighteenth century' in Helen Berry and Elizabeth Foyster (eds), *The family in early modern England* (Cambridge, 2007), p. 185; Michèle Cohen, *Fashioning masculinity: national identity and language in the eighteenth century* (London, 1996), p. 66; eadem, '"To think, to compare, to combine, to methodise": girls' education in Enlightenment Britain' in Sarah Knott and Barbara Taylor (eds), *Women, gender and enlightenment* (New York, 2005), pp 226, 238; Barclay, *Love, intimacy and power*, p. 149; Amanda Flather, *Gender and space in early modern England* (Woodbridge, 2007); Vickery, *Behind closed doors*, pp 26–7.

9 Richardson, '"Well-neighboured houses"', p. 67; Lewis, '1784 and all that', p. 99.

10 Linda Colley, *Britons: forging the nation 1707–1837* (3rd edn, London, 2009), p. 287; Flather, *Gender and space*, pp 35, 42, 52, 54, 129–30; K.D. Reynolds, *Aristocratic women and political society in Victorian Britain* (Oxford, 1998), p. 41.

11 Linda Kerber, 'Separate spheres, female worlds, woman's place: the rhetoric of women's history', *The Journal of American History*, lxxv (1988), p. 38.

12 Ibid., p. 39; Amanda Vickery, 'Golden age to separate spheres? A review of the categories and chronology of English women's history', *Historical Journal*, xxxvi (1993), p. 401.

The emergence of this literature and theory is to be applauded, but what of Ireland? Despite the agenda for Irish women's history laid out over twenty years ago by Mary O'Dowd, Margaret MacCurtain and Maria Luddy, historians have been slow to pick up the gauntlet. The best overview of Irish women's lives during this period and the book that has done the most to open up the field, is that by O'Dowd herself, which examines the lives of Irish women from 1500 to 1800 and in all walks of life. More recently, Jane Ohlmeyer has written at length on the Irish elite in the seventeenth century, but her approach is gender neutral and in any case, concludes at the point at which this book begins, with the fallout from the Glorious Revolution of 1688. Roger Sawyer's work, though valuable, is mainly concerned with the women of post-Union (1801) Ireland.[13] As in the English and Scottish literature, there are also a number (albeit a much smaller number) of works which target one aspect of elite women's lives, such as marriage or philanthropy and a few case studies of specific women or families, including work by Sean Connolly on Letitia Bushe and Stella Tillyard's book on the Lennox sisters, who, although themselves English, were heavily entwined with the Irish elite through marriage.[14] General histories of Ireland and its social scene during the late Stuart and early Hanoverian period have fleshed out the historiography a little further, but do not prioritise, or even offer equal attention to, the female experience, with the exception of the work of Toby Barnard.[15] Further issues arise from the fact that, by their very nature, case studies deal with one particular individual or theme, while overviews must sacrifice a certain amount of detail to facilitate a greater chronological scope. In addition, those case studies which do exist favour the mid to late eighteenth century, offering little concrete information on the earlier decades. What is needed, and what this

13 Margaret MacCurtain, Mary O'Dowd and Maria Luddy, 'An agenda for women's history in Ireland, 1500–1900', *Irish Historical Studies*, xxviii (1992), pp 1–37; Mary O'Dowd, *A history of women in Ireland, 1500–1800* (Harlow, 2004); Jane Ohlmeyer, *Making Ireland English: the Irish aristocracy in the seventeenth century* (London, 2012); Roger Sawyer, *We are but women: women in Ireland's history* (London, 1993).

14 A.P.W. Malcomson, *The pursuit of the heiress: aristocratic marriage in Ireland 1740–1840* (2nd edn, Belfast, 2006); Deborah Wilson, *Women, marriage and property in wealthy landed families in Ireland, 1750–1850* (Manchester, 2009); Rosemary Raughter, 'A natural tenderness: the ideal and the reality of eighteenth-century female philanthropy' in M.G. Valiulis and Mary O'Dowd (eds), *Women and Irish history: essays in honour of Margaret MacCurtain* (Dublin, 1997), pp 71–88; S.J. Connolly, 'A woman's life in eighteenth-century Ireland: the case of Letitia Bushe', *Historical Journal*, xliii (2000), pp 433–51; Stella Tillyard, *Aristocrats: Caroline, Emily, Louisa and Sarah Lennox 1740–1832* (London, 1994).

15 L.A. Clarkson, 'Hospitality, housekeeping and high living in eighteenth-century Ireland' in J.R. Hill and Colm Lennon (eds), *Luxury and austerity. Historical Studies xxi* (Dublin, 1999), pp 84–105; Tighernan Mooney and Fiona White, 'The gentry's winter season' in David Dickson (ed.), *The gorgeous mask: Dublin, 1700–1850* (Dublin, 1987), pp 1–16; S.J. Connolly, *Divided kingdom: Ireland 1630–1800* (Oxford, 2008); idem, *Religion, law, and power: the making of Protestant Ireland 1660–1760* (Oxford, 1992); David Dickson, *New foundations: Ireland, 1660–1800* (2nd edn, Dublin, 2000); D.A. Fleming, *Politics and provincial people: Sligo and Limerick, 1691–1761* (Manchester, 2010); Padhraig Higgins, *A nation of politicians: gender, patriotism, and political culture in late eighteenth-century Ireland* (Wisconsin, 2010); Toby Barnard, *A new anatomy of Ireland: the Irish Protestants, 1640–1770* (London, 2003); idem, *Irish Protestant ascents and descents, 1641–1770* (Dublin, 2004); idem, *Making the grand figure: lives and possessions in Ireland, 1641–1770* (London, 2004).

book will seek to provide, is an examination of the lives of elite women in Ireland which deals with more subjects than a case study, in a tighter timeframe than that employed by current surveys. This will allow for the women to take centre stage, for their individual experiences to be collated into a detailed, collective narrative, in which any trends within the group can be identified, and for their hitherto obscure contribution to Irish history during this period to be uncovered. The book will question how far their lives changed, and situate its findings within the wider historiography on the rest of the British Isles to establish to what extent women in Ireland were influenced by their closest neighbours.

When this book opens in 1690, Ireland was on the brink of great social, political and economic change. In the 1650s, large quantities of freehold landed property had been redistributed by Oliver Cromwell, until the acreage owned by Catholics, which had stood at 59% of Irish land in 1641, had fallen to just 8–9% in 1660. After the Restoration, the new government unrealistically promised not only to restore all forfeited estates to Catholics who had remained loyal to the monarchy during the Civil War and the Interregnum, but also to allow those soldiers and adventurers who had benefited from the Cromwellian land settlement to keep their estates and use any remaining land to pay pre-1649 salary arrears to Royalist officers. Needless to say, there was not enough to go around, and although a certain number of the Cromwellian forfeitures were reversed, Catholic landowners were not returned to their 1641 position, instead holding only a little over a fifth of Irish lands in 1665.[16] The events of the 1690s were to build on these changes.

After William III's victory over his father-in-law, James II, at the Battle of the Boyne in 1690 and the signing of the articles of Limerick the following year, the English parliament confiscated much of the land which had belonged to William's political adversaries and the king proceeded to grant it to his supporters. It was then reclaimed in 1700 by the parliament, given over to trustees and sold at auction.[17] This turn of events, though detrimental to William's grantees, was considerably more so to those who had purchased land from them in the interim, and Sean Connolly has shown that along with the Cromwellian settlement, it allowed many more self-made men, who were of modest, rather than aristocratic birth, to enter the elite.[18] Catholics were barred from buying the forfeited land freehold and by 1703, their share of Irish freehold land stood at just 14%.[19]

Aided by the land settlements, the relative legal, social and political positions of Protestants and Catholics also changed considerably after the war. Protestants soon

16 S.J. Connolly, *Religion, law and power: the making of Protestant Ireland 1660–1760* (Oxford, 1992), pp 13–15.

17 Dickson, *New foundations*, pp 37, 41; *Oxford D.N.B.* (William III and II (1650–1702)); Patrick Walsh, *The making of the Irish Protestant ascendancy: the life of William Conolly, 1662–1729* (Woodbridge, 2010), p. 50.

18 Walsh, *Making of the Irish Protestant ascendancy*, p. 50; Connolly, *Religion, law and power*, pp 64–5.

19 J.G. Simms, *The Williamite confiscation in Ireland, 1690–1703* (London, 1956), p. 195. Ian McBride agrees that the land redistribution caused by the Williamite forfeitures was small in comparison to the Cromwellian settlement (Ian McBride, *Eighteenth-century Ireland: the isle of slaves* (Dublin, 2009), pp 113–14). See also W.A. Maguire, 'The land settlement' in idem, *Kings in conflict: the revolutionary war in Ireland and its aftermath 1689–1750* (Belfast, 1990), pp 139–56.

came to enjoy a new 'Ascendancy', while Catholics, who had experienced a period of greater tolerance and power under James II, were increasingly repressed by a series of penal laws designed to limit their economic, social and political power.[20] The articles of Limerick, which had included clauses to protect their rights, were not fully implemented, and over the next few decades, more and more legal disabilities were placed upon them.[21] Among other things, they could not carry arms, lands had to be divided between all sons upon the death of their father, rather than passed down through primogeniture, and there were severe restrictions upon the purchase of new land. Catholic voting rights were also severely restricted, before being entirely removed in 1728.[22] Yet despite these changes, Connolly has argued that the effects of the penal laws on the structure of Irish society should not be overestimated and that their impact lay more in their effect on the daily lives of Catholics 'than their declared aim of controlling access to the upper levels of the political system'.[23]

As for the Irish economy, although its health fluctuated between the 1690s and 1740s and did occasionally improve, historians are more or less in agreement that it was in a generally poor condition throughout this period. Initially it was hindered by the 1689–91 war and its after-effects, which caused long-term disruption to 'Irish trade, agriculture, manufacture, the economy in general, and the administration of government'.[24] The remainder of the decade was overshadowed by the collapse of the revenue system during the war and the huge rental and pay arrears accrued as a result.[25] The increasing numbers of soldiers stationed in Ireland during the reigns of William, Anne and George I, put an additional strain on a country which by 1717 was burdened with a national debt of £80,000, and matters were not helped by Ireland's primarily agrarian and backward economy. Although its woollen manufacture had been facilitating an economic recovery in certain parts of the country, this was neutralised in 1699 by an act which prevented Irish wool being exported anywhere but England, where it was heavily taxed through customs duties.[26] Though some historians take a slightly more optimistic view, arguing for an economic recovery in the 1690s, they acknowledge that even this was negated at the turn of the century by what David Dickson has summarised as 'depressed export prices, unfortunately timed currency adjustments and bad harvests'.[27] In addition to the Woollen Act, there were other restrictions: trade with the colonies was prohibited, as was cattle trade with England. Although Connolly has argued that economic diversification and the domestic market compensated to a certain extent for these limitations, the effects were not felt in time to save Ireland from severe

20 C.I. McGrath, *The making of the eighteenth-century Irish constitution: government, parliament and the revenue, 1692–1714* (Dublin, 2000), pp 15–16. See also J.G. Simms, 'The making of a penal law (2 Anne, c. 6), 1703–4', *Irish Historical Studies*, xii (1960–1), pp 105–18.

21 D.W. Hayton, *Ruling Ireland, 1685–1742: politics, politicians and parties* (Woodbridge, 2004), p. 31.

22 Connolly, *Divided kingdom*, pp 198–9. These pages also give a fuller summary of the penal laws.

23 Ibid., pp 258–9.

24 McGrath, *The making of the eighteenth-century Irish constitution*, pp 50–1.

25 Ibid., pp 51–3, 59.

26 Hayton, *Ruling Ireland*, p. 213; 10 & 11 Will. III, c. 10 [Eng.] (4 May 1699).

27 Dickson, *New foundations*, p. 115. See also Connolly, *Divided kingdom*, p. 344.

famines in the late 1720s and early 1740s, which killed hundreds of thousands and caused many more to emigrate.[28] Nor was the situation helped by the number of absentee Irish landlords, often living in England and taking around £300,000 out of Ireland each year in rents.[29] Some tried to improve their estates, but many more did not, or could not, being constrained by their own poor financial situation, or the fact that their lands were rented out on long-term leases to middlemen, who then sublet them to peasant tenants.[30] Internal absentees were a problem as well, splitting their time, often very unequally, between rustication on far-flung, piecemeal provincial estates and a busy social life in Dublin.[31]

The Irish political system between the 1690s and 1740s was a blend of both old and new. The use of lords lieutenant (and occasionally lords deputy) as the monarch's representative in Ireland was carried over from earlier times, and they were supplemented by a team of lord justices when the office was vacant, or its occupant out of the country.[32] In a break from the past, sessions of the Irish parliament became far more regular after the Glorious Revolution, a development governed primarily by financial reasons. Beforehand, the hereditary revenues allowed to the monarch had been enough to enable them to govern Ireland without parliament. Afterwards, given the state of Ireland's economy, these funds were no longer sufficient and the government had to turn to MPs for further supplies. Irish MPs soon developed the habit of granting additional revenues on a short-term basis, a strategy which helped to ensure that parliament would have to be regularly reconvened to vote further supplies.[33] If there were any doubts that its recall depended on its financial powers, these were removed after MPs were particularly generous in the 1695–9 parliament, only to then find that their services were not required again until 1703, when the money ran out. After this, revenues were usually granted for two years at a time.[34]

Post-war Ireland also saw the development of the 'undertaker' system of government, through which the most powerful Irish politicians 'undertook' to use their connexions and influence to manage the governing of the country for the lord lieutenant (known informally as the viceroy), in exchange for a share of the patronage he had at his disposal.[35] Though it has been argued that this system only developed in the early 1720s, David Hayton has demonstrated that it in fact originated in the late 1690s and early 1700s, a position supported by Sean Connolly, who has pointed out that what was new in the 1720s, 'was not the concept of undertakers, but the emergence of one individual as chief undertaker, and his acceptance as in effect a partner in the government of the kingdom'.[36] Lords lieutenant had few

28 Connolly, *Divided kingdom*, pp 346–7.

29 McBride, *Eighteenth-century Ireland*, pp 115–16.

30 Connolly, *Divided kingdom*, p. 348.

31 McBride, *Eighteenth-century Ireland*, p. 116. See also David Dickson, 'The place of Dublin in the eighteenth-century Irish economy' in T.M. Devine and David Dickson (eds), *Ireland and Scotland 1600–1850: parallels and contrasts in economic and social development* (Edinburgh, 1983), pp 177–92.

32 McGrath, *The making of the eighteenth-century Irish constitution*, p. 17.

33 Ibid., p. 35.

34 Ibid., pp 153–4.

35 Patrick McNally, *Parties, patriots and undertakers: parliamentary politics in early Hanoverian Ireland* (Dublin, 1997), p. 95.

36 J.L. McCracken, 'The political structure, 1714–60' in T.W. Moody and W.E. Vaughan (eds), A

options but to acquiesce to this development, as (with one exception) they were themselves English and unfamiliar with Ireland and its politicians, making undertakers necessary if a viceroy was to gain the support he needed in the Irish House of Commons to pass legislation.[37]

Ireland was also affected by the changing and sometimes volatile political and social scene in England and Scotland. In the period covered by this book, England and Scotland faced the upheavals not just of 1688, but of union in 1707, the change from the Stuart to the Hanoverian dynasty in 1714, the fall of the Tory party and the supremacy of the Whigs and the threat of Jacobite rebellions and attempts to restore the descendants of James II.[38] The royal court underwent a massive expansion from the days when it had revolved solely around Queen Anne, and in addition to the influx of German politicians and courtiers, the royal family itself was larger, gaining a prince and princess of Wales, their children and a collection of royal mistresses. The Irish peerage and exchequer often had to absorb some of the demands of these new courtiers, and George I's mistress, Melusine von der Schulenburg and his half-sister, Sophia von Kielmansegg, were created duchess of Munster and countess of Leinster respectively, before being granted the English titles of duchess of Kendal and countess of Darlington.[39] Melusine also helped to cause a major political crisis in Ireland in the early 1720s, when she sold the patent the King had granted her controlling Irish coinage production to a Birmingham ironmaster named William Wood, who was then accused of flooding the market with debased money, 'an act that for many in Ireland epitomized their economic exploitation by the British government'.[40] This incident aside, and despite their Irish titles, she and Sophia do not feature in this book, for as German women living in England and holding their titles *suo jure*, rather than through a connexion to an Irish family, they do not qualify for inclusion.

The women researched for this study conform to the following criteria: they belonged to an Irish family by either birth or marriage and were members of the upper orders of society (the elite). Defining the term 'elite' is difficult, for membership was based on a flexible mixture of wealth and rank, and the presence of one did not guarantee the other. David Fleming has also pointed out the potential for disparities between the lives of those living in rural and urban areas who would both have considered themselves as members of the social elite and the 'increasing commercialisation of society and the growth of the "middling sorts"' which 'introduced luxury and politeness to an increasingly large portion of the population'.[41] In

new history of Ireland, iv: *Eighteenth century Ireland, 1691–1800* (Oxford, 1986), pp 61–3; Hayton, *Ruling Ireland*, pp 107, 130; Connolly, *Divided kingdom*, p. 233.

37 Hayton, *Ruling Ireland*, pp 111–12.

38 There were two Jacobite invasions in this period, one in 1715 and another in 1745.

39 *Oxford D.N.B.* (Schulenburg, (Ehrengard) Melusine von der, *suo jure* duchess of Kendal and *suo jure* duchess of Munster (1667–1743)); ibid. (Kielmansegg, Sophia Charlotte von [*formerly* Countess Sophia Charlotte von Platen und Hallermund], *suo jure* countess of Darlington and *suo jure* countess of Leinster (1675–1725)).

40 Ibid. (Schulenburg, (Ehrengard) Melusine von der, *suo jure* duchess of Kendal and *suo jure* duchess of Munster (1667–1743)). See also ibid. (Wood, William (1671–1730)).

41 David Fleming 'Diversions of the people: sociability among the orders of early eighteenth-century Ireland', *Eighteenth-Century Ireland*, xvii (2002), p. 101.

addition to this, personal circumstances were mutable and people and families could enter into or drop out of the elite. The term has therefore been applied quite liberally and encompasses people and families who were titled, those who derived the bulk of their income from landed estates, as well as high-ranking churchmen, such as deans, bishops and cathedral clergy, MPs, and government officials, together with their immediate relations.[42] In many cases overlap occurred, as those with landed wealth obtained posts in parliament, government or even the royal household, but the key point is that while everyone under the umbrella of the 'elite' meets a baseline in terms of income and status, there could be considerable variation, much like the rungs on a ladder. There is no specific residency requirement, so long as individuals had a discernible effect upon Irish affairs, but almost all spent at least eighteen consecutive months in the country. Only one never visited at all. Technically, the book covers elite women in Ireland during the period, rather than just those who were members of the 'Protestant' Ascendancy. However, the effects of the land forfeitures and restrictions on Catholic job opportunities mean that, in practice, the vast majority of elite families were Anglican, as were their women. Still, the odd Catholic lady is mentioned and even if Protestant examples are used, some shared experiences, such as childbirth, and many social routines hinged primarily on status and gender, not religion, so that the conclusions drawn can be applied to all.

Very occasional exceptions have been made to these rules. First, for Mary Pendarves (*née* Granville), an English widow who visited and travelled around Ireland for eighteenth months in the early 1730s and left an extensive written record of her interactions with polite society.[43] Second, there will be the occasional mention in the later chapters of the wives of the lords lieutenant, the vicereines. These women are not considered in-depth for they were predominantly English by birth and marriage and, as the wives of the monarch's representative, were in a position that set them apart from the rest of the elite, much as a queen consort differed from the courtiers and English elite surrounding her. This makes their experiences unrepresentative. That being said, it is not feasible to examine the viceregal court, even from the point of view of the resident female elite, without mentioning them.[44]

The identification of specific elite women as subjects of study has been dictated, to a large extent, by surviving archival sources. Those who appear most frequently belong to five core families, represented by large collections of documents: the Butlers, Boyles, Brodricks, O'Briens and Conollys. Women outside these families, but who were known to them and discussed in their correspondence are also included. Other smaller, or less female-orientated collections of letters and

42 Patrick Walsh has pointed out that 'the purchase of a country estate had long been recognised as one of the final steps towards attaining a place in the social elite'. See *Making of the Irish Protestant ascendancy*, p. 7.

43 Coincidentally, Mary would later marry into the Irish elite anyway, becoming the wife of Patrick Delany, dean of Down, in 1743 and relocating to Ireland for the duration of that marriage. See *Oxford D.N.B.* (Delany [*née* Granville; *other married name* Pendarves], Mary (1700–1788).

44 For information on the social and to an extent, political and artistic activities of the vicereines during this period, see Rachel Wilson 'The vicereines of Ireland and the transformation of the Dublin court', *The Court Historian*, xix (2014), pp 3–28.

documents, have been used to increase the geographical scope of the book and to ensure a greater breadth across elite society. The resulting sample provides an invaluable cross-section of the Irish elite between 1690 and 1745, particularly as each of the core families had varying levels of wealth, rank and political status. The trajectories they followed were also quite different, with some on the ascent and others in decline. In addition, their women hailed from across Ireland, England and even Wales, allowing for a marked variation in the strength of the families' connexions and loyalty to the English regime and a better insight into how outside values did or did not translate to Ireland.

The Butler family held the only Irish dukedom of the time, that of Ormond (along with the earldoms of Ossory and Arran). Although multiple members of the family will be mentioned, the most attention will be given to the wife of the 2nd duke. Formerly Lady Mary Somerset, daughter of the 1st duke of Beaufort, she was born in 1665 and married James Butler, then earl of Ossory, in August 1685 as his second wife (his first being Anne Hyde, who had died six months earlier and who was the daughter of Laurence, 1st earl of Rochester). Ossory's father had died in 1680, so that when his grandfather, the 1st duke of Ormond, passed away in 1688, James and Mary became the 2nd duke and duchess. During the time period covered by this book, the Butler family's fortunes were in a downward spiral, due to huge debts (some of which were inherited from the 1st duke) and the extravagance of the 2nd duke and duchess, who, aside from their lavish spending habits, visited Ireland increasingly rarely, preferring to reside in England at great additional cost to the estate. Thus, the Ormonds provide an opportunity to observe the decline of a once great Irish family and the role Mary played in attempting to retain their political and social hegemony.[45]

The Boyle family were descended from Richard Boyle, 1st earl of Cork. His son, the 2nd earl, was created earl of Burlington in 1665 and it was primarily by this title that Burlington's descendants were known, though other branches of the family descended from his father included the earls of Orrery and eventually Shannon.[46] Of primary interest to this book will be Juliana Noel, who was born in England in 1672, the daughter of Henry Noel and granddaughter of the 4th Viscount Campden. After the death of her parents, she was raised by her paternal aunt, Mary, dowager countess of Northampton, before marrying Charles Boyle, grandson of the 1st earl of Burlington, in 1688. The earl's eldest son, Viscount Dungarvan, who was Charles's father, died in 1694, so that when Lord Burlington himself died four years later, Charles and Juliana became the next earl and countess.[47] Juliana was widowed in 1704, and left to raise her son, Richard, now 4th earl of Cork and 3rd earl of

[45] D.W. Hayton, *The Anglo-Irish experience, 1680–1730: religion, identity and patriotism* (Woodbridge, 2012), pp 49–75; *Oxford D.N.B.* (Butler, James, 1st duke of Ormond (1610–1688)); ibid. (Butler, James, 2nd duke of Ormond (1665–1745)); *D.I.B.* (Butler, James (1665–1745)).

[46] *Oxford D.N.B.* (Boyle, Richard, 1st earl of Burlington and 2nd earl of Cork (1612–1698)); ibid. (Boyle, Roger, 1st earl of Orrery (1621–1679)).

[47] Journal of Elizabeth (Clifford), Lady Burlington, 1650s–1688 (Chatsworth, Cork MSS, miscellaneous box 5); marriage settlement of Charles Boyle and Juliana Noel, 4 Jan. 1687/8 (ibid., MS L/46/28); *Oxford D.N.B.* (Boyle, Richard, 1st earl of Burlington and 2nd earl of Cork (1612–1698)).

Burlington, and four surviving daughters, the Ladies Elizabeth, Juliana, Henrietta and Jane Boyle. Although the Boyles owned huge estates in Ireland, by the time of Juliana's widowhood they had become absentee landowners, arguably more interested in their English lands and position. This pattern was to be continued by the dowager countess and her son, and would have a great impact upon their dealings with and understanding of Ireland and Irish affairs. She is also the only woman discussed who never came to Ireland.[48]

The Brodricks were headed by Alan Brodrick, later 1st Viscount Midleton. A lawyer by profession, he became a prominent politician and held many posts during his long career, including those of lord justice and lord chancellor of Ireland. Brodrick was married three times, and though little information survives about his first wife, Catherine Barry, much more is available on her successors, Lucy Courthope and Ann Hill (*née* Trevor). Lucy was the daughter of Sir Peter Courthope of Little Island, County Cork, and married Alan in 1693. She produced three children before her death in 1703, including her daughter Alice, who was born in 1697, but after her mother's death, was raised primarily by her aunt, Martha Courthope, in England.[49] It was not until 1716 that Alan married Ann Hill, whose father, Sir John Trevor of Brynkinalt in Wales, was the Speaker of the English House of Commons. Born in 1670, she had previously been married to Michael Hill of Hillsborough from 1690 until his death in 1699, which had left her with two sons and a daughter, also called Anne, who was married to Alan Brodrick and Catherine Barry's son, St John, in 1710.[50] The Brodrick family made great efforts throughout the early eighteenth century to maintain a healthy political and landowning presence in both England and Ireland, and were perhaps the most determined and successful of all the families mentioned here at straddling both worlds. Lord Midleton's father was originally from Surrey, but had been granted lands in County Cork during the Cromwellian land settlement and Midleton was to become MP for Cork city three times between 1692 and 1710, then for County Cork between 1713 and 1714 and finally for Midhurst in Sussex between 1717 and his death in 1728. His brother, Thomas Brodrick, and son, St John, operated in much the same way, also holding seats in both countries, while another brother, William, was MP for Mallow, County Cork, from 1716 to 1727.[51]

48 Arthur Collins and Sir Egerton Brydges, *Collins's peerage of England; genealogical, biographical and historical. …* (9 vols, London, 1756), v, 170. Two other daughters, Mary and Catherine, died young. See also *Oxford D.N.B.* (Boyle, Richard, 3rd earl of Burlington and 4th earl of Cork (1694–1753)); *D.I.B.* (Boyle, Charles (1670?–1704)).

49 *Oxford D.N.B.* (Brodrick, Alan, 1st Viscount Midleton (1655/6–1728)); Alan Brodrick to St John Brodrick, 9 Dec. 1697 (Surrey History Centre, MS 1248/1/296–297). Letters show that Alice and her younger brother, Alan Brodrick, junior, had been dispatched to England by July 1704 to stay with Martha. See same to same, 11 July 1704 (ibid., MS 1248/2/141–142).

50 *Oxford D.N.B.* (Brodrick, Alan, 1st Viscount Midleton (1655/6–1728)); Brian Mackey, 'The creation of Knockbreda parish church and Belvoir Park' in Lydia Wilson (ed.), *Knockbreda: its monuments and people* (Belfast, 2009), pp 10–11.

51 *Oxford D.N.B.* (Brodrick, Alan, 1st Viscount Midleton (1655/6–1728)); Edith Johnston-Liik, *History of the Irish parliament, 1692–1800: commons, constituencies and statues* (6 vols, Belfast, 2002), iii, 266–75. For a more detailed discussion of the Brodrick family, see D.W. Hayton, *The Anglo-Irish experience, 1680–1730: religion, identity and patriotism* (Woodbridge, 2012), pp 76–103.

The branch of the O'Brien family of particular interest to this book were the descendants and in-laws of Sir Donat O'Brien, 1st Bt. He had two sons, Lucius and Henry, and it is Lucius's wife, Catherine Keightley, who is the key member of the family studied here.[52] She was born in England in 1676, the daughter of Thomas Keightley and Lady Frances Hyde, and through her mother (a daughter of the 1st earl of Clarendon and sister of Anne, duchess of York), was a cousin of Queen Mary II and Queen Anne. The Keightleys moved to Ireland in the late 1670s, and her father was increasingly employed in the Irish government, aided by Frances's brothers, Henry Hyde, 2nd earl of Clarendon and Laurence Hyde, 1st earl of Rochester, who were the country's lord deputy and lord lieutenant from 1685 to 1689 and from 1700 to 1703 respectively.[53] Despite her family connexions, place of birth and the fact that later letters indicate that Catherine spent at least some time in England before her marriage, she appears to have been more familiar with Ireland than anywhere else.[54] After her marriage to Lucius, which took place in late 1701 or early 1702, she spent most of her time there (though their eldest son, Edward, was born in England in 1705) and continued in the country for many years after Lucius and Sir Donat had died in 1717, despite her mother's pleas to return to England, where Lady Frances was once again living.[55] The O'Briens were much more entrenched in Ireland and concerned with its wellbeing than the Butlers, Boyles and Brodricks. They claimed descent from the Gaelic king, Brian Boru (d. 1014), and all their lands and income were located in Ireland, primarily in County Clare, for which constituency Sir Donat was MP four times between 1692 and 1714. He and Catherine both lived upon and personally managed the family estates, so that compared to those of their contemporaries who were absent from Ireland on a regular basis, they had the opportunity to become much more familiar with their tenants and lands and with Irish affairs and society.[56]

Finally, there is the extended Conolly family. Katherine Conyngham was born in around 1662, the eldest child of Sir Albert Conyngham and Margaret Leslie of Mount Charles in Donegal. In 1694, she married William Conolly, who also came from Donegal, specifically Ballyshannon, and was the son of Patrick and Jane Conolly. While details of his family background are scarce, the story that his father was a publican is most likely untrue and the family were instead minor landowners. Like Alan Brodrick, first a friend and then a political rival, William had trained as a lawyer (though an attorney, rather than a barrister) before rising to political prominence. As his career progressed, he held various government

52 Grania O'Brien, *These my friends and forebears: the O'Briens of Dromoland* (Ballinakella, 1991), pp 15–16.

53 *Gentleman's Magazine* ... (London, 1829), xcix, 322; *Oxford D.N.B.* (Keightley, Thomas (c.1650–1719)); ibid. (Hyde, Henry, 2nd earl of Clarendon (1638–1709)).

54 Marriage settlement of Lucius O'Brien and Catherine Keightley, 29 Dec. 1701 (NLI, MS 45, 290/4); Mary Chapman to Catherine O'Brien, 22 Apr. 1712 (ibid., MS 45, 296/8).

55 Thomas Keightley to Sir Donat O'Brien, 19 Apr. 1705 (ibid., MS 45, 295/4); Lady Frances Keightley to Catherine O'Brien, 15 Jan. 1723/4 (ibid., MS 45, 348/5).

56 'Inchiquin papers' (http://www.nli.ie/pdfs/mss%20lists/143_Inchiquin.pdf) (3 Aug. 2012); Johnston-Liik, *History of the Irish parliament*, v, 367–8.

posts, including serving multiple terms as a lord justice of Ireland, and became Speaker of the Irish House of Commons in 1715, a position which he held for the rest of his life. He was also a powerful figure within the revenue commission, particularly after the Hanoverian succession, and was MP for Donegal borough twice in the 1690s and for County Londonderry from 1703 until his death. Though he never held a title, by the end of his life in 1729, he was credited with being the richest man in Ireland and left his wife well provided for during her widowhood. While Katherine is the principal member of her family who will be examined here, her sisters, Jane Bonnell and Mary Jones, will also feature, as will various other women connected to her, through both her own and her husband's family, for although the Conollys had no children of their own, they each had multiple nieces and nephews, many of whom played an important part in their lives. The Conollys were in many ways very different from the other four families mentioned. Far from being well-established financially, socially or politically at the beginning of this period, they were a non-aristocratic family on the rise, and their relatively humble origins, which had not prepared them to deal with the world of high society in Dublin, make their activities once there all the more interesting.[57]

For the most part, little notice has previously been paid to these women by historians. None have had biographies written about them, and only Katherine Conolly has an entry in the *Dictionary of Irish Biography*. She and her sisters are also the only women in the book who have received considerable attention before now, principally through the work of Toby Barnard, supplemented by Lena Boylan and Patrick Walsh, the latter of whom has written on William Conolly. Catherine O'Brien and her mother, Lady Frances Keightley, have been researched by Finola O'Kane, who has focused on Catherine's architectural interests and by their descendants, who have produced histories of the family which include summaries of the women's lives.[58] However, they have always been viewed in isolation, rather than as part of the wider social group to which they belonged. As for the Boyle family, most of the literature available on Juliana consists of passing references made to her in works about her son. Much the same is true of the women of the Ormond and Brodrick

57 Walsh, *Making of the Irish Protestant ascendancy*, pp 11–24; *D.I.B.* (Conolly, Katherine (Catherine) (*c.*1662–1752)); ibid. (Conolly, William (1662–1729)).

58 Ibid. (Conolly, Katherine (Catherine) (*c.*1662–1752)); Toby Barnard, 'A tale of three sisters: Katherine Conolly of Castletown' in idem, *Irish Protestant ascents and descents*, pp 266–89; Walsh, *The making of the Irish Protestant ascendancy*; idem, 'The career of William Conolly, 1689–1729' (Trinity College Dublin, Ph.D. thesis, 2007); Lena Boylan, 'The Conollys of Castletown: a family history', *Quarterly Bulletin of the Irish Georgian society*, xi (1968), pp 1–46. On William Conolly, see also Michael Quane, 'Speaker Conolly', *Dublin Historical Record*, xxv (1971), pp 25–32. On the O'Briens, see Finola O'Kane, 'Design and rule: women in the Irish countryside 1715–1831', *Eighteenth-Century Ireland*, xix (2004), pp 56–74; eadem, '"Obliges me to dip my hands in mortar": Catherine O'Brien's influence at Dromoland', *Journal of the Irish Georgian Society*, vii (2004), pp 80–105; Grania O'Brien, *These my friends and forebears*; Ivar O'Brien, *O'Brien of Thomond: the O'Briens in Irish history 1500–1865* (Chichester, 1986). There is also a short article by Michael McMahon, 'Lucius and Catherine O'Brien of Corofin' in *The Other Clare*, xxv (2001), pp 51–9.

families, though work by Toby Barnard, David Hayton, Jane Ohlmeyer and Steven Zwicker has provided a gateway into their lives.[59]

The structure of the book reflects some of the most common life experiences of the female elite in Ireland, details of which occur again and again in their correspondence and papers. It is arranged in seven chapters. To begin, there will be an examination of the process by which marriages were brought about and what options were open to women if their relationships with their husbands broke down. Chapter 2 will detail the pressures of having to produce and raise children, Chapter 3 the domestic responsibilities of elite women during marriage, and Chapter 4 the ways in which widows managed the estates of their underage sons. Though this type of estate management was not especially uncommon, not all guardians have left enough evidence of their activities to provide a clear picture of them, and so the fourth chapter will break with the pattern used elsewhere, of examining many women from multiple families, and instead focus on the experiences of only two, for whom excellent source material survives. The remaining three chapters will then deal in turn with women's social, political and philanthropic roles. Limitations of space preclude a chapter dealing specifically with religion, but the topic appears in one form or another throughout the book, thanks in large part to the conflicts which arose from having a predominantly Anglican ruling class in an overwhelmingly Catholic country.

Keeping track of the various titles by which aristocrats were known throughout their lives can, at times, prove difficult. The many titled women in this study will be referred to by whichever name they held at the time in question, though these will sometimes be shortened for convenience and to avoid constant repetition. For instance, Juliana Boyle, dowager countess of Cork and Burlington, will often be referred to simply as Lady Burlington. The lack of standardised spelling used in the seventeenth and eighteenth centuries can also be problematic, as names, both first and second, were often spelt in a variety of ways. For the sake of clarity and continuity, one spelling has been selected for each person or family mentioned and used throughout this book. So Sir Donat O'Brien is never Sir Donough, despite the fact that the latter spelling sometimes appears in contemporary documents and has been used by other historians. The term 'lady' or 'ladies' (without capital letters) refer to women of the elite in general, not necessarily women who held the title of 'Lady'. In the latter instances, the word will always begin with a capital.

This book does not claim to be an exhaustive study of all of the elite women living in Ireland between 1690 and 1745, or of every possible aspect of their lives, for that would be impractical. What it does provide, though, is a window into their world through which more detail than ever before can be seen and hopefully, an impetus for further research in the field.

[59] Juliana is briefly mentioned in various chapters of Edward Corp (ed.), *Lord Burlington – the man and his politics: questions of loyalty* (New York, 1998); Toby Barnard and Jane Fenlon (eds), *The dukes of Ormond, 1610–1745* (Woodbridge, 2001); W.G. Neely, 'The Ormond Butlers of county Kilkenny 1515–1715' in William Nolan and Kevin Whelan (eds), *Kilkenny: history and society: interdisciplinary essays on the history of an Irish county* (Dublin, 1990), pp 107–26; Hayton, *The Anglo-Irish experience*; Jane Ohlmeyer and Steven Zwicker, 'John Dryden, the house of Ormond, and the politics of Anglo-Irish patronage', *Historical Journal*, xlix (2006), pp 677–706.

1

The making and breaking of a marriage

> On Thursday evening last Sir St. George Gore St George, Bart. eldest son of the late Sir Ralph Gore, Bart. who was one of the Lords Justices, Chancellor of the Exchequer, and Speaker of the House of Commons of this Kingdom, was married to Miss Burton, daughter of the Right Hon. Francis Burton, Esq. Knight of the Shire for the County of Clare, and one of his Majesty's most honourable privy councillors, a young lady of great beauty and merit, with a fortune of 20,000l.[1]

So ran a typical announcement for a marriage within the eighteenth-century Irish elite. Though comparatively brief, it exposes a great deal regarding contemporary attitudes towards such unions and women's place within them. From this short paragraph can be gleaned details of the social, financial and personal attributes sought in a prospective spouse, the importance of the marriage not just to the couple, but to their families, and the legal subordination of women within the entire process (note the absence of the bride's first name and of any mention of her mother or mother-in-law).

For all that they revealed, published announcements such as this concealed much more, for they gave only brief, sanitised and businesslike views of an event which was merely the end-point of a long and often much more complex journey. They said nothing of the months, sometimes years, of delicate negotiations which had taken place in order to bring a union about, omitted the stories of frustrated hopes and failed engagements, glossed over the less attractive qualities of many a bride and groom, and disguised the reality of women's input into their own marriages and the marriages of others. It is this more rounded view of how matches were mooted and made which will be provided here. Using the Irish elite's own words, this chapter will trace the customs and legalities which surrounded unions from courtship to altar to (occasionally), separation and divorce.

Past scholars have done much to pave the way for such a task, and the historiography on early modern English marriage is particularly strong. Social and legal historians including Lawrence Stone, R.B. Outhwaite, Lloyd Bonfield and Sir John Habakkuk have produced a variety of studies examining the institution as a whole, or focusing on its various forms and constituent parts, while those working in the field of women's and gender studies have used the female point of view to expand upon and push forward our understanding of the intricacies of early modern marriage and widowhood.[2] More recent research by Katie Barclay, Anthony

1 *London Evening Post*, 1–4 Oct. 1743.

2 See, for example, Lawrence Stone, *The family, sex and marriage in England, 1500–1800* (London, 1977); R.B. Outhwaite (ed.), *Marriage and society: studies in the social history of marriage* (London, 1981); Lloyd Bonfield, *Marriage settlements, 1601–1740: the adoption of the strict settlement* (Cambridge, 1983); John Habakkuk, *Marriage, debt and the estates system: English landownership,*

Malcomson and Deborah Wilson has begun to retrieve the history of early modern Scottish and Irish unions and has considerable parallels to English patterns, though Malcomson and Wilson have focused on the mid eighteenth century, rather than the post-Revolution decades.[3]

Controlled choice

Across Britain and Ireland, the pressure was on from a girl's teenage years to marry and to marry well. In a world where there were few job opportunities for a lady of the elite, her financial security (and by extension, her place on the social ladder) often depended on acquiring a husband with the means to support her in the manner to which she was accustomed, for even the wealthiest woman would have struggled to survive on the interest accruing from an inheritance or an unused marriage portion.[4] Yet there were considerable drawbacks in taking a husband, for under the laws of coverture, once married, a woman in England, Wales and Ireland (Scotland's laws were less stringent) 'fell prey to a whole series of disabilities which placed her in the same legal category as wards, lunatics, idiots and outlaws' and firmly under her husband's control.[5] Her financial assets became his, unless well protected by either her marriage settlement, or the will of any person who bequeathed such assets to her, and he was perfectly within his rights to beat her and to keep her children from her.[6] With her economic and personal wellbeing destined to depend so heavily upon this one person, selecting a suitable husband was paramount, yet here women found their freedom of choice restricted.

Marriage in Ireland in the late seventeenth and early eighteenth centuries was governed by an unusually strict legal framework. Thanks to the Cromwellian and Williamite land forfeitures and the emergence of the Protestant Ascendancy in a predominantly Catholic country, Irish marital laws were updated several decades

1650–1950 (Oxford, 1994); R.B. Outhwaite, *Clandestine marriage in England, 1500–1850* (London, 1995); Amy Erickson, *Women and property in early modern England* (London, 1993); eadem, 'Property and widowhood in England 1660–1840' in Sandra Cavallo and Lyndan Warner (eds), *Widowhood in medieval and early modern Europe* (Harlow, 1999); Eileen Spring, *Law, land, and family: aristocratic inheritance in England, 1300–1800* (London, 1993). See also Amanda Vickery, *The gentleman's daughter: women's lives in Georgian England* (London, 1998), esp. ch. 2; Tanya Evans, 'Women, marriage and the family' in Hannah Barker and Elaine Chalus (eds), *Women's history: Britain, 1700–1850* (New York, 2005), pp 57–77; Ingrid Tague, *Women of quality: accepting and contesting ideals of femininity in England, 1690–1760* (Woodbridge, 2002), esp. ch. 3.

3 Katie Barclay, *Love, intimacy and power: marriage and patriarchy in Scotland, 1650–1850* (Manchester, 2011); A.P.W. Malcomson, *The pursuit of the heiress: aristocratic marriage in Ireland 1740–1840* (2nd edn, Belfast, 2006); Deborah Wilson, *Women, marriage and property in wealthy landed families in Ireland, 1750–1850* (Manchester, 2009).

4 Robert Shoemaker, *Gender in English society, 1650–1850: the emergence of separate spheres?* (London, 1998), pp 91–2; Malcomson, *Pursuit of the heiress*, pp 116–17.

5 Janelle Greenberg, 'The legal status of the English woman in early eighteenth-century common law and equity', *Studies in Eighteenth-Century Culture*, iv (1975), p. 172. On the rights of Scottish wives, see Barclay, *Love, intimacy and power*, p. 51.

6 Greenberg, 'The legal status of the English woman', pp 174–7; Wilson, *Women, marriage and property*, p. 127; Shoemaker, *Gender in English society*, p. 52.

sooner than those in England and permitted a level of familial and legal control over unions not seen in England until the 1753 Hardwicke Marriage Act, which decreed that the only legal unions were those which took place in an Anglican church either after banns, or with a licence.[7] Officially, the legal age for marriage on both sides of the Irish Sea was fourteen for a boy and just twelve for a girl,[8] but in Ireland no girl under 16 had been allowed to marry without her father or guardian's consent since 1634, in order to help combat the abductions of heiresses (maternal consent being no substitute unless a mother was her child's legal guardian).[9] As the protection and promotion of Protestant landownership became more important, further restrictions were brought in. From 1697 onwards, any Protestant Irish woman worth more than £500 who married a Catholic immediately forfeited her estate to her nearest Protestant family member, though if the positions were reversed, a husband was given a year to convert his wife and could retain her estate if successful, a distinction which Deborah Wilson has argued paid homage to the idea of wifely submission.[10] After 1735, no minor, male or female, could marry without paternal consent if they or their parents owned a real estate worth more than £100, nor were they free do so if their personal estate totalled more than £500, or £2,000 in the case of their parents.[11] In theory, those legally and financially independent of their parents were free of such impediments, but in practice, filial respect and the continued pecuniary considerations surrounding inheritance ensured that many fathers and mothers had a determining influence in the identity of their sons- and daughters-in-law, even after their children had turned 21. This was partly to control and protect familial and estate interests. Marriages were financial mergers, useful for creating and strengthening social, political and kinship networks which promoted the welfare of each family involved and the Ascendancy as a whole. As such, they were too valuable to be left in the hands of the young and impressionable, whose actions might be guided by personal concerns over familial duty and who might be persuaded into a union with an unsuitable candidate if one was permitted to approach them. There were emotional considerations too. Negotiations often failed and it was best to avoid allowing a child to become invested in a union which

7 26 Geo. II, c. 32 [Eng.] (1753) reproduced in Outhwaite, *Clandestine marriage*, pp 173–80; Evans, 'Women, marriage and the family', p. 61. Evans points out that Jews, Quakers and royalty were exempt from these rules, but Roman Catholics were not, which posed a considerable problem for England's Irish communities.

8 Bridget Hill, 'The marriage age of women and the demographers', *History Workshop Journal*, xxviii (1989), p. 130. While this law was amended in England by the 1753 Hardwicke Marriage Act, it theoretically survived for much longer in Ireland, which was not mentioned by the act. See 26 Geo. II, c. 32 [Eng.] (1753) reproduced in Outhwaite, *Clandestine marriage*, pp 173–80. In Scotland, 12 and 14 remained the legal ages for marriage until 1929 (Barclay, *Love, intimacy and power*, p. 42).

9 Wilson, *Women, marriage and property*, pp 24, 29. The abduction of heiresses was rare among the Irish elite during the period under consideration here, and is therefore not discussed in detail, however further information on the phenomenon may be found in Malcomson, *Pursuit of the heiress*, pp 155–6; Wilson, *Women, marriage and property*, pp 24–7; James Kelly, 'The abduction of women of fortune in eighteenth-century Ireland', *Eighteenth-century Ireland*, ix (1994), pp 7–43. For Scotland, see Barclay, *Love, intimacy and power*, p. 77.

10 Wilson, *Women, marriage and property*, pp 25–6.

11 Ibid., p. 29.

would not happen. The organisation of marriages therefore remained primarily in the hands of parents.

In the case of a first marriage, if a young man or woman's father was alive, he would take the lead in organising their union, though the input of mothers and even grandmothers was frequently welcome and often sought. In the late 1690s Mary, countess of Drogheda, with the assistance of her mother, took a leading role in the ultimately doomed negotiations for a union between her son, Lord Moore, and Catherine Keightley, a first cousin of Mary II and Queen Anne. In 1710, Robert Molesworth (later Viscount Molesworth) specifically requested the help of his wife, Letitia, when their daughter Charlotte's marriage was being arranged.[12] In England too, negotiations 'were largely carried on by women, whether their husbands were alive or not', but maternal involvement was a courtesy rather than a right, and it was only when family patriarchs were dead that a mother, or other female relative left as guardian, would have power and influence equal to a father's.[13] This subjugation of maternal to paternal power was epitomised by the treatment of Catherine's mother, Lady Frances Keightley. Having separated from her husband in the 1680s, she was repeatedly excluded from the discussions surrounding their daughter's marriage. When Catherine eventually wed Lucius O'Brien, Frances was not even informed until after the event.[14]

The opening move in negotiations was typically made by the groom's side and directed towards the bride's parents or guardians, a convention which furthered parental control, but also allowed for discreet enquiries to be made with minimal embarrassment to the prospective bride or groom should they be rejected. Attempts to circumvent normal procedures were not well received, and the orphaned County Limerick heiress, Frances Ingoldsby, was disgusted and alarmed when she was approached by a Mr Oliver Crofton in 1733 and pelted with a stream of unsolicited, rambling love letters, begging for her hand.[15] Far from accepting him, she passed the letters to her guardian, who threatened Crofton with legal action if he persisted, and confessed himself 'not a little surprised that a person of whom I had received so good an impression should make pretensions to a lady under my wardship in the manner you did'.[16] If an offer was received warmly, however, it would be followed by a flurry of polite, but determined letters, as the two sides haggled over financial details while simultaneously trying to befriend future in-laws. Though the couple in question might already know one another and be aware of and even promoting their engagement, it was rare that they would correspond directly on the subject until the match was all but certain.

12 Mary, countess of Drogheda to Thomas Keightley, 22 June 1698 (NLI, MS 45, 722/3); Robert Molesworth to the Hon. Letitia Molesworth, 8 Apr. 1710 (*The Clements archive*, ed. Malcomson (Dublin, 2010), p. 128).

13 Erickson, *Women and property*, p. 93.

14 Laurence, earl of Rochester to Catherine O'Brien, 24 Jan. 1701/2 (NLI, MS 45, 295/2).

15 See, for example, Oliver Crofton to Frances Ingoldsby, [1733] (ibid., MS 41, 581/11).

16 James Smythe to Crofton, 18 Mar. 1732/33 (ibid.). Frances Ingoldsby turned out to be too much of a catch for her own good. She was ultimately abducted and married in 1743 by Hugh Fitzjohn Massy. See Malcomson, *Pursuit of the heiress*, p. 64; Toby Barnard, *The abduction of a Limerick heiress: social and political relations in mid-eighteenth century Ireland* (Dublin, 1998).

This system, though overbearing in many ways, succeeded because parental control was not routinely pushed to its limits. While there were instances of forced marriage on both sides of the Irish Sea (such as the 2nd earl of Sunderland's daughter, Lady Elizabeth Spencer, who was made to marry Donough MacCarthy, 4th earl of Clancarty in 1684 at the age of no more than 13) the practice was becoming increasingly unpopular across Britain and it should not be inferred that those in, or about to enter, the Irish elite had no control over who they married.[17] Generally, while their families and even friends might express a preference for a particular candidate and encourage a young man or woman to accept the match, if they expressed a great aversion to it, their feelings were usually taken into account and the union did not proceed, no matter how favourable it would have been to the families involved. As one father put it,

> I should not press any of my children beyond their inclinations. I have reason to believe they will pay that deference to my judgement as not to engage without my advice and consent and I will be so just to them as not to force their inclination, but allow them a vote in their own choice.[18]

Of the multiple proposals of marriage the Honourable Alice Brodrick (daughter of the 1st Viscount Midleton) received, at least two failed because she refused to marry either of the gentlemen in question, much to the chagrin of her uncle, Thomas Brodrick. He reported with regard to one suitor, of whom both he and her father approved, that although he asked for her reasons for refusing the proposal, which was 'very honourable and great', he 'could get no other answer than that she was sure she could never be happy with him, and would rather live on fifty pounds a year rather than marry him' despite his great wealth. In frustration, Thomas wrote to his brother that he could not 'guess at the reason which none but her self can unriddle'.[19] Sir Edward O'Brien was just as intransigent and, even as a minor, successfully resisted for several years requests from his mother and grandmother to wed Miss Mary Hickman from County Clare. His motives are more easily discerned than Alice's, for his hesitancy and eventual change of heart were grounded in a determination to make the most profitable match possible and an inflated sense of his own worth in the marriage market.[20]

The basic selection criteria which the Irish elite used to choose a spouse were essentially the same for both men and women. One gentleman summed up the perfect wife as having 'quality, fortune, friends, and ... good humour and virtue', while another listed his own attributes as being wealth, character, education and

17 *Oxford D.N.B.* (Spencer, Robert, 2nd earl of Sunderland) and (MacCarthy, Donough, styled 4th earl of Clancarty). For the increasingly rarity of forced marriages in Scotland from the later seventeenth century onwards, see Barclay, *Love, intimacy and power*, p. 77; Katharine Glover, *Elite women and polite society in eighteenth-century Scotland* (Woodbridge, 2011), p. 22.

18 Thomas Knox to Thomas Knox, 16 Nov. 1704 (PRONI, D2860/4/13). These two men were cousins, thus their identical names.

19 Thomas Brodrick to Alan, Viscount Midleton, 7 July 1724 (SHC, MS 1248/6/41–42); quote from same to same, 1 Aug. 1724 (ibid., MS 1248/6/47–48).

20 See, for example, Lady Frances Keightley to Catherine O'Brien, 31 Aug. 1723 (NLI, MS 45, 348/6).

reputation, all supported by connexions which left him 'nearly allied on all sides to families no one need blush to own'.[21] Female education will be discussed in greater detail in Chapter 2, but it is useful to note here the growing trend to instruct girls in a variety of subjects which would enable them to function as companions to their husbands, capable of engaging their interest on a cerebral level. Jonathan Swift, despite being a life-long bachelor, was a great believer in this practice, warning a young lady of his acquaintance that her youth and beauty would soon fade (and nowhere faster than in the eyes of her husband), necessitating their replacement 'with more durable qualities', for 'the endowments of your mind will even make your person more agreeable to him'.[22] Without such mental acuity, 'it is impossible to acquire or preserve the friendship and esteem of a wise man, who soon grows weary of acting the lover, and treating his wife like a mistress, but wants a reasonable companion, and a true friend through every stage of his life'.[23] As Swift acknowledged, despite the limited value he placed upon them, good looks were a frequent demand made of brides, though less so of grooms, who instead found their characters subjected to greater scrutiny by those assessing their suitability as husbands; an unsurprising variation when the legal control a husband would have over a wife and the rudimentary state of divorce at this time are taken into consideration. Jane Bonnell, widow of the accountant general of Ireland, James Bonnell and sister-in-law of William Conolly, Speaker of the Irish House of Commons, even received a report in the late 1720s that an acquaintance, Miss Silver, had broken off her engagement to a Mr Barry after he 'fell in to a passion' in her presence, for 'she said if he showed that temper beforehand what must she expect when a wife'.[24]

Drawing on these prerequisites, each individual and family had a customised list of requirements for a spouse, at the head of which was invariably money, a boon which could cloak many defects. At 17 years old, Sir Edward O'Brien had already made it clear that he wanted an advantageous union with a wife who came with good looks and 'match money', but so blinded was he by the size of the fortune which would accompany Lady Betty Barry, daughter of the 4th earl of Barrymore, that he apparently overlooked her many flaws.[25] His grandmother, Lady Frances Keightley, soon reminded him. The lady was 'very plain', had 'no manner of wit like her father', and was in short 'extremely insipid', and almost mute, whether at home or in company. Her excellent connexions might have helped, but her mother 'was of an odd behaviour and all her family though of great quality had strange tempers'. To cap it all, she had 'been brought up with a mother-in-law [*stepmother*] who though

21 Terence McDonogh to Kean O'Hara, 8 Mar. [1700/1] (PRONI, T2812/5/21); Crofton to [Frances Ingoldsby], [n.d., c.1733] (ibid., MS 41, 581/11).

22 Jonathan Swift, 'A letter to a very young lady on her marriage' in *The prose works of Jonathan Swift*, ed. Herbert Davis (14 vols, Oxford, 1939–68), ix, 89.

23 Ibid., 86. See also Shoemaker, *Gender in English society*, pp 47–9; Glover, *Elite women and polite society*, p. 30; Katharine Glover, 'The female mind: Scottish enlightenment femininity and the world of letters. A case study of the women of the Fletcher of Saltoun family in the mid-eighteenth century', *Journal of Scottish Historical Studies*, xxv (2005), pp 5, 20; Christina De Bellaigue, *Educating women: schooling and identity in England and France, 1800–1867* (Oxford, 2007), p. 16.

24 Sarah Worth to Jane Bonnell, 11 Dec. [1729?] (NLI, MS 41, 580/27).

25 Lady Frances Keightley to Catherine O'Brien, 29 Nov. 1722 (ibid., MS 45, 348/5); same to same, 5 Nov. 1723 (ibid., MS 45, 348/6).

extremely good will never be thought to have found out gun powder or any other mystery'.[26] Such a woman would never do for Edward, and his grandmother instead advised his mother that 'your chiefest care must be the temper of the woman or both will be miserable to excess'.[27] Edward's view, though unromantic, was the more typical, however. The determination to marry someone with resources equal to, or better than, your own was endemic throughout the elite, and marriages between those who were financially unequal were unusual. Edward was warned off two potential brides who were too rich for him (including Lady Betty) and who would, his grandmother explained, 'claim a title to a way of life which holds full proportion to what they bring', while Sir John Frederick did not even approach Alice Brodick's family about a possible match in 1724 until he was sure she had £10,000 to her name. These financial barriers in turn led to social endogamy, for people of similar means and standing frequented the same circles while those who tried to reach beyond them, as Edward had done, discovered the futility of doing so. By the early eighteenth century, more than half the MPs in the Irish House of Commons were related to one or more of their colleagues.[28]

Social and financial restrictions were added to by those of a geographical nature. Wives typically settled in their husbands' homes, but many baulked at the idea of moving far from all they knew. Mary Aldworth, sister of Kean O'Hara of County Sligo, raised this issue, among others, with her brother when he was hoping to marry Lady Betty Moore, daughter of the 3rd earl of Drogheda. Though her letter to him does not survive, its tenor and contents can be reconstructed from Kean's reply. As well as the problems which would be caused by the disparity in rank between the pair, she was convinced that 'if the house were never so fine and complete ... the young lady would not like living in the country', but Kean sought to 'assure you to the contrary'. He could not afford to live in Dublin, but Betty was both 'as willing to live in this country as I am myself' and 'satisfied to live under her quality, and according to my present fortune'. More telling than all his protests, however, is the fact that the wedding did not take place. Lady Betty married George Rochfort, MP for Westmeath and someone who would therefore spend considerable time in parliament in Dublin, while Kean married Eleanor Matthew, of County Tipperary, a woman of lower birth and fewer demands and one of the few Catholic women mentioned in this book (though Kean was Protestant).[29]

With Irish women often unwilling to relocate permanently within their own country, it is no surprise to find that an English or Scottish bride, with no prior connexions, or experience of Ireland, was a rare thing indeed among the resident

26 Same to same, 5 Nov. 1723 (ibid., MS 45, 348/6); same to same, 2 Jan. 1724/25 (ibid.); same to same, 28 Sept. 1723 (ibid.).

27 Same to same, 18 Nov. 1723 (ibid.).

28 Same to same, 28 Sept. 1723 (ibid); Thomas Brodrick to Midleton, 7 July 1724 (SHC, MS 1248/6/41–42); Habakkuk, *Marriage, debt and the estates system*, p. 163; Mary O'Dowd, *A history of women in Ireland, 1500–1800* (Harlow, 2004), p. 44.

29 Kean O'Hara to Mary Aldworth, 14 Mar. 1701/2 (PRONI, T2812/5/39); *D.I.B.* (Rochfort, George Augustus (1738–1815)); Bernard Burke, *A genealogical and heraldic dictionary of the landed gentry of Great Britain and Ireland* (4th edn, 2 vols, London, 1863), ii, 1111; J.G. Simms, 'County Sligo in the eighteenth century', *Journal of the Royal Society of Antiquaries of Ireland*, xci (1961), pp 154–5.

peerage. One of the many reasons Lady Frances Keightley deemed the English-born Lady Charlotte Hyde an unsuitable bride for her grandson was the fact that 'I am certain Dromoland [*the O'Brien family seat in County Clare*] should never agree with her', a gentle warning that an English lady was unlikely to voluntarily migrate to the west coast of Ireland.[30] Even the most cosmopolitan families were deceptively provincial. The 2nd duke of Ormond's mother was Dutch and his wives were first Lady Anne Hyde, daughter of Laurence, earl of Rochester and second, Lady Mary Somerset, daughter of the duke of Beaufort, yet the family retained strong connexions with the Irish elite. Rochester and his brother, Lord Clarendon, were both heavily involved in the running of Ireland in the 1680s and Anne's mother was Lady Henrietta Boyle, a daughter of the 2nd earl of Cork. Lady Mary may have had no obvious Irish connexions at the time of her marriage, but a year after her wedding, her sister, Henrietta, was married to the heir of the earl of Thomond. In fact, it was generally only permanent absentees, like the doubly ennobled earls of Cork and Burlington, who frequently married into undiluted English families (the 3rd earl of Cork was wed to Juliana Noel from Yorkshire, the 4th to the marquis of Halifax's daughter, Lady Dorothy Savile), and even they did not entirely forget their Irish roots. Another Lady Henrietta Boyle, this time the daughter of the 3rd earl and countess of Burlington (4th of Cork), married her distant cousin, Henry Boyle, later 1st earl of Shannon.[31] There were practical obstacles to international marriages too, even between Irish women and Englishmen or Scots. The parties and their families could be 'utterly strangers' to each other and 'living in several kingdoms makes contracts of this kind attended with several difficulties that otherwise would not occur'.[32]

The tight-knit nature of the elite also explains how rarely titles were explicitly asked for in a spouse. A homogeneous social circle and by extension, marriage pool, ensured that like would marry like, making it unnecessary to specify specific ranks. Beyond their servants, the elite were unlikely to know anyone of a significantly higher or lower station than their own and if they did, personal pride usually prevented unequal matches. The position of a woman's family was of the utmost importance, despite the fact that she could rarely pass a title to her children, and Malcomson has shown that by the mid-century it was rare for an Irish peer to 'condescend' to marry the daughter of even the wealthiest of commoners, notwithstanding the possible financial inducements.[33] This trait may be projected back to the early 1700s, but it is not to be found in England or Scotland, where there was a clearer pattern of cash-strapped peers and sons of peers marrying what J.V. Beckett has called 'commoner heiresses', as well as members of the elite. For their part, women were not immune to the lure of becoming Ladies (widows who married lower a

30 Lady Frances Keightley to Catherine O'Brien, 31 Aug. 1723 (NLI, MS 45, 348/6).

31 *Oxford D.N.B.* (Butler, James, 2nd duke of Ormond (1665–1745), Hyde, Laurence, 1st earl of Rochester (*bap.* 1642, *d.* 1711), Somerset, Henry, 1st duke of Beaufort (1629–1700), Boyle, Henry, 1st earl of Shannon (1681x7–1764)).

32 Thomas Knox to Thomas Knox, 16 Nov. 1704 (PRONI, D2860/4/13).

33 For an example of a woman who could pass her title to her children, see Elizabeth Boyle, the English-born countess of Cork and Burlington, who inherited the title of Baroness Clifford and was able to pass it on to her descendants (*Oxford D.N.B.* (Clifford, Henry, 5th earl of Cumberland (1592–1643)); Malcomson, *Pursuit of the heiress*, p. 49).

second or third time, kept their prior titles), but most knew that rank was only as good as the fortune underpinning it. Katie Barclay has argued that in Scotland, the elite were willing to overlook a lower social status if it was compensated for by wealth, but 'suitors who could not suitably match their beloved in rank and fortune risked their authority within marriage'. In Ireland in 1738 Frances Ingoldsby refused the marriage proposal of the financially challenged Francis de Bermingham, 14th Baron Athenry, saying that she 'did not want gentility'. She knew as well as he, that money was the real asset.[34]

Inappropriate marriages

Occasionally, someone would flout the rules and make a wholly inappropriate match, much to the shock (and delight) of the gossip-mongers, who condemned those who had married down for having succumbed to lust, and those who had married up for being fortune hunters.[35] Alan Brodrick, Viscount Midleton, was sure that William Vesey, the third husband of Ursula, dowager Baroness Altham, 'neither chose her for youth or beauty: and if the estate was in her power when he married her, I doubt not it either is not so now, or will not long be so'.[36] Meanwhile the 66-year-old Katherine, dowager countess of Barrymore, upon taking as her third husband the 51-year-old Sir Henry Piers, 3rd Bt, felt compelled to make him promise 'not to bed in four days for she told the minister that married them she hoped no one supposed she married out of wantonness'.[37] Katherine's 'wantonness' did her no harm though, for she lived for eight years after this wedding, more than could be said for one unlucky male newlywed, whose demise moved his cousin to remark that 'a young wife is indeed no good prescription when a man is turned of sixty'.[38]

Matches made solely on the strength of love, rather than advancement, were rare. If a couple were lucky, love might emerge during marriage, but while marriage negotiations spoke of men and women's characters and brokers usually looked for a degree of compatibility between intended spouses, romantic love was barely mentioned, either in Ireland, or elsewhere.[39] John Boyle, 5th earl of Orrery, professed

34 J.V. Beckett, *The aristocracy in England, 1660–1914* (Oxford, 1986), p. 105; Arthur Blennerhassett to William Smyth, 26 Dec. 1738 (NLI, MS 41, 581/13); Barclay, *Love, intimacy and power*, p. 81.

35 In England too, 'widows were thought to marry for lust' (Shoemaker, *Gender in English society*, p. 137). See also Tague, 'Aristocratic women and ideas of family in the eighteenth century' in Helen Berry and Elizabeth Foyster (eds), *The family in early modern England* (Cambridge, 2007), p. 192.

36 Midleton to Thomas Brodrick, 20 Mar. 1720/1 (SHC, MS 1248/4/434–435).

37 [Sarah Worth?] to Bonnell, 13 Dec. [1729] (NLI, MS 41, 580/27). This letter incorrectly gives the couple's ages as 70 and 40; however, Katherine was born in 1663 and Henry in 1678. See John Lodge and Mervyn Archdall, *The peerage of Ireland, or a genealogical history of the present nobility of that kingdom* (7 vols, Dublin, 1789), i, 308; ibid., ii, 203.

38 Charles O'Hara to [Kean O'Hara?], 12 Feb. 1703/4 (PRONI, T2812/8/8).

39 Katie Barclay, 'Love and courtship in eighteenth-century Scotland' in eadem and Deborah Simonton (eds), *Women in eighteenth-century Scotland: intimate, intellectual and public lives* (Farnham, 2013), pp 37–54. Tague, *Women of quality*, ch. 2.

adoration for his new wife, the wealthy heiress, Margaret Hamilton of Caledon, County Tyrone, in 1739, but he was equally enamoured of her fortune, if not more so. In announcing the marriage, he boasted that she had brought him 'a heart fill'd with love and a hand with money'. One wonders how far the former would have got her without the latter.[40] Some unions could be attributed to nothing but strong affection, though. Chaworth Brabazon, 6th earl of Meath, completely ignored all financial, social and even aesthetic considerations in his marriages, taking as his first wife his aunt's chambermaid and then, in his widowhood, Juliana, daughter of Sir Thomas Prendergast, 1st Bt. The English-born Mary Pendarves (later wife of Patrick Delany, dean of Down), who was then visiting Ireland, was convinced that this second marriage was for love as the lady had 'little or no fortune, and is far from handsome'.[41] Another observer was less diplomatic in his description of the countess, who was, he declared

> as large and rosy as her lady mother [*Penelope Cadogan*] or her uncle [*the 1st Earl*] Cadogan. She is as broad backed as Tom Christmas. She has a stomach capable of supporting such infinite hugeness of bulk. There is in my sense as much reason to think her with child in her cheeks as where she should swell naturally. Her hands have literally verified the gross hyperbole of potato fingers.

He also predicted (correctly) that the marriage would never produce any children.[42]

As inadvisable as these marriages were, they were at least made openly and between free agents, under no obligations to their immediate families. As such, they did not occasion the same vitriol that was directed at those who contracted a clandestine match. Clandestine marriages were those willingly entered into by two individuals of marriageable age, but without the knowledge or permission of one or both of their parents or guardians. In Scotland, they were fairly common in the seventeenth century, before petering out over the course of the eighteenth, as children were given a greater say by their parents in who their spouse would be, while the practice may have faded even faster in England, where R.B. Outhwaite has shown that they were relatively rare in the upper orders by the early 1700s.[43] Evidence for their popularity in Ireland is sketchy at best, but there were calls for them to be made illegal as early as the 1690s and for the clergy involved to be prosecuted. The eventual amendments to the Irish laws discussed earlier also show that they raised more concern among the Irish than the British, for the title of the 1735 act ('For the more effectual preventing clandestine marriages') made it clear

40 John, earl of Orrery to John Kempe, 1 July 1739 (*The Orrery papers*, ed. Emily, countess of Cork and Orrery (2 vols, London, 1903), i, 240); *D.I.B.* (Boyle, John (1707–62)). See also Everard Hamilton, *Hamilton memoirs: being historical and genealogical notices of a branch of that family which settled in Ireland in the reign of King James I* (2nd edn, Dundalk, 1920), pp 5, 8–12.

41 Mary Pendarves to Anne Granville, 14 Dec. 1731 (*The autobiography and correspondence of Mary Granville, Mrs Delany: with interesting reminiscences of King George III and Queen Charlotte*, ed. Lady Llanover (ser. 1, 3 vols, London, 1861), i, 330).

42 Robert Bettesworth to Henry Boyle, 15 Feb. 1732/3 (PRONI, D2707/A/1/11/59). See also Malcomson, *Pursuit of the heiress*, p. 10.

43 Barclay, *Love, intimacy and power*, pp 75–8; Outhwaite, *Clandestine marriage*, p. 62. One eighteenth-century example can be found in Glover, *Elite women and polite society*, p. 93.

that it was explicitly intended to help eradicate them.[44] Whether this was because of a surfeit of such marriages is highly debatable, though. The wording and property qualifications in both this act and that of 1634 show that they were aimed at only the wealthier inhabitants of Ireland (who would have been primarily Protestant by 1735), and Deborah Wilson sees the later measure as being another facet of the ongoing battle to strengthen the Protestant Ascendancy in Ireland. She argues that the Irish legislation was more akin to a penal law than to the Hardwicke Act (which applied to all persons in England and Wales, irrespective of wealth, but did not extend to Ireland) and was motivated by the need to deal with 'specific perceived threats to Protestant interests', which were not felt in England.[45] Other deterrents that concerned parents availed of suggest a desire to protect family interests and included financial penalties which would make children less attractive prospects (or targets). In his will of 1689, Matthew Plunkett, 7th Baron Louth, stipulated that after his death, if his daughters Ally, Frances and Rose married with their mother's consent, they would each be entitled to a marriage portion of £600. If not, he left them only £50 apiece.[46]

All the financial obstacles in the world were not enough to stop the determined, however, and the 1735 act came too late to thwart some marriages, nor could it prevent or nullify those weddings which took place outside of Ireland.[47] These unions were frowned upon by families and society at large for the financial uncertainties they brought, but even a new son- or daughter-in-law who might otherwise have been considered a worthy partner was unwelcome, given 'the disappointment and disrespect' shown to their parents or guardians. Men and women were denounced in equal measure for making such a move, and the damage to family relations was often irreparable.[48] Williams Conyngham, the wayward nephew of Speaker William Conolly and his wife Katherine, was practically disowned by his family after he married Adamina Wilhemina Nierops in Amsterdam in about 1717. Though he represented her as being an heiress who 'neither in fortune nor in family is in any way unequal to me', and wrote many pleading leaders to his aunt Conolly and her sister, Jane Bonnell, seeking their help in reconciling him with his uncle, William, the letters to Katherine went unanswered.[49] Following Adamina's early death and another hasty, unvetted marriage, this time to the slightly more

44 Reverend John Hawkins to Sir Donat O'Brien, 1st Bt, 9 Feb. 1698/9 (NLI, MS 45, 293/4); 9 Geo. II, c. 11 [Ire.] (1735). For more information on the various unsuccessful attempts in England between the Restoration and the 1753 Hardwicke Marriage Act to create laws against clandestine marriages, including the practice of fining the clergy involved, see Outhwaite, *Clandestine marriage*, pp 13–19.

45 Wilson, *Women, marriage and property*, pp 32–3.

46 Will of Matthew Plunkett, 7th Baron Louth, 16 Dec. 1689 (NLI, MS 40, 094/1).

47 Malcomson has pointed out that, particularly after 1753, Irish couples took advantage of the fact that the Hardwicke Act did not apply in Scotland and travelled there to be wed, something they were able to do in the first half of the century as well, money permitting (Malcomson, *The pursuit of the heiress*, p. 157).

48 Ibid.; Barclay, *Love, intimacy and power*, p. 75; Evans, 'Women, marriage and the family', p. 60. Quote from Hawkins to Sir Donat O'Brien, 1st Bt, 9 Feb. 1698/9 (NLI, MS 45, 293/4).

49 Williams Conyngham to Bonnell, 18 Apr. 1718 (NLI, MS 41, 579/1); same to same, 17 Apr. 1718 (ibid.).

suitable Constance Middleton, daughter of an English MP, Williams was ultimately disinherited.[50]

Marriage settlements

The financial uncertainty clandestine marriages posed, particularly to women, also indicates that they were used only by the impetuous or the desperate, for they did not come with the security of a marriage settlement, the cornerstone of an elite marriage.[51] The poor and the lowly rarely had such settlements, the wealthy and the high-born were rarely without. They were drawn up before the wedding, signed by the bride and groom and, in the case of the marriages of minors or dependants, by their parents or guardians. Lengthy, technical and jargon-filled, they detailed the financial aspects of the union and the pecuniary rights of all those involved. The key sums involved were the amount of money or land a bride brought to the union (known alternatively as her portion or dowry), the amount of money she would be allotted out of her husband's estate for maintenance should he predecease her (known as her jointure) and, as an optional extra, the amount she might receive in predetermined instalments throughout the year as a kind of allowance in excess of her household budget for 'clothes, amusements, charities and, and such other out-of-pocket expenses'.[52] This was her 'pin money'. A settlement also established the portions which would be given to any and all sons and daughters of the marriage upon their majorities or marriages, so allowing the system to run from one generation to the next.

Portions, jointures and 'pin money' were all interconnected, and the more a woman brought to a marriage the better treated she would be financially during and after it. In the early seventeenth century English jointures tended to be around a fifth of the size of the portion, with the provision for widows gradually decreasing as the century wore on so that by the early eighteenth, the typical ratio was that of ten to one (that is, ten pounds of portion for every one pound of jointure).[53] Even

50 Patrick Walsh, *The making of the Irish Protestant ascendancy: the life of William Conolly, 1662–1729* (Woodbridge, 2010), p. 10.

51 An extensive historiography has traced the development of these settlements in England, though to date little has been written on the Irish experience. See John Habakkuk, 'The rise and fall of English landed families, 1600–1800', *Transactions of the Royal Historical Society*, ser. 5, xxix (1979), pp 187–207; Lloyd Bonfield, 'Marriage settlements, 1660–1740: the adoption of the strict settlement in Kent and Northamptonshire' in R.B. Outhwaite (ed.), *Marriage and society*, pp 101–16; Christopher Clay, 'Property settlements, financial provision for the family, and sale of land by the greater landowners 1660–1790', *Journal of British Studies*, xxi (1981), pp 18–38; Bonfield, *Marriage settlements, 1601–1740*; Habakkuk, *Marriage, debt and the estates system*; Spring, *Law, land, and family*; Susan Staves, *Married women's separate property in England, 1660–1833* (London, 1990). For Ireland, see Wilson, *Women, marriage and property*; Malcomson, *Pursuit of the heiress*.

52 Erickson, *Women and property*, p. 103; Staves, *Married women's separate property*, p. 132. The quote is from Staves.

53 Erickson, *Women and property*, p. 119; Habakkuk, 'Rise and fall of English landed families', p. 192; Spring, *Law, land, and family*, pp 50–1. Occasionally a reference will be seen to dower, rather than jointure, an older method of widow maintenance which was petering out by the late

when one half of the couple had Irish connexions, if both were living in England, the ten per cent formula was usually followed. Lady Dorothy Savile brought £30,000 to her marriage in 1720 and in return was allotted a £3,000 jointure from her husband, Richard, earl of Cork and Burlington.[54] Many women were allotted the income from a specific piece of land rather than a cash payment, so that the amount intended for the jointure was not specified in the settlement, and if and when it became due, could fluctuate depending on the economy and on how difficult it was to rent out land. However, land jointures were decreasing in popularity by the early eighteenth century, allowing scholars of Irish settlements to find that the older ratio of five to one survived longer for those couples who were actually resident in Ireland and continued into the Hanoverian regime.[55] Catherine O'Brien brought a £3,000 portion and received a jointure of £500 in 1701/2 and Sir John Frederick was prepared to offer the very generous jointure of £3,000 for Alice Brodrick's £10,000 dowry in 1724.[56] The English practice of giving roughly a ten per cent return was increasingly followed, even when both spouses were Irish, born and bred. Barbara Ingoldsby (great-aunt of Frances Ingoldsby) from County Limerick was allotted £200 in recognition of the £2,000 she brought to her union with William Smyth in 1713, and when James Barlow of Dublin married Althmia Leigh from Drogheda in 1731, the portion and jointure were £3,000 and £350 respectively.[57] Confusing the matter further were those who completely ignored the trend. Lady Anne Wentworth, daughter of the earl of Strafford, brought £5,000 to her marriage with William Conolly, junior, in 1733, yet still secured a jointure of £3,000, to give her an incredibly high return of sixty per cent.[58] She stands as an exception, and other reasons should be looked to for her unusual allowance. As noted earlier, peers were rarely paid extra in order to marry, or allow their children to marry, into a commoner family, however 'if any cash was going for "condescension", it is likely to have been paid by Irishmen or Irishwomen marrying into English high society'.[59] This was the case with the Conolly/Wentworth connexion. William came from a family which had only recently climbed to the top of the social ladder in Ireland through the efforts of his uncle and namesake the Speaker, and so, when faced with the opportunity to ally himself with the daughter of an English earl, who also

seventeenth century, but which had entitled women to a lifelong interest in a third of their late husbands' estates and as such, was arguably more favourable than jointure. For discussions of this change, see Malcomson, *Pursuit of the heiress*, pp 20–2; Wilson, *Women, marriage and property*, pp 42–6, 62, 75–6; Staves, *Married women's separate property*, pp 97–100; Spring, *Law, land, and family*, pp 40–52.

54 Marriage settlement of Richard, 3rd earl of Burlington and 4th earl of Cork and Lady Dorothy Savile, 18 Mar. 1720 (Chatsworth, MS L/17/93).

55 On the decrease of land jointures, see Barclay, *Love, intimacy and power*, p. 83; Spring, *Law, land, and family*, p. 50. On Irish settlements, see Clay, 'Property settlements', p. 28; Malcomson, *Pursuit of the heiress*, p. 27.

56 Marriage settlement of Lucius O'Brien and Catherine Keightley, 29 Dec. 1701 (NLI, MS 45, 290/4); Thomas Brodrick to Midleton, 7 July 1724 (SHC, MS 1248/6/41–42).

57 Marriage settlement of William Smyth and Barbara Ingoldsby, 16 Mar. 1712/13 (NLI, MS 41, 568/1); marriage settlement of James Barlow and Althmia Leigh, 14 Jan. 1730/1 (ibid.).

58 Marriage settlement of William Conolly and Lady Anne Wentworth, 1733 (IAA, MS G/9/1).

59 Malcomson, *Pursuit of the heiress*, p. 49.

happened to be a potential heiress, he was willing to allow a high jointure to be placed on his estate.[60]

Next to a jointure, 'pin money' was the most important aspect of a marriage settlement for a bride. A relatively new phenomenon, it is not often found in Irish marriage settlements of the late 1600s and early 1700s, though it was common by the 1720s and 1730s, as was also the case in England.[61] Legally speaking, it was illogical and unenforceable, for a husband was already required to provide for his wife and the laws of coverture meant that he owned her financial assets.[62] To try to circumvent this problem, trustees were often appointed at the time of the marriage to manage the money on a wife's behalf (though they were not a legal requirement), but, confusingly, arrears of more than one year could not be collected, seemingly confirming the idea that the wife did not have full rights to the money and presenting it as nothing more than a favour from her husband. On top of this, even if the money was hers, the items she bought with it could become his.[63] These incongruities did not affect the popularity of 'pin money', probably because, as Susan Staves and Eileen Spring have pointed out, it gave women a certain sense of independence, a source of income in case of marital breakdown or particularly tight-fisted or careless husbands and, by sparing them from having to go to their spouses each time they wished to make a purchase, it made life more convenient for both.[64] Like jointure, it was related to the size of the bride's marriage portion, though this relationship was fluid and it is difficult to compare the two. Spring has suggested that it gradually came to match the interest accruing from the portion, and Deborah Wilson gives a figure of between four and ten per cent of the portion.[65] Thus, Lady Dorothy Savile was given £800 a year during her marriage, Lady Anne Wentworth received £450, and Sir John Frederick suggested £300 for Alice Brodrick.[66]

60 Walsh, *Making of the Irish Protestant ascendancy*, p. 8; A.P.W. Malcomson, 'The fall of the house of Conolly 1758–1803' in Allan Blackstock and Eoin Magennis (eds), *Politics and political culture in Britain and Ireland, 1750–1850* (Belfast, 2007), p. 130.

61 Erickson, *Women and property*, p. 150; Habakkuk, *Marriage, debt and the estate system*, pp 79–80; Staves, *Married women's separate property*, p. 132.

62 Staves, *Married women's separate property*, pp 133–5. Both Staves and Deborah Wilson note that 'pin money' should arguably not be referred to as separate estate, and, as Staves writes, though a distinction would be helpful, none was forthcoming in the eighteenth century (ibid., p. 134; Wilson, *Women, marriage and property*, pp 66–70). Coverture meant that a married women's legal rights, property and even debts became her husband's upon marriage and she was known as *femme covert*, as opposed to a widow or an unmarried adult woman, both of whom were known as *femme soles*. At the time of the Glorious Revolution, some argued that William III need not share the throne with his wife, Mary II, despite her stronger hereditary claim to it, because as a *femme covert*, all that she had belonged to him. See Lois Schwoerer, 'Images of Queen Mary II, 1698–95', *Renaissance Quarterly*, lxii (1989), pp 728–30.

63 Staves, *Married women's separate property*, pp 133–6; Wilson, *Women, marriage and property*, p. 67.

64 Staves, *Married women's separate property*, p. 44; Spring, *Law, land, and family*, p. 53.

65 Spring, *Law, land, and family*, p. 53; Wilson, *Women, marriage and property*, p. 128.

66 Marriage settlement of Richard, 3rd earl of Burlington and 4th earl of Cork and Lady Dorothy Savile; marriage settlement of William Conolly and Lady Anne Wentworth; Thomas Brodrick to Midleton, 1 Aug. 1724 (SHC, MS 1248/6/47–48).

The treatment of as yet unborn children in a marriage settlement was a source of some difficulty. To help avoid the potential financial problem of multiple daughters surviving into adulthood and all requiring portions, Scottish families often provided eldest daughters with larger sums than their sisters, making the younger girls less attractive marriage prospects.[67] In England and Ireland, on the other hand, 'it was very unusual to observe either primogeniture or any other distinction among daughters', and settlements frequently granted a specific sum of money for a single girl, or a larger lump sum to be divided equally among multiple daughters and payable either upon either their 18th or 21st birthdays, or their marriages, whichever came first.[68] The settlement of Charles and Juliana, 2nd earl and countess of Burlington (3rd of Cork) gave £10,000 for the use of one daughter, or to be divided between multiple sisters. A generation later, their son's settlement set aside £30,000 if he should have one daughter, or £40,000 to be divided among multiple girls, assuming they reached the age of 18, or were married.[69]

The pot might have to be shared with brothers, so that a woman would suffer financially if she acquired a sibling, but gain from their deaths, as long as they died before they were married or had attained their majorities. The young Molly Burton, whose marriage was mentioned at the beginning of this chapter, was raised by her great-aunt, Katherine Conolly and was bitterly disappointed when she learned that the birth of her little brother had cost her £3,000 from her dowry. She soon thought of a way around the problem, for according to Katherine, 'she looked blank and after some time silent she said, well then I'll stick close to my own dear mama [*Katherine*] and she will give me a portion and never left me all day'.[70] The £20,000 ascribed to her by newspaper reports at the time of her marriage indicates that it was a shrewd move. Conversely, by the terms of their parents' marriage settlement, the remaining daughters of the 3rd earl and countess of Burlington and 4th of Cork, gained significantly by the death of their sister, Lady Juliana Boyle, as the £40,000 stipulated for their shared portions had only to be divided into two, rather than three.[71]

Depending on how stringent a marriage settlement had been, portions could be increased by later legal documents once it became apparent how many surviving children a marriage was likely to produce. Charles, earl of Cork and Burlington, whose marriage settlement included a clause allowing him do just that, used it in 1701 to boost his four daughters' dowries from the £10,000 they would otherwise have had to share, to £5,000 each. Additionally, if even one of them died before claiming this money, her sisters' dowries would have automatically risen to

67 Glover, *Elite women and polite society*, p. 21; Stana Nenadic, 'Experience and expectations in the transformation of the Highland gentlewoman, 1680 to 1820', *Scottish Historical Review*, lxxx (2001), pp 205, 209.

68 Malcomson, *Pursuit of the heiress*, p. 32. See also Clay, 'Property settlements', p. 33; Spring, *Law, land, and family*, p. 77.

69 Settlement on the marriage of Charles Boyle, Lord Clifford (later 2nd earl of Burlington and 3rd earl of Cork) with the Hon. Juliana Noel; marriage settlement of Richard, 3rd earl of Burlington and 4th of Cork and Lady Dorothy Savile.

70 Katherine Conolly to Bonnell, 17 Mar. 1732/3 (NLI, MS 41, 578/7).

71 Marriage settlement of Richard, 3rd earl of Burlington and 4th of Cork and Lady Dorothy Savile.

£10,000.[72] This did not happen, but when his daughter Juliana married Lord Bruce in 1719, her brother increased her dowry to £10,000 anyway.[73] Later in the century, William Conolly, junior, also increased his daughters' portions, from the £4,000 stipulated in his marriage settlement, to £8,000 apiece, though his eldest daughter, Kitty, benefited even further by virtue of a bequest left to her by her great-aunt, Katherine Conolly, which brought her portion up to £10,000.[74]

Failed unions and second chances

One contingency for which marriage settlements failed to make provision was a failed union, which resulted in the parting of the spouses. It is difficult to be sure how often this occurred in late seventeenth- and early eighteenth-century Ireland, for the nomadic lifestyle of the elite, frequently moving between different houses, could help to hide separations, some of which were less formal than others.[75] A couple could simply stop cohabiting and agree, either verbally or in a written deed of separation, the new financial and living arrangements which they and their children were to abide by.[76] Alternatively, they could obtain a judicial separation, known as separation *a mensa et thoro* (literally from bed and board), which also laid out what maintenance a wife was to receive, relieved her husband of responsibility for her debts and established custody arrangements for any children. Some have pointed out these deeds' rather dubious claims to legality, for, like 'pin money', they ignored coverture and as a result were sometimes overturned in court, but they were often the best option for a couple who, for whatever reason, were unable to cohabit or divorce.[77]

While a wife had to prove adultery and cruelty before she could obtain a legal separation from her husband, he had only to prove adultery in order to separate from her (a distinction based on the implications of a wife's unfaithfulness for the paternity of her children). Normally a husband's unfaithfulness, if discovered, was virtually ignored by wives and society at large and instead of seeking legal redress, women were advised that 'meekness and complacency are the only weapons

72 Settlement on the marriage of Charles Boyle, Lord Clifford (later 2nd earl of Burlington and 3rd earl of Cork) with the Hon. Juliana Noel; the Right Honourable Charles earl of Burlington's appointment of portions for his four daughters, the ladies Elizabeth, Juliana, Jane and Henrietta Boyle, 25 Mar. 1701 (Chatsworth, MS L/46/25).

73 Lord Bruce to the earl of Burlington and Cork, release for the marriage portion of Lady Juliana Boyle, 28 Apr. 1738 (ibid., MS L/6/14).

74 Malcomson, *Pursuit of the heiress*, p. 32. It was not uncommon for a girl's portion to be increased by an inheritance from a female family member, and Barbara Harris has traced this practice back to at least the fifteenth century for England (Barbara Harris, 'Sisterhood, friendship and the power of English aristocratic women, 1450–1550' in James Daybell (ed.), *Women and politics in early modern England, 1450–1700* (Aldershot, 2004), pp 27–8).

75 Malcomson, *Pursuit of the heiress*, p. 146.

76 Erickson, *Women and property*, p. 112; Wilson, *Women, marriage and property*, pp 134–5.

77 Wilson, *Women, marriage and property*, pp 134–5; John Bergin, 'Irish private divorce bills and acts of the eighteenth century' in James Kelly, John McCafferty and Charles Ivar McGrath (eds), *People, politics and power: essays on Irish history 1660–1850, in honour of James I. McGuire* (Dublin, 2009), p. 94. On the legality of these deeds, see Shoemaker, *Gender in English society*, p. 108.

wherewith to combat an irregular husband' (though the fact that this tract was written by a man may have had some bearing on its contents).[78] It was much more likely that a separation would be precipitated by mutual dislike, cruelty or even abandonment. Anne Burke, Lady Dunkellin (later countess of Clanricard), had a stormy relationship with her second husband, Michael. Her letters show that she strongly disliked his friends and advisers, and constantly disagreed with him over financial matters.[79] In March 1721 her children from her first marriage opted to live with their paternal grandmother, as they feared 'unkind and barbarous treatment from my Lord Dunkellin', and shortly afterwards, Anne decided to sail for the continent, without her husband, arriving in Utrecht by July.[80]

It was not always men who were the offending party, though. Only three years into their marriage, Jonathan Swift wrote that the Irish politician, Richard Tighe and his wife Barbara were going to live separately, saying that Tighe 'solemnly vows never to live with her' and had been known to beat her on more than one occasion. Yet Swift laid the blame for this unhappy union at the feet of both spouses, saying that 'she is the most urging, provoking devil that ever was born; and he a hot, whiffling puppy, very apt to resent'.[81] In other cases the fault lay primarily with the wife. Having moved out of their marital home in Dublin in 1698, Sir John Peyton described his wife Rose as 'a monster of woman', who was 'a plague to herself and all others'. He was confident his correspondent would provide an understanding and sympathetic ear, for it was Rose's son by her previous marriage, Kean O'Hara.[82]

In cases where a husband had abandoned his wife, many women fought for some kind of *rapprochement* with their errant spouses, a seemingly odd decision, until the financial, practical and social obstacles facing a deserted wife are considered. As marriage settlements made no financial provisions for marital splits ('pin money' was no substitute), most women found themselves obliged to take whatever their husbands gave them. Catherine O'Brien was left in Ireland in 1715 by her husband, Lucius, and barred by him from following him first to England and then the continent. She had access to the lands settled on her and her husband at their marriage, but her income had also to be supplemented by her father-in-law, an uncomfortable situation for them both, as letters and accounts between them show.[83] Then there was the issue of where a woman would live, if not with her husband. Some couples had multiple houses to ease this burden, but many did not. Lady Frances Keightley was fortunate to have had a brother willing to take her in after she separated from Catherine's father, Thomas, in 1686 and a husband who

78 Wilson, *Women, marriage and property*, pp 134–5. Quote from Wetenhall Wilkes, *A letter of genteel and moral advice to a young lady. …* (Dublin, 1740), p. 117. Malcomson has shown that many women did not discover their husbands' unfaithfulness, in *Pursuit of the heiress*, pp 134–5.

79 See, for example, Anne, Lady Dunkellin to Robert Taylor, 14 May 1720 (NLI, MS 25, 430).

80 Same to same, 23 Mar. 1720/1 (ibid.); same to same, 20 May 1721 and 28 July 1721 (ibid.).

81 Jonathan Swift to Esther Johnson, 24 Aug. 1711 (Jonathan Swift, *Journal to Stella: letters to Esther Johnson and Rebecca Dingley, 1710–1713*, ed. Abigail Williams (Cambridge, 2013), p. 266. Even discounting this incident, Swift had a particular dislike for Tighe and wrote several disparaging tracts about him (*D.I.B.* (Tighe, Richard (1678–1736))).

82 Sir John Peyton to Kean O'Hara, 22 Feb. 1697/8 (PRONI, T2812/4/225).

83 Sir Donat O'Brien to Catherine O'Brien, 8 Mar. 1713/14 (NLI, MS 45, 295/3); accounts of Sir Donat, Lucius and Catherine O'Brien 1711–14 (ibid., MS 45, 339/10).

allowed her to take whatever she wanted and needed from what had been their home.[84] Last, separations were heavily frowned upon by society, and couples were expected to stay together, even in the face of marital misery.[85] Lady Dunkellin was so concerned about leaving for England without her husband that she asked her friend, Robert Taylor, dean of Clonfert, to try to convince her hated husband to go with her in order to avoid the situation appearing suspicious to the outside world.[86] When she felt she had to leave without him, she asked Taylor to be sure to tell people that she would be returning to Ireland and her husband after she had dealt with her affairs in England, which she hoped would only take a few months.[87] How much easier her life and the lives of so many others would have been, had they only been able to obtain a divorce.

The modern concept of divorce, whereby a person is free to marry again during the lifetime of their previous spouse, was still in its infancy in England, Wales and Ireland in the early eighteenth century. Scotland had its own, much more progressive laws, which allowed both men and women to seek a divorce on the grounds of adultery or desertion from 1560 onwards, but the earliest case in England was that of Lord Roos and Lady Anne Pierrepoint in 1670.[88] An extensive and impressive historiography on the matter, much of which relates directly to Ireland, has shown that divorce was a lengthy, expensive and difficult process and as such, was extremely rare.[89] Sybil Wolfram has stated that only fourteen cases occurred across Great Britain (excluding Scotland) between 1700 and 1749, although she has omitted a further two, which were passed in the Irish parliament during that time, bringing the total to sixteen. Of the initial fourteen, three involved Irish couples, though there were several other failed attempts from Irish petitioners.[90] As with separations, there was a social stigma attached to the couple involved and the laws of the time were weighted heavily in favour of husbands, who had only to show that their wives had been unfaithful in order to be able to divorce them, while a wife had to prove adultery along with some other crime, such as bigamy. Divorce by mutual consent was not permissible.[91] The procedure itself required first

84 Henry, earl of Clarendon to Rochester, 6 Sept. 1686 (*The correspondence of Henry Hyde, earl of Clarendon, and his brother Laurence Hyde, earl of Rochester: …*, ed. S.W. Singer (2 vols, London, 1828), i, 577); Thomas Keightley to Flower, countess of Clarendon, 4 Sept. 1686 (NLI, MS 45, 720/2).

85 Ingrid Tague, 'Love, honor, and obedience: fashionable women and the discourse of marriage in the early eighteenth century', *Journal of British Studies*, xl (2001), p. 97.

86 See, for example, Dunkellin to Taylor, 24 May 1720 (NLI, MS 25, 430).

87 Same to same, 27 Aug. 1720 (ibid.).

88 Barclay, *Love, intimacy and power*, p. 48; *Oxford D.N.B.* (Manners, John, 1st duke of Rutland (1638–1711)).

89 See Stone, *Broken lives*; idem, *Road to divorce: England 1530–1987* (Oxford, 1990); Rachel Weil, *Political passions: gender, the family and political argument in England, 1680–1714* (Manchester, 2009), p. 125; Sybil Wolfram, 'Divorce in England 1700–1857', *Oxford Journal of Legal Studies*, v (1985), pp 155–86; Bergin, 'Irish private divorce bills', pp 94–121; Diane Urquhart, 'Irish divorce and domestic violence, 1857–1922', *Women's History Review*, xxii (2013), pp 820–37. Wolfram, Bergin and Urquhart's work is particularly useful for scholars of Irish divorce law.

90 Bergin, 'Irish private divorce bills', pp 118–19; Wolfram, 'Divorce in England', pp 156–7.

91 Malcomson, *Pursuit of the heiress*, p. 145; Wolfram, 'Divorce in England', p. 157; Bergin, 'Irish private divorce bills', p. 102.

an ecclesiastical divorce from bed and board, which then had to be followed by a successful suit against the wife's supposed lover for adultery with her (known as criminal conversation, or 'crim. con.'), before a final act of parliament, to dissolve the marriage. The compensation from the 'crim. con.' proceedings could help to offset a husband's expenditure, but it remained a costly process, confined to the wealthier members of society and, for most, only death truly freed them from their spouses and gave the survivor the chance of a happier remarriage.[92]

Remarriage presented its own unique set of issues for women. First and foremost were the familial and economic considerations to be weighed before a new union could be entered into, and these could range far beyond the loss of financial independence that a widow would suffer if she re-entered coverture. The will of Arthur Chichester, 3rd earl of Donegall (1660–1706), decreed that if his wife, Katherine, remarried after his death, not only would she forfeit guardianship of their children, but also her 'plate, household goods, jewels, ready money and other personal estate (except the debts due to me)'.[93] Jointures could likewise be lost by a remarriage or left at the mercy of a second husband, as Arthur's sister Anne discovered. Having been widowed by John Butler, 1st earl of Gowran, her second husband, Francis Aungier, 1st earl of Longford, used this income to pay his debts.[94]

Second were the social implications. A widow could be condemned both for the timing of her remarriage and her choice of husband. Mary, Lady Shelburne (who had married Henry Conyngham, brother of Katherine Conolly and Jane Bonnell, but retained her title from her first marriage) was criticised by Catherine O'Brien when rumours surfaced of a third marriage, for showing a great disrespect to the memory of her second husband by moving to replace him so quickly. As Catherine wrote to Jane, 'I hear from Dublin by several hands that my Lady Shelburne is to marry the speaker [*Alan Brodrick*] which I confess gives me a great concern; for I know not how to fancy so good a wife can have so short a memory and so soon forget such a loss as I know hers to be.' These particular rumours turned out to be false, but Lady Shelburne did indeed remarry before the end of 1706 (her second husband having died that January) to Colonel Robert Dallway.[95] The practice of a man and woman already related to each other by their first marriages choosing to then marry each other at a later date, could be deplored or accepted, depending on the circumstances. Lady Henrietta O'Brien was lambasted for her 'dismal conjunction' in 1705 with her brother-in-law, Henry Howard, Lord Walden, partly because of the reckless way in which the pair were spending the inheritance of her young son, the 8th earl of Thomond, and partly because of Walden's poor treatment

92 Wilson, *Women, marriage and property*, p. 134; Bergin, 'Irish private divorce bills', p. 99. Wolfram points out that a Mr Box, who obtained a divorce in 1701, was a London grocer, however she admits elsewhere that his wife was the daughter of a baronet and her lover held the title of Esq., indicating that Box was of a higher social rank than he appeared (Wolfram, 'Divorce in England', p. 162; eadem, *In-laws and outlaws: kinship and marriage in England* (London, 1987), p. 80).

93 Will of Arthur, earl of Donegall, 30 July 1705 (TNA, Prob. 11/504, f. 178); Outhwaite, *Clandestine marriage*, p. 59; Malcomson, *Pursuit of the heiress*, p. 17.

94 Francis, earl of Longford to Charles Gosling, 28 Jan. 1695/6 (NLI, MS 2456).

95 Catherine O'Brien to Bonnell, 30 June 1706 (ibid., MS 41, 580/22); Walsh, *The making of the Irish Protestant ascendancy*, p. 18.

of his first wife (the sister of Henrietta's first husband).[96] Yet Ann Hill's daughter had been married to Alan Brodrick's son for six years before their parents' union in 1716, and although Ann did not get on well with her stepchildren, this seems to have been for financial reasons rather than any objection to the level of intermarriage in the family.[97]

Women looking to remarry could also face hostility, resentment and jealousy from single women, as the supply of possible husbands was diminished, concerns which reinforce how parochial and restricted the marriage pool really was. Wealthy widows free to select their own spouses were apparently quite a distraction for the unmarried men around them and could be pursued by multiple, supposedly ardent, suitors, as Mrs Ann Worth pointed out to her friend, Jane Bonnell. Writing in 1722, she claimed that 'nothing makes so great a talk in town as the many rich widows we have, and she who has made the greatest noise is Dean Story's widow, lovers she has in abundance and all received but has now fixed her choice on Colonel Whichet'.[98] Often young, single women and their families could do little but watch and grumble as eligible bachelors were snapped up, a problem of which Ann was acutely aware, telling Jane that while she very much wanted to see her daughters married to good men, 'they say the maidens must not think of marrying while so much riches in the widows dazzle their eyes'.[99]

Last was the threat that a woman's second husband would be less interested in her than in her finances, though women were frequently guilty of the same thing, which balanced the system out. Although later husbands had to be genuinely loved, rather than merely tolerated by their new wives (the opposite of which was true for first unions), it was still rare for a woman to cross social boundaries when choosing a new spouse. Instead, she would follow the vetting procedures employed by parents and guardians when their first marriages had been arranged, and marry a man of the same, or close to the same, rank as herself, with the financial health to match. As Samuel Waring commented to Ann Hill on her marriage to Baron Brodrick, her choice was prudent, and the world would know that 'it was not place or title only that prevailed upon her to become a Lady', implying that they nevertheless played a part in her decision.[100]

96 Michael Hickie to Sir Donat O'Brien, 24 May 1705 (NLI, MS 45, 311/2); same to same, 2 Dec. 1704 (ibid.).

97 Brian Mackey, 'The creation of Knockbreda parish church and Belvoir Park' in Lydia Wilson (ed.), *Knockbreda: its monuments and people* (Belfast, 2009), p. 10. Brodrick's children seem to have been concerned about the effect of a remarriage on the size of their inheritances. See Ld Brodrick to Thomas Brodrick, 17 Jan. 1716/17 (SHC, MS 1248/3/400–401).

98 A[nn] Worth to Bonnell, 21 Aug. 1722 (NLI, MS 41, 580/27). George Story was Dean of Limerick from 1705 until his death in November 1721. His widow was Catherine, *née* Warter (*D.I.B.* (Story, George Warter (*d.* 1721))).

99 A[nn] Worth to Bonnell, 21 Aug. 1722 (NLI, MS 41, 580/27).

100 Samuel Waring to Ann, Baroness Brodrick, 8 Dec. 1716 (ibid., MS 8897). Robert Shoemaker has noted similar concerns about fortune hunters among English women (Shoemaker, *Gender in English society*, p. 137).

Conclusion

Marriage was at once the most personal and impersonal event in a woman's existence. The culmination of lengthy and complicated planning, it dictated the course the rest of her life would take, yet at the same time, usually represented a strategic power play made by two families, rather than the mutual affection of two people. Designed to advertise and bolster the social, financial and political credentials of all involved, a cynic would say that emotions were lost in the shuffle, as young men and women were positioned by their kin (and themselves) to marry for maximum gain, but the truth was more nuanced. Financial considerations were certainly important, for they were the driving force behind the number of state and parental controls imposed on young couples, the primary criteria used to select a spouse, the main theme of settlements and the reason clandestine marriages were hated and unequal unions ridiculed. Yet secret and imbalanced matches show that money could be trumped by love, and the detailed descriptions provided by relatives and friends of the personal attributes of potential spouses indicate a recognition and acceptance of the idea of a happy marriage, made between compatible parties and worth sacrificing a little money or position for. Marriage was, after all, almost invariably for life. Separations were unpopular and divorce almost impossible.

But there was more at stake than familial pride and personal happiness. A strong, if insular, marriage network also functioned as a way to pick up the pieces and move forward after the political, social and religious upheavals of the Glorious Revolution. Marriage alliances were the framework upon which the now mainly Protestant elite built their power and shaped a new group identity, which incorporated the old and the new. Geographical proximity and political allegiance to England allowed an easy exchange of ideas between the two countries and ensured that the latter's marriage practices were mimicked, giving the Ascendancy an Anglo-Irish flavour, even when both parties were Irish born and raised. At the same time, a unique set of marital laws, endogamy and the longer survival of more favourable jointures gave a distinctly Irish bent to this most universal of institutions. It was in this world that the women discussed here came to the altar and lived out their married lives, for better or for worse.

2

Mothers and children

On 3 December 1734, Lady Anne Conolly was at home in Leixlip Castle, County Kildare, entertaining her husband's widowed aunt, Katherine Conolly, when she suddenly fell into an unexpected and abnormally fast labour with her second child. Katherine had just time to send for an elderly woman who lived nearby to attend on Anne, before the baby, a boy, arrived. He was premature and small, wrote Katherine, and it was 'a great providence I was here or in all human probability both mother and child had been lost'.[1] It was a month later before Anne could write to her father, Thomas Wentworth, earl of Strafford, offering her thoughts on her ordeal and her first son. When she did, she explained that she was:

> very sensible of my happiness in having this dreadful affair so well over, and to be sure having a son, is so much to Mr Conolly and all his friends' satisfaction, tis a joy to me, but the doubts I still have, of his doing well, makes me afraid of growing fond of him, so my pretty girl is still my favourite, and she is so strong and healthy she gives me no fears for her welfare. We had the child privately christened the night he was born, and Mr Conolly has a mind to defer the other christening till the child is better.[2]

Anne's experiences exemplify many of the joys, risks and harsh realities of becoming a mother in eighteenth-century Ireland. Her own letter and that written by Katherine are evidence of the dangers of pregnancy and labour, the threat of infant mortality, the pressure on women to produce a male heir and the rate at which ladies of the elite might have their children (Anne had married in April 1733, had her 'pretty girl', Kitty, on 30 January 1734 and would go on to have nine children in total).[3] It is these issues (and others) surrounding pregnancy and childbirth which this chapter will consider, along with how children were raised, cared for and educated, and the part their mothers played therein.

There is already a robust scholarship available on early modern pregnancy and infancy within the British elite, which has tackled issues including maternal and infant mortality, miscarriages, gender preferences within the family and society at large and the familial, social and psychological effects of childlessness.[4] There

1 Katherine Conolly to Jane Bonnell, 9 Dec. 1734 (NLI, MS 41, 578/7).

2 Lady Anne Conolly to Thomas, earl of Strafford, 3 Jan. 1734/5 (BL, Add. MS 22228, f. 141).

3 *D.I.B.* (Conolly, Thomas (1738?–1803)); marriage settlement of William Conolly and Lady Anne Wentworth, 1733 (IAA, MS G/9/1); Katherine Conolly to Anne, countess of Strafford, 31 Jan. 1733/4 (BL, Add. MS 22228, f. 168).

4 Robert Shoemaker, *Gender in English society, 1650–1850: the emergence of separate spheres?* (London, 1998), p. 129. Shoemaker draws attention to the slightly higher mortality rates for female children and considers the idea that they were neglected because of their gender. On the preference for boys, see also Ingrid Tague, 'Aristocratic women and ideas of family in the

is general agreement that boys were preferred to girls, as heirs to the estate and progenitors of the family name, although some have noted that even if their birth was a disappointment, daughters were still loved and valued by their family, especially if the proverbial heir and spare had already been produced.[5] More thorny is the issue of parental responses to child mortality. Some adhere to an older argument that in an era when young children died more frequently than today, parents were hardened to the loss of at least some offspring.[6] Others cite contemporary letters and journals as evidence that bereavement was felt just as heavily in the seventeenth and eighteenth centuries as in modern times.[7] There is however no study which examines how these issues translated to the upper orders of early modern Irish society.

Pregnancy: Responsibility and risks

'Breeding', as it was often termed at the time, was the most important responsibility of any young bride, and she was under constant scrutiny from family and friends, to the point that any deviation from expected routines could raise hopes. Sir Edward O'Brien's mother, Catherine, wrongly assumed that his wife, Mary, was expecting because the couple failed to attend George II's coronation in 1727.[8] Short- or long-term infertility and miscarriages were not uncommon, but the burden for conception rested more heavily upon women than men, and the double standard surrounding marital fidelity meant that although husbands could prove their ability to father children by producing bastards with little or no fallout from family and society, wives had no such recourse. Any illegitimate child on their part would have to be passed off as their spouse's – a risky move given the marital strife and breakdown which could ensue if the lie was discovered.

eighteenth century' in Helen Berry and Elizabeth Foyster (eds), *The family in early modern England* (Cambridge, 2007), p. 197; Helen Payne, 'Aristocratic women, power, patronage and family networks at the Jacobean court, 1603–1625' in James Daybell (ed.), *Women and politics in early modern England, 1450–1700* (Aldershot, 2004), p. 166; Katharine Glover, *Elite women and polite society in eighteenth-century Scotland* (Woodbridge, 2011), pp 20–1. On maternal mortality, see Judith Lewis, '"Tis a misfortune to be a great ladie": maternal mortality in the British aristocracy, 1558–1959', *Journal of British Studies*, xxxvii (1998), pp 26–53; Roger Schofield, 'Did the mothers really die? Three centuries of maternal mortality' in Lloyd Bonfield, R.M. Smith and Keith Wrightson (eds), *The world we have gained: histories of population and social structure: essays presented to Peter Laslett on his seventieth birthday* (Oxford, 1986), pp 131–60. On the effects of childlessness on men, see Berry and Foyster, 'Childless men in early modern England' in eadem (eds), *The family in early modern England*, pp 158–83.

5 Glover, *Elite women and polite society*, p. 21; Shoemaker, *Gender in English society*, p. 129.

6 Lawrence Stone, *The family, sex and marriage in England, 1500–1800* (London, 1977), pp 105–6; Clare Gittings, *Death, burial and the individual in early modern England* (London, 1988), p. 81; Mark Porter, *Cultural history and postmodernity: disciplinary readings and challenges* (New York, 1997), pp 26–7.

7 Tanya Evans, 'Women, marriage and the family' in Hannah Barker and Elaine Chalus (eds), *Women's history: Britain, 1700–1850* (New York, 2005), p. 69; Linda Pollock, *Forgotten children: parent–child relations from 1500 to 1900* (Cambridge, 1983), pp 51, 127–8, 135.

8 Catherine O'Brien to Mary, Lady O'Brien, 26 Oct. 1727 (NLI, MS 45, 352/1).

Miscarriages were typically viewed as the result of some mishap, rather than a natural occurrence which could befall any woman, and correspondents frequently offered or demanded the supposed reason for them, the most common being over-exertion on the part of the mother, or some kind of physical or mental trauma. Inherent in such letters was the assumption that women had considerable control over the success or failure of their pregnancies and the health of their newborns. Catherine O'Brien and her doctors blamed the death from convulsions of her infant daughter, Lucia, on the 'the great melancholy and troubles I lay under' while pregnant. Another lady from County Waterford fell on her back several days before miscarrying, which she believed killed her child, though she was not blamed as she had deliberately thrown herself backwards upon stumbling, in an effort 'to save her belly'. Lady Anne Conolly, however, when purportedly in danger of a late miscarriage in 1740, was criticised by Katherine Conolly for having 'routed about too much when here', although Katherine commented that 'young people is not to be advised especially those that loves diversions'. Travelling while pregnant was also discouraged. Catherine O'Brien's uncle, Laurence Hyde, earl of Rochester, was torn in 1702 as to whether or not she should be allowed to go to England. The trip was for the sake of her health; however, she was pregnant and 'still is in danger of miscarrying', which would possibly negate any potential benefits. It is unclear whether or not she made the trip, but she certainly lost the pregnancy, for her first child was not born until 1705.[9]

In an age before modern medicine everyone, male or female, old or young, parent or childless, could have an opinion on pregnancy, and those whose lifestyle offered no obvious explanation for their fertility problems were offered a range of advice and so-called remedies from family, friends and doctors. Such 'cures' included bloodletting for women thought to be in danger of miscarrying, sending ladies to Bath to improve their fertility or restore their health after a failed pregnancy, and having them carry particular herbs about with them.[10] In response to earlier miscarriages, Katherine Chichester, countess of Donegall embarked on 'a fancy diet even before being with child at least she drinks pansy [poset?] twice a day'.[11] Doubtless, many of these measures were unnecessary, useless and sometimes even harmful, but they were lapped up by desperate would-be mothers all the same.

In spite of the potions and treatments which promised a successful delivery, pregnancy was still a dangerous undertaking and there were no guarantees for the life of either child or mother. Given the rudimentary state of health care at the time, a miscarriage, or even a normal delivery, could be fatal. Jane Pearson, sister of Speaker William Conolly, suffered a particularly traumatic miscarriage during which

9 Same to Bonnell, 24 June 1710 (ibid., MS 41, 580/22); Mary Mason to John Mason, 17 Dec. 1737 (PRONI, T3131/B/1/37); Katherine Conolly to Bonnell, 3 Apr. 1740 (NLI, MS 41, 578/13); Laurence, earl of Rochester to Thomas Keightley, 20 June 1702 (ibid., MS 45, 721/1); *D.I.B.* (O'Brien, Sir Edward (1705–65)).

10 [Sarah Mason?] to John Mason, 7 Apr. [n.d.] (PRONI, T3131/B/1/4); Marmaduke Coghill to Edward Southwell Jn, 21 June 1733 in *Letters of Marmaduke Coghill: 1722–1728*, ed. D.W. Hayton (Dublin, 2005), p. 128; Laura Blood to Dorothy, countess of Cork and Burlington, 16 Mar. 1730/1 (PRONI, T3158/10, T3158/11); Andrew Crotty to same, 23 Mar. 1730/1 (ibid., T3158/12).

11 Agnes Hamilton to Margaret, countess of Panmure, 19 June [n.d.] (NRS, GD45/14/238/64).

there was 'such violent shedding that they thought she would have died', while Ann Hickman, the mother of Mary, Lady O'Brien, warned her to be especially careful during pregnancy, 'on the consideration that not only the life of your infant, but your own future health, and safety, depend on it'.[12] Wealth and station offered little protection. The first wife of the 2nd duke of Ormond, Anne, countess of Ossory (daughter of the 1st earl of Rochester), died after a miscarriage in 1685, and Mary Mason of County Waterford, whose brother John was then MP for Waterford City, wrote to him of three acquaintances who had died in one night in childbirth in 1737.[13] Such stories, while frightening for early modern Irish women, obscure the reality of their situation though. Many, including Catherine O'Brien, survived multiple miscarriages and despite a popular belief that the wealthy faced a greater risk in childbirth due to their inherent delicacy, recent scholarship has shown that during the first half of the eighteenth century, the chance of a lady of the British aristocracy dying in childbirth was only 4.6–7.1%.[14] Statistics would have meant little, though, to those who faced lost pregnancies or difficult deliveries.

The reaction of women to a miscarriage was to take it in their stride as much as possible. After a failed pregnancy in 1697, Mary, duchess of Ormond and her family focused much more on the delays caused to her plans to travel to Ireland, coupled with relief that it had happened before she set sail, than any emotional outburst. This practical attitude reflected the frequency of miscarriages at this time, but also covered the disappointment Mary must have felt at losing a chance to produce a boy. Her only son, Thomas, had already died and her surviving children were both daughters.[15]

The need for a male heir

Irish landed families, like those in England and Scotland, were obsessed with the need to produce a male heir. For those like the duchess of Ormond, at the apex of society, pressure also came from other directions. Her position as Ireland's only duchess, the eldest daughter of the 1st duke of Beaufort and a lady of the bedchamber to Queen Anne, made her one of the celebrities of her day. Such was the interest in the Butler dynasty's fortunes, that the writer John Dryden felt comfortable, when dedicating a selection of his work to her, in undercutting his compliments of her otherwise excellent wifely behaviour with the observation that:

12 Thomas Pearson to Bonnell, 16 July 1719 (NLI, MS 41, 580/24); Ann Hickman to Mary O'Brien, 1 Aug. 1728 (ibid., MS 45, 352/1).

13 James, earl of Ossory to Rochester, 13 Feb. 1684/5 (*The correspondence of Henry Hyde, earl of Clarendon, and his brother Laurence Hyde, earl of Rochester: ...* ed. S.W. Singer (2 vols, London, 1828), i, 107–8); Mary Mason to John Mason, 7 Nov. 1737 (PRONI, T3131/B/1/20).

14 Aside from the 1702 pregnancy mentioned by her uncle Rochester, Catherine also lost at least one other pregnancy in April 1707 (Catherine O'Brien to Bonnell, 30 June 1707 (NLI, MS 41, 580/22)). For the maternal mortality statistics, see Lewis, '"Tis a misfortune to be a great ladie"', p. 32. See also Schofield, 'Did the mothers really die?', p. 259.

15 Charles, marquis of Worcester to John Ellis, 12 May 1697 (BL, Add. MS 28927, f. 67); Samuel Stebbing, A *genealogical history of the kings and queens of England and monarchs of Great Britain, ...* (London, 1707), p. 371.

All other parts of pious duty done,
You owe your Ormond nothing but a son.[16]

The implication was clear. No matter how good a wife she was, nothing could compensate for the lack of an heir, for without it, the direct Butler line would die out. The prevention of such a catastrophe lay with Mary and it was a 'duty' and a debt she 'owed' to her husband, though one which she would ultimately not fulfil.

The overwhelming pressure to have a boy was heightened even further if a family was literally in the ascent; that is a new dynasty with new money, which had come to prominence in the aftermath of the Glorious Revolution and was not yet well established. With no cadet branches to inherit if the main line failed, the production of sons was of critical importance. William and Katherine Conolly were childless, necessitating the promotion of William's nephew to heir and leaving the future of the family with his children. Thus, while Katherine was relieved when Lady Anne was safely delivered of her first baby in January 1734, her happiness was tempered by the fact that the child was only a girl, even if it was named after her. She told Anne outright that she hoped to see a boy within the year and commiserated with the baby's maternal grandfather over the birth of a mere daughter, for he was likewise unimpressed.[17] As we have seen, Anne obliged by producing the desired boy within ten months, but, as she herself acknowledged, the risk of child mortality was ever present so that one son was never enough and multiple spares were sought.[18] Even after the birth of her second son in 1708, Catherine O'Brien's uncle, Lord Rochester, wrote to her husband that 'you have now two strings to your bow, and which will be as comfortable to you, you have as good as two bows too, a man of your age being generally not contented with one'. To emphasise the point, he finished the letter with hopes that Catherine 'may bring you more of the same sort'. This desire for boys even overrode the possible dangers to expectant mothers, and one gentleman, when discussing his wife's thoughts upon his sister-in-law's pregnancy, said that 'poor Kate begins to be in pain for my sister, but I must confess to you, I should not be concerned, provided she would give us a boy every year, for I believe you may remember it was my desire formerly, and I assure you it is so still'. So pervasive was this gender preference that even those second wives, who, unlike the duchess of Ormond, were theoretically free of dynastic responsibility and much lower down the social ladder, felt the need to produce a boy.[19]

Alan Brodrick's first wife, Catherine Barry, had already provided him with a son, St John, but he still wrote in 1702, upon the birth of a second son to his second wife, Lucy, that the child was 'very likely to live and make her amends for the loss of her other boy'. Why such amends were necessary, given that St John was due to inherit, no matter how many boys Lucy produced, may be explained as no more

16 John Dryden, *Fables ancient and modern* ... (London, 1721), unpaginated.

17 Katherine Conolly to [Lady Anne Conolly], 23 Feb. 1733/4 (IAA, MS J/2); same to Ld Strafford, 28 Feb. 1733/4 (BL, Add. MS 22228, f. 170).

18 Lady Anne Conolly to Ld Strafford, 3 Jan. 1734/5 (BL, Add. MS 22228, f. 141). See also Katherine Conolly to Bonnell, 6 Aug. 1741 (NLI, MS 41, 578/14).

19 Rochester to Lucius O'Brien, 18 Mar. 1707/8 (NLI, MS 45, 296/6); James Smyth to William Smyth, 12 Dec. 1715 (ibid., MS 41, 582/2).

than a matter of female pride on her part, proof that she could produce healthy sons just as her husband's first wife had done. There was also the possibility though that her stepson would die, leaving her child as the heir and, in fact, this is exactly what happened, though Lucy did not live to see it.[20]

Though this all-consuming drive for a son could make the arrival of a daughter a slight disappointment, parents (especially, but not exclusively, mothers) still loved their girls. When her daughter Alice was born in 1697 (before the all important boy), Lucy Brodrick boasted proudly that she had 'the finest girl in the world', while Lady Anne Conolly adored her daughter Kitty and chastised her father for his lack of interest in his first grandchild, telling him even after she had produced a son, 'you affronted me extremely in seeming to make so light of her. I am sure you would think her as worthy [*of*] care as if she had been a son and I assure you I would not change her for one.' Her husband too, despite having hoped for a boy, was entranced by his little girl, telling his father-in-law when the child was only four weeks old that 'the little one can already express her thoughts, or at least we pretend to understand her'.[21]

Inevitably, some couples had only girls, or no surviving children at all. In the first instance, this left daughters as heiresses, which, in the case of multiple sisters, could lead to the breakup of the estate. In cases where a couple were completely childless, many favoured the route taken by William and Katherine Conolly and adopted a favourite niece or nephew. This not only provided them with an outlet for any parental instincts they may have had, but also supplied a single heir and ensured the continued cohesion of the estate. As a bonus, if an earlier marriage settlement did not enforce their rights, it allowed for disappointing relations to be overlooked and the estate directed towards more suitable candidates. It was for this reason that the vast Conolly inheritance eventually came to the Speaker's nephew, William Conolly, junior. Although it was Katherine's niece and nephews, the Conynghams, who were raised by their aunt and uncle, they proved unacceptable successors.[22]

Child mortality and illnesses

Childhood illnesses were as inevitable as they were dangerous and the ever-present threat of smallpox, measles and the like was a constant worry to parents.[23] Catherine O'Brien fretted over her son Edward's recovery from smallpox and the possibility of her younger son catching it, saying, 'he is I hope out of all danger but I need not tell you the fright and trouble I have been in and now heartily expect

20 Alan Brodrick to St John Brodrick, 20 Jan. 1701/2 (SHC, MS 1248/2/51–52); *D.I.B.* (Brodrick, Alan (c.1655–1728)).

21 Alan Brodrick to St John Brodrick sn, 9 Dec. 1697 (SHC, MS 1248/1/296–297); Lady Anne Conolly to Ld Strafford, 3 Feb. 1734/5 (BL, Add. MS 22228, f. 145); William Conolly, jr, to same, 26 Feb. 1733/4 (ibid., f. 110).

22 *Oxford D.N.B.* (Boyle, Richard, 3rd earl of Burlington and 4th earl of Cork (1694–1753)); Patrick Walsh, *The making of the Irish Protestant ascendancy: the life of William Conolly, 1662–1729* (Woodbridge, 2010), p. 10.

23 Pollock, *Forgotten children*, pp 133–4.

Tom and my own maid to have them neither being well'.[24] Mothers played an integral part in the formulation and administration of remedies to treat children and, although they often consulted doctors and heeded their advice, did not rely upon them. Instead, the collaborative nature of such relationships speaks to the confidence many had in their own knowledge and abilities to heal their children, often over and above those of the supposed professionals and certainly without the latters' supervision. Great store was set by treatments such as bloodletting and purges, in use for centuries, but women also requested and offered advice to each other on how best to treat illnesses, and created and shared their own 'cures' for common ailments. Jane Bonnell even travelled around Ireland and England to take her daughter, Rebekah, to the 'healing waters' of Bath and the cleansing air of the County Down countryside.[25] Widows such as Jane was had the freedom to do as they wished, but even those who were married met little resistance. Husbands accepted and respected their wives' instincts as to how best to protect and care for their children while widowers turned to other female relatives. His wife having died in 1741, Andrew Savage of Portaferry in County Down took the advice of her mother, Lady Catherine Nugent (daughter of the earl of Westmeath), and sister, Barbara Reilly, as to how best to treat his son's hives. On their say-so, the child was given goat's whey mixed with sulphur for several months to combat what his aunt called his 'gross humours'.[26]

It was also a mother's responsibility to prevent her children becoming ill in the first place. Some preventative measures show the discrepancies in the advice for healing ailments and avoiding them, but women seemed oblivious to the inconsistencies. Catherine O'Brien was unimpressed with the repeated decisions of Mary, dowager Lady Shelburne, to take her young children to Dublin for the winter, writing to Mary's sister-in-law, Jane Bonnell, 'God send the children their health there, though it is what they have all been used to every winter so I hope it may not do amiss with them'. No criticism was levelled at Jane, though, for dragging Rebekah from one side of the Irish Sea to the other in search of a miracle cure, before the child died at the age of six.[27] The reason for the difference? One pattern of behaviour respected accepted knowledge; the other did not. Deviations from tried and tested methods were viewed with mistrust, and the idea that a mother knew what was best for her children crumbled if a collection of other mothers did

24 Catherine O'Brien to Bonnell, 14 Feb. 1709/10 (NLI, MS 41, 580/22).

25 Molly Burton to Bonnell, [n.d., 1720s?] (ibid., MS 41, 579/8); Juliana, dowager countess of Cork and Burlington to Dorothy, countess of Cork and Burlington, 4 Oct. 1744 (Chatsworth, Devonshire MSS, 1st series, no. 232.3); Bonnell to William King, 24 Sept. 1700 (TCD, MS 1995–2008/724); same to same, 6 Aug. 1701 (ibid., MS 1995–2008/820). Note that the Molly Burton mentioned here was the mother of the woman who would later become Lady Gore.

26 Lady Catherine Nugent to Andrew Savage, 9 Dec. 1743 (PRONI, D552/A/2/4/6); Barbara Reilly to same, 16 June 1744 (ibid., D552/A/2/7/10). For the contemporary notion, influenced by the ideology of separate spheres, that women were better suited to the task of raising children, see Shoemaker, *Gender in English society*, pp 30–2, 122–3. Tanya Evans has made the similar argument that 'good mothering and responsible childrearing became women's social duty' in 'Women, marriage and the family', p. 68.

27 Catherine O'Brien to Bonnell, 29 Nov. 1707 (NLI, MS 41, 580/22); Bonnell to King, 24 Sept. 1700 (TCD, MS 1995–2008/724); same to same, 6 Aug. 1701 (ibid., MS 1995–2008/820).

not agree with her. Thus, the fact that Mary was not respecting the group wisdom of her peers was enough to condemn her, despite the fact that Catherine herself had to admit that previous trips to the capital had done the children no harm. Ironically, this herd mentality and the off-putting barrage of criticism levelled at those who broke from it held back real medical progress, and the use of inoculations, which, with the support of Princess Caroline, was just beginning to gain acceptance in England, was deeply mistrusted. When the daughter of Ireland's lord lieutenant, John, Lord Carteret, was vaccinated against smallpox in 1725, newspapers wrote of the event as though it was an assault and 'hoped her fine complexion and features will not suffer by the inoculation lately performed upon her'.[28]

When the worst happened and a child died, women's reactions varied considerably depending on the age of the deceased and the circumstances of their death. An adult would be spoken of for months or years after their passing and openly and extensively mourned by their mothers through the wearing of black clothing. Lady Mary Boyle (a member of the O'Brien family by birth and mother of Henry Boyle, the future Speaker of the Irish House of Commons and 1st earl of Shannon) was nearly suicidal when she lost one of her adult sons, telling Henry that her thoughts were 'altogether in the grave with the dear creature that is so lately gone to it, I wish I could be laid by him'. Even the usually blasé Katherine Conolly was deeply affected when her turn came and she outlived her favourite niece, Molly, Lady Gore, whom she had raised from a small child. Writing to Lady Anne Conolly, she told her that 'my loss you know is great for my dear dear child was dearer to me than all the world'.[29]

The deaths of very small children were treated rather differently. When studying English practices during the period between 1500 and 1900, Linda Pollock has found that 'in every century studied, young infants were not mourned as deeply as older children'.[30] On the face of it, this was true in Ireland also, for the deaths of such children were rarely mentioned after the initial announcement. This suggests a certain ambivalence towards their fate, but the truth was less straightforward. To begin with, there were issues of finance and convenience. Official mourning, with its black clothing and social restrictions, was lengthy and expensive, and given the high rate of infant mortality, it was neither desirable nor cost-effective to employ it for those whose time in the world had been so brief.[31] Then there were the psychological factors. Some mothers tried to avoid becoming immediately attached to their newborns, particularly those they viewed as being at risk of death, to lessen the grief they would feel (and therefore exhibit), if and when such children died. Lady Anne Conolly's comment at the beginning of this chapter, that she was 'afraid to grow fond' of her premature son, is not indicative of an emotionally cold

28 *Daily Journal*, 14 Aug. 1725. On Caroline's early support for inoculation and the inoculation of her daughters, see Hannah Smith, *The Georgian monarchy: politics and culture, 1714–1760* (Cambridge, 2006), pp 92–5.

29 *Oxford D.N.B.* (Boyle, Henry, 1st earl of Shannon (1681x7–1764)); Lady Mary Boyle to Henry Boyle, 3 Mar. 1725/6 (PRONI, D2707/A/1/1/7F); Katherine Conolly to Lady Anne Conolly, 16 May 1745 (IAA, MS A/9).

30 Pollock, *Forgotten children*, p. 141.

31 Lou Taylor, *Mourning dress: a costume and social history* (London, 1983).

woman, but of one who recognised how deeply she could love her little boy and who was afraid of the pain she would endure should she allow herself to do so, only for the baby to die. The response of those around her to the birth encouraged her behaviour. Her husband, William Conolly, Jr, agreed to having their son christened the night he was born, betraying his own early concerns for the boy's survival, and Katherine Conolly noted that the baby was 'called William [*after her husband, rather than the baby's father*] but not till I had a promise that if it died I would have another William'.[32] Little William's quick baptism, the readiness with which his great-aunt requested and received his parents' assurances that his name would be recycled if he did not live long enough to stamp it with his own individuality and Katherine's relegation of him to an 'it' rather than a 'he', all combine to form a picture of a family who recognised and accepted the child's low chances of long-term survival and therefore refused to invest too much emotion in him. It is in this context that both Anne's and society's, aloofness regarding the loss of young children must be placed. It does not follow that they were forgotten, though, and anecdotal evidence indicates that at least some women grieved over their lost babies for much longer than they admitted to publicly. Lady Frances Keightley kept a careful list of the names, births, deaths and burials of all seven of the children she lost while they were young, including a daughter who lived only a few minutes and twin boys who lived for a week. She later did the same for her grandchildren.[33]

Emotional detachment was also employed, especially among more distant family members, when dealing with older children with frequent or ongoing health problems. Although Katherine Conolly expressed sympathy for her niece Jenny Sampson (who was constantly suffering bereavements) in 1736, this did not prevent her from writing a damning, seemingly callous, report on the situation, observing that, 'I think so likely a healthy father and mother never had so rotten miserable creatures: fine handsome children till they come to 3 or 4 years old, then they die like so many rotten sheep'. Her sister Mary Jones (the children's grandmother) wrote on another occasion that the 'youngest daughter is very ill, it will not be any great loss if she dies'.[34] Comments such as these are shocking to modern eyes, but within the context of life (and death) in Ascendancy Ireland, they were taken as sensible, even kind. As well as trying to protect themselves from great grief when one of these ailing children passed away, the sisters' attitudes also stemmed from a desire not to see the youngsters suffer. When Katherine wrote that everyone was glad that one of the Sampson boys had died, she explained that it was because of 'the miserable condition he was in a pallapass [*sic*] or hard lump in his throat could not be cut out nor help given him [*he*] could swallow nothing but liquids this way for above 2 years'.[35] To her, an early death was inevitable for this child and the quicker it came, the better, both for him and for those who had to care for him and watch his pain.

32 Lady Anne Conolly to Ld Strafford, 3 Jan. 1734/5 (BL, Add. MS 22228, f. 141); Katherine Conolly to Bonnell, 9 Dec. 1734 (NLI, MS 41, 578/7).
33 *Gentleman's Magazine* ... (London, 1829), xcix, 322.
34 Katherine Conolly to Bonnell, 25 May 1736 (NLI, MS 41, 578/9); Jones to same, 5 Feb. [n.d.] (ibid., MS 41, 577/3).
35 Katherine Conolly to same, 3 Apr. 1740 (ibid., MS 41, 578/13).

An Ascendancy education

The children who did survive infancy, with all its dangers and sometimes misguided attempts to protect them from death, had then to be educated according to gender and status. This was easier said than done, and some attempts fell flat. In March 1734 Lady Anne Conolly described a ball in Dublin Castle which she herself had not attended (having given birth only five weeks previously), but which she had quickly heard about. In the course of the evening, she reported, one young lady 'undertook to amuse the audience by dancing the Britain ... but could not dance a step of it, and was forced to leave off in the middle but nobody was sorry for her, for she is much hated by everyone, for her impertinent behaviour'.[36] Safe in the belief that she would never make such a spectacle of herself, Anne's smug description of this woman's very public failure to perform properly, and her pre-existing knowledge and dislike of the lady's personal qualities, which she claimed was shared 'by everyone', are a cautionary tale on the importance for elite women of obtaining what contemporaries deemed a 'proper' education. It was only through the acquisition and perfection of a very particular skill-set, both practical and personal, that one could avoid having limitations dissected and circulated within polite society in the manner of Anne's letter.

The education given to a young lady in Ireland during the Ascendancy era was, for the most part, the same as that given to girls of the English and Scottish elites, for whom there is already an impressive historiography led by scholars such as Michèle Cohen, Philip Carter, Peter Borsay, Christina De Bellaigue and Katharine Glover. Recent co-authored contributions from Deirdre Raftery and Susan M. Parks and Gerardine Meaney, Mary O'Dowd and Bernadette Whelan have likewise pushed forward our understanding of Irish education. Together, they have examined the way in which contemporary notions of gender affected curricula and educational experiences, the logic behind the use of distinct learning models for the two sexes and the separate and shared sites of learning in which boys and girls were taught.[37]

36 Lady Anne Conolly to Ld Strafford, 9 Mar. 1733/4 (BL, Add. MS 22228, f. 114).

37 Michèle Cohen, '"To think, to compare, to combine, to methodise": girls' education in Enlightenment Britain' in Sarah Knott and Barbara Taylor (eds), *Women, gender and enlightenment* (New York, 2005), pp 224–42; Philip Carter, *Men and the emergence of polite society, Britain 1660–1800* (Harlow, 2001); Peter Borsay, 'Children, adolescents and fashionable urban society in eighteenth-century England' in Anja Müller (ed.), *Fashioning childhood in the eighteenth century: age and identity* (Burlington, VT, 2006), pp 53–62; Christina De Bellaigue, *Educating women: schooling and identity in England and France, 1800–1867* (Oxford, 2007); Katharine Glover, 'The female mind: Scottish enlightenment femininity and the world of letters. A case study of the women of the Fletcher of Saltoun family in the mid-eighteenth century', *Journal of Scottish Historical Studies*, xxv (2005), pp 1–20; eadem, '"Polite London children": educating the daughters of the Scottish elite in mid-eighteenth-century London' in Stana Nenadic (ed.), *Scots in London in the eighteenth-century* (Cranbury, 2010), pp 253–71; Deirdre Raftery and Susan M. Parkes, *Female education in Ireland 1700–1900: Minerva or Madonna* (Dublin, 2007); Gerardine Meaney, Mary O'Dowd and Bernadette Whelan, *Reading the Irish woman: studies in cultural encounter and exchange, 1714–1960* (Liverpool, 2013). See also L.M. Cullen, 'Patrons, teachers and literacy in Irish: 1700–1850' in Mary Daly and David Dickson (eds), *The origins of popular literacy in Ireland: language change and educational development 1700–1920* (Dublin, 1990), pp 15–44; Kenneth Milne, *The Irish charter*

Each country was heavily influenced by the conduct literature of the day, written by authors such as Richard Allestree, John Locke, Mary Astell and François Fénelon.[38] The Irish were aware 'of contemporary English publications on the education and ideal behavior of women', and the opening decades of the eighteenth century were a 'peak' for the production of such tracts in Ireland.[39] During the 1720s and 1730s, Irish editions of the most popular education manuals began appearing, endorsed by subscriptions from members of the Ascendancy, and in 1740, Irishman Wetenhall Wilkes published his *Letter of genteel and moral advice to a young lady*, printed first in Dublin by subscription and with a specifically Irish audience in mind, having been written initially for his niece.[40] The advice contained within these manuals varied, depending on how conservative or liberal the author was, but a girl's curriculum was challenging, robust and broadly speaking, comprised of two parts.

The first might be called 'book learning' or learning by rote, and consisted of a combination of subjects, knowledge of which could be easily tested. She was given a solid grounding in religion, the ability to raise children, manage accounts, run a household (and even an estate) and proficiency in a selection of 'polite accomplishments'. These accomplishments included history, modern languages, music and dancing, which, if learned correctly, were useful for display at social events and for attracting a husband looking for a companionable wife. They would even (the liberals hoped) improve a girl's mind and bring her enjoyment.[41] This model was in use from the earliest days of the Ascendancy, and during the 1690s Sir Donat O'Brien's daughter, Elizabeth, was taught 'writing and dancing, German and to play on the spinet'. Elizabeth, like the vast majority of the elite, was Protestant, but the advice of Lady Frances Keightley (a convert to Catholicism) to her daughter Catherine followed the same model, the only difference being its comments on the possibility of Catherine joining a religious community, despite the fact that the girl was raised as a Protestant.[42]

The second was her interpersonal skills, often referred to as 'politeness' or 'civility'. These skills were far less easily quantified than book learning, but they

schools: 1730–1830 (Dublin, 1997); D.W. Hayton, *The Anglo-Irish experience, 1680–1730: religion, identity and patriotism* (Woodbridge, 2012).

38 Richard Allestree, *The ladies calling* … (Oxford, 1673); John Locke, *Some thoughts concerning education* (London, 1693); Mary Astell, *A serious proposal to the ladies, for the advancement of their true and greatest interest* (London, 1694); François de Salignac de La Mothe Fénelon, *Instructions for the education of a daughter* … (London, 1707).

39 Meaney, O'Dowd and Whelan, *Reading the Irish woman*, pp 17, 51 (quote from p. 17).

40 For instance, Richard Allestree, *The works of the learned and pious author of the whole duty of man* (Dublin, 1723); John Locke, *Some thoughts concerning education* (9th edn, Dublin, 1728); Wetenhall Wilkes, *A letter of genteel and moral advice* … (Dublin, 1740); *Oxford D.N.B.* (Wilkes, Wetenhall (1705/6–1751)). For a list of the subscribers to the Irish editions of Locke and Wilkes' works, see 'Inventing and reinventing the Irish woman' (http://www.ul.ie/inventing/content/resources) (accessed 09 July 2014). See also Meaney, O'Dowd and Whelan, *Reading the Irish woman*, pp 17–20.

41 For an example of a curriculum recommended by a conduct writer of the Ascendancy era, see George Berkeley, *The ladies library* (3 vols, London, 1714), i, 13–29. For a comparison to Scotland, see Glover, '"Polite London children"', pp 260–1.

42 Dorothy Berkeley to Sir Donat O'Brien, 4 Feb. 1692/3 (NLI, MS 45, 293/3); Lady Frances Keightley to Catherine O'Brien, 26 Sept. 1681 (ibid., MS 45, 720/1).

were of the utmost importance if a girl wished to build and maintain a good reputation and avoid being 'hated by everyone'. They rested on a good deportment, a pleasing manner and the ability to carry on a polite conversation – a subjective mix, difficult to define and best obtained through practice and guidance.[43] When advising a young female friend on proper conduct, Letitia Bushe, originally of County Kilkenny, cautioned that:

> the world whom you please by the advantage of your fortune, polite people by gentleness of your manners, others by the agreeableness of your person ... an attention more general on your part for all sorts of people will fortify the whole world in the pleasure of saying good of you, and the good that will be said of you, will even help to fix you the firmer in the possession of everything which can contribute to your honour.[44]

Wealth and status were not a sure path to success, nor a satisfactory replacement for good behaviour, and Letitia complained that the people of Cork and Bristol were 'without any politeness' and instead valued 'their riches, as if they were supplied by money, with every valuable qualification, of mind and body'.[45] On the issue of conversational skills, which were themselves a fine art, *The Ladies Library* (published in 1714 and long attributed to Richard Steele, but in fact compiled by another Irishman, the philosopher George Berkeley, later bishop of Cloyne), advised that:

> a young lady should never speak but for necessity, and even then with diffidence and deference. She should never talk of things above the common reach of her age or sex, however she may be informed of them by the advantages of her quality and education ... Her behaviour should be exact and regular, her temper even and orderly, her judgment just and upright, to know when to talk and when to be silent.[46]

Confusingly, though, she should also have been able to adapt her behaviour to whatever company she was in.[47] Lady Shelburne boasted in 1706 that she had never been accused of any fault in her manners, 'my education and conversation having always been such as would teach me how to behave myself towards all men'. Yet her comment was made in response to accusations circulating among her acquaintance in Ireland that she had been 'disrespectful, or scurrilous' in her correspondence with her absent husband's Scottish landlord, and in fact she had acted towards him in a

43 On the importance of conversation skills among the English elite, see Michèle Cohen, '"Familiar conversation": the role of the "familiar format" in education in eighteenth- and nineteenth-century England' in Mary Hilton and Jill Shefrin (eds), *Educating the child in Enlightenment Britain: beliefs, cultures, practices* (Farnham, 2009), pp 99–116.

44 Letitia Bushe to unknown, [c.1739–40] (PRONI, D2092/1/6).

45 Same to Lady Anne Bligh, 19 Aug. 1740 (ibid.). For more on Letitia Bushe, see S.J. Connolly, 'A woman's life in eighteenth-century Ireland: the case of Letitia Bushe', *Historical Journal*, xliii (2000), pp 433–51.

46 Berkeley, *The ladies library*, i, 56. On the change in attribution from Steele to Berkeley, see Stephen Parks, 'George Berkeley, Sir Richard Steele and *The Ladies Library*', *Scriblerian*, xii (1980), pp 1–2; E.J.F. and D.B., 'George Berkeley and *The Ladies Library*', *Berkeley Newsletter*, iv (1980), pp 5–13; *Oxford D.N.B.* (Berkeley, George (1685–1753)).

47 Berkeley, *The ladies library*, i, 58.

very high-handed manner. Clearly the image she wanted to portray did not always match with that which was presented, though her bungled attempt at damage control (she offered only a half-hearted apology, wrapped in further insults) shows that she realised it should have.[48] With sociability such a tricky feat to master and a young girl's reputation and position within society dependent upon its acquisition, the choices of where to educate her and to whom to entrust her instruction were of critical importance.

Female boarding schools were not popular among the higher ranks of the elite, for contemporary wisdom dictated that a school could not impart the same moral and social education as a parent, being more concerned with academic subjects – a moot point for boys, who were not subject to the same expectations of chastity as their sisters and might very well need a strong academic grounding in order to pursue a career.[49] Women were also warned not to 'take up the confidence, the boldness of men, under a notion of good breeding', an idea which also appeared later in the century in the argument that schools were dangerous to girls in case they should give them too much confidence (an advantage in a boy, who would have to make his way in the world), thereby eroding their meek and pliable personalities.[50] The expense of certain schools also ruled them out for those slightly lower down the social ladder, with gentle, rather than aristocratic backgrounds, but pretentions to more. The Rev. James Smyth, writing from County Antrim, briefly entertained the idea of sending his daughter, Anne, to a Dublin establishment for a year, but had to abandon the plan when he realised the cost.[51] Nor could a school provide the kind of environment needed for certain types of situation-based learning. It was only at the family residence that a girl could undertake 'part of the management of her mother's house', and thereby 'learn how to go through her domestic offices when she comes to one of her own'.[52] For these reasons, her primary learning space was her home, and though professionals were brought in to teach particular skills (references to dancing masters for daughters are common within female correspondence and account books), her first and overall governess was her mother.[53] If the mother had died or was unavailable for any reason, girls were sent to female relatives to be educated, rather than remaining in their father's house. Elizabeth O'Brien was taught by her father's sister, Dorothy Berkeley, and

48 Mary, dowager Lady Shelburne to Alexander Murray, 7 Dec. 1706 (PRONI, D2860/9/16).

49 Cohen, '"To think, to compare"', p. 227; Glover, '"Polite London children"', p. 257.

50 Quote from Berkely, *The ladies library*, i, 187–8, in which he also criticised those men who 'fall into the effeminacy and delicacy of women'; Cohen, '"To think, to compare"' p. 229. For the argument that home schooling for boys led to 'foppish' behaviour, see Carter, *Men and the emergence of polite society*, pp 146–7.

51 James Smyth to William Smyth, 31 May 1728 (NLI, MS 41, 582/6). On the similar attitudes of the English elite towards boarding schools for girls, see De Bellaigue, *Educating women*, pp 140–1. Cohen agrees that the upper orders preferred a home education for their daughters (Cohen, '"To think, to compare"', pp 227–8).

52 Wilkes, *A letter of genteel and moral advice …*, p. 120.

53 See, for example, Elizabeth, dowager countess of Kildare to Thomas, Lord Coningsby, 6 Sept. 1716 (PRONI, D638/42/4). Official governesses, employed by the family to teach their daughters, were not yet popular in Ireland at this time and references to them do not appear in correspondence.

Alan Brodrick sent his daughter Alice to her maternal aunt in England after the death of her mother, Lucy, in 1703.[54]

The bad dancer Lady Anne Conolly so decisively lampooned had doomed herself to the position of social reject because of her failure in the arenas of both technical ability and sociability. Mediocrity in either was unacceptable, and the hallmark of a well-educated lady was her ability to excel in both. Taught at home under the eye of Katherine Conolly, her great-aunt and guardian, Molly Burton was, Katherine boasted, an excellent sewer who 'writes well, dances well and plays well on the spinet as well for her age as any child in Dublin'.[55] The problem was that here her education stopped. One of Katherine's sisters, Mary Jones, complained that 'she spends little of her time in the drawing room with company but with the servants, and as great ado with her baby house as if she were but seven year old, I think this is strange education for a young lady near 14 year old'.[56] She could see what Katherine could not, that rather than being allowed to live her life in the nursery, interacting primarily with servants, by 13 social events should have been Molly's schoolroom and polite society her instructors. At the same age at which Miss Burton was playing with her 'baby house', Lady Mary Butler, daughter of the duke and duchess of Ormond, had the ability and composure needed to open the dancing at a ball in Dublin with the earl of Abercorn.[57] To provide Molly with the similar civility and adroitness she would need to be accepted and respected within the Ascendancy, Katherine ought to have insisted that she be exposed to the company of other women of a similar rank, to whose manners, conversation and conduct she should then have drawn her niece's attention, directing her in what to emulate and what to avoid. Instead, Mary wrote 'there is no care taken of her education nor principals and my sister makes no enquiries whether she tells her lies which she does every day'.[58] As a result, she was spoilt and ill-mannered, with an incomplete and therefore inferior education which did not fit her for elite society. One can only imagine what Lady Anne made of her.

At the core of Molly's problems was the fact that she was caught in a cycle of poor education. Katherine was not a learned lady, and what had been fit for the daughter of a knight in Restoration Ireland was nowhere near enough for a lady of one the wealthiest Ascendancy families sixty years later.[59] Mrs Conolly was not oblivious to the changed times, nor to the conduct literature of the day, having subscribed to Wetenhall Wilkes' *A letter of genteel advice* in 1740 (though whether she read it or attempted to implement its strictures is another matter), but she took little care to set a good example for Molly and was ultimately unequal to the task of raising the child to be any more socially adept than herself. At the time of her

54 Dorothy Berkeley to Sir Donat O'Brien, 4 Feb. 1692/3 (NLI, MS 45, 293/3); Alan Brodrick to St John Brodrick, 21 June 1705 (SHC, MS 1248/2/213–214).

55 Katherine Conolly to Bonnell, 21 June 1735 (NLI, MS 41, 578/8).

56 Jones to same, 3 July [n.d., c.1736] (ibid., MS 41, 577/5).

57 Abel Boyer, *The history of the reign of Queen Anne, digested into annals. Year the first. …* (London, 1703), p. 80. Borsay records English children as young as six or seven attending recreational events (Borsay, 'Children, adolescents and fashionable urban society', p. 59).

58 Jones to Bonnell, 25 July [n.d.] (NLI, MS 41, 577/3).

59 *D.I.B.* (Conolly, Katherine (Catherine) (c.1662–1752)).

death in 1752, Mary Delany described her as 'a plain and vulgar woman in her manner', and like her great-niece prone to fits of rudeness and lying, neglecting to invite Mary Jones to Molly's wedding in 1743, then telling those who inquired that she had implored her to come, a lie which Mary was quick to refute.[60] With an almost total disregard for what others thought of her, a habit of coasting by on her money and connexions and the knowledge that her education was no more lacking than that of many other women of her generation, it was Katherine's failure to recognise the extent of her own limitations which blinded her to Molly's.[61] Even Miss Burton's father commented that his daughter did not always show him proper respect, being 'sometimes very fond and at others quite contrary' and was 'possibly too much indulged'. Katherine by contrast, wrote that she was 'really a good girl very dutiful and much liked by all that knows her she is very civil and humble'.[62] Either she was easily manipulated and fooled, or she did not consider Molly's inconsistent behaviour a problem. Whatever the answer, the girl's education had serious flaws.

Given its informal setting, administration by mothers, and focus on the ornamental and domestic, female education seems, at first glance, to have had little in common with that given to boys, whom conduct literature urged be instructed in 'masculine' subjects such as 'politicks, the military art, law, philosophy, and divinity', all of which had clear professional applications.[63] Early learning was imparted through a combination of hired tutors and Irish schools, and Sir Donat O'Brien sent his younger son, Henry, to Enniskillen in 1695 'for want of a fit master, which I could not meet with'.[64] By their teenage years though, while their sisters were being taught social graces in the drawing room and at assemblies, boys were invariably being sent across the Irish Sea to complete their education in English schools and universities. Sir Donat's elder son, Lucius, undertook law studies in Gray's Inn in the 1690s, his distant cousin, Henry O'Brien, 8th earl of Thomond, was a pupil at Eton in the early 1700s, and roughly twenty years later, Lucius's son, Edward, despite occasional stints at home with a tutor, had attended at least three different schools in Ireland by the age of 14 and was sent to Oxford at 16. The formal education of Edward's brother, Thomas, seems to taken place exclusively in England.[65] Had the younger O'Briens been the first in their family to attend English schools, one might put the decision down to the backgrounds and social

60 Mary Delany to Anne Dewes, 26 Sept. 1752 (*Letters from Georgian Ireland: the correspondence of Mary Delany, 1731–68*, ed. Angélique Day (Belfast, 1991), p. 53); Jones to Bonnell, 1 Dec. [1743] (NLI, MS 41, 577/5).

61 Anthony Malcomson has pointed out the astonishment ladies of the later eighteenth century expressed when they saw their Irish mothers' and grandmothers' poor handwriting and phonetic spelling, traits Katherine shared (A.P.W. Malcomson, *The pursuit of the heiress: aristocratic marriage in Ireland 1740–1840* (2nd edn, Belfast, 2006), pp 120–1).

62 Francis Burton to Bonnell, 19 Nov. 1729 (NLI, MS 41, 579/9); Katherine Conolly to same, 28 Jan. 1741/2 (ibid., MS 41, 578/15).

63 Fénelon, *Instructions for the education of a daughter*, p. 3.

64 Sir Donat O'Brien to Lucius O'Brien, 22 Mar. 1694/5 (NLI, MS 45, 293/6).

65 Ibid.; Michael Hickie to Sir Donat O'Brien, 18 Sept. 1703 (ibid., MS 45, 311/2); Lucius O'Brien to Catherine O'Brien, 22 July 1714 (ibid., MS 45, 297/1); David England to same, 30 Sept. 1717 (ibid., MS 45, 346/5); Joshua Dawson to same, 5 Feb. 1718/19 (ibid., MS 45, 346/3);

aspirations of their English mothers, for Catherine O'Brien, who managed her sons' education from 1717 onwards, was a cousin of Mary II and Queen Anne and Lord Thomond's mother, widowed in 1690 when her son was a toddler, was a daughter of the 1st duke of Beaufort.[66] The fact that their educational trajectory followed that of brothers Lucius and Henry a generation earlier, however, reflects the trend, well established by the early eighteenth century, of using education to Anglicise the Ascendancy.

Sending Irish children to English schools was not unheard of in the pre-Revolutionary period, but why the trend was adopted with such fervour by Irish Protestant landowners can be explained by their recent history.[67] In the aftermath of the Glorious Revolution, as they struggled to create for themselves a distinct national identity, an English education for their children created a sense of belonging, allowing them to think of themselves as extensions of the English elite, equally sophisticated and able to pursue opportunities in both countries. It also demonstrated their loyalty to the ruling regime by hopefully quashing any Jacobite leanings and transmitting English values back to Ireland. In addition, an English education was seen as being of a better quality, and the idea of dispatching a child of Anglo-Irish birth from England to Ireland to be taught was rarely contemplated.[68] The duke of Dorset, in his capacity as lord lieutenant, tried to reverse the trend by sending his son, Lord George Sackville, to Trinity College, Dublin in 1731, but it was a wasted effort; England was still preferred.[69] This was despite a disparity in wealth and position between members of the two elites which could sometimes lead to discomfort.[70] Sir Edward's grandmother, Lady Frances Keightley, warned that, like his father, he would find his life in England a severe comedown after his Irish education, 'for Sir Edward O'Brien in Ireland where he is amongst his tenants and followers with servants suitable to his estate and rank, will find it a mighty fall to be at Oxford, with only one servant and a tutor, and where there will be many on an equal foot and not a few above him'. She believed 'a trial may not be amiss', though, and the boy remained at Oxford, a little ego-deflation was clearly seen as worth the chance to mingle and integrate with the English elite.[71] Afterwards, he set off on his

Lady Frances Keightley to same, 3 May 1721 (ibid., MS 45, 348/5); same to same, 15 Feb. 1723/4 (ibid., MS 45, 348/6).

66 *D.I.B.* (Keightley, Thomas (*c.*1650–1719)); John Lodge, *The peerage of Ireland* ... (7 vols, London, 1789), ii, 40.

67 The Butlers and the Boyles sent their sons to England to be educated, but this may be explained by their position at the top of Ireland's social hierarchy and strong marital ties to the English aristocracy, which meant that they always had one foot on each side of the Irish Sea. The 1st duke of Ormond was also a prominent supporter of Charles II during the Interregnum. See *Oxford D.N.B.* (Butler, James, 1st duke of Ormond (1610–1688); Butler, James, 2nd duke of Ormond (1665–1745); Boyle, Richard, 1st earl of Burlington and 2nd earl of Cork (1612–1698); Boyle, Roger, 1st earl of Orrery (1621–1679); Boyle, Robert (1627–1691)).

68 Toby Barnard, *A new anatomy of Ireland: the Irish Protestants, 1640–1770* (London, 2003), p. 109.

69 Marmaduke Coghill to Edward Southwell, jr, 18 Oct. 1733 (*Letters of Marmaduke Coghill*, p. 136).

70 Barnard, *A new anatomy of Ireland*, p. 109.

71 Lady Frances Keightley to Catherine O'Brien, 3 May 1721 (NLI, MS 45, 348/5).

Grand Tour, the spell of European travel which a young man took at the end of his education in order to broaden his horizons and expand his knowledge.[72]

The differing locales of male and female learning meant that a mother's input into her son's education was typically more restricted than for her daughters, the rare exception being a boy who was educated at home, such as Richard Boyle, 4th earl of Cork and 3rd earl of Burlington.[73] Catherine O'Brien oversaw the majority of her boys' education only because their father and grandfathers had died. Previously, all decisions had been made for the boys by Sir Donat, as male head of the family, and even their father, Lucius, had only a limited role in organising their education.[74] After Lucius's death, Sir Donat insisted on sending Edward to a school in Limerick, despite Catherine's reservations and her assertion that 'I part with the only true comfort I have in this world when that child leaves me'.[75] She understood the reality of her position, though, and the futility of fighting, for she needed Sir Donat's help financially.[76] So she made every effort to appear amenable to her father-in-law's wishes, insisting that she believed it was his right to have control over his heir and even offering him guardianship of Edward. The only hint of uneasiness was her plea that allowances be made for Edward's behaviour, for ''tis not possible for thirteen to have so much thought as five and twenty', an oblique reference to her loss of control over how he would now be disciplined as well.[77]

The disciplining of boys was the province of men, though women would step in when necessary and particularly in the reprimanding of young children still living in the family home. Writing to her brother, John, in 1718, Sarah Mason of Waterford reported the punishment meted out to his son, Aland, by another of his aunts:

> my sister Alcock whipped Aland this morning, he cried half an hour and his maid could by no means quiet him, then my sister threatened him, but that would not do, so she whipped him, and he was immediately quiet, wiped his eyes and promised to be a good boy, tis the first time he was so corrected since you went hence, or (I believe) deserved it.[78]

There was no doubt in the minds of either of Aland's aunts that he deserved what he got, or that Mrs Alcock was perfectly within her rights to hit him, but Sarah's comment that this was his first such punishment since John had left the boy in their care indicates that it was he who usually disciplined his son. The whipping had the

72 M[ary] Long to same, [n.d., 1723?] (ibid., MS 45, 346/4). See also Jeremy Black, *The British abroad: the Grand Tour in the eighteenth century* (New York, 1992).

73 *Oxford D.N.B.* (Boyle, Richard, 3rd earl of Burlington and 4th earl of Cork (1694–1753)).

74 Lucius O'Brien to Catherine O'Brien, 22 July 1714 (NLI, MS 45, 297/1).

75 Catherine O'Brien to England, 14 Sept. 1717 (ibid., MS 45, 346/5). See also England to Catherine O'Brien, 30 Sept. 1717 (ibid.).

76 James Davoren to Catherine O'Brien, 13 Sept. 1717 (ibid., MS 45, 347/1).

77 Catherine O'Brien to England, 14 Sept. 1717 (ibid., MS 45, 346/5). Edward O'Brien was actually 12 at the time, having been born in April 1705 (Rochester to Thomas Keightley, 7 Apr. 1705 (ibid., MS 45, 295/7)).

78 Sarah Mason to John Mason, 8 July 1718 (PRONI, T3131/B/1/12). Sarah and John had two sisters, Elizabeth and Jane, who had both married men with the surname Alcock. It is therefore impossible to be sure which one Sarah is referring to here.

desired effect by obtaining Aland's submission, but women were less successful and comfortable when dealing with older boys. Their residence at school and the wish of all to avoid 'feminising' them made it both impractical and undesirable to have them beaten by their mothers (or aunts); nor can one imagine many teenagers acquiescing to such measures. This presented obvious problems for women dealing with particularly unruly and fatherless boys. Despite earlier problems with Sir Edward O'Brien's behaviour, his grandmother still turned to him for assistance in disciplining his much wilder brother, having already been reduced to threatening Thomas with a seven-year stint on an Indian ship to achieve a degree of control over his bad behaviour, which included running away from and vandalising his school.[79]

Despite the differences, on close inspection, considerable similarities between male and female education are discernible and the two complimented each other well. Though intended for occupational, rather than domestic purposes, many of the same topics were routinely taught to boys as girls, including reading, writing and arithmetic.[80] Catherine Keightley was allowed by her mother to study 'plays and romances', seen as typically female fare, but more important to Lady Frances was that her daughter also had a grounding in religion, history, morality and philosophy.[81] The need for men, as well as women, to be able to manoeuvre society meant that dancing lessons were taken alongside fencing and learning environments sometimes overlapped.[82] When boys emerged from school and attended society events (long the scene of a girl's education), their manners and personalities were thought to be improved by the opportunity to socialise with their more refined female contemporaries, who had been having the finer points of decorum drilled into them since childhood. Girls meanwhile could benefit from the conversation of their better travelled and supposedly better-read male acquaintances.[83] The Grand Tour was another opportunity for young men to hone these hitherto neglected skills, but it was a double-edged sword, for without the parental guidance meted out to daughters, it could lead to disingenuous behaviour. Having been reintroduced to a Mr Mills in Waterford in 1737, Mary Mason remarked that he 'seemed well pleased to see me, but as he has been so lately visiting the several courts of Europe, I won't build too much on his complaisance, which may be only the effects of polite

79 Lady Frances Keightley to Catherine O'Brien, 28 Mar. 1721 (NLI, MS 45, 348/5); same to Sir Edward O'Brien, 2nd Bt, [n.d., c. Feb. 1724/5] (ibid., MS 45, 348/6); same to Catherine O'Brien, 29 Nov. 1722 (ibid.).

80 Catherine O'Brien's accounts from September 1724 show a back payment to a Mr Tim Conningham [*sic*] 'for instructing Sir Edward in his writing and arithmetic, to August 1721' (account of Catherine O'Brien with Sir Edward O'Brien, 1723–4 (ibid., MS 45, 350/5)).

81 Lady Frances Keightley to Catherine O'Brien, 26 Sept. 1681 (ibid., MS 45, 720/1).

82 Katherine Conolly to Bonnell, 15 Mar. 1719/20 (ibid., MS 41, 578/3). For the pressure on men and women to perform well on the dance floor and the nerves they sometimes experienced when faced with this task, see Glover, *Elite women and polite society*, p. 89; Carter, *Men and the emergence of polite society*, p. 167.

83 Carter, *Men and the emergence of polite society*, pp 67–9, 75; Glover, *Elite women and polite society*, pp 79, 84; Jonathan Swift, 'A letter to a very young lady on her marriage' in *The prose works of Jonathan Swift*, ed. Herbert Davis (14 vols, Oxford, 1939–68), ix, 91. This tract was originally written in 1723.

education, and signify no more than the sincere bows that you may meet with at the Castle [*Dublin Castle*]'.[84]

Languages were also prized among both genders, though the ability to speak Irish counted for little and was even viewed as a problem. 'My little boy speaks nothing but Irish which I fear will prevent his being a scholar so soon [*as his cousin*],' wrote Barbara Reilly, of County Roscommon, in 1744, her son having apparently picked up the language of the nurse she had just brought him home from.[85] The Irish elite wanted their children to look outwards, not inwards and to become part of the British and European world. As such, it was European languages which were sought and European travel which was used to improve a young gentleman's linguistic skills. Having previously been told by his father to work on his French in order to aid his career at court, Alan Brodrick, junior, wrote from Hanover in 1725 that:

> I have done what has been in my power towards perfecting myself in French; and have learnt as much Italian as the small share of conversation, which strangers can have with the people of the country, would admit of. As for the German language it is so extremely difficult, my stay has been so short in any one place, and the accents and manner of speaking so different all over Germany, that I could not propose to myself to make any progress in it; so that I have entirely let alone, what I could not hope to arrive at.[86]

While the kind of travel enjoyed by Alan was not an option for a woman, the quest for educational and social uniformity with England which boarding schools and the Grand Tour afforded men, was replicated by elite women in Ireland in the visits they made to Dublin, or even London, to be 'finished' and to learn the most fashionable etiquette. The wealthy County Tyrone heiress, Margaret Hamilton, who would later become countess of Orrery, planned to travel to England for six months as soon as she was of age in 1732, and by so doing, wrote a female acquaintance, 'shows to the world her taste in going'.[87] Her 'taste' was rooted in the fact that the trip provided an opportunity not only for pleasure and to advertise her wealth and position, but to complete her education by improving and refining the social graces she had already picked up in Ireland and giving them that cosmopolitan flavour which was the mark of time spent in a great urban centre. England was the preferred place to obtain this educational polish, not only because of the novelty of leaving Ireland, but because its larger, better-established elite and the permanent presence of a royal court gave it an air of sophistication and provided girls with the opportunity to perfect the bi-culturalism necessary to traverse both the English and Irish elites while also contributing to the ongoing Anglicisation of the latter. In pursuit of this

84 Mary Mason to John Mason, 12 Dec. 1737 (PRONI, T3131/B/1/35). Though Mary spelt this young man's name 'Mills' he may in fact have been called Milles and a relation of Thomas Milles, then bishop of Waterford and Lismore. See *D.I.B.* (Milles, Thomas (1671–1740)).

85 Reilly to Savage, 21 Aug. 1744 (ibid., D552/A/2/7/11).

86 Alan, Baron Brodrick to Hon. Alan Brodrick, 7 May 1717 (SHC, MS 1248/4/19–20); Hon. Alan Brodrick to Alan, Viscount Midleton, 11 Sept. 1725 [n.s.] (ibid., MS 1248/6/302–303).

87 Sa[rah] Worth to Bonnell, 9 Oct. 1732 (NLI, MS 41, 580/27). Scottish girls visited Edinburgh as well as London, see Barclay, *Love, intimacy and power*, pp 33, 44; Nenadic, 'Experience and expectations', p. 206; Glover, '"Polite London children"', pp 253–71.

goal, a spell in London was also the surest way to soften or even remove one of the clearest markers of a girl's Irishness, her native accent. This made it time and money well spent.

A good accent, which was increasingly one which copied the received pronunciation of the English court, showed that a person moved in and belonged to, polite society, but its acquisition by Irish (and Scottish) children caused many a headache for their parents. Boys could be expected to learn correct inflections at their English schools, and the Scottish benefited from touring English theatre companies, but it was difficult in Ireland, particularly in rural areas, to find English people of a suitable rank for children to converse with, and the problem became another reason to send country girls to the city.[88] James Smyth, when writing of his daughter's education in 1728, told his brother that 'it is impossible she can improve in this country except it be in the dialect of Scotland for which reason I have thoughts of sending her soon to Dublin'.[89] For those with aspirations of high society, especially in England, it was worth the effort to correct this 'defect', for outsiders had a low tolerance for parochial accents. Horace Walpole, despite his otherwise disparaging remarks on the education of the poor, but famously beautiful, Gunning sisters, admitted that their mother had ensured 'that they avoided the provincial brogue of their Irish neighbours', a measure of which he clearly approved.[90] There were disadvantages to trying to remove this tell-tale brogue, though, for some could never quite master the switch, leaving them with a mangled, hybrid accent and at the mercy of their peers' teasing.[91]

Conclusion

The continuous theme to be found in women's experiences of motherhood and childhood was expectation. The expectation that she would produce a family of healthy children; the expectation that even after some losses, this family would contain a high percentage of boys; the expectation that she would know how best to protect and care for her offspring; and the expectation that she would have an education suitable to her rank and would see to it that her daughters did too. This

88 Glover, *Elite women and polite society*, pp 41, 98, 103; eadem, '"Polite London Children"', p. 261; Angela Dain, 'Assemblies and politeness 1660–1840' (University of East Anglia, Ph.D. thesis, 2000), pp 153–4. Dain also writes that schools increasingly offered instruction in correct English pronunciation and that some chose to converse in French to hide their parochial accents (ibid., pp 158–9, 165).

89 James Smyth to William Smyth, 24 May 1728 (NLI, MS 41, 582/6).

90 Quoted in Malcomson, *Pursuit of the heiress*, p. 121. Maria and Elizabeth Gunning were born in England to Irish parents, moving back to Ireland as children. Maria became the countess of Coventry, Elizabeth (through two marriages) the duchess of Hamilton and Brandon, then Argyll. See *Oxford D.N.B.* (Campbell [*née* Gunning], Elizabeth, duchess of Argyll and *suo jure* Baroness Hamilton of Hameldon [*other married name* Elizabeth Hamilton, duchess of Hamilton and Brandon] (*bap.* 1733, *d.* 1790)).

91 Toby Barnard, 'Protestantism, ethnicity and Irish identities, 1660–1760' in Tony Claydon and Ian McBride (eds), *Protestantism and national identity: Britain and Ireland, c.1650–c.1850* (Cambridge, 2007), p. 216.

last point had implications for the entire Irish elite, for if the birth and survival of children was a way to expand and secure the fortunes of an individual family, their education was a way to expand and secure the reach of their whole social group, allowing it to integrate with the English elite and the wider European community, without the wholesale abandonment of the endogamous marriage pattern discussed in Chapter 1. Even daughters, educated at home, had a part to play in this juggling game, dispatched to England to learn supposedly more sophisticated manners and speech patterns, then import them back into their communities and families, creating an ever more Anglo-Irish elite.

Running alongside these expectations was the inevitable mixture of success and failure, blame and sympathy, which came from women's efforts to meet them. The emotional highs experienced by some from producing the longed-for male heir were matched by the lows of repeated miscarriages and infant mortality. Compliments on a woman's accomplishments could be offset by criticisms of her limitations. Yet what shines through most clearly is the web of support women wove for each which transcended the generations and prevented the weight of these expectations from becoming crushing. Family and friends were always available for help and advice, whether it was guiding each other through the perils of childbirth, or dealing with children's illnesses, education and bad behaviour. Katherine Conolly, disappointed though she was that Lady Anne's first child was a girl, showered the baby with gifts and insisted on paying the costs of Anne's lying-in (that is, the weeks before and after the birth, during which Anne withdrew from society).[92] One may even detect, in the grumblings of her sister, Mary, over the poor manners of their great-niece, Molly Burton, a familial concern for the girl's future and desire to protect her from the kind of derision levelled by the likes of Lady Anne at those who failed to meet society's behavioural and educational standards.

This support network was no weaker or less important when it came to assisting and supporting women in the challenges they faced within their marriages, as household and estate managers, and it is to these challenges that we will now turn.

92 Katherine Conolly to Lady Anne Conolly, 23 Feb. 1733 (IAA, MS J/2).

3

The lady of the house

Writing from her home in Holymount, County Down, in 1745, Mary Delany, wife of the dean of Down, expressed her concern to her sister over the state of the household of their brother, Bernard Granville:

> I find his domestics [*meaning servants*] are not right yet, nor can they ever be in good order till he has a wife to manage them, for men are no judges of domestic affairs; we were designed for that purpose, and have the talents that are fit for the purpose.[1]

There were few areas outside of childbirth in which a woman could have made such a sweeping generalisation as to the superiority of her own sex over the other without risking a serious backlash, but household management was one of them. There was no question in Mary's mind that a wife, any wife, would be preferable to Bernard's singleton status. All of his household problems were caused by his bachelorhood and all would be solved by his marriage, for domestic dominance was a task for which women were born, educated and uniquely fitted, having been granted greater abilities to any man by the Almighty himself. Even ladies of the elite, the social group of which Mary considered herself, her brother and any potential sister-in-law, members, were not exempt.

Though such ideas went against the general consensus that male trumped female, Mary's belief that her brother was handicapped by his gender in a way in which a wife would not be, were typical for one of her station and time and across her native England and adopted Ireland, conduct writers and the men and women of both elites echoed her views. Just five years earlier, Wetenhall Wilkes in his *Letter of genteel and moral advice to a young lady* published in Dublin, dictated that 'oeconomy, or the art of house-keeping, is the most immediate female business' and one from which 'neither wealth nor greatness can totally absolve you'.[2] His ideas were not new, for George Savile, marquis of Halifax, had advised his daughter Elizabeth in 1688, that household management was 'the province allotted to your sex'.[3] Mrs Delany would have approved of the actions of Sir Donat O'Brien, 1st Bt, of County Clare. Having been widowed twice, he employed a housekeeper to manage his home and in later years, offered his cash-strapped son and daughter-in-law the chance to live with him, with 'Mrs O'Brien to manage and govern all as much as she does now and to

1 Mary Delany to Ann Dewes, 10 Aug. 1745 (*The autobiography and correspondence of Mary Granville, Mrs Delany* ..., ed. Lady Llanover (ser. 1, 3 vols, London, 1861), ii, 375).

2 Wetenhall Wilkes, *A letter of genteel and moral advice* ... (Dublin, 1740), pp 119, 120.

3 George Savile, 1st marquis of Halifax, *The lady's new-year's gift: or, advice to a daughter* (London, 1688), p. 69.

be at no expense for it'.[4] This was obviously meant to be an incentive for Catherine O'Brien, who would not be subordinate to either her father-in-law or his servants, and illustrates the typical domestic roles envisaged for and by each sex.

Interest in the history of the 'big house' in early modern Ireland has been growing in recent years, and a number of books and articles, some with a distinctly female bent, now afford us a glimpse into their internal workings and power structures, providing information on the physical layout of elite homes, the costs involved in running them and the interactions between employers and servants.[5] As of yet, little of this work concerns itself with the late seventeenth and early eighteenth centuries, although it is supplemented by the much better established English and Scottish historiographies, which more often take in the earlier period. This scholarship has shown that dependent women (that is, those who were married or managing the home of a male relation, as opposed to living independently in their own residences) found power rather than subjugation in their place as mistress of the household, for this was an area in which traditional gender roles did not always apply.[6] A person's rank could supersede their sex, allowing female to supersede male. Women held authority over male employees and the lady of the house made the majority of the daily decisions for it.[7] Attempts to subvert this chain of command were typically met with hostility and could, as Anne Kugler has shown in her study of Sarah, Lady Cowper, put severe stress upon marriages and the internal harmony of a home.[8] This was unusual, though, for early modern men generally had great respect for women's domestic abilities and their rights over the household. Echoing Sir Donat's choices, Amanda Vickery points to the speed with which unmarried English men who had their own households, or widowers, married in order to secure a mistress for their home, and Stana Nenadic has noted the value of domestic skills for Scottish widows re-entering the marriage market, who would find it easier to secure a second or third husband, courtesy of their proven ability to efficiently manage a house.[9] Despite these gendered stereotypes, scholars also acknowledge the

4 Mary, Lady Jervis to Sir Donat O'Brien, 14 Nov. 1700 in *The Inchiquin manuscripts*, ed. John Ainsworth (Dublin, 1961), p. 58; quote from Sir Donat O'Brien to Thomas Keightley, 10 Jan. 1706/7 (NLI, MS 45, 295/4).

5 Olwen Purdue, *The big house in the north of Ireland: land, power and social elites, 1878–1960* (Dublin, 2009); Maeve O'Riordan, 'Assuming control: elite women as household managers in late nineteenth-century Ireland' in Ciarán O'Neill (ed.), *Irish elites in the nineteenth century* (Dublin, 2013), pp 83–98; Terence Dooley, '"Till my further orders": rules governing servants at Carton in the mid-eighteenth century' in idem, Patrick J. Cosgrove and Karol Mullaney-Dignam (eds), *Aspects of Irish aristocratic life: essays on the FitzGeralds and Carton House* (Dublin, 2014), pp 106–17.

6 Amanda Vickery, *Behind closed doors: at home in Georgian England* (London, 2009).

7 Amanda Flather, *Gender and space in early modern England* (Woodbridge, 2007), pp 34–8; Ingrid Tague, *Women of quality: accepting and contesting ideals of femininity in England, 1690–1760* (Woodbridge, 2002), p. 131.

8 Anne Kugler, *Errant plagiary: the life and writing of Lady Sarah Cowper, 1644–1720* (Stanford, 2002).

9 Vickery, *Behind closed doors*, ch. 7; eadem, *The Gentleman's daughter: women's lives in Georgian England* (London, 1998), pp 128–9; Stana Nenadic, 'Experience and expectations in the transformation of the Highland gentlewoman, 1680 to 1820', *Scottish Historical Review*, lxxx (2001), p. 207.

joint, if uneven, efforts of spouses in managing their homes. Vickery for instance, has traced the gendered spending habits of elite couples during the eighteenth century and come to the conclusion that women's purchases were 'an element in a bigger system, locked in relationship with the consumption of their husbands and households'.[10]

The story of early modern Scottish and English houses is a complicated one, in which the boundaries for correct male and female behaviour were fluid and the role of a woman was as important as it was challenging. The question remains, though, as to how and why these patterns were either replicated in Ireland, or replaced by something else.

Budgets, budgeting and spending

Wilkes' choice of the word 'oeconomy' was particularly fitting, for an elite household was a micro-economy, gathering its income from the family estate and perhaps the master's salary while requiring the expenditure of sometimes vast sums to keep itself running. Co-ordinating the spending, as a kind of chancellor of the Exchequer, was the lady of the house. The best sources of information as to how she did this are account books, but despite being trained in their use from childhood and badgered by frustrated husbands to keep good records, not all women complied. According to her husband Francis, Molly Burton (*née* Conyngham) was consistently poor at keeping track of her finances and nothing, save a few stray comments in her family's letters, survives to show how she spent the money he gave her.[11] The wealthier, such as the 2nd duke and duchess of Ormond, had servants to keep their records for them, but the accuracy of these records depended upon the diligence of secretaries and how meticulous the employer was in monitoring outgoings and keeping receipts. Where records do exist, they can vary widely in terms of detail and accuracy. This variation, coupled with the difference in income among elite families and the changing economic circumstances of Ireland during the years encompassed by this book, make it unwise, if not impossible to make direct comparisons between different households. What can be established, though, are the operating budgets of some of the ladies of the Anglo-Irish elite and the percentage of the family's income allotted to them.

Mary, duchess of Ormond, had an allowance of £70 per week specifically for 'household expenses' in 1694, which then fluctuated up within a few years to between £100 and £120 per payment, though the instalments were not as steady. While these allowances related to her London establishment and terminated with her trip to Ireland in 1697, they nevertheless provide a guide as to what she was used to receiving and spending – a staggering £4,040 in the year between March

[10] Amanda Vickery, 'His and hers: gender, consumption and household accounting in eighteenth-century England', *Past and Present*, supplement, i (2006), p. 35.

[11] Francis Burton to Jane Bonnell, 14 Feb. 1729/30 (NLI, MS 41, 579/10). Molly Conyngham Burton will be referred to here by both her maiden and married surnames to avoid confusion with her daughter, also called Molly Burton (later Lady Gore).

1695 and March 1696.[12] The Butler family's income at this time stood at around £17,000 *per annum* (at the most), which means that Mary was using nearly 28% of the total, if not more.[13] By contrast, Catherine O'Brien, while managing Dromoland Castle in County Clare for her underage son, Sir Edward O'Brien, 2nd Bt, spent only £550 (an average of around £9 per week) between 15 July 1720 and 11 August 1721.[14] The O'Brien estate brought in £14,031 4*s.* 11¼*d.* in rents during the first five years of Edward's minority (a little over £2,806 per annum) so that Catherine was spending around 19% of Edward's income on his house at the start of the decade, considerably less than the duchess.[15] Even this was too much, and of the £550 mentioned, she requested and was reimbursed only £360 from his estate by the court of Chancery. The shortfall she made up herself, no doubt from of her jointure, worth £500 per year.[16]

Falling under the umbrella of household spending were food, furnishings, household paraphernalia (such as plateware and candles), building maintenance, personal items for the family and servants' wages. Catherine's accounts of the 'sundry disbursements' she was making on behalf of her son show that, between 1719 and 1722, she spent £70 'for the firing' at Dromoland Castle, including £10 for coals.[17] In January 1724, she spent ten shillings for six cups and saucers, and the following month there were payments of £0 5*s.* 5*d.* to mend the clock at Dromoland and £1 7*s.* 4*d.* 'for a stewpan, 2 large saucepans and a pair of candlesticks'.[18] In May there was £4 10s. for a chamber pot, and between January 1723 and June 1724, it cost £15 5s. 1½*d.* just to keep the house in butter.[19] Some food she acquired from the demesne, much she bought. Not one to deny herself the finer things, her family's diet was remarkably varied, and though their home in western Clare was far from any large urban centre, they enjoyed wine, rum, brandy, tea, coffee, a variety of meats, seafish, poultry and citrus fruits, and treats such as sugared almonds, strawberries and spices. Little wonder Mrs O'Brien needed to draw upon her own and her son's income to make ends meet.[20]

12 Accounts of James, duke of Ormond, Sept. 1694–Dec. 1707, and of Mary, duchess of Ormond, Mar. 1694–May 1697 (ibid., MS 2547, unfoliated).

13 D.W. Hayton, *The Anglo-Irish experience, 1680–1730: religion, identity and patriotism* (Woodbridge, 2012), p. 51.

14 Account of Catherine O'Brien with her son Sir Edward O'Brien, 2nd Bt, mainly relating to tenants and workmen, during the minority of the said Sir Edward, 1719–22 (NLI, MS 14, 369, f. 26).

15 Account of Catherine O'Brien with her son Sir Edward O'Brien, 2nd Bt, 1719–23 (ibid., MS 14, 370, unfoliated).

16 Account of Catherine O'Brien with her son Sir Edward O'Brien, 2nd Bt, mainly relating to tenants and workmen, during the minority of the said Sir Edward, 1719–22 (ibid., MS 14, 369, f. 26); marriage settlement of Lucius O'Brien and Catherine Keightley, 29 Dec. 1701 (ibid., MS 45, 290/4).

17 Account of Catherine O'Brien with her son Sir Edward O'Brien, 2nd Bt, mainly relating to tenants and workmen, during the minority of the said Sir Edward, 1719–22 (ibid., MS 14, 369, f. 26).

18 Account of Catherine O'Brien with Sir Edward O'Brien, 2nd Bart, 1723–1724 (ibid., MS 45, 350/5, ff 25, 26).

19 Ibid., ff 27, 32.

20 Ibid., ff 32–6.

Perpetual bachelor Jonathan Swift once expressed an idealised, but popular view of how a wife should manage her husband's money. She ought, he wrote, 'to be well informed how much your husband's revenue amounts to, and be so good a computer, as to keep within it in that part of the management, which falls to your share'. Mothers too advised their daughters to 'be careful in your expenses not to exceed your husband's fortune', and instead, they were to strike a balance between what was wanted, what was needed and what could be realistically obtained on the family budget, a task easier said than done, as some discovered.[21]

Some were hampered by pre-existing financial obligations which then spiralled out of control. Catherine O'Brien's problems had begun long before her widowhood, and she fought to conceal debts from her husband, Lucius, contracted both before and after their marriage, and often had to rely on handouts from her father-in-law to pay her servants and bills. The duchess of Ormond also faced an uphill fight from the outset, as income from the Butler estates fell (by 1715, they were bringing in less than half of the expected £16,000), and she and her husband were burdened with debts of between £98,500 and £150,000 inherited from his grandfather, the 1st duke of Ormond. Nor did either woman show any great concept of the value of money, or how best to handle it, a weakness also displayed by Molly Conyngham Burton.[22]

Extravagance exacerbated Molly's inability or unwillingness to keep good account books. Her husband, Francis, begged her aunt, Jane Bonnell, to write to her, 'recommending it to her to manage the money I send with the utmost prudence, for I must tell you she has very little notion of money, and when she has it she is too generous'.[23] His complaints and recourse to Jane show the seriousness of the situation, for spontaneously intervening in a wife's domestic affairs risked open marital conflict and was something most men were loathe to do.[24] Having had it drummed into them since childhood that the household was their domain, women could be territorial over their rights there, easily irked by unwanted interference (with its underlying suggestion that they were overwhelmed or incompetent) and, like Mary Delany at the beginning of this chapter, scathing of the idea that any man would know better than they did. Francis's letter to Jane not only shows his failure to rein in Molly's expenditure, but his unwillingness to push his authority over his wife any further. Better to let some other family member bear the brunt of her displeasure and himself maintain as much plausible deniability as possible. Older, female relations, like Jane, with credentials gained from having run their own homes for many years, were best for this job, for their advice would hopefully be taken as informed, well-intentioned and helpful and accepted with grace, rather than disdain. If not, then at least a wife's ire would not be directed towards her husband. Nevertheless, this self-preservation was mingled with kindness, and

21 Jonathan Swift, 'A letter to a very young lady on her marriage' in *The prose works of Jonathan Swift*, ed. Herbert Davis (14 vols, Oxford, 1939–68), ix, 94. This tract was originally written in 1723. See also Lady Frances Keightley to Catherine O'Brien, 26 Sept. 1681 (NLI, MS 45, 720/1).

22 Catherine O'Brien to Bonnell, 7 Nov. [1704?] (ibid., MS 41, 580/22); accounts between Sir Donat, Lucius and Catherine O'Brien, Apr. 1711–June 1714 (ibid., MS 45, 339/10); *Oxford D.N.B.* (Butler, James, 2nd duke of Ormond (1665–1745)).

23 Francis Burton to Bonnell, 14 Feb. 1729/30 (NLI., MS 41, 579/10).

24 For an example of this conflict, see Kugler, *Errant plagiary*.

Francis asked Jane not to tell Molly of his letter, in part to prevent an argument with her, but also to spare his wife's feelings by leaving her unaware that he was complaining about her. He and Jane's discretion also allowed Molly to save face in front of him, for greater importance could be attached to appearances than reality, and women were usually anxious to present themselves to their husbands as capable and prudent managers and explain unforeseen expenditures. It was with this in mind that Hugh Howard (a prominent Irish painter and art collector) was assured by his wife Thomasine, when she received money from him, that 'I will be as good a housewife of [*it*] as I can'.[25] When asking for more, she explained that 'I have not spent upon myself in plat[e] or anyway idle 3 guineas'.[26]

Molly and Thomasine's difficulties were intensified by having to live separately from their husbands for prolonged periods, splitting the family income and raising overall expenditure as two households were maintained instead of one. As another of Molly Conyngham Burton's aunts, Katherine Conolly, commented to Jane Bonnell, 'when you write to Molly I would have you advise frugality to her especially now in her husband's absence for it's now double expenses'.[27] Molly's continued spending and slowness to return from a stay in Paris to her husband in Ireland did not help the situation and exasperated him.[28] The duchess of Ormond suffered similar problems when she planned to relocate from England to Ireland with her daughters in 1697 while the duke went campaigning in Flanders.[29] In barely one week in April she spent £481 on unspecified items (despite having done no more than remove to her father's home in Badminton, before finally reaching Ireland in June), while the duke laid out £800 between 8 and 17 September in France.[30] The relocation may have been intended as a cost-saving measure (Mary certainly found life at Kilkenny to be at a much slower pace than in London), but this and later separations helped to cripple the family finances to the extent that she was having to fend off bailiffs at their Richmond home while the duke was in Ireland in 1711.[31] Even when they were together, the very existence of multiple residences created problems. Vickery has argued that ladies in Mary's position were at a particular disadvantage compared to those of a lower rank, as constant moves between homes 'weakened the association between ladies and their houses', inflating expenses while making them harder to monitor.[32] Intensifying this issue for the duchess was the fact that one of the Butler homes was in Ireland, while she spent most of her time in England. The sea journey made it difficult and (as the figures above show) very

25 *Oxford D.N.B.* (Howard, Hugh (1675–1738)); Thomasine Howard to Hugh Howard, 2 Apr. 1726 (NLI, MS 38, 600/7).

26 Thomasine Howard to Hugh Howard, 2 Apr. 1726 (NLI, MS 38, 600/7).

27 Katherine Conolly to Bonnell, 18 Oct. 1729 (ibid., MS 41, 578/4).

28 Francis Burton to same, 24 May 1730 (ibid., MS 41, 579/10).

29 Valentine Smyth to Charles Gosling, 10 Apr. 1697 (ibid., MS 11, 058/3).

30 Accounts of James, duke of Ormond, Sept. 1694–Dec. 1707, and of Mary, duchess of Ormond, Mar. 1694–May 1697 (ibid., MS 2547, unfoliated); Smyth to John Ellis, 23 June 1697 (BL, Add. MS 28881, f. 331).

31 On Mary's experiences (and boredom) at Kilkenny, see Mary, duchess of Ormond to Benjamin Portlock, 12 Feb. 1697/8 (NLI, MS 2502). On her dealings with the bailiffs, see [D?] Kennedy to Sir William Robinson, 12 Nov. 1711 (ibid., MS 2474).

32 Vickery, *Behind closed doors*, p. 160.

expensive to visit often.[33] Her contemporary, Juliana Boyle, dowager countess of Cork and Burlington, likewise complained of the difficulty of managing her son's Irish seat, Lismore Castle, from England during his minority, and of her worries that servants whom she had never met were taking advantage of her absence to live in the Castle at her son's expense and thereby increase household bills. Writing to his estate agents in 1704, she complained that 'I told you plainly before that I would not allow firing, candles, or an assistant, and I wonder that you will trouble me again on the same subject, for I think it a needless expense to my son'.[34]

Extravagant husbands were another problem. Katherine Conolly felt that responsibility for the financial problems which had left the Burtons heavily in debt by 1730 lay with Francis as well as Molly, saying that 'they have both an extravagant, squandering way'.[35] As his campaign expenditure suggests, the duke of Ormond was also a profligate spender, determined to project the 'required' ducal splendour whether he could afford it or not, while Lucius O'Brien accumulated debts of £3,543 16*s.* in the first five years of his marriage alone.[36] He spent his and his wife's income on fruitless trips to England without her, running up debts there in addition to those she already owed, borrowing money from his father to pay them and driving the latter to distraction, along with Catherine's father, Thomas Keightley, as the couple fell further and further into debt. Lucius even admitted to being lazy when it came to making something of himself and supporting his family, yet attempted to write this off as a natural disability within him for which allowances should be made.[37] When the young people were offered the cost-saving option of moving in with Sir Donat in early 1707, they refused, on Lucius's instigation, and despite the fact that Catherine indicated that she would be agreeable to the scheme.[38] With such a husband, it is little wonder she had trouble controlling expenditure.

Whatever the mitigating factors, it was still wives who were judged (even from the outset of their marriages) according to how successfully homes were run and family finances managed. Though it may have been the husband who contracted the debts, it was her job to bring the problem under control and her reputation that would suffer if she did not. Katherine Conolly wrote, with some sympathy, that, thanks to her nephew, Roger Jones, his wife would have no easy task managing their family's finances, 'for he is so in debt [*that*] without selling he cannot get the better

33 Mary was in Ireland between 1697 and 1699 and again between 1703 and 1705. During the latter visit her husband was lord lieutenant of the country, however, and they were primarily based in Dublin Castle (*Post Man*, 8–10 July 1697; Richard Cox to James, duke of Ormond, 16 May 1699 (NLI, MS 2456); *D.I.B.* (Butler, James (1665–1745)).

34 Juliana, dowager countess of Cork and Burlington to Roger Power, Richard Bagge and Thomas Baker, 7 Oct. 1704 (NLI, MS 43, 361/2).

35 Katherine Conolly to Bonnell, 16 Sept. 1729 (ibid., MS 41, 578/4).

36 *D.I.B.* (Butler, James (1665–1745)); Sir Donat O'Brien to Thomas Keightley, 21 Feb. 1706/7 (NLI, MS 45, 295/4).

37 Lucius O'Brien to Catherine O'Brien, 3 Jan. 1712/13 (NLI, MS 45, 297/1).

38 Same to same, 22 July 1714 (ibid.); accounts between Sir Donat, Lucius and Catherine O'Brien, Apr. 1711–June 1714 (ibid., MS 45, 339/10); Thomas Keightley to Sir Donat O'Brien, 2 Dec. 1706 (ibid., MS 45, 295/4); Sir Donat O'Brien to Thomas Keightley, 10 Jan. 1706/7 (ibid.); Thomas Keightley to Sir Donat O'Brien, 16 Jan. 1706/7 (ibid.).

of it and selling above the half'.[39] However, Roger's mother, Katherine's sister, Mary Jones, expected that her son's wife should remedy the situation and went to stay with them in order to 'judge what a manager his wife will prove to be'.[40] Sympathy notwithstanding, Katherine ultimately had similar views, and although her great wealth ensured that budgeting was not something she needed to concern herself with, she still expected those of more limited means to perfect the art. Writing of the problems of Molly Conyngham Burton when her husband Francis was away, Katherine mused that 'it's much more prudent it should be the wife should save than the husband'.[41] To her, a wife's outgoings were of less import than a husband's and more likely to include frivolous items which could be trimmed from the family expenditure. These were tough expectations to meet, and more than one wife must have bristled at being expected to do without when her husband was not. Molly certainly did not toe the line. Yet the disagreements the Burtons had with each other over household costs belie the true nature of male and female participation in domestic spending, for despite their prominence within the household, wives did not have unilateral control over it, nor in fact, did they usually want this. Instead, a controlling interest, with the option of heavily directed input from husbands, was the preference.

Teamwork

Katie Barclay and Amanda Vickery have shown that Scottish and English couples functioned as 'domestic allies', sharing the responsibility for purchasing household items.[42] To an extent, the same may be said of Ireland, but a distinction must be made between country and town and between women who were with their husbands and those temporarily separated from them. Compared to urban residents, women in the country were obliged to be more flexible regarding how they would obtain the goods they wanted, and their husbands often played a larger role in their acquisition, especially if they were away, visiting areas with better shopping districts than could be found at home.

Margaret Savage of Portaferry and Anne Ward of Castle Ward (both living in County Down and very close together) repeatedly issued their husbands, Andrew Savage and Judge Michael Ward, with lengthy shopping lists when the men were in Dublin. Along with clothing and dress patterns for the women and their children were goods clearly intended for the house and estate. Michael was ordered to send

39 Katherine Conolly to Bonnell, 29 May 1733 (ibid., MS 41, 578/7).

40 Same to same, 12 June 1733 (ibid.).

41 Same to same, 18 Oct. 1729 (ibid., MS 41, 578/4). Ingrid Tague has argued that for the English, 'if domestic economy suggested feminine virtue, its absence was a sign of moral failing' (Tague, *Women of quality*, p. 110).

42 Katie Barclay, *Love, intimacy and power: marriage and patriarchy in Scotland, 1650–1850* (Manchester, 2011), pp 152–4; Vickery, *Behind closed doors*, p. 9 (quote from Vickery). See also Claire Walsh, 'Shops, shopping, and the art of decision marking eighteenth century England' in John Styles and Amanda Vickery (eds), *Gender, taste, and material culture in Britain and North America, 1700–1830* (New Haven, 2006), pp 151–78.

nails and iron to shoe the Ward horses so that they could be put to work, three iron locks, shot and six shovels of powder 'for the fowler', a barrel of peas, for 'we want the peas for the garden very much' and 'a pair of boxes, the boxes to be made by the man in Damask Street'. Margaret had Andrew 'order Hugh McMullie [*a servant he had taken to Dublin*] to buy a stone of the best English flour for paste and them things it will be wanting and order him to buy 12 pounds of mole's candles five to the pound, tell him that I believe he will get the flour at Mr Kennedy's'.[43] More exotic foods were also popular. Each woman requested oranges, and Margaret also sent for 'one pound of capers' and 'two pounds of saltpeter and a crock of anchovies'.[44]

In some ways, using husbands as 'proxy shoppers' was advantageous. Anne and Margaret saved themselves, or one of their household servants, from the trouble of having to make the purchases, and at least some of the receipts issued for these items may well have been placed on their husbands' accounts, preserving their wives' control over the choice of goods arriving at their doors, but saving on their official household expenses and allowing them to divert their allowance elsewhere. Female power was likewise maintained thanks to the very detailed instructions issued to husbands as to exactly what should be bought, from whom and at what price. Yet by involving men in the purchase process, wives made them complicit in the household spending and less able to complain about it later. Had Molly Conyngham Burton done the same when Francis was absent, she might well have avoided some of the complaints he levelled at her.[45]

There are hints, though, of inconveniences. Michael was chided for not sending an inventory with an earlier package of goods, and Andrew was told to desist from buying Margaret anything she had not particularly asked for.[46] Nor was importation quick or cheap. In addition to the cost of the goods themselves, delivery necessitated a boat trip or a lengthy road journey, and both ladies acknowledged the costs involved would be steep. Anne wanted a dozen oranges only if they could be bought cheaply, and Margaret, in a comment which again spoke to her determination to maintain control over the house, told Andrew not to buy everything the family cook had asked for, for 'if people was to buy everything that servants desired they would be very extravagant and soon run out their fortunes'.[47] Why then, despite this added trouble and expense, was outsourcing so popular?

First was the problem of supply and demand associated with certain items. This was a particular issue for women such as Anne and Margaret managing households in rural Ireland. Exotic foodstuffs such as oranges, capers and anchovies were

43 Anne Ward to Michael Ward, [c. 1723] (PRONI, D2092/1/2); Margaret Savage to Andrew Savage, 5 Dec. 1738 (ibid., D552/A/2/9/2); same to same, Dublin, 8 June 1741 (ibid., D552/A/2/9/3).
44 Margaret Savage to Andrew Savage, [1738–41] (ibid., D552/A/2/9/12).
45 On 'proxy shopping', see Walsh, 'Shops, shopping and the art of decision making', pp 170–1. Toby Barnard has noted the ambiguity historians face as to when a 'grandee', male or female, might deign to enter a shop, as opposed to having a servant do it. See 'Hamilton's "Cries of Dublin"; the society and economy of mid-eighteenth Dublin' in William Laffan (ed.), *The cries of Dublin etc.: drawn from the life of Hugh Douglas Hamilton, 1760* (Dublin, 2003), pp 27–8.
46 Anne Ward to Michael Ward, [c. 1723] (PRONI, D2092/1/2); Margaret Savage to Andrew Savage, 5 Dec. 1738 (ibid., D552/A/2/9/2).
47 Anne Ward to Michael Ward, [c. 1723] (ibid., D2092/1/2); Margaret Savage to Andrew Savage, [1738–40] (ibid., D552/A/2/9/12).

unavailable within the vicinity of their homes and, given the urgency in her tone, even the type of peas Anne wanted for the garden were unobtainable. This left importation, slow and costly though it was, as the only viable option if wishes were to be met.

Second was the matter of quality, which in some measure counteracted the inconveniences and cost of importation (better goods being worth a little extra money and effort). When it came to commonplace items, like those Anne requested for the horses and fowler, which must have been available in some form closer to home, the decision to wait until her letter could reach Dublin and Michael or a servant could buy, pack and send goods back to her, indicate a belief in the superiority of items from the capital which was worth the delay and added expense incurred. She and Margaret's directions as to which vendors to patronise also show that they had either checked with family or friends as to which were the best, or were repeat customers. Either way, they believed that there were none as good who could suit their needs in County Down.

A third and alternative way to look at Anne and Margaret's requests is to see them as a deliberate ploy on their part (with their husbands' acquiescence) designed to take advantage of the social benefits of being able to afford importation. The desire to maintain a 'grand figure' before friends, neighbours and tenants made carting in wares from Dublin (especially non-essential, luxury goods) a useful method of advertising a family's financial health and high status. This in turn possibly reinforced the idea of their ability and right to rule over their local area as landlords, politicians and law enforcers. This consumer posturing granted women's purchase choices and role as household managers an additional level of importance beyond the provision of comfort and luxury for their families, for they were also helping to promote the social and political wellbeing of the elite, and in most cases, the Protestant Ascendancy as a whole and demonstrating, as one historian recently put it, that even provincial Irish families 'were part of the wider British Atlantic world'.[48]

Whatever the motives, Michael and Andrew's presence in Dublin and by extension, their ability to make purchases for their wives of items they might otherwise have had difficulty in obtaining, was a convenience the women clearly appreciated and made the most of, as did many others in their position.[49] Yet we may still detect some unease on their part over their inability to buy what they wanted themselves. Their very precise instructions and complaints when these were not followed to the letter show two women who were used to having a greater degree of control over their purchases and were not entirely comfortable delegating. Despite their determination to take full advantage of the shopping possibilities opened by their husbands' trips, the management of their households was ultimately their sphere (a stereotype all the more deeply entrenched by a husband's absence), and they were prepared to share the load only when they calculated that the benefits of doing so outweighed the drawbacks.

48 Madeline Shanahan, '"Dining on words": manuscript recipe books, culinary change and elite food culture in Ireland, 1660–1830', *Irish Architectural and Decorative Studies*, xv (2012), p. 94.
49 Barnard, 'Hamilton's "Cries of Dublin"', p. 28.

In the city, a lady might maintain greater autonomy in her consumer choices and activities, thanks to the proximity of a wide variety of shops and merchants. Mary Delany spent one Wednesday in 1750 travelling 'all over Dublin shopping, bespeaking paper for hangings, linen for beds, and a thousand things too tedious to be here inserted'. The tedium she experienced was balanced out, though, by the ability to see the goods before she purchased them and make an informed, independent decision as to whether or not to buy. No third party was required and she was in no way reliant upon her husband to make or carry out her choices for her.[50] Husbands might better be termed as domestic assets then, rather than allies, for wives maintained overall power. Men, when they entered the process at all, appear as instruments carrying out their wives' wishes. With servants, though, the situation was slightly more complex.

Servants

Depending on a family's wealth and the size of their household, its complement of staff might include a combination of workers such as maids, footmen, grooms, kitchen workers, a butler and a housekeeper. During the viceroyalty of the duke of Shrewsbury in 1713–14, Dublin Castle had a staff of 106, but it was a government building as well as a family residence. The wealthy and ever extravagant Conollys had a 'family' (to use the term favoured by contemporaries to describe their employees) of 70 in 1729, but others had far fewer to manage. Mrs Delany called her household 'large and consequently expensive', but these are relative terms, and she mentioned in her correspondence only a housekeeper, butler, several maids and some servants of the dean.[51]

The distinction between those servants who 'belonged' to a wife and those who were her husband's is of particular importance in understanding the internal workings of an elite house and the dynamics between master and mistress, employer and servant. Just like finances and shopping, a wife was the dominant force, though there were instances in which she deferred to her spouse. Mrs Delany felt personally possessive and responsible for most of the household servants, male or female, and frequently slipped into referring to them as 'my housekeeper' or 'my maids' rather than using the word 'our' and so acknowledging her husband's place as employer.[52]

50 Delany to Dewes, 8 June 1750 (*Autobiography and correspondence*, ser. 1, ii, 552). See also Sarah Foster, '"Ornaments and splendour": shops and shopping in Georgian Dublin', *Irish Architectural and Decorative Studies: the Journal of the Irish Georgian Society*, xv (2002), p. 25. Mainly focusing on the period following the mid eighteenth century, Foster finds that by that time 'going shopping was seen as a female preserve, and sometimes merely as a leisure pursuit'.

51 '*The establishment of H.G. the Duke of Shrewsbury's house in Dublin Castle*', 1713 (Royal Irish Academy, MS 24 H 22, ff 1–46); Katherine Conolly to Bonnell, 9 Dec. 1729 (NLI, MS 41, 578/4). Delany to Dewes, 17 Aug. 1745 (*Autobiography and correspondence*, ser. 1, ii, 379). For references to specific servants, see same to same, 5 Apr. 1746 (ibid., 434); same to same, 6 June 1747 (ibid., 462); same to same, 13 Oct. 1747 (ibid., 476). For the size of nineteenth-century Irish households, see O'Riordan, 'Assuming control', p. 86.

52 See, for example, Delany to Dewes, 6 June 1747 (*Autobiography and correspondence*, ser. 1, ii, 462).

Her phrasing was indicative of a widely acknowledged difference between general staff (such as cooks and butlers), whose work directly benefited all members of the family, and the personal attendants of each family member. The first were associated with a particular residence, the second with a particular person. A housekeeper would stay with the house, a lady's maid or a groom would go wherever their employer went. It was this mobility, coupled with the greater access and physical proximity to an employer that resulted from it, which dictated those servants who would report to the mistress and those who would report to the master, not the gender of a particular employee.[53]

Husbands were happy for their wives to manage the main staff of the family home or homes and their own and the children's attendants, but when it came to the choice of groom or secretary, the husband remained in control. This made sense, for it was these servants who would spend the most time with him, travelling with him even when his wife did not. Thus, Lucius O'Brien wrote in 1705 that he and his wife Catherine would not be hiring any further servants at that time, because Catherine had deemed it unnecessary, but the duke of Ormond, on his way to Ireland in 1698 where his wife and children awaited him, personally dealt with the imprisonment and dismissal of his disgraced 'gentleman' when he discovered the man had been stealing from him.[54] Slightly different was the case of Andrew Savage of Portaferry. In need of a temporary cook during a trip to Dublin, he sought the assistance of his wife, Margaret, at home in the north. She had him compile a shortlist then send her details of 'where the cooks lived, them that you would think look likely to be fittest for your purpose and set it down that I might see by that if I liked any of them. I could send up for to have them hired after you came down but don't you hire any of them.'[55] Though Margaret was not there, a cook was the type of servant for which female input was required, and neither she nor Andrew wholly trusted his judgement.

Good servants were a prized possession and finding just the right one was a serious business. Ladies swapped stories of employees who had pleased and those who had not, acting as an informal recruitment agency and screening service for each other and for those bachelors and widowers who had no one else to perform this customarily female task for them. Elizabeth, Lady Rogerson, whose husband Sir John had been lord mayor of Dublin in 1693–94 'thought highly' of her housekeeper during that time and repeated as much to Mary, Lady Jervis. She in turn recommended the woman to Sir Donat O'Brien in 1700 when he was in search of a new housekeeper, relating details of her birth, marriage, general employment background and conduct, and calling her 'the best [*housekeeper*] in Ireland that ever I knew'.[56] Residential employees (that is, those who would live permanently in their employer's home), were especially important, for ladies might be absent from the home for prolonged periods of time and obliged to leave it in the hands

53 On female authority over male servants, see also Flather, *Gender and space*, pp 34–8.

54 Lucius O'Brien to Richard Wilson, 5 Nov. 1705 (NLI, MS 45, 296/3); *Flying Post (London)*, 11–13 Aug. 1698. See also O'Riordan, 'Assuming control', p. 96.

55 Margaret Savage to Andrew Savage, [1738–41] (PRONI, D552/A/2/9/10).

56 Jervis to Sir Donat O'Brien, 14 Nov. 1700 (*Inchiquin manuscripts*, p. 58); *D.I.B.* (Rogerson, Sir John I (*c.*1648–1724)).

of employees with whom communication might be slow and faltering. Mrs Delany worried when her housekeeper took ill in 1746, writing that 'she would have been a great loss to me, as she is I think an excellent servant, and one that I may trust with the care of my house in my absence.'[57]

Once employed, the advice of the day was that servants be well treated, though not over-indulged, so that they would be obedient and industrious. Mrs Delany found these responsibilities 'teazing' but she nevertheless recognised that in order to be a good manager, her staff required 'both my care and attention'.[58] Occasional disputes between them were anticipated, but it was the job of the mistress to ensure that arguments were quickly resolved and harmony restored.[59] When the offence was serious and punishment was required, Lady Frances Keightley recommended that there be no 'scolding and wrangling, for a few words well placed will signify more than a week's railing but if after 3 or 4 reproves they will not mend part with them and by this proceeding you will be feared and esteemed by your servants'.[60] Her daughter, Catherine O'Brien, took this advice to heart, dictating when her servants would be employed, insisting that if any displeased her she would show no hesitation in dismissing them and avoiding over-familiarity with them (something her mother had also warned against).[61] Others were not so careful. Katherine Conolly disapproved of Molly Conyngham Burton's overly friendly dealings with servants and generosity to them, complaining that 'what used to vex me was seeing her often give her maid such clothes, stays, and head clothes, as was fit for any gentlewoman in the kingdom to make their best appearances'.[62] Such actions not only blurred the lines between mistress and servant, making discipline all the harder, but also between social orders. If the servants were dressed like gentlewomen, they might be mistaken for such, undermining the elite's sense of superiority and otherness from the general Irish population and weakening their control, a particularly delicate issue for the vastly outnumbered Protestant Ascendancy. Yet Molly was not the only one at fault. Many wealthy women left servants money and goods in their wills, and the distance they were told to keep was often much greater than was actually observed.[63]

Advice on servants might be ignored for a variety of reasons, but particularly if it was unsolicited, or perceived as unnecessary and therefore bothersome and insulting. Mary Jones warned her sister, Katherine Conolly, not to interfere in Lady Anne Conolly's choice of servants, Anne having already made it clear that 'when she hired servants it should be to please herself', but Katherine responded that 'she

57 Delany to Dewes, 5 Apr. 1746 (*Autobiography and correspondence*, ser. 1, ii, 434).

58 Same to same, 17 Aug. 1745 (ibid., 379).

59 Wilkes, *A letter of genteel and moral advice* ..., p. 120; Katherine Conolly to Molly Burton, 12 June 1720 (NLI, MS 41, 579/8); Fénelon, *Instructions for the education of a daughter*, pp 228–33.

60 Lady Frances Keightley to Catherine O'Brien, 26 Sept. 1681 (NLI, MS 45, 720/1).

61 Lucius O'Brien to Wilson, 5 Nov. 1705 (ibid., MS 45, 296/3); Catherine O'Brien to Henry O'Brien, 12 Mar. 1712/13 (ibid., MS 45, 297/4). Lady Frances Keightley to Catherine O'Brien, 26 Sept. 1681 (ibid., MS 45, 720/1).

62 Katherine Conolly to Bonnell, 23 Feb. 1729/30 (ibid., MS 41, 578/5).

63 For example, Alice, dowager countess of Drogheda left multiple bequests of money and clothing to her servants (will of Alice, countess of Drogheda, 14 Jan. 1712 [/13?] (TNA, Prob. 11/525, f. 48)).

could not answer it to her conscience if she did not and that she would always do it so'.[64] As an older woman, the matriarch of the family and a lady managing the greatest house in Ireland, she felt it was her place, her right, and even her duty, to guide the younger generation, whether they liked it or not.

Personal space and communal living

By law, a house would belong to its master only, a woman having lost her independent status and property rights upon marriage, so that it was only single women or widows who might own their own homes.[65] In practice, though, things were a little different. Mary Delany frequently referred to 'my house' or 'our house', but never did she call her and her husband's home his only, reflecting her sense of its shared possession.[66] Her phrasing was partly for convenience, but it also allowed her to construct a necessary fiction to bolster her position within the home, for if she was to manage it and its staff, she needed to occupy the position of their undisputed mistress, not a quasi-guest or lodger, hamstrung by her gender and her husband.

Female ideas of equal ownership (usually respected in reality, if not on paper) related only to the overall structure of the home. Once within its walls, the situation shifted, and in the same way in which certain servants were more a wife's than a husband's, so too were certain rooms.[67] An inventory taken at Kilkenny Castle in 1705 lists the duke and duchess of Ormond's separate bedrooms, dressing rooms and closets, while other areas were for their dual use, including the drawing room and the great dining room, though these rooms had gendered connotations, the drawing room being seen as female, the dining room as male. Certain living spaces could nominally belong to wife or husband, however, and Mrs Delany was particularly possessive of her 'English room' in her house in Dublin.[68] Homes were also divided according to status, and some areas were rarely entered by its mistress, being designated for the servants' quarters. Kilkenny Castle contained, along with the family's separate and joint living spaces, 'the stewards' eating room', 'the room where the house maids lay' and a lodging room for Mrs Butler, who was presumably

64 Mary Jones to Bonnell, 11 Apr. [n.d.] (NLI, MS 41, 577/3).

65 For a summary of the English laws surrounding male home ownership versus female, see Flather, *Gender and space*, pp 41–2.

66 See for example, Delany to Dewes, 12 July 1744 (*Autobiography and correspondence*, ser. 1, ii, 309); same to same, 28 Aug. 1744 (ibid., 321).

67 The debates discussed in the main introduction to this book, on what constituted public and private, are useful to bear in mind when considering room use in an elite home. See, for example, Flather, *Gender and space*; Markman Ellis, 'Coffee-women, *The Spectator* and the public in the early eighteenth century' in Elizabeth Eger, Charlotte Grant, Clíona Ó Gallchoir and Penny Warburton (eds), *Women, writing and the public sphere, 1700–1830* (Cambridge, 2001), pp 27–52; John Brewer, 'This, that and the other: public, social and private in the seventeenth and eighteenth centuries' in Dario Castiglione and Lesley Sharpe (eds), *Shifting the boundaries: transformations of the languages of public and private in the eighteenth century* (Exeter, 1995); Amanda Vickery, 'Golden age to separate spheres? A review of the categories and chronology of English women's history', *Historical Journal*, xxxvi (1993), pp 383–414.

68 Delany to Dewes, 12 July 1744 (*Autobiography and correspondence*, ser. 1, ii, 310).

the housekeeper and thus entitled to the luxury of her own bedchamber. Nor did the lady of the house like the servants to move within the areas she frequented any more than was necessary. Mary Delany wanted the layout of her house at Delville altered so that 'that which is now my kitchen to be turned into a room for my maids, that they may have no call upstairs but when they are about their business there'.[69]

Having enough space within the home to demarcate it in this way was a sign of a family's comparative wealth, social standing and comfortable living standards. This helps explain why gendered and social segregation filtered down from the aristocracy, living in castles like the Ormonds, to the lower levels of the elite like the Delanys, with their smaller houses. There were practical benefits too. A combination of single-sex and mixed living spaces was useful for couples who were incompatible in some way, whether in sleep patterns, or more seriously, in their personalities, but they also allowed for alone time for women, away from their husbands (and vice versa) during which activities such as letter writing could be pursued. Personal apartments even provided storage for belongings which were designated as 'hers' rather than 'his' (though again, legally speaking, the husband owned all). Mrs Delany's closet and bedroom at Delville were where she dealt with her correspondence, and the duchess of Ormond's closet was where she stored her china.[70] Fluid interpretations of public and private meant that spouses could visit and use each other's supposedly separate rooms, without undermining their individual ownership. Bedrooms were the most obvious example, but in extenuating circumstances and if it was to be for a short period of time only, theoretically gendered living spaces overlapped too. When Patrick Delany caught a bad cold, Mary was 'so gracious as to indulge him with my English room, which is very warm when the wind is easterly. We lived four days in it.'[71]

Decorative details

It was a husband's job to provide the home upon marriage, and Vickery has noted that an inability to do so showed that a man's financial circumstances were too poor for him to be eligible for marriage and postponed or prevented many weddings. After marriage, though, it was a wife's responsibility to ensure that the house was comfortable, functional and fashionably decorated, both for the family's enjoyment and so that it would be impressive to visitors and indicative of the owner's social status.[72] In the early years of her second marriage, Mary Delany often had 'workmen

69 Kilkenny Castle inventory, 1705 (NLI, MS 2553); Delany to Dewes, 20 Aug. 1748 (*Autobiography and correspondence*, ser. 1, ii, 500). On the emergence of separate living spaces in Dublin town houses, see Jane Fenlon, 'Moving towards the formal house: room usage in early modern Ireland', *Proceedings of the Royal Irish Academy*, sect. C, cxi (2010), pp 160–1. See also Conor Lucey, 'Keeping up appearances: redecorating the domestic interior in late eighteenth-century Dublin' in ibid., pp 174–6.

70 Kilkenny Castle inventory, 1705 (NLI, MS 2553, f. 12); Delany to Dewes, 11 July 1747 (*Autobiography and correspondence*, ser. 1, ii, 471).

71 Delany to Dewes, 11 July 1747 (*Autobiography and correspondence*, ser. 1, ii, 409).

72 Vickery, *Behind closed doors*, p. 87.

of all sorts in the house – upholsters, joiners, glaziers, and carpenters – and am obliged to watch them all, or their work would be but ill-finished'.[73] In her dealings with these workmen, Mary inverted traditional gender roles by taking authority over them despite being female, but in such cases, rank outstripped gender and her actions were acceptable.

Taste was a nebulous concept, but depended upon more than just the acquisition of beautiful, expensive or exotic possessions; it was about knowing how best to place them and display them in relation to one and other and the rest of the house. A lady's choices were tangible proof of her own taste and creative abilities (whether good or bad), and a well-chosen item could serve as a convenient conversation piece for guests and spark compliments upon its selection, while a poorly executed interior invited ridicule from peers.[74] The inventories for the 2nd duke and duchess of Ormond's various homes in Ireland and England show that they lived an enviable lifestyle, and the duchess was surely involved in the accumulation of some of the luxury items which adorned their houses. These included tapestries, Persian carpets, looking glasses, a huge collection of paintings, Dutch and Indian furniture, a dining room in Kilkenny Castle that was completely hung with gilt leather, and private apartments furnished with feather beds, silk cushions and damask curtains.[75] The importance afforded to such displays of wealth and pomp can be gauged from the detailed descriptions provided of them, and Kilkenny left casual observers in awe. When visiting the castle in 1699, John Dunton, an English bookseller, wrote enthusiastically of its remarkable qualities, saying that the gallery 'for length, variety of gilded chairs, and the curious pictures that adorn it, has no equal in the three kingdoms, and perhaps not in Europe; so that this castle may properly be called the Elisium of Ireland'.[76] Less favourable was the review delivered by Mary Pendarves (later Delany) in 1732 on Castletown House, home of Katherine Conolly. It was 'a large heavy building, a vast deal of room in it, but not laid out with a good taste, the furniture good but not disposed to the best advantage'.[77] Though much smaller and less expensive, she preferred the apartments of her friend, Katherine Clayton, wife of the bishop of Killala. She described in detail the measurements of the rooms and the carvings, pictures, busts, marble tables, Persian carpets and furnishings of Genoa damask that adorned them, including many 'virtues, and busts, and pictures the bishop brought with him from Italy'. In her decorative choices, Mrs Clayton had achieved the perfect balance between content and layout, foreign and native, traditional and innovative. There were no complaints regarding the disposition of

73 Delany to Dewes, 26 July 1744 (*Autobiography and correspondence*, ser. 1, ii, 319).

74 Tague, *Women of quality*, p. 100; Vickery, *Behind closed doors*, p. 150; eadem, 'His and hers', pp 14–15. See also Marcia Pointon, *Strategies for showing: women, possession, and representation in English visual culture, 1665–1800* (Oxford, 1997).

75 An inventory of his grace the duke of Ormond's goods at his house in St James's Square London taken the 14th day of November 1689 (NLI, MS 2529, f. 6); Kilkenny Castle inventory, 1705 (ibid., MS 2553, ff 1, 4).

76 John Dunton with introduction and notes by Andrew Carpenter, *The Dublin scuffle* (Dublin, 2000), p. 211; *Oxford D.N.B.* (Dunton, John (1659–1732)).

77 Mary Pendarves to Ann Granville, 11 Mar. 1731/2 (*Autobiography and correspondence*, ser. 1, i, 342).

her furniture, and Mary was charmed by the way in which the more conventional oak carvings had been mixed with imported textiles and ornaments.[78]

The use of continental and Asian goods and furnishings to indicate taste and status was increasingly popular among the Irish elite and not just those, who, like the Ormonds, were of English or European extraction.[79] Stephen Conway has suggested that such ostentatious displays were particularly important to the Ascendancy as a way of distinguishing them from poorer Protestants and the earlier Catholic landowners they had displaced. By showcasing their wealth and foreign links, they were demonstrating 'their right to rule' not only 'from conquest and approbation, but from their superior culture'.[80] As the arbiters of good taste and interior decoration, women had a crucial role to play in making this point. Thus, Mrs Clayton's inclusion of some of her husband's Italian purchases made the house his as well as hers, but also reminded visitors of his expensive education and broad cultural horizons, which he could now share with his wife and their visitors. To make sure this message was received, she made a point of opening up her apartments every Wednesday to 'all her acquaintance'.[81]

Homes were not only for public display when their owners were in residence, nor were they designed to impress just friends and relatives. Dunton was not personally acquainted with the Butler family and he visited Kilkenny soon after it had been vacated by the duke and duchess of Ormond in 1699. Mary Delany knew Katherine Conolly in later years, but when she went to Castletown in 1732, it was to see the house, not its mistress, who was then in Dublin.[82] A home was a surrogate for its absent owner. It needed to look its best the whole year round, for the proprietor was judged by its appearance. This proxy role was especially important for families of the Irish elite, who, like the Ormonds, split their time (often very unevenly) between Ireland and England, for their houses remained behind as the main, perhaps only, visual reminder of an absent lord and lady. This added to the pressure on women to get it right when it came to décor. If they succeeded, their homes would constantly project and reinforce the air of wealth, power, refinement and endurance that so impressed Dunton and transmute it to them and their families. If they failed, the reaction would be more akin to that of Mrs Delany at Castletown.

78 Same to same, 22 Sept., 21 Oct. 1731 (ibid., 289, 305).

79 Stephen Conway, *Britain, Ireland and continental Europe in the eighteenth century: similarities, connections, identities* (Oxford, 2011), pp 117–20. Edward Corp traces the popularity of many of these continental imports to the influence of Charles II's Portuguese wife, Catherine of Braganza. Edward Corp, 'Catherine of Braganza and cultural politics' in Clarissa Campbell Orr (ed.), *Queenship in Britain 1660–1837: royal patronage, court culture and dynastic politics* (Manchester, 2002), pp 64–5. See also Gertrude Thomas, *Richer than spices: how a royal bride's dowry introduced cane, lacquer, cottons, tea and porcelain to England, and so revolutionized taste, manners, craftsmanship, and history in both England and America* (New York, 1965).

80 Conway, *Britain, Ireland and continental Europe*, pp 129–30.

81 Pendarves to Granville, 21 Oct. 1731 (*Autobiography and correspondence*, ser. 1, i, 305). On decoration as a display of political affiliations a generation earlier, see Fenlon, 'Moving towards the formal house', pp 150–1.

82 Katherine Conolly to Bonnell, 10 Mar. 1731/2 (NLI, MS 41, 578/6). This letter was written from Dublin at almost the exact same time at which Mrs Delany was at Castletown in County Kildare.

What Katherine Conolly lacked was not the money and sense to buy similarly good furnishings to those favoured by her contemporaries (a japanned cabinet, supposedly painted by her as a wedding gift to her great-niece, Molly Burton, can still be viewed at Castletown), but the knowledge, apparently, of how to make the most of these items. If taste was a relative concept, hers may have been lost in translation and subject to English snobbery and xenophobia, which was determined to see anything which did not replicate a preordained combination of English and continental fashions, as substandard. Later in the century, English decorative fashions were slavishly promoted and followed by the Irish, but Mrs Pendarves's comments and her assignment, fourteen years later, of one room in her house as her 'English room', suggest that this trend was not yet well established in the 1730s and 1740s, and marked differences still existed between the two countries.[83] By comparison, exterior disparities should not be overplayed. Although Lady Anne Conolly preferred the ruin of Rathfarnham Castle to Castletown, describing it as 'a place I own I like the best of any I have seen, in this country' because it had 'much the air of an English nobleman's seat', in fact, after the Glorious Revolution, Rolf Loeber and Livia Hurley have shown that 'no clear style of Irish building emerged' and 'influences were, with the exception of absentee landlords, almost solely from Britain to Ireland'.[84] Anne seemed not to appreciate that the look and grandeur of Castletown were exceptional within Ireland or that most new Irish architecture imitated England's.

The marital estate

If the household was the wife's fiefdom, with occasional input from a husband, then the opposite was true of the family estate, for contemporary writers recommended that while wives should have some knowledge of estate matters, husbands were expected to deal with such things.[85] This remained the case in nineteenth-century Britain, when the task would 'generally fall on the husband, by convention, convenience, or choice'.[86] Yet women could function as 'incorporated wives' who, although they had 'little formal involvement in the running of estates' and limited training for such a task, could step into the breach to represent their ill or absent husbands and independently administer the estate with confidence and success.[87] This incorporation may also be found in seventeenth- and eighteenth-century Ireland where it was of even greater importance than in Britain, for despite the great distances between London and some parts of England and Scotland, Irishmen

83 Delany to Dewes, 4 Jan. 1745/6 (*Autobiography and correspondence*, ser. 1, ii, 409); Lucey, 'Keeping up appearances', pp 176–7.
84 Lady Anne Conolly to Thomas, earl of Strafford, 24 May [c. 1734] (BL, Add. MS 22228, f. 120); Rolf Loeber and Livia Hurley, 'The architecture of Irish country houses, 1691–1739' in Raymond Gillespie and R.F. Foster (eds), *Irish provincial cultures in the long eighteenth century: making the middle sort* (Dublin, 2012), p. 218.
85 Fénelon, *Instructions for the education of a daughter*, pp 215–16, 236.
86 K.D. Reynolds, *Aristocratic women and political society in Victorian Britain* (Oxford, 1998), p. 44.
87 Ibid., pp 43–5. See also O'Riordan, 'Assuming control', pp 85, 98.

who wished to go to court, unlike their mainland counterparts, were automatically separated from their lands by a sea journey. This made even communication by letter slow and unreliable, and frequently prevented their wives from awaiting instructions before making decisions. Much more trust had therefore to be placed in these women to manage estates.[88]

Some wives worked more closely with their spouses than others. The Honourable Letitia Molesworth (later Viscountess Molesworth) regularly discussed estate matters with her husband Robert, and took constant instructions from him while he was in England on everything from making leases to the disposition of pigeon-houses and the planting of trees.[89] Enthusiasm was no substitute for ability, however. When writing to their son in 1722, Robert declared that he had made a mistake in 'giving her an entire power over my whole estate', for his debts had increased as a result, his rents had gone into arrears and he was 'forced in my old age, when I expected ease and idleness, to turn my own receiver and manager again'.[90] Quite why it took so long for him to notice the problems, or why he blamed Letitia if she had merely been following his instructions, is another matter, but his experiences may have had some impact on the opinions he expressed in print the following year on the topics of agriculture and the management of land by landlords.[91]

Catherine O'Brien had even greater latitude in dealing with her husband's lands, for Lucius was frequently absent and his interest in managing his estate swung like a pendulum from exacting to non-existent. She could find herself one day left to her own devices ('do what you will with the barn and the garden for I am too far off to direct in those matters')[92] and another having to follow detailed instructions ('let not the foundation [*of a wall in their garden*] be laid or the palisades be set up till I return'[93]). No matter how slight Lucius's input, Catherine's duties remained comparatively light compared to what was to come during her son's minority. Until then, most of the O'Brien lands were still under the control of her father-in-law, Sir Donat, and her knowledge of estate management continued to be underdeveloped. Not so for Mary, dowager Lady Shelburne. She married as her second husband, Henry Conyngham, brother of Katherine Conolly, Mary Jones and Jane Bonnell. When Henry went off campaigning in 1704 (never to return, as it transpired), he left Mary in control of their lands in counties Meath and Donegal. Despite her assertions that she was 'both a bad and lazy writer, especially in business', Mary wrote lengthy letters on estate matters in which she demonstrated a considerable understanding of everything from rental arrears and abatements to debt management,

88 Letters could be lost if the boat they were carried on sank, or was raided by privateers. See Mary, dowager Lady Shelburne to Alexander Murray, 13 May 1710 (PRONI, D2860/9/25); Alan, Viscount Midleton to Thomas Brodrick, 12 Dec. 1725 (SHC, MS 1248/6/345–346).

89 See, for example, Robert Molesworth to the Hon. Letitia Molesworth, 7 Aug. 1704 (*The Clements archive*, ed. A.P.W. Malcomson (Dublin, 2010), pp 123–6).

90 Same to the Hon. John Molesworth, 20 Oct. 1722 (ibid., p. 350).

91 Robert, Viscount Molesworth, *Some considerations for the promoting of agriculture, and employing the poor* (Dublin, 1723).

92 Lucius O'Brien to Catherine O'Brien, 9 [Sept.?] 1712 (NLI, MS 45, 297/1).

93 Same to same, 8 Feb. 1712/13 (ibid.).

the proper execution of legal documents and the state of the Irish economy.[94] She boasted of her ability to influence her husband's decisions and was not afraid to speak her mind, berating Henry's landlord, Alexander Murray of Broughton in Scotland, for making her repeat herself in their correspondence and for his method of managing his estates.[95] Some went one step further, showing enough confidence to criticise even their husbands. Anne Burke, Lady Dunkellin, felt Lord Dunkellin's choice of a new tenant in 1720 to be a very poor one and was perfectly open about it, though whether this had any effect on her difficult and inept spouse is unknown.[96] Her conduct was unusual, though, especially given that her husband was neither unwell, nor absent from his estate, and it was a symptom of a deteriorating marriage rather than a standard of behaviour to which Irish women aspired.

In a more difficult position were those women left in charge of estates with which they had previously had only limited contact. In some cases this was caused by internal absenteeism, when families owned lands scattered across the country, some of which they rarely visited. In others, both husband and wife were frequent external absentees, spending much of their time outside Ireland. Into this latter category fell Mary, duchess of Ormond, as she shuttled between Ireland and England, sometimes with the duke, sometimes not. She was prepared to receive the rents from her husband's estates, but, where possible, deferred all decisions until she could confer with him, or he could deal with them himself, making for a hesitant, but competent enough stand-in.[97]

Then there were the permanent absentees. Born and raised in England, Dorothy, countess of Cork and Burlington never visited Ireland and had little confidence in dealing with her husband's estates there.[98] If he were away from home and she could avoid it, she refused even to open letters to the earl on his Irish affairs, telling him 'I expect you so soon, and perhaps there may be bills in them'.[99] Hers was the nadir of estate involvement, for the earl apparently had no issue with her opening his estate correspondence if he was travelling, and it was her choice not to.

If partial or total absenteeism made the job of some women difficult, it was only another problem to be added to the more general hindrance caused by the pitiable state of the Irish economy after the Glorious Revolution. Alan Brodrick, then Speaker of the Irish House of Commons, complained from Tipperary in 1704 of 'the scarcity of money, not a penny of silver is to be seen in most country people's houses whatever their condition is'.[100] Simultaneously, in Donegal, Lady Shelburne described being unable to 'command £50 money, but am forced to take cattle and butter at such rents as the tenants will please to give them and after being at the expense to bring them to Dublin sell them at five or six shillings in the pound

94 Shelburne to Murray, 14 Nov. 1704 (ibid., D2860/9/1).
95 Ibid.; same to same, 20 June 1705 (ibid., D2860/9/3).
96 A[nne?] King to Robert Taylor, 10 May 1720 (NLI, MS 25, 430).
97 Mary Ormond to Ellis, [n.d.] (BL, Add. MS 28927, f. 202).
98 Reynolds has made the same argument for nineteenth-century Ireland (Reynolds, *Aristocratic women*, pp 48–9).
99 Dorothy, countess of Cork and Burlington to Richard, earl of Cork and Burlington, 28 May 1728 (BL, Add. MS 75358, 806e).
100 Alan Brodrick to Thomas Brodrick, 21 Oct 1704 (SHC, MS 1248/2/152–153).

less'. Unsympathetic outside landlords did not help. Writing to Alexander Murray about obtaining an abatement in her husband's rents, Lady Shelburne told him, 'I wish you would come over yourself then you would be convinced of the deplorable condition of this poor kingdom'.[101] Murray declined.

Conclusion

Domestic duties were something in which female authority and competence were not only assumed, but promoted and expected. Controlling expenditure, servants and even the family estate was all part and parcel of a wife's lot, and though mistakes were common and disasters could happen, quitting was not an option. Thanks to the social conditioning and education to which they were subjected from early childhood, teaching that household management was their God-given right and purpose, these ladies took a role foisted upon them by society and made it so much their own that even the most incompetent among them was fiercely protective of her 'rights'. To be the lady of the house became part of their identities as women and a bulwark against being discarded by men, to whom most were legally, socially and financially subordinate. It offered a way to provide women with a means to present themselves as indispensable assets and gave them a sense of purpose, usefulness and power, even if they felt their responsibilities to be a burden.

Yet husbands and wives (or occasionally some other combination of male and female relations) found a strict gender divide undesirable and impractical and instead shared the workload. Responsibility for purchase choices and expenditure was not gender specific and something for which both men and women were equally susceptible to error, though it was the latter who were generally liable for the blame. Stepping into traditionally male shoes, wives of absentee husbands could assume control of estates with which they may or may not have been familiar, and manage them with only limited and intermittent instructions from their spouses. It was experience that some must have been grateful for, if and when they found themselves widowed and responsible for their children's landed inheritance, as did the two ladies whose experiences form the basis of the next chapter.

[101] Shelburne to Murray, 20 June 1705 (PRONI, D2860/9/3).

4

Widows, guardians and estate managers

On 9 February 1704, Charles Boyle, 3rd earl of Cork and 4th earl of Burlington died in England. His will, signed just five days earlier, named his 32-year-old wife, Juliana, as guardian to their four surviving daughters and only son, Richard. It also named her as custodian of the vast Boyle estates for the duration of the new earl's minority. In Ireland, this meant huge swathes of counties Cork and Waterford, including the principal Irish family seat at Lismore Castle. In England, it gave her control of the family's lands in Yorkshire, along with Burlington House in London and Chiswick House. As Richard was still two months short of his tenth birthday, Juliana was to have the care of his inheritance for over eleven years.[1]

Finding herself in a similar situation in 1717 was Catherine O'Brien. Widowed at the start of the year, when her feckless husband, Lucius, died in France, having abandoned her in Ireland with their three children two years earlier, she had at first been subservient to her domineering father-in-law, Sir Donat O'Brien 1st Bt. Then, in November, he too died. It was at this point that the 41-year-old Catherine (who up until then had always been controlled by the men in her life and reliant upon their good will to pay her debts and provide for her and her children) suddenly experienced a complete reversal of power and fortune, finding herself in control of the O'Brien estates in County Clare on behalf of her 12-year-old son, Sir Edward and with access to more responsibility and money than she could ever have dreamed of.[2]

Though female guardians were far from unheard of, these two women are particularly useful for a study of how ladies managed their sons' estates in Ireland. Both have left behind unusually large archives detailing their time as guardians. Both controlled large estates on behalf of two of Ireland's oldest and best-established families, and did so for a significant and comparable amount of time, and both remained widows, and therefore sole guardians of their sons. Equally important are the differences in their respective positions. Though each was English by birth and had married into a great Irish house, Catherine had been raised in Ireland from the age of about five and (barring occasional visits to her homeland) had been living on the O'Brien estates since her marriage in around 1701. Juliana had never and would never set foot on her son's Irish lands. Where Catherine would manage Edward's estates with the personal touch, Lady Burlington would deal with Richard's Irish inheritance remotely.

1 Will of Charles, earl of Burlington, 26 Feb. 1703/4 (TNA, Prob. 11/475, f. 331); *Oxford D.N.B.* (Boyle, Richard, 3rd earl of Burlington and 4th earl of Cork (1694–1753)).

2 Sir Donat O'Brien, 1st Bt to Counsellor Molony, 31 Jan. 1716/17 (NLI, MS 45, 298/3); Margaret Forde to Catherine O'Brien, 23 Jan. [n.d., 1717/18?] (ibid., MS 45, 346/4); David England to same, 19 Nov. 1717 (ibid., MS 45, 346/5).

Juliana, though, had a prior example to follow. As an orphaned heiress in the 1680s, she and her inheritance had been placed under the guardianship of her paternal aunt, Mary Compton, dowager countess of Northampton, to whom she and her husband Charles had remained close. Mary was even recommended as a source of advice and guidance for her niece in Charles's will.[3] Lady Burlington had also been countess for six years before she became dowager, living with her husband and able to observe his own management not just of his distant Irish estate, but of his familiar English one. It was Catherine, ironically, despite her Irish residency, who had less experience. She was never Lady O'Brien and had never had the opportunity to study, up close, the management of the main O'Brien lands, nor did she come from landed stock herself. Her father, Thomas Keightley, had sold his lands in England before relocating to Ireland and thereafter survived on pensions and salaries from political posts.[4] Catherine had overseen hers and Lucius's personal estate for some time, but only with the assistance of her father-in-law. She did benefit from fewer distractions than Juliana, however. The care of Edward's Irish estate was her primary concern, while Lady Burlington had also to manage an English estate for her son. In addition, the countess was a lady of the bedchamber to Queen Anne for her entire reign and was periodically needed at court for almost all of Richard's minority, leading to delays in her responses to agents' letters and consequently in the issuing of fresh orders regarding the estates.[5] She was also a society hostess (not something Catherine could ever have been accused of), and on at least one occasion her secretary wrote that she was entertaining, among others, the duke and duchess of Queensberry and was too 'busy with company all afternoon' to deal with estate business.[6]

Lady Burlington's court duties appear to have provided her with an airtight reason for never visiting Ireland, but in fact they were not as binding as they seemed. R.O. Bucholz has noted that although the ladies of the bedchamber 'formed the one set of great household officers whose personal attendance was regular and indispensable', there were ten women filling these posts and often only one in attendance at any given time. Unlike men, whose commitments at court or in parliament may have unavoidably kept them from their estates for long periods, the ladies of the bedchamber, with their nine substitutes, were much freer to come and go. Attendance rotated on a weekly basis, but allowances were made for illness, and Mary, duchess of Ormond took a two-year sojourn to go to Ireland from 1703 to 1705 when her husband was lord lieutenant. It seems reasonable to suppose that had she asked for it (and there is no evidence that she ever did), Juliana would have been allowed a much briefer visit in order to deal with her son's estates.[7]

3 Will of Henry Noel, 13 [Nov.?] 1677 (Chatsworth, MS L/24/89); will of Charles earl of Burlington.

4 *D.I.B.* (Keightley, Thomas (*c.*1650–1719)).

5 Juliana, dowager countess of Cork and Burlington to Thomas Baker and Roger Power, 28 Aug. 1707 (NLI, MS 13, 231); Joseph Waite to Richard Musgrave and Baker, 28 June 1711 (ibid., MS 13, 242/5); same to Thomas Brown, 14 May 1709 (Chatsworth, Joseph Waite's letter book 1708–10, Burlington MSS, miscellaneous, box 1).

6 Anthony Spurret to George Myers, 20 Jan. 1704/5 (Chatsworth, Anthony Spurret's letter book 1703–4, Burlington MSS, miscellaneous, box 1).

7 R.O. Bucholz, *The Augustan court: Queen Anne and the decline of court culture* (Stanford, 1993), p. 118.

Female estate management among the elite in Ireland is still largely a neglected topic, but there is a developing historiography. Deborah Wilson has written on the legal practicalities of maternal guardianship, and W.A. Maguire has provided a brief study of Katherine, countess of Donegall's management of her son's lands between 1706 and 1715. Anthony Malcomson has outlined the management by Lady Anne Conolly of the Conolly estates in the mid eighteenth century, as has D.W. Hayton for Helen Rawdon's guardianship of the inheritance of her son, Sir John Rawdon, between 1695 and 1710. Biographies of some of the better-known English women who undertook this task in the seventeenth and eighteenth centuries supply further insights. Molly McClain provides information on the achievements and failures of Mary Somerset, 1st duchess of Beaufort, who, between 1654 and 1671, managed the inheritance of her son from her first marriage, William, 3rd duke of Somerset, as well as details of her later battles with her daughter-in-law, Rebecca, marchioness of Worcester, regarding the inheritance of the 2nd duke of Beaufort, Mary's grandson from her second marriage. Lois Schowerer's book on Rachel, Lady Russell, is also of use in examining how Rachel cared for her son's estates after his father had been executed in 1683 for involvement in the Rye House Plot. More general surveys of English women's lives provide further information.[8] This limited literature is bolstered by works on the role of early modern men in dealing with their estates. David Hainsworth has elucidated the experiences of estate agents, with considerable reference to relationships with employers (usually male, though there are occasional references to wives and landladies). Philip Jenkins's work on the Welsh gentry, though not exclusively concerned with estates, provides similar information, while Toby Barnard provides an Irish perspective on the position of agents, and (helpfully for this chapter) includes many references to the Boyle family, including the Burlington branch.[9]

Between them, Juliana and Catherine, who at once had so much and so little in common, provide a way of examining not only their individual styles of estate management and their separate successes and failures, but also how location, background and personal circumstances could combine to help or hinder a widow

[8] Deborah Wilson, *Women, marriage and property in wealthy landed families in Ireland, 1750–1850* (Manchester, 2009), pp 88–97; W.A. Maguire, 'A question of arithmetic: Arthur Chichester, fourth earl of Donegall, 1695–1757' in Brenda Collins, Philip Ollerenshaw and Trevor Parkhill (eds), *Industry, trade and people in Ireland 1650–1950, essays in honour of W.H. Crawford* (Belfast, 2005), pp 33–8; A.P.W. Malcomson, 'The fall of the house of Conolly 1758–1803' in Allan Blackstock and Eoin Magennis (eds), *Politics and political culture in Britain and Ireland, 1750–1850* (Belfast, 2007), pp 107–56; D.W. Hayton, 'Thomas Prior, Sir John Rawdon, third baronet, and the mentality and ideology of 'improvement': a question of upbringing' in Raymond Gillespie and R.F. Foster (eds), *Irish provincial cultures in the long eighteenth century: making the middle sort: essays for Toby Barnard* (Dublin, 2012), pp 112–13; Molly McClain, *Beaufort: the duke and his duchess, 1657–1715* (London, 2001); Lois Schwoerer, *Lady Rachel Russell (1637–1732): 'one of the best of women'* (London, 1988); Ingrid Tague, *Women of quality: accepting and contesting ideals of femininity in England, 1690–1760* (Woodbridge, 2002), pp 123–31.

[9] D.R. Hainsworth, *Stewards, lords and people: the estate steward and his world in later Stuart England* (Cambridge, 1992); Philip Jenkins, *The making of a ruling class: the Glamorgan gentry 1640–1790* (Cambridge, 1983); Toby Barnard, *A new anatomy of Ireland: the Irish Protestants, 1640–1770* (London, 2003), ch. 8.

in managing a great landed estate. This chapter will deal with the many challenges they faced and their responses. It will first consider the legal limitations and requirements imposed on female guardians, before moving on to the difficulties posed by tenants, particularly over the collection of rents, then the women's relationships with land agents, and finally, their responsibility to protect their sons' inheritances from physical or legal attacks by tenants and outside parties.

The task facing each woman was mammoth. Barnard has compared the work involved in managing a great estate to that needed to run a government department, and it is easy to see why, for estates required entire teams of people to keep them functioning.[10] At the top of the pyramid was the guardian herself, aided by her secretaries and her son's agents, who were resident on the estates, managing their day-to-day running. They in turn were assisted by clerks and family members, along with a bevy of 'lawyers, surveyors, seneschals, bailiffs, and sergeants of woods', who were often either the agents themselves acting in a dual role, or others who were essentially in the pocket of the landlady.[11] The tenants who actually farmed the land, and who could easily number in the hundreds or even thousands on the greatest estates, were at the bottom of this managerial structure.

Legal limits

The fact that Juliana and Catherine obtained physical and legal custody over their children and their inheritances was by no means inevitable. As Wilson has explained, 'there was no assumption in law that on the death of her husband a woman would be guardian to her children'. This depended almost entirely upon his last will and testament. The guardianship of children whose fathers died intestate went to their nearest male relation, and 'a mother could contest this, only if these guardians by default refused to act as such'. Wilson also suggests that female guardianship over estates was becoming less common in this period, as a distinction was made between who would have custody of children and those who would control their estates.[12] Furthermore, even if a mother was put in charge of her children and their inheritances, such power could come with strings attached in the form of remarriage penalties, stripping them of guardianship if they took another husband so that he could not gain control of his stepchildren and their estates.[13] Neither Juliana nor Catherine were hampered by such a clause, though, as it happened, neither of them remarried.

Even if granted guardianship, a mother's legal powers were not infinite. There were restrictions on how she could handle and lease out her child's assets, what kind of maintenance and alterations she could authorise to lands and buildings, and how she could spend his income. Certain expenditures were forbidden, while others

10 Barnard, *A new anatomy*, pp 208, 216.

11 Ibid., pp 208, 218–21, 236. Quote from p. 208. For further information on the practice of agents holding multiple jobs, including as agents to other landowners, see ibid., pp 209, 218.

12 Wilson, *Women, marriage and property*, p. 88.

13 Ibid., p. 94. For an example, see the will of Arthur, earl of Donegall, 30 July 1705 (TNA, Prob. 11/504, f. 178).

were insisted upon. Renting out land and other possessions, such as mills, mines and fisheries, was fine, but nothing could be done that would outlive the minority, and leases had to be made for shorter and shorter terms as a boy's majority approached. The most a mother could do was to promise, as Lady Burlington did when renting out her son's English coal mines for the remainder of his minority, to 'use her interest with his lordship to continue that agreement for a longer term', after he had come of age.[14] Catherine O'Brien did not take these restrictions as seriously. When she built a new church (calling it St Catherine's) and attempted to endow it with some of her son's lands, she exceeded her powers and had to be warned by his agent, James Davoren, that 'as tis not in the power of a guardian to do in behalf of a minor all that the minor can do when he is of age, it is much less in the guardian's power to do what that minor can't do when of age'. Given the complexity of the arrangement by which Edward held the land in question (he was a tenant in tail of the 3rd earl of Inchiquin), even as an adult, he would have been unable to confer it upon the church. Catherine certainly could not. 'I won't pretend to judge whether it will look well that a guardian and a bishop should prevail on a minor of 13 years of age to make any promises of granting and continuing any endowment to the church.' Instead, Davoren wished 'with all my heart it could be deferred till Sir Edward came of age'.[15]

Maintenance versus alteration

Mothers could spend their son's money to maintain his estate, but unnecessary alterations were prohibited, the aim of guardianship being to preserve as much of the minor's income and existing inheritance as possible. In 1713, the countess of Burlington agreed to expand the prison at Tallow, County Waterford, and to employ as many people as were needed to fix the wall around her son's park, but in 1708 the walls around the town of Bandon, County Cork, were to be repaired only if it could be done 'at an easy expense',[16] and as no member of the family was living at Lismore Castle, she stopped paying for newspapers and candles, which were being used only by its caretakers.[17] Actual alterations were anathema to her. She agreed 'that Richard Clarke's house in Bandon be speedily repaired at my son's expense to prevent it falling', but only because the agents informed her that 'Clarke is able and may be obliged to pay back the rent and the charge of repairing it'. New buildings were out of the question: 'such other houses in Bandon as are in danger of falling may be likewise put into repair, but I can't think it for my son's advantage to undertake the building of new houses'. If the tenants wanted to carry

14 Waite to Myers, 4 July 1710 (Chatsworth, Joseph Waite's letter book 1708–10, Burlington MSS, miscellaneous, box 1).

15 James Davoren to Catherine O'Brien, 23 Oct. 1718 (NLI, MS 45, 347/1).

16 Waite to Musgrave and Baker, 28 May 1713 (ibid., MS 13, 249/9); same to same, 13 Mar. 1707/8 (Chatsworth, Joseph Waite's letter book 1706–8 (Ireland and Yorkshire), Burlington MSS, miscellaneous, box 1).

17 Spurret to Mr [?] Smith, 18 July 1704 (Chatsworth, Anthony Spurret's letter book 1703–4, Burlington MSS, miscellaneous, box 1); Burlington to Digby Foulke, Power, Richard Bagge and Baker, 20 June 1704 (NLI, MS 43, 361/2).

out the building themselves and at their own expense, the most Juliana would do was 'encourage them by granting leases at small acknowledgments during my son's minority'.[18] When the corporation of Bandon sent a petition asking that the cost of rebuilding their market house be met by her son, her secretary, Joseph Waite, wrote that 'her ladyship being only guardian to my lord, can't order them anything towards the charge they have been at in rebuilding the market house'.[19]

Catherine O'Brien, although indicating her awareness of the rule, either believed it could be interpreted far more leniently, or made a conscious decision to ignore it, allowing herself to be carried away by her enthusiasm to renovate one of her son's homes, Dromoland Castle. Her father-in-law had left it in a dilapidated condition, and soon after his death Catherine was writing of her plans to tear down the front part of the castle, before rebuilding. She justified her actions as being 'an employment, which however agreeable it is to me, I should hardly engage in at present, were there not an absolute necessity for it', and claimed that she was limiting her activities, so as not to risk doing anything of which her son would later disapprove.[20] Her actions were not particularly unusual and even had a certain logic to them. Unlike the Burlingtons and Lismore Castle, she and her children actually occupied Dromoland and, as a close relation of two queens, it was fitting that Edward have a home reflecting his social status and bolstering his right to own and ultimately help to rule, Ireland. Barnard has pointed out the great improvements many Irish landowners of this period were making to their Irish holdings and homes in an attempt to Anglicise the country and improve the income of their estates, the general condition of society and its lower orders.[21] The problem was that, as a mere custodian, Catherine was not at liberty to copy their example and authorise extensive and expensive alterations, a point of which her advisers had soon to remind her. In 1718, one of them, Joshua Dawson, wrote that 'you ought not to lay out any of your son's money in building or other improvements, you cannot answer expending a minor's money in any way but in preserving and keeping in repair what is already built and done'. He questioned whether

> your son will care to live at Dromoland when he comes of age, can you answer for him that he will like what you do when he comes to the possession of it, how do you know what new schemes he may have when he arrives to 21, that may be very different from yours, then you have laid out his money and have no thanks for your pains, but perhaps rather disoblige him.

He went on to discuss the alterations Catherine wished to make to the gardens of the castle, but finished by saying, 'if you are resolved to go on with these works I

18 Burlington to Power, Bagge, Baker and Jeremy Coughlan, 6 Dec. 1705 (NLI, MS 43, 361/3).

19 Waite to George Howse, 19 Feb. 1707/8 (Chatsworth, Joseph Waite's letter book 1706–8 (Ireland and Yorkshire), Burlington MSS, miscellaneous, box 1).

20 [Catherine O'Brien?] to [Thomas Burgh] [c. 1718?] [Letter is endorsed 'copy to Mr Burgh about house of Dromoland and changes required'] (NLI, MS 45, 346/4). See also Finola O'Kane, '"Obliges me to dip my hands in mortar": Catherine O'Brien's influence at Dromoland', *Journal of the Irish Georgian Society*, vii (2004), pp 80–105.

21 Toby Barnard, Improving Ireland?: projectors, prophets and profiteers, 1641–1786 (Dublin, 2008), pp 16–18.

will, when I hear from you again, give you my best thoughts, but I flatter myself you will consider again before you proceed'.[22] He was indeed flattering himself by thinking he could hold Catherine back, for she proceeded with her plans, and her accounts show payments to workmen at Dromoland the following year and well into the 1720s, including some for having the walks in the orchards and gardens altered, something that was surely not vital, as Dawson had implied. On top of this, she was also having to pay (with her son's money) for the upkeep of his other houses at Leamanah and Corofin.[23] Perhaps, after so many years of financial woes, she did not know how to properly handle any degree of wealth; or perhaps she simply had a careless and extravagant nature and was happy to indulge her interest in building at her son's expense. Whatever the reason, her heavy expenditure quickly caused problems, and in 1719 she was informed that unless she could find a way to boost the estate's revenue and 'lessen the work and other expenses, you will have a continual uneasiness'.[24]

Cash flow and creditors

Increasing an estate's revenue was easier said than done for tenants were notoriously difficult to extract money from. In Catherine's case, her own actions did not always help, sometimes counteracting the advantages of her living on site. She was criticised in September 1719 by James Davoren for her method of collecting the rents, which was unusual and harmful to the estate, for

> had your ladyship left the collection and payments to me and ordered somebody to settle the accounts with your labourers and such of your servants as work with you and bring the sum stated to me, the collection would not be half so anxious to me and that is the method you'll find that is observed twixt every landlord of note and his receiver.[25]

He did little better himself, however. In the following December he admitted that he did not 'find any of your principal tenants disposed to pay a farthing'. After eight days trying to collect the money she was owed, he had received very little, 'and what is worse that I do not see I am to receive much more'.[26] Such tales would have been familiar to Juliana. In 1707, three years into her son's minority, there were 'arrears accrued upon the estate since my late lord's death, amounting to upwards of £15,000'. By 1712, the figure was £19,273 15*s*. 7½*d*.; this on an estate with an estimated income (in 1729) of £17,000.[27]

22 Joshua Dawson to Catherine O'Brien, 12 Mar. 1717/18 (NLI, MS 45, 346/3).
23 'Killeran labourer's work for Sir Edward O'Brien and Mrs Catherine O'Brien from the first of May 1719 to the first of November following according to Frank [Barnaby's?] his son's returns' (ibid., MS 45, 350/4); account of Catherine O'Brien with Sir Edward O'Brien, 1723–4 (ibid., MS 45, 350/5).
24 Davoren to Catherine O'Brien, 21 Dec. 1719 (ibid., MS 45, 347/3).
25 Same to same, 24 Sept. 1719 (ibid.).
26 Same to same, 11 Dec. 1719 (ibid.); same to same, 21 Dec. 1719 (ibid.).
27 Waite to Musgrave, 9 Sept. 1707 (Chatsworth, Joseph Waite's letter book 1706–8 (Ireland and Yorkshire), Burlington MSS, miscellaneous, box 1). Waite is likely talking about the 1st earl, who

Without doubt, one of the biggest problems was the condition of the Irish economy. The Boyle agents wrote in 1710 that the town of Youghal, in County Cork, was in dire straits because of 'the wars and want of due encouragement for trade which have been the principal cause of reducing that town to so great extremities'.[28] Juliana was bombarded with petitions from her son's tenants for leniency, abatement of rents and arrears, more time to pay, alterations to the terms of leases and even to be released from them, while the Burlington account books are littered with annotations beside the names of tenants who were insolvent, or had run away.[29] It was difficult to find tenants to replace those who had been lost, or that the countess wanted rid of, for lease agreements that had to expire at the end of the landlord's minority and in an economically challenged country were not attractive to potential farmers. Moreover, Protestant tenants were preferred, despite the overwhelming Catholic majority among the local population. In an effort to attract diligent farmers and compensate for the disadvantages imposed on them by her son's minority and the general economic situation, the countess had new leases contain 'war clauses', which stated that the rent charged on the land would be lower while hostilities continued, and looked into the possibility of having an Act of Parliament passed to allow her to make leases for lives renewable.[30] She kept herself well informed of the economic situation in Ireland and the prices of commodities such as butter and corn, so that any improvement could be used to her son's advantage and when she could, she intervened directly with her powerful friends to try to improve the country's lot.[31] Knowing the problems caused by export restrictions placed on Irish goods, in 1710, she had Joseph Waite approach her brother-in-law, Henry Boyle, later Lord Carleton, then a secretary of state in England, and convey her concerns regarding 'the great hardship that had fallen upon my lord and his honourable tenants by the embargo that was laid upon shipping for preventing exportation of corn, which was the chief commodity they had to raise their rents by'. Boyle assured him 'that application to the government about it at present would be of service, for he believed the reason of the embargo was the same there [*Ireland*] as here (which is reported to be the exporting of corn to France)'. The hint had the desired effect. Four months later, Waite wrote that:

had died in 1698, as £15,000 would have been a huge sum to have accumulated in only three years. See also list of arrears taken out of Michaelmas rental 1711 and brought into Lady Day rental 1712 (NLI, MS 43, 747/3); Thomas Prior, *A list of the absentees of Ireland, and the yearly value of their estates and incomes spent abroad. ...* (London, 1729), p. 2. On the similar difficulties experienced by English landlords at this time, see Hainsworth, *Stewards, lords and people*, pp 50, 54, 62.

28 Waite to Musgrave and Baker, 3 Nov. 1710 (Chatsworth, Joseph Waite's letter book 1708–10, Burlington MSS, miscellaneous, box 1); Waite to Foulke, 30 Apr. 1709 (NLI, MS 13, 254/3).

29 Burlington to Power, Bagge and Baker, 11 Jan. 1704/5 (NLI, MS 13, 254/3); Waite to Musgrave and Baker, 30 Oct. 1708 (ibid., MS 43, 364/4); same to Foulke, 25 Nov. 1707 (Chatsworth, Joseph Waite's letter book 1706–8 (Ireland and Yorkshire), Burlington MSS, miscellaneous, box 1); Lady Day rental 1706 (NLI, MS 43, 747/2).

30 Waite to Foulke, 3 Apr. 1708 (Chatsworth, Joseph Waite's letter book 1706–8 (Ireland and Yorkshire), Burlington MSS, miscellaneous, box 1); Richard Turner to [Burlington], 8 Mar. 1704/5 (NLI, MS 43, 361/3).

31 Burlington to Power, Bagge and Baker, 11 Jan. 1704/5 (NLI, MS 43, 361/2); Waite to Howse, 26 Oct. 1709 (Chatsworth, Joseph Waite's letter book 1708–10, Burlington MSS, miscellaneous, box 1).

> my lady is pleased to inform me that she has a very good reason to believe the embargo against exporting corn will be taken off in a short time after the arrival of my lord lieutenant [*the earl of Wharton*] at Dublin who is now on the road thither for application has been made to his Excellency on that account setting forth the great disadvantage it has been at to the farms and country in general.[32]

She made further use of Henry 'and other friends' later that year, so that 'the bill for encouraging tillage etc. may [*pass*] the council board here in regard it will be so beneficial an act for the Kingdom of Ireland and particularly in relation to my lord's estate', but their efforts were in vain.[33]

Catherine had no such friends in high places. By the time of her guardianship, her own and her husband's family were dead, or of fairly low social and political status and, unlike Juliana, she was not at court in England, in a position to have her grievances heard by those in a position to do something about them. Her guardianship began three years after the war ended and 'war clauses' in leases were never part of her arsenal in her fight to obtain rents. Yet the economy was far from recovered and many of the issues which affected Juliana were ongoing. A Tillage Bill which Lady Burlington supported and which it was hoped would increase crop yields and by extension, incoming rents, was proposed nine times in the Irish parliament between 1710 and 1727, but did not finally pass until 1730, four years after Edward O'Brien's majority.[34]

What to do, then, when tenants missed the deadline for their rents? Both women were theoretically willing to prosecute those who failed to pay, but each was hesitant to actually engage in legal proceedings. Davoren had to urge Catherine to have the sheriff seize a man who owed her £24, and Juliana's numerous threats to prosecute those who were very behind with their payments often came to nothing.[35] Even when her son's agents failed to initiate proceedings she had ordered, her letters to them contained no reprimands.[36] She wavered, she explained, because placing people in jail was a harsh expedient and one which, incidentally, would have left them completely unable to pay more money while putting her to the expense of costly legal fees.[37] Compromise was the preferred course of action. Juliana ordered that problem tenants on her son's estate be summoned to explain themselves, and both she and Catherine allowed some to pay off arrears through unpaid work on the estate, if it was deemed necessary maintenance or improvements.[38] But tenants

32 Waite to Musgrave and Baker, 3 Jan. 1709/10 (Chatsworth, Joseph Waite's letter book 1708–10, Burlington MSS, miscellaneous, box 1).

33 Same to same, 6 May 1710 (NLI, MS 13, 242/2); same to same, 13 July 1710 (ibid.).

34 3 Geo. II c. 3 [Ire.] (1730).

35 Waite to Howse, 19 Apr. 1709 (Chatsworth, Joseph Waite's letter book 1708–10, Burlington MSS, miscellaneous, box 1); Davoren to Catherine O'Brien, 23 Jan. 1718/19 (NLI, MS 45, 347/2).

36 See, for example, Waite to Howse, 17 May 1709 (Chatsworth, Joseph Waite's letter book 1708–10, Burlington MSS, miscellaneous, box 1); same to same, 4 June 1709 (ibid.); same to same, 27 Oct. 1709 (ibid.); same to same, 10 Nov. 1709 (ibid.).

37 Same to Foulke, 6 May 1707 (Chatsworth, Joseph Waite's letter book 1706–8 (Ireland and Yorkshire), Burlington MSS, miscellaneous, box 1).

38 Burlington to Power, Bagge and Baker, 21 Nov. 1704 (NLI, MS 43, 361/2); same to same, 10 May 1705 (ibid., MS 43, 361/3); Davoren to Catherine O'Brien, 21 Dec. 1709 (ibid., MS 45, 347/3).

often ignored summonses, or had arrears which were too hefty to be exchanged for labour. In such cases, harsher measures had to be employed. Juliana sympathised with tenants' difficult circumstances and told the agents not to arrest those whose condition was particularly bad.[39] When she could, she showed favour and leniency towards 'good paymasters and improving tenants', who might still pay money if given a little extra time. Others who did not meet these criteria, or who had already been granted extensions, were pressed for immediate payment.[40] Mimicking how she dealt with her son's English estates, she had the lands of these offending tenants distrained (seized) and their possessions and livestock taken and sold to raise money.[41]

Though she could not abate arrears, Lady Burlington could, if pushed, abate future rents, provided that she had 'very good reasons to bear me out'.[42] This loophole, combined with the necessity of easing the burden tenants were under if she hoped to make money out of them and keep the better ones, meant that she was occasionally brought to reduce some rents, saying of one man in 1706 that she would 'make him a small abatement if you can't get the rent from another tenant that he is obliged to pay', and reducing the rent of another in 1710 by £5 during the war 'rather than part with so able a tenant'. She was loath to exercise this power, however, and often sent instructions that these kindnesses be kept private, so that her favouritism would not be known and encourage other claimants.[43]

It was little wonder Juliana and Catherine were so desperate to obtain their sons' rents, for in addition to the titles and estates the boys had inherited, they had also acquired the debts of their fathers and, in the case of the new Lord Burlington, his great-grandfather. Juliana was plagued by creditors and obliged, at the suggestion of her husband's will, to obtain an Act of Parliament in 1705 to allow her to exceed the normal restrictions placed upon a guardian and sell some of her son's lands to raise funds.[44] This was still not enough, and in 1707 there remained 'so very many creditors that if her ladyship should pay some and not others, she would never be at quiet, so she chooses rather at present to deny them'.[45] It was this pressure on her which filtered down to her son's tenants. Rental arrears could not be absolved or

39 Spurret to Foulke, 4 Sept. 1705 (ibid., MS 13, 249/1).

40 Quote from Waite to Musgrave and Baker, 29 Apr. 1710 (Chatsworth, Joseph Waite's letter book 1708–10, Burlington MSS, miscellaneous, box 1). See also same to Foulke, 12 Oct. 1708 (ibid.); Burlington to Foulke, Power, Bagge and Baker, 8 July 1704 (NLI, MS 43, 361/2); same to Power, Bagge and Baker, 11 Jan. 1704/5 (ibid.).

41 Burlington to Power, Bagge and Baker, 7 Oct. 1704 (NLI, MS 43, 361/2); Waite to Foulke, 19 Aug. 1707 (Chatsworth, Joseph Waite's letter book 1706–8 (Ireland and Yorkshire), Burlington MSS, miscellaneous, box 1); same to Howse, 26 Oct. 1709 (ibid., Joseph Waite's letter book 1708–10, Burlington MSS, miscellaneous, box 1); same to Myers, 19 Dec. 1706 (ibid., Joseph Waite's letter book 1706–8 (Ireland and Yorkshire), Burlington MSS, miscellaneous, box 1).

42 Burlington to Power, Bagge and Baker, 11 Jan. 1704/5 (NLI, MS 43, 361/2).

43 Same to same, 21 Feb. 1705/6 (ibid.); Waite to Musgrave and Baker, 30 Sept. 1710 (Chatsworth, Joseph Waite's letter book 1708–10, Burlington MSS, miscellaneous, box 1); same to same, 1 Mar. 1708/9 (NLI, MS 13, 242/1).

44 Will of Charles earl of Burlington; 'An act for the sale of several estates in England and Ireland for payment of debts of Charles, earl of Burlington and Cork, 1705' (Chatsworth, MS L/28/109).

45 Waite to Mr [?] Keld, 27 Sept. 1707 (Chatsworth, Joseph Waite's letter book 1706–8 (Ireland and Yorkshire), Burlington MSS, miscellaneous, box 1).

decreased by a guardian without a judgement of Chancery since the money belonged to the creditors, nor could Juliana remit money due on bonds to any creditors, or stop them from initiating bond debt prosecutions, for she was only their trustee.[46]

Catherine was in a similarly difficult position, for as well as her own extravagance at Dromoland, James Davoren wrote that 'nobody alive suffers more than you do by debts that are properly Mr [*Lucius*] O'Brien's, and your accounts will plainly show what a sufferer you are, and that people are mightily mistaken if they think you have any money in your hands'.[47] Unless their evidence was airtight and they had the means to pursue her for the money, those who came to her looking for restitution of debts contracted by her husband met with disappointment. Lucius's cousin, Captain Christopher O'Brien, complained in 1719 of a debt to the executors of a Captain Long for which he 'stood bound for Mr Lucius O'Brien', swearing that he was liable to be 'ransacked' at any time and begging Catherine for 'so much of Sir Edward's money as will answer the contents of the executions, for madam I cannot otherwise raise the money'.[48] The debt was genuine – Sir Donat had paid the interest on it during his son's lifetime – but Davoren thought the request ridiculous and Christopher to be trying his luck, for 'he does not think or expect you are capable or able to pay it'. He advised Catherine to 'be cautious in giving anything under your hand, it will be very honourable and conscionable to pay these debts in proper time'.[49] Three years later, Christopher was still waiting, and selling his goods at the Ennis fair to obtain the cash.[50]

Indispensable assistants or *agents provocateurs*?

Agents such as Davoren were relied upon by their mistresses to handle the day-to-day running of a child's estates. Given the level of trust placed in them, the competence and reliability of these men was arguably even more important than the personal ability of a young lord's mother, for they typically had greater hands-on experience than women who had previously been subordinate to husbands (even allowing for possible stints as managers when their spouses had been absent). Yet they 'belonged to no professional body and had undergone no uniform preparation'.[51] Those who had come to their posts through family connexions were perhaps best prepared, having likely served a form of apprenticeship under a father or uncle, but many of the earl of Burlington's employees had no such background.[52] Nevertheless,

46 Spurret to Bagge, 28 Mar. 1704 (ibid., Anthony Spurret's letter book 1703–4, Burlington MSS, miscellaneous, box 1); Burlington to Power, Bagge and Baker, 21 Nov. 1704 (NLI, MS 43, 361/2); Waite to Foulke and John Walker, 5 Dec. 1712 (ibid., MS 13, 249/3).

47 Davoren to Catherine O'Brien, 24 Dec. 1719 (ibid., MS 45, 347/3).

48 Christopher O'Brien to same, 3 Dec. 1719 (ibid., MS 45, 348/3).

49 Accounts between Sir Donat, Lucius and Catherine O'Brien, Apr. 1711–June 1714 (ibid., MS 45, 339/10); Davoren to Catherine O'Brien, 24 Dec. 1719 (ibid., MS 45, 347/3).

50 Christopher O'Brien to Catherine O'Brien, 15 Aug. 1722 (ibid., MS 45, 348/3).

51 Barnard, *A new anatomy*, p. 212.

52 For a brief discussion of the background of the Burlington agents in Ireland between the 1690s and 1730s, see ibid., pp 218–25.

agents were the people to whom tenants actually answered, they were the men who advised the family matriarch how to proceed and the ones who collected rents and drew up accounts. An estate was only as good as the sum of its parts and the agents were critical parts, though there were days when both Juliana and Catherine could have seen them far enough.

Lady Burlington, as an absentee responsible for estates in two different countries, was particularly reliant upon her son's agents, yet she rarely if ever met some of those based in Ireland. She had to take their letters, news and advice on trust, a trust which she sensed was often misplaced. Many had been allowed to rent lands on the Irish estate, which caused her considerable annoyance. She found it strange 'that stewards of an estate should be farmers to it' and was understandably angry when they slipped into arrears, pointing out the poor example it set for other tenants and the bad impression it made on creditors.[53] More concerning was the serious conflict of interest produced. The agents did not inform her of the true value of the lands they were renting until after their lease agreements had been made, and she wrote that

> I have sometimes thought that you argued with me more like tenants than agents, but now I am convinced that you are so far from being good stewards that I can hardly esteem you honest tenants and I have reason to be on my guard when I deal with you, and not only to suspect your proposals for your farms but your management and advice in other matters, for this is a fault which proceeds from habitual unfaithfulness and is the last that ought to be pardoned.[54]

In an effort to minimise, and eventually remove, the problem, she tried to limit the lands let out to them, but in her desperation for tenants she broke her own rule when agent Richard Bagge requested a further lease, writing that 'it is against my rule to let anymore lands to my agents, but I desire to know your opinion of his offer, and what you think is a reasonable rent for that ground by the acre, and whether any other tenant offers for it'.[55] She had her fingers burned when it became apparent that Bagge owed her son vast sums of money, and quickly decreed that 'no agent shall be suffered to be in arrears but before the half year's account is closed if he does not pay what he owes that he shall be distrained on'.[56] It was too late to retrieve much of the money from Bagge, and only six months later Juliana had dismissed him from his post and issued orders that his goods be seized if necessary, to help pay his debts.[57]

As it transpired, the problems with Bagge were the tip of the iceberg. The diligence of her son's agents often left much to be desired, and Lady Burlington was constantly complaining that they were slow to collect in rents and arrears and

53 Burlington to Power, Bagge, Baker and Coughlan, 6 Dec. 1705 (NLI, MS 43, 361/3).

54 Same to Power, Bagge and Baker, 7 Oct. 1704 (ibid., MS 43, 361/2). This was not an uncommon problem in Ireland. See Barnard, *A new anatomy*, p. 233. It has to be wondered if the shortage of Protestant tenants had any bearing on the number of agents renting land from their employers.

55 Burlington to Power, Bagge and Baker, 8 Sept. 1705 (NLI, MS 43, 361/3).

56 Same to Power, Musgrave, Baker and Coughlan, 6 Dec. 1705 (ibid.).

57 Spurett to Musgrave and Baker, 28 May 1706 (ibid., MS 43, 364/3). None of the joint letters written to the Irish agents after January 1706 have Bagge's name on them.

remit her the funds she required.[58] She was forced to borrow money to meet her needs, and protested that the Irish agents were too lenient on tenants who failed to pay, allowing them to run up arrears on 'trifling pretentions', while ignoring her instructions to distrain, forcing her to repeat herself in an effort to produce results.[59] In fact, she was convinced that 'the tenants do almost what they please without any manner of restraint from my son's agents on the spot, though not altogether, without their countenance and encouragement', a complaint echoed by other landlords in England, who, according to Hainsworth, also frequently felt that 'their stewards were too sympathetic to the interest of the tenants, pursuing policies which favoured them, rather than the employer'.[60] The Burlington agents were prone to leaving their mistress in the dark regarding her son's estate and tenants, failing to alert her to the severity of certain farmers' arrears and even to crimes committed on the earl's lands.[61] They would request increases in salary despite knowing her difficult financial situation, lease out farms at low rents without her permission and make use of the estate for their own ends, as Irish agent, Thomas Baker, did, when he enclosed some of the earl's lands for his own horses.[62]

To make matters worse, their working relationship with each other was appalling at times, with constant bickering and vying for precedence. They were petulant if one seemed more in favour than another, sent Juliana separate instead of joint letters, with differing recommendations and complained about each other so much that she was led to comment that 'your differences are grown so high that I believe you are more industrious a great deal to find occasions to complain of one another, than to do your duty'.[63] Other absentee Irish landlords met with similar problems, as agents tried to oust one another so that they and their families could gain further control over their employer's lands, often to disguise and further their fraudulent and self-motivated handling of the estate.[64] The Boyle stewards often refused even to meet with each other to discuss estate matters, and their disagreements and poor relationship proved costly.[65] When the countess told them to threaten the tenants

58 Burlington to Baker and Power, 23 Oct. 1705 (ibid., MS 13, 231); Waite to Musgrave and Baker, 2 Aug. 1712 (ibid., MS 13, 242/8).

59 Burlington to Power, Bagge and Baker, 6 Jan. 1704/5 (ibid., MS 43, 361/2). Quote from same to Foulke, Power, Bagge and Baker, 20 May 1704 (ibid.). See also same to Baker and Power, 23 Oct. 1705 (ibid., MS 13, 231).

60 Same to Power, Bagge and Baker, 21 Feb. 1705/6 (ibid., MS 43, 361/3); Hainsworth, *Stewards, lords and people*, p. 49.

61 See, for example, Waite to Foulke, 5 Apr. 1707 (Chatsworth, Joseph Waite's letter book 1706–8 (Ireland and Yorkshire), Burlington MSS, miscellaneous, box 1); same to Coughlan, 25 June 1707 (ibid.).

62 Same to Baker, 21 June 1707 (ibid.); Burlington to Baker and Power, 23 Oct. 1705 (NLI, MS 13, 231); same to Power, Bagge and Baker, 21 Feb. 1705/6 (ibid., MS 43, 361/3). For information on the typical salaries of agents, see Barnard, *A new anatomy*, pp 226–7.

63 Waite to Baker, 26 Feb. 1706/7 (Chatsworth, Joseph Waite's letter book 1706–8 (Ireland and Yorkshire), Burlington MSS, miscellaneous, box 1); Burlington to Power, Bagge and Baker, 7 Oct. 1704 (NLI, MS 43, 361/2); same to same, 10 May 1705 (ibid., MS 43, 361/3). Quote from Burlington to Power, Baker, Baker and Coughlan, 6 Dec. 1705 (ibid.).

64 Barnard, *A new anatomy*, pp 210–11.

65 Spurret to Baker, 16 Nov. 1704 (Chatsworth, Anthony Spurret's letter book 1703–4, Burlington MSS, miscellaneous, box 1).

with distraining (without any intention of carrying it out), Richard Bagge and Thomas Baker let the information slip, 'I suppose out of pure opposition', so that the tenants were fearless in their refusals to give security for their rents.[66] Such failings grated with a woman who was obsessed with protecting her son's income and limiting his expenditure. She constantly scrutinised her own outgoings and those of the agents, reducing their travel expenses when they were on estate business by setting them a daily allowance of five shillings, rather than reimbursing them after the event.[67] When they needlessly cost her son money despite her best efforts, it is little wonder that she was at her wits' end as to what to do with them for she fretted that the slow collection of rents which was the result of their incompetence would be blamed on her by the creditors and that she would be accused of mismanagement.[68] Venting her frustration in October 1705, she complained that 'there is not a great estate in the Kingdom, managed to so little advantage to the owner as my son's has been for a year or two past'.[69]

Her difficulties raise the issue of whether it was better for an Irish estate to have an absentee landlord in possession, or an absentee landlady as guardian. Though she might have found it hard to believe, Juliana's example actually supports the latter conclusion, for she was more vigilant than some of her male counterparts, who were often willing to overlook a certain amount of incompetence on the part of their agents (if they were even aware of it), in exchange for an easier life.[70] In the long term, she was motivated by a desire to protect her son and by the knowledge that he would one day be able to look back over her guardianship and establish if she had done well; in the short term, she was driven by the scrutiny of a collection of creditors and the Court of Chancery. This led her to monitor and question the activities of her son's agents much more rigorously than many landlords (including her adult son), and none were able to perpetuate large-scale, long-term fraud against the estate, though this did happen in the 1720s, after Richard had taken over management of his inheritance.[71]

Juliana's main recourse for the agents' shortcomings was to reprimand them constantly, and she sent numerous letters with orders as to how they could improve. They were to be far stricter with the tenants and force them to pay where at all possible. Accounts were to be laid out in a manner specified by her and drawn up every Saturday night. The money was to be stored in an iron chest, agents were not to keep it for considerable periods of time before entering it in the books, and it was to be sent to her every time they had collected £100.[72] More than once her

66 Burlington to Power, Bagge and Baker, 7 Oct. 1704 (NLI, MS 43, 361/2).

67 Same to Foulke, Power, Bagge and Baker, 20 June 1704 (ibid.).

68 Waite to Musgrave and Baker, 2 Aug. 1712 (ibid., MS 13, 242/8).

69 Burlington to Baker and Power, 23 Oct. 1705 (ibid., MS 13, 231).

70 Barnard, *A new anatomy*, p. 213.

71 Ibid., pp 225–6.

72 Burlington to Power, Bagge and Baker, 11 Jan. 1704/5 (NLI, MS 43, 361/2); Spurret to Baker, 10 Jan. 1704/5 (Chatsworth, Anthony Spurret's letter book 1703–4, Burlington MSS, miscellaneous, box 1); Burlington to Power, Bagge and Baker, 21 Feb. 1705/6 (NLI, MS 43, 361/3); same to same, 21 Nov. 1704 (ibid., MS 43, 361/2); Waite to Musgrave and Baker, 14 Dec. 1706 (Chatsworth, Joseph Waite's letter book 1706–8 (Ireland and Yorkshire), Burlington MSS, miscellaneous, box 1).

irritation with their incompetence boiled over and she threatened to dismiss them, writing only five months after her husband's death that if they did not do better, she would 'be obliged to put my affairs into other hands'. Sixteen months later, the situation had not improved, and she wrote to them that 'if you will not observe my orders, I desire you would tell me so, that I may employ others that will'.[73] Pay rises were out of the question and even their existing salaries were sometimes delayed for lack of funds, though Juliana perhaps hoped that if their own pockets were hit, they would be better motivated to collect her son's money.[74] As for their personal difficulties with each other, unless compelling evidence could be produced as to why she should do so, she would not dismiss one at the request of the other, as Richard Musgrave had requested she do to Thomas Baker and George Howse. Instead they were all to immediately put aside their differences if they wished to keep their jobs.[75] To help ease mutual jealousy, she strove to treat each fairly. When she was compelled by her late husband's instructions to give the seneschalship of Dungarvan to Jeremy Coughlan against her own inclinations, she compensated the aggrieved Richard Musgrave, who thought he should have had the job, by making him a commissioner for 'taking affidavits for the courts above especially in the chancery and exchequer', and later asking him to be made a justice of the peace.[76] He still proved difficult, though, receiving neither favour with grace. He was slow to take his oaths as commissioner and to thank Juliana for the offer of being made a JP, then refused the latter position, to the surprise and annoyance of Joseph Waite, who felt that Musgrave risked offending the countess by such behaviour.[77]

Juliana herself bore some blame for the scale of these problems. She was diligent in many respects, enquiring how other landlords dealt with their property and tenants to provide her with a template for how to act, and looking back to how her husband and his grandfather had run the Boyle estates for guidance and to provide some continuity in their management.[78] However, she never once took the trouble to visit Ireland, and her physical distance from her son's Irish agents (and even his English ones on occasion) exacerbated the problems she faced, while limiting the options available for dealing with them. She and her secretaries were constantly exchanging long letters with the various agents in Ireland and Yorkshire, but sheer

73 Burlington to Power, Bagge and Baker, 7 Oct. 1704 (NLI, MS 43, 361/2); same to same, 21 Feb. 1705/6 (ibid., MS 43, 361/3).

74 Waite to Baker, [2?] Aug. 1707 (Chatsworth, Joseph Waite's letter book 1706–8 (Ireland and Yorkshire), Burlington MSS, miscellaneous, box 1); Spurret to Andrew Holden, 29 Aug. 1704 (ibid., Anthony Spurret's letter book 1703–4, Burlington MSS, miscellaneous, box 1).

75 Waite to Musgrave, 26 Feb. 1707/8 (ibid., Joseph Waite's letter book 1706–8 (Ireland and Yorkshire), Burlington MSS, miscellaneous, box 1); Spurret to Power, 10 Jan. 1704/5 (ibid., Anthony Spurret's letter book 1703–4, Burlington MSS, miscellaneous, box 1).

76 Waite to Musgrave, 22 Nov. 1707 (ibid., Joseph Waite's letter book 1706–8 (Ireland and Yorkshire), Burlington MSS, miscellaneous, box 1); same to same, 13 Jan. 1707/8 (ibid.). Quote from same to Coughlan, 18 Dec. 1707 (ibid.).

77 Same to Musgrave, 6 Nov. 1708 (ibid., Joseph Waite's letter book 1708–10, Burlington MSS, miscellaneous, box 1); same to Baker, 3 Feb. 1708/9 (ibid.).

78 Spurret to Foulke, 28 June 1705 (NLI, MS 13, 249/3); Burlington to Foulke, Power, Bagge and Baker, 20 June 1704 (ibid., MS 43, 361/2); Spurret to Sir Richard Cox, 23 Mar. 1703/4 (Chatsworth, Anthony Spurret's letter book 1703–4, Burlington MSS, miscellaneous, box 1).

distance necessitated far heavier reliance upon those who were 'on the spot', as she so often put it, than would have been required had she been there herself. On numerous occasions she had to delegate decisions, responsibilities and powers to men whose abilities and dedication she openly doubted and who constantly failed her.

The obvious answer to Juliana's problems with the agents would have been to dismiss them, but there were good reasons for her reluctance to do so. First, the difficulties involved in finding competent replacements quickly from such a distance, men who were familiar with the land and capable of running an estate the size of the young earl's, made removing the current agents an unattractive and unrealistic option, and both sides knew it. It made even her threats to dismiss them (noteworthy for how often they were repeated and how rarely they were acted upon) little more than empty words.[79] Second, was the occasional bout of sentimentality. When age and health made it difficult for the Irish agent, Digby Foulke, to manage his duties, Juliana allowed him to hire his son-in-law to help him, rather than relieving him of his post, a common enough practice among landowners and their elderly agents.[80] She acted in a similarly lenient way with the incompetent English agent, Thomas Brown. Despite his constant failures to respond to letters and carry out his duties, she threatened, but continually failed, to dismiss him, citing respect for both him and his family. Yet she had Richard Musgrave told in 1708 that if he wished to relocate to England, he could have the post instead, as Brown's inadequacies had left it as good as vacant.[81]

Last were the advantages which warring agents brought: not immediately apparent, but very much present. With Juliana so far away and unable to monitor their behaviour closely, leaving them in place had tactical benefits, for their misdemeanours were often only brought to her attention when one exposed another. Had they worked as a team, they could have acted almost as they pleased. Had she replaced them slowly, the newer agents might have been too cowed by the older ones to report them. Though she dismissed Richard Bagge, she was brought to do it by reason of his great debts and allegations of corruption from the other agents who (in a rare instance of agreement), collectively showed a strong dislike for him, rather than for other failures which his colleagues shared, but which did not cost them their jobs.[82] Dismissing one agent who all agreed was a problem removed him as a scapegoat and made her other threats to dismiss more credible. For a time at least, it seemed to work. In January 1708, Richard Musgrave had 'a better opinion of Mr Baker than you seemed to have not long ago', and although he was already

79 See, for example, Burlington to Power, Bagge and Baker, 7 Oct. 1704 (NLI, MS 43, 361/2); same to Foulke, Power, Bagge and Baker, 17 Jan. 1705/6 (ibid., MS 43, 361/3).

80 Waite to [Foulke?], 27 Feb. 1710/11 (ibid., MS 13, 254/3); Barnard, *A new anatomy*, p. 236.

81 Same to Keld, 14 Aug. 1707 (Chatsworth, Joseph Waite's letter book 1706–8 (Ireland and Yorkshire), Burlington MSS, miscellaneous, box 1); same to Mr [?] Simondson, 9 Dec. 1707 (ibid.); same to Musgrave, 13 Jan. 1707/8 (ibid., Joseph Waite's letter book 1706–8 (Ireland and Yorkshire), Burlington MSS, miscellaneous, box 1). Brown was still in Juliana's employ in May 1709 (same to Brown, 14 May 1709 (ibid., Joseph Waite's letter book 1708–10, Burlington MSS, miscellaneous, box 1)).

82 Barnard, *A new anatomy*, p. 219.

starting to complain of the incompetence of Andrew Crotty, Crotty's later misdemeanours (he was the agent mentioned earlier who defrauded the estate in the 1720s) lend credence to his observations.[83]

Catherine O'Brien likewise experienced problems with her son's agent, James Davoren, and was also partially responsible for the situation. Davoren had his faults, among them occasionally drinking so much that he was rendered temporarily incapable of carrying out his job, but Catherine blew his failings out of proportion while ignoring her own.[84] She was annoyed by the attention he paid to Sir Edward's orders, without clearing them with her first, telling him not to release money to her son 'without my knowledge for whilst he is under my guardianship all remittances must go through my hands'.[85] Yet by this time she was allowing Edward to give orders to his servants, leading to confusion as to whose instructions should be followed, while his later inability to manage his income well suggests that Edward was trying to pull the wool over the eyes of his mother and agent in order to be given double the amount of money. Despite their problems, it was not until 1724 that she finally 'attacked me with fury', as Davoren put it, and dismissed him.[86] Had he been as incompetent as she claimed, so too was she for keeping him so long, particularly as, unlike Juliana, she lived in Ireland, could observe his actions at close quarters and replace him more easily. If he was, in fact, generally good at his job, but too honest for his own good when it came to telling her of her failings (which seems more likely), then she was foolish to remove, only two years before her son's majority, an agent who had more experience running the estate than she and who was a devoted servant. Her own mother, Lady Frances Keightley, hinted that Catherine should think twice before dismissing him: 'I have always heard him spoken of as a person that would sacrifice all he has for the good of your children.'[87] Sir Edward, his tutor Mr Campbell, and even Catherine herself had often spoken very highly of him, and Frances had heard he was rich and 'has a sort of inclination as well as a good power to make your children the better for him, and therefore in my opinion it were good to keep him a friend'.[88] She even suggested that he could be persuaded to help Catherine with her considerable financial problems during his lifetime.[89] Ultimately, though, she left the decision to her daughter, admitting that she knew nothing of the man personally and that if Catherine felt Davoren was trying to turn Edward against his mother, he deserved all he got.[90] Yet she urged her to 'act upon substantial and demonstrable grounds, otherwise it will not have the end I truly wish for your satisfaction'.[91] Whether or not Catherine did this is

83 Waite to Musgrave, 13 Jan. 1707/8 (Chatsworth, Joseph Waite's letter book 1706–8 (Ireland and Yorkshire), Burlington MSS, miscellaneous, box 1). For more on Andrew Crotty, see Barnard, *A new anatomy*, pp 223–5.

84 Grania O'Brien, *These my friends and forebears: the O'Briens of Dromoland* (Ballinakella, 1991), pp 45–6.

85 Catherine O'Brien to Davoren, 13 May [1722?] (NLI, MS 45, 347/4).

86 Davoren to Catherine O'Brien, 23 Jan. 1724/5 (ibid.).

87 Lady Frances Keightley to same, 3 Dec. 1723 (ibid., MS 45, 348/6).

88 Same to same, 21 Dec. 1723 (ibid.).

89 Same to same, 2 Jan. 1724/5 (ibid.).

90 Same to same, 3 Dec. 1723 (ibid.); same to same, 2 Jan. 1724/5 (ibid.).

91 Same to same, 2 Jan. 1724/5 (ibid.).

questionable, and Davoren certainly felt that his removal was completely unwarranted and was shocked and hurt by her actions. He cited his nine years' service to the O'Briens, swore that his letters to the family would bear out his claims that he had never acted the part of anything but a faithful servant, and told her that 'our term in this world is but short and that endeavouring to stain our neighbours reputation, is one of the difficult articles to be repented for. I appeal to your own conscience if you have not done me that way the greatest of injuries.'[92]

Not all dealings with agents were problematic. When a good one was found 'he was looked after as a treasure', and ladies in nineteenth-century England sent condolences to each other when a valued agent died, in recognition of the trouble his mistress would be put to in replacing him.[93] Those who were in constant face-to-face contact with their master or mistress were viewed as members of their household family and often held in great affection in their own right.[94] Though distance (and their incompetence) made this affection weaker, Juliana expressed similar feelings for her son's Irish agents, and despite the problems they caused, there were many instances in which she told them that she was satisfied with agreements they had made, or actions they had pursued for the good of the estate. She even made a particular effort to make Thomas Baker feel valued in 1709, when he wrote to her complaining of his large workload, small salary and the difficulties involved in dealing with Richard Musgrave.[95] She responded that she was well aware of Baker's worth, appreciated his great efforts and fatigue on her son's behalf and granted him a one-off gift of twenty guineas from her son's money to show her gratitude – a considerable favour, given how reluctant she was to spend the earl's cash.[96] It was the English agent, George Myers, with whom she was much more familiar and well-satisfied, who brought out the best in her, though. She valued him so greatly that she enquired after him when he was ill, ordered him to take care of his health and even had him send her a list of his symptoms so that she could consult her own doctors for him.[97] Even Catherine O'Brien and James Davoren originally got along well, and she had 'a vast opinion of him', perhaps because, far from showing favouritism towards the tenants and making excuses for them, as the Boyle agents did, he wrote that 'I am sure I lay aside all [ceremony?] and disoblige every one of your tenants rather than see yours and Sir Edward's interest and credit suffer by their neglect'.[98] Again, familiarity and competence (both enhanced by a resident landlady) went a long way towards a good working relationship between employer and employee.

92 Davoren to same, 23 Jan. 1724/5 (ibid., MS 45, 347/4).

93 K.D. Reynolds, *Aristocratic women and political society in Victorian Britain* (Oxford, 1998), pp 49–50 (quote is from p. 49).

94 Hainsworth, *Stewards, lords and people*, pp 259–60.

95 Waite to Foulke, 22 June 1710 (Chatsworth, Joseph Waite's letter book 1708–10, Burlington MSS, miscellaneous, box 1); same to Baker, 6 Dec. 1709 (ibid., Joseph Waite's letter book 1706–8 (Ireland and Yorkshire), Burlington MSS, miscellaneous, box 1).

96 Ibid.

97 Same to Myers, 7 Nov. 1706 (ibid.).

98 Keightley to Catherine O'Brien, 21 Dec. 1723 (NLI, MS 45, 348/6); Davoren to same, 24 Sept. 1719 (ibid., MS 45, 347/3).

Legal issues

Legal challenges were another headache for guardians to endure. Between June 1723 and May 1724 Catherine O'Brien spent £181 *6s. 9d.* on 'law charges for Sir Edward', no doubt in large part due to the legal proceedings her brother-in-law, Henry O'Brien, had initiated against her concerning the will of his father, Sir Donat, and Henry's share of the inheritance.[99] In Cork and Waterford, the Boyle bailiffs, like the agents, were slow to collect in rents and arrears, because they were 'very partial to many of the tenants'.[100] They tried to claim salaries to which they were not entitled and use them to offset their own debts, but Juliana responded that if they would 'not do the business for the fees which belong to the office, I make no doubt but other honest men may be had to that employment', before chastising the agents for allowing them 'to run in arrears on a groundless pretension to salaries, when you own that they never had any allowed them'.[101] She faced further problems when it emerged that lands her son owned were out of his possession and not bringing in any revenue. To complicate matters, various people (including the bishop of Waterford and Viscount Grandison) disputed which lands were actually Richard's and where the boundaries of his estate lay.[102] Juliana responded by ordering that the paperwork showing exactly what her son owned be found and that any alienated lands be brought back into the rental.[103] She had the agents find living witnesses who could swear as to where the boundaries were, and refused to make any agreements or concessions which would be disadvantageous to her son.[104] When the mayor of Youghal tried to supersede the rights of the earls of Cork over the north and south abbeys in the town, she quickly established that 'my son's title to all the liberties, franchises, privileges etc. formerly belonging to those religious houses is indisputable', and ordered that the mayor be prosecuted for infringing not just them, but also her son's rights over the college at Youghal and for mistreating her constable and bailiffs when they tried to stop him.[105] When Richard's ownership of Dungarvan prison was threatened by the justices of the peace and the grand jury at the Waterford assizes, along with lord chief justice, Richard Pyne, Juliana wrote that, 'as my son's affairs are now under my care they may assure themselves, I will support and defend his right against all invaders let the persons or the expense

99 Account of Catherine O'Brien with Sir Edward O'Brien, 1723–4 (ibid., MS 45, 350/5); Counsellor Thomas Staunton to Catherine O'Brien, 10 Dec. 1720 (ibid., MS 45, 348/4).

100 Burlington to Power, Bagge and Baker, 7 Oct. 1704 (ibid., MS 43, 361/2).

101 Same to Foulke, Power, Bagge, Baker, 20 June 1704 (ibid.).

102 Spurret to Power, 10 Jan. 1704/5 (Chatsworth, Anthony Spurret's letter book 1703–4, Burlington MSS, miscellaneous, box 1); Waite to Musgrave and Baker, 28 July 1707 (ibid., Joseph Waite's letter book 1706–8 (Ireland and Yorkshire), Burlington MSS, miscellaneous, box 1).

103 Waite to Coughlan, 6 July 1708 (ibid., Joseph Waite's letter book 1708–10, Burlington MSS, miscellaneous, box 1).

104 Spurret to Power, 10 Jan. 1704/5 (ibid., Anthony Spurret's letter book 1703–4, Burlington MSS, miscellaneous, box 1); Waite to Musgrave and Baker, 28 July 1707 (ibid., Joseph Waite's letter book 1706–8 (Ireland and Yorkshire), Burlington MSS, miscellaneous, box 1).

105 Burlington to Musgrave and Baker, 13 Dec. 1707 (ibid., Cork MSS, vol. xxxv, no. 40*). See also Waite to Foulke, 25 Nov. 1707 (ibid., Joseph Waite's letter book 1706–8 (Ireland and Yorkshire), Burlington MSS, miscellaneous, box 1).

be never so great. His minority shall be no manner of advantage to his enemies.'[106] Strong words, but not always followed up by strong actions.

Just as the countess threatened, but was slow to actually prosecute those who owed her son money, so she threatened but was slow to seek legal redress from those who damaged his estate, whether tenants or not. When trees were felled without permission, Juliana expressed her anger but overlooked the offence as the timber had been used to carry out repairs on her son's estate and was only worth £50, though she ordered that all such future offences were to be prosecuted.[107] When the walls of the towns on the estate were broken down and the stones taken for the perpetrators' own use, she ordered that those responsible be 'made public examples, and that they may be obliged to make full satisfaction for such abuses to deter others from the like bad practices for the future'.[108] Yet her anger soon cooled and her natural reluctance to spend time and money on legal proceedings reappeared, when her agents informed her that the stones had been used to repair buildings on the estate (which would be to her son's advantage) and that the walls were not strictly necessary for security any more, as the war in Ireland was over. She therefore amended her orders, so that only those people who were not tenants would be prosecuted.[109] An acknowledgement of fault, along with a humble apology from an offender and a promise to pay for any damage inflicted on the estate, could also halt a prosecution in its tracks, and at least one man (Richard Fitzgerald, who had broken into the jail at Tallow and freed a prisoner there) saved himself from retribution in this way.[110] In the end, money trumped all. Legal proceedings were costly and the potential gains had to be weighed against the expense. It is this which explains the mismatch between Juliana's bark and her bite.

Conclusion

What made a mother a good guardian? The ideal woman would have lived on her son's estates, had a good business head and prior experience of estate management, a team of competent and trustworthy agents to help her, well-placed political and social connexions, but, somewhat incongruously, few distractions from her job as manager. Yet even she would have faced challenges beyond her control. Legal limits on her powers, second-, even third-generation debts which demanded payment, problematic employees, impoverished tenants (courtesy of an economy which was on its knees and further hampered by English-imposed trade restrictions) and legal disputes with family members, local officials and other landholders: all would have tried the abilities of even the best and best prepared of guardians. For Catherine and Juliana, neither of whom started in an optimal position, they made the task infinitely more difficult. Though both worked hard, it was virtually an impossible

106 Burlington to Musgrave and Baker, 1 May 1708 (NLI, MS 43, 364/1).
107 Waite to Howse, 9 Dec. 1707 (Chatsworth, Joseph Waite's letter book 1706–8 (Ireland and Yorkshire), Burlington MSS, miscellaneous, box 1).
108 Same to Musgrave, 9 Sept. 1707 (ibid.).
109 Same to Howse, 9 Dec. 1707 (ibid.).
110 Same to Coughlan, 25 June 1707 (ibid.); same to same, 27 Jan. 1707/8 (ibid.).

job to keep their sons' estates entirely solvent in the circumstances they faced, and neither boy's inheritance was in a healthy condition at the end of his minority. The account books of the earl of Cork and Burlington show that by 1717, his Irish lands alone were saddled with arrears of £12,910 9*s*. 3¾*d*. and Catherine's spending and problems collecting in rents had left her over £7,000 in debt to her son by 1729, forcing her to sign over land in Counties Clare and Galway to repay him.[111]

Despite efforts by both women to involve their sons in the management of their estates before their 21st birthdays and so prepare them for life as a great landlord, neither man would prove to be diligent or competent enough to reverse these downward trends.[112] Sir Edward was a profligate spender whose sons had to take control of his estate in later life before all was lost, and the arrears on Lord Burlington's Irish estate had already climbed to £24,116 5*s*. 12½*d*. by 1723.[113] These were problems for the next generation, though, and when their sons' majorities arrived, neither Lady Burlington, nor Mrs O'Brien continued to try to impose their authority upon the lands. Juliana handled Richard's affairs for a few weeks after his birthday until he returned from his Grand Tour, but he then assumed total control.[114] In 1727, just a year after her son turned 21, Catherine moved to France, where she died in around 1731.[115] Neither she nor the countess expressed any desire for a continuation or a return to their days at the head of two of Ireland's great estates.

111 Arrears taken out of Lady Day rental and brought into Michaelmas rental 1717 (NLI, MS 43, 747/4); Memorial of an indenture quadripartite between Lady Catherine O'Brien, Henry, earl of Sherbourn, Sir Edward O'Brien, 2nd Bart. and William O'Brien, earl of Inchiquin, 17 Sept. 1729 (ibid., MS 45, 361/3).

112 See, for example, Thornton to Catherine O'Brien, 19 Feb. 1723/4 (ibid., MS 45, 348/8); same to same, 13 Feb. 1723/4 (ibid.); Mr [?] O'Brien to Davoren, 3 Nov. 1724 (ibid., MS 45, 347/4); Waite to Foulke and Walker, 24 Mar. 1712 (ibid., MS 13, 249/3).

113 *D.I.B.* (O'Brien, Sir Edward (1705–65)); Arrears taken out of Lady Day rental and brought into Michaelmas rental 1723 (ibid., MS 43, 747/4).

114 Waite to Foulke and John Walker, 9 Apr. 1715 (NLI, MS 13, 249/3); same to same, 21 July 1715 (ibid.).

115 O'Brien, *These my friends and forebears*, pp 54, 56.

5

Society queens

Writing from Dublin to her brother John, in May 1718, Sarah Mason, a native of County Waterford, described how she and their sister, Harriet, were putting in their days: 'We spend our time in visiting and receiving visits, and buying for our Waterford friends etc. Harriet is very tired, very little stirring in the town, and few people, almost everyone at their country house.'[1] In analysing her words, one begins to get a sense of the female experience of Ascendancy society. In her comment that most people had retreated to their country homes and there was 'very little stirring in the town', Sarah is alluding to Dublin's recently finished social season, which ran from roughly November to March, with another brief flurry of activity in April and May. This season dictated the ebb and flow of the elite population between city and country, and elite women organised their year around it. When exactly it was established is unclear, but as early as 1695 ladies spoke of 'passing 3 or 4 months of this winter in Dublin'.[2] It is tempting to connect the season to the sittings of the Irish parliament, as historians have done for England, but in Ireland these were only biennial, and in the later eighteenth century at least, parliamentary sessions made little, if any difference to the social programme available in the capital.[3] Outside the season, few entertainments remained beyond the staple activity of 'visiting and receiving visits', but Harriet's fatigue suggests that the season itself was as punishing as it was enjoyable (she had been in Dublin for some time by this point, while Sarah had only just arrived).[4] Much more is needed, though, before we can understand the social landscape, both urban and rural, which was inhabited by the two sisters and their peers.

Thanks to the efforts of a number of historians, there is already a considerable literature on the amusements available to the Irish during the eighteenth century.[5]

1 Sarah Mason and [Harriet] Alcock to John Mason, 19 May 1718 (PRONI, T3131/B/1/7).
2 Tighernan Mooney and Fiona White, 'The gentry's winter season' in David Dickson (ed.), *The gorgeous mask: Dublin, 1700–1850* (Dublin, 1987), p. 1; Agnes Hamilton to Margaret, countess of Panmure, 9 Sept. 1695 (NRS, GD45/14/238/10).
3 Elaine Chalus and Fiona Montgomery, 'Women and politics' in Hannah Barker and Chalus (eds), *Women's history: Britain, 1700–1850* (New York, 2005), p. 225; Peter Jupp, 'The roles of royal and aristocratic women in British politics, c. 1782–1832' in Mary O'Dowd and Sabine Wichert (eds), *Chattel, servant or citizen: women's status in church, state and society. Historical Studies xix* (Belfast, 1995), p. 109; Mooney and White, 'The gentry's winter season', p. 2.
4 Sarah and Harry Mason to John Mason, 7 May 1718 (PRONI, T3131/B/1/6).
5 See, for example, Toby Barnard, '"Grand Metropolis" or "The anus of the world"? The cultural life of eighteenth-century Dublin' in Peter Clark and Raymond Gillespie (eds), *Two capitals: London and Dublin, 1500–1840* (Oxford, 2001), pp 185–210; idem, 'Integration or separation? Hospitality and display in Protestant Ireland, c. 1660–1800' in Laurence Brockliss and David Eastwood (eds), *A union of multiple identities: the British Isles, c. 1750–1850* (Manchester, 1997), pp 127–46; idem, *Making the grand figure: lives and possessions in Ireland, 1641–1770* (London,

David Fleming has shown that the upper, middling and lower orders enjoyed certain events together, including local fairs and state celebrations, with their firework displays and bonfires. However, he has cautioned against employing rigid definitions of what constituted elite culture, pointing to the presence of different faiths (Catholic, Anglican and Dissenter), different social groups (English, Irish or Old Irish) and the increasing accessibility of culture and entertainment to those who could afford it, but who might not be part of the aristocracy or gentry.[6] The role of Dublin Castle as a site of elite sociability has come under scrutiny from Toby Barnard, while the Dublin season, as it was enjoyed by the upper orders during the later eighteenth century, has been examined by Tighernan Mooney and Fiona White.[7] This historiography does not focus on elite women, however, and with the exception of some case studies undertaken by Barnard and Sean Connolly, our understanding of their experiences in Ireland, distinct from those of men, remains hazy.[8] This leaves Irish scholarship far behind that of England and Scotland, where, for some time, historians have been uncovering how female sociability was expressed within a variety of contexts and activities, whether within or without the home, in single-sex or mixed company and in urban or rural environments.[9] It is this broader picture, adapted for an Irish context, which the present chapter seeks to provide.

Historians once designated the home as a private and female space. However, scholars have pointed out the flaws in this classification, which fails to take into account the multitude of visitors, tradesmen and servants, both male and female, who passed through elite houses on a daily basis. Likewise, amusements available outside the home may have been available to only a select few, making the use of the word 'public' hard to justify. With no clear lines defining public and private, new terminology must be sought to express these ideas. For our purposes, those social activities which took place inside the home will be called domestic, while those which took place outside of it will be dealt with on a case-by-case basis, to determine how inclusive or exclusive they really were.[10]

2004); Lindsay Proudfoot, 'Market fairs and towns in Ireland, c.1600–1853' in eadem and Peter Borsay (eds), *Provincial towns in early modern England and Ireland: change, convergence and divergence* (Oxford, 2002), pp 69–96.

6 David Fleming, 'Diversions of the people: sociability among the orders of early eighteenth-century Ireland', *Eighteenth-Century Ireland*, xvii (2002), pp 100–1.

7 Toby Barnard, 'The vice-regal court in later seventeenth-century Ireland' in Eveline Cruickshanks (ed.), *The Stuart courts* (Stroud, 2000), pp 256–65; Mooney and White, 'The gentry's winter season', pp 1–16. See also Rachel Wilson, 'The vicereines of Ireland and the transformation of the Dublin court, c. 1703–1737', *The Court Historian*, xix (2014), pp 3–28.

8 Toby Barnard, 'A tale of three sisters: Katherine Conolly of Castletown' in idem, *Irish Protestant ascents and descents, 1641–1770* (Dublin, 2004), pp 266–89; S.J. Connolly, 'A woman's life in eighteenth-century Ireland: the case of Letitia Bushe', *Historical Journal*, xliii (2000), pp 433–51.

9 For a sample of this historiography, see Katharine Glover, *Elite women and polite society in eighteenth-century Scotland* (Woodbridge, 2011), esp. ch. 4; Ingrid Tague, *Women of quality: accepting and contesting ideals of femininity in England, 1690–1760* (Woodbridge, 2002), esp. chs 2 and 6; Amanda Vickery, *The gentleman's daughter: women's lives in Georgian England* (London, 1998); Susan Whyman, *Sociability and power in late-Stuart England: the cultural worlds of the Verneys 1660–1720* (Oxford, 1999).

10 For a greater discussion of public and private and the historiography available on it, see above pp 2–3.

House calls and home visits

Visits were the ultimate form of domestic sociability, for they were immune to the changing social seasons and could facilitate a variety of people from beyond the family. Benjamin Heller has pointed to their frequency as evidence of the superiority of domestic leisure over that which took place in other spaces and sees them, as do many other historians, as promoting the creation, renewal and strengthening of social, political and familial links by creating a network of sociability between different houses.[11] They were bound up with ideas of politeness and civility, and for girls, and women in particular, this meant perfecting and displaying the social skills which formed such an integral part of their education by observing how other, more experienced ladies conducted themselves. Scholars have also pointed to the opportunities which receiving visitors afforded young girls to practise their skills as a hostess under the tutelage of their mothers, before they married and obtained houses of their own.[12] During a tour of Ireland in the early 1730s, Mary Pendarves (who would later marry Patrick Delany, dean of Down) was particularly impressed with the endeavours of a young Miss Wesley, the daughter of her host and hostess, who carried out 'the honours of the house as well as if she was a woman'.[13] This training was not meted out to boys, giving ladies an important and unique role within domestic sociability, which men could not assume and which they struggled to compensate for in its absence. Those who did not have a wife but still wished to attract visitors, typically sought alternatives, with daughters and sisters making popular stand-ins.[14]

The timing and length of visits depended on location. Those living in towns and cities, within easy reach of each other, were able to accomplish several calls in a day, each relatively short and with little or no organisation needed. Evening engagements were typically by invitation only, making them a useful way of showing favour to a particular person or persons. Sarah Mason's other sister, Mary Mason, basked in the prestige of dining at a friend's home in Dublin 'by invitation' in 1737.[15] In the countryside, visits between neighbours might also be carried out unannounced, but made to last the whole day. For those which stretched into the night, there might be an *ad hoc* invitation to dinner. In Caledon, County Tyrone, Margaret Boyle, countess of Orrery, called on Robert Clayton, bishop of Clogher and his wife Katherine one morning after breakfast in 1746, and was 'most violently pressed to stay all night'. She declined, though, citing a desire to get home and obviously aware that the impromptu invite stemmed from a wish to appear polite,

[11] Benjamin Heller, 'Leisure and the use of domestic space in Georgian London', *Historical Journal*, liii (2010), p. 624; Glover, *Elite women and polite society*, p. 82. Second quote is from Janet Mullin, '"We had carding": hospitable card play and polite domestic sociability among the middling sort in eighteenth-century England', *Journal of Social History*, lvii (2009), p. 993.

[12] Glover, *Elite women and polite society*, pp 82–3.

[13] Mary Pendarves to Ann Granville, 27 May 1732 (*The autobiography and correspondence of Mary Granville, Mrs Delany: with interesting reminiscences of King George III and Queen Charlotte*, ed. Lady Llanover (ser. 1, 3 vols, London, 1861), i, 348).

[14] See, for instance, same to same, 22 Dec. 1747 (ibid., ii, 481).

[15] Mary Mason to John Mason, 10 Dec. 1737 (PRONI, T3131/B/1/34).

rather than a premeditated design to flatter her.[16] Thanks to the greater distances involved, journeys between town and country were longer in length and fewer in number. Mary, dowager Lady Shelburne, spent a month and a half travelling back to Conyngham Hall, County Meath from Mount Charles, County Donegal, calling on various friends along the way with whom she stayed days or weeks, as opposed to the minutes or hours which a local visit would encompass.[17] It was not just geography which dictated who might call at a lady's door however, or vice versa.

The Irish elite was not a homogeneous group. All existed at the top of the social pyramid, but within that uppermost wedge were tiers of subdivisions. At the beginning of this period, these subdivisions held considerable sway over who socialised with whom. Left in Kilkenny Castle in 1698 by her husband, Mary, duchess of Ormond complained of being 'shut up in a Castle by all the sorts of ill weather' and of having 'no company but men that think themselves very dully entertained by a woman they never saw before and are upon the high respect with'. Apart from a Mrs Stanley, who was 'with much ado much prevailed upon to come down' and join her, Mary had not 'one woman besides myself to have sat down at table with me this whole winter, (when generally there is twelve or fourteen men)', and was soon begging that all efforts be made to persuade her absent husband to either come to her, or send for her.[18] As the duchess herself acknowledged, there were plenty of people around her, but as they were all men, strangers to her and of a much lower rank than she, all concerned felt awkward at the prospect of socialising together. Her title was obviously off-putting to women also. While it might be assumed that Mrs Stanley would have jumped at the chance to be received by Ireland's first lady, in fact, the idea of having single-handedly to amuse the country's only duchess, who usually spent her time at the royal court, was likely more nerve-racking than exciting. Mary learnt the hard way that the elite of post-Revolutionary Ireland was simply too small and comprised of too many absentees to sustain rigid social boundaries based on rank, especially for incoming strangers with few, if any, pre-existing social connexions and who were living in the more sparsely populated countryside. Fortunately, things were already changing.

In place of the system Mary had known in the 1690s, the new Ascendancy elite slowly emerged over the following decades, blending together those with rank and the newly moneyed commoners who had risen to prominence in the wake of the Glorious Revolution. Now, ladies of at least genteel, but otherwise varying backgrounds socialised together, and the highest title in the room did not necessarily signify the greatest riches. By the early 1720s, the untitled but fabulously wealthy Katherine Conolly was welcomed to Dublin Castle by Henrietta, duchess of Grafton, the duchess of Ormond's niece and wife of the then lord lieutenant. On

16 Margaret, countess of Orrery to John, earl of Orrery, 2 June, 4 June 1746 (*The Orrery papers*, ed. Emily, countess of Cork and Orrery (2 vols, London, 1903), ii, 222). On contemporary interpretations of politeness and how it related to sociability, see Lawrence Klein, 'Politeness and the interpretation of the British eighteenth century', *Historical Journal*, xliv (2002), pp 869–98; Paul Langford, 'The uses of eighteenth century politeness', *Transactions of the Royal Historical Society*, ser. 6, xii (2002), pp 311–31.

17 Mary, dowager Lady Shelburne to Alexander Murray, 7 Dec. 1706 (PRONI, D2860/9/16).

18 Mary, duchess of Ormond to Benjamin Portlock, 12 Feb. 1697/8 (NLI, MS 2505).

one occasion, Katherine even brought with her Constance Conyngham, the wife of her disreputable nephew, Williams.[19] There is no mention of what Henrietta made of this arrangement, but like her aunt, there was no one in the kingdom of her own status, and the alternative to lowering her standards was loneliness and boredom. Gender divisions were also breaking down. While the duchess of Ormond and the less eminent men around her at Kilkenny Castle had shrunk from the idea of socialising together in the absence of the duke, fifty years later, Margaret, countess of Orrery thought nothing of mixing with bishops and their wives. Although her rank placed her well above them, their wealth put them on a par with her. She took return visits from the Claytons (who were said to live particularly well) and received local doctors and churchmen even when her husband was in England, though always in pairs or groups, no doubt to avoid the gossip which solo visits might have caused.[20] Such a social routine would have been the envy of many a Scottish lady, where no resident husband often meant no visitors for those in rural areas.[21]

The mixing of ranks had practical benefits for ladies socialising beneath themselves. Those of a lower station did not require the same level of attention and civility that those of a higher one took for granted, and some enjoyed the simplicity this allowed for: 'Monday we made visits to some of the townspeople; there are none better than Mrs. Herbert or some of her rank, which eases us of much ceremony,' wrote Mary Pendarves in 1732.[22] There were limits, though. Katherine Conolly was ridiculed for inviting the famous actress, Kitty Clive, to her house, Castletown, specifically because 'though there was so much company as to have three tables at dinner she [*Katherine*] had her [*Kitty*] at the table with herself, where there was company of the first rank'.[23] No matter how much social boundaries had softened, there were still some people with whom a lady simply should not have associated.

Status was conferred by having visitors come to you, rather than going to them, a rule which recognised the inconvenience of travel and the expense of many types of hospitality. Katherine Conolly boasted in 1722 that her outings to see the duchess of Grafton were the only visits she had made for five years previously and, had she wished, she could have excused even this concession as a kindness motivated by the duchess's pregnancy.[24] Nor did she change her ways as she grew older, for at the time of her death in 1752, she had 'never made a visit since Mr Conolly died', twenty-three years earlier.[25] Her guests were often her extended family; however, she arrived home one day in 1744 to find Castletown contained 'a vast deal of company, 3 tables quite full and I know only of 3 or 4 of my good neighbours, but when I came from church I found a house full of them'; this was further evidence of the relaxed

19 Katherine Conolly to Jane Bonnell, 22 Jan. 1721/2 (ibid., MS 41, 578/3).
20 Margaret Orrery to Ld Orrery, 11 Sept. 1746 (*Orrery papers*, ii, 246); same to same, 20 July 1748 (ibid., 252–3). On the Claytons' lifestyle, see Mary Delany to Ann Dewes, 15 Oct. and 23 Nov. 1745 (*Autobiography and correspondence*, ser. 1, ii, 394, 399).
21 Glover, *Elite women in polite society*, p. 87.
22 Pendarves to Granville, 21 June 1732 (*Autobiography and correspondence*, ser. 1, i, 355).
23 Jones to Bonnell, 27 Oct. [n.d., 1734–42] (NLI, MS 41, 577/5).
24 Katherine Conolly to same, 22 Jan. 1721/2 (ibid., MS 41, 578/3).
25 Delany to Dewes, 26 Sept. 1752 (*Autobiography and correspondence*, ser. 1, iii, 159).

social code governing Irish sociability.[26] In some ways, Katherine demonstrated and improved her reputation for magnanimity by acting in this way; in others she showed an intransigence which most women could not afford to indulge and who in any case, would have recognised the inherent rudeness of refusing to attend on others in their homes and sought to avoid it. Good manners demanded a *quid pro quo* approach to visits to spread the compliment of being waited upon. Having been visited at home in 1745 by Philip and Petronilla Stanhope, earl and countess of Chesterfield, who were then the lord lieutenant and vicereine, Mary Delany was anxious to go to Dublin Castle just two days later 'to return thanks for the honour they did us'.[27] For similar reasons, women who had just arrived in the area after a spell away, or to stay with friends or family who lived in the neighbourhood, could expect a veritable onslaught of callers from among the local female elite, though these social demands could be taxing. Mary Pendarves, visiting Killala in 1732, complained of the burden of repeatedly becoming the subject of visits herself while she was travelling, for she and her friends had 'almost as much company here as in Dublin' yet were 'never are so well pleased as when we are by ourselves'.[28] Being alone was not an option, though. On the day of her arrival from England, while she and her companions were still recovering from the fatigue of the journey, their hosts, Robert Clayton, then bishop of Killala and his wife Katherine (who was the sister of Mary's fellow traveller, Anne Donellan), ensured that they were 'denied to all but particular friends', but a Mrs Usher and her son and daughter still came to visit. Had the Claytons not stepped in, there would have been far more. This was despite the fact that women sometimes resented having to make such calls. In 1746, Lady Orrery complained that the Claytons were 'at Mr. Lowry's and I must make them a visit', an excursion she obviously felt obliged to make to avoid rudeness, but which she would rather have avoided.[29]

Even entertaining in your own home could be disagreeable. Mrs Pendarves worried that the prospect of entertaining the lord lieutenant, the duke of Dorset and possibly his duchess, would 'put my cousins in a fuss, and give them very little pleasure', not because of the rank of their visitors, but because 'they are as awkward as ever at entertaining strangers'.[30] Other women were simply in no mood to entertain, even for people they knew. Lady Orrery noted glumly that if the Claytons stayed overnight at Mr Lowry's, she would have to invite them to dinner the following day. Two weeks earlier, she had positively despaired, when, in the middle of her otherwise quiet Saturday breakfast 'a Coach stoped [*sic*] at the Door, and up came Dr. Premium [*Samuel*] Madden, a tall, thin, wide mouthed Wife and two daughters, each of them fat and brown as Ma King'. Nevertheless, she put a brave face on the matter, and despite being 'ready to cry' received 'a multitude of Kisses and embraces with seeming joy', and entertained her guests for 'the intolerable length of a day from ten to five'.[31] She had that talent, which Mary Pendarves felt

26 Katherine Conolly to Bonnell, 31 July 1744 (NLI, MS 41, 578/17).
27 Delany to Dewes, 22 Oct. 1745 (*Autobiography and correspondence*, ser. 1, ii, 396).
28 Same to same, 7 Aug. 1732 (ibid., i, 368).
29 Margaret Orrery to Ld Orrery, 11 Sept. 1746 (*Orrery papers*, ii, 246).
30 Pendarves to Granville, 11 Mar. 1732 (*Autobiography and correspondence*, ser. 1, ii, 342).
31 Margaret Orrery to Ld Orrery, 11 Sept. 1746 (*Orrery papers*, ii, 246); same to same, 25 Aug.

her cousins lacked, of putting even unwelcome guests at their ease and entertaining them in a manner which seemed easy, seamless and enjoyable.

A hostess could deal with her guests in many ways. The consumption of food and drink, card playing, embroidery, tours of the house and gardens, and musical performances by the lady of the house, or perhaps her daughter, were all standard fare, even for short visits of a day or less. Lengthier trips, during which the guests stayed at the home of their hosts, opened up further possibilities. Mary Pendarves enjoyed walking and fishing expeditions, complete with picnics, with her friends during their tour of Ireland in 1732, and even attended the local Killala fair, where she had 'excellent sport' thanks to the horse races and competitions which were put on for the spectators and the birthday party for her hostess, Mrs Clayton, which rounded off the day's entertainments.[32] Each visit was a little different, depending on the number and composition of its guests, how familiar they were with their hostess and with each other, the time of day they called at and the length of time they stayed. The best hostesses knew how to choose entertainments which would suit whatever combination of guests and circumstances they were faced with, and create a pleasing, relaxed atmosphere for all.

When she was in exclusively female company, Katherine Conolly and her visitors whiled away the hours with needlework. She boasted in 1729 that she 'had set all the idle ladies at work' in 'knotting', much to the delight of their husbands and fathers, though had these men been present, doubtless other employments would have been found which were less overtly feminine.[33] This would not have been difficult, for most diversions could be adapted to both heterosocial and homosocial settings. Some, such as tours of the garden, were obviously weather-dependent, but the presence of plants and flowers to be noticed and discussed also provided prompts to the conversation which were particularly useful when dealing with unfamiliar or awkward guests. The countess of Orrery chose this measure to pass the time with the unwelcome Madden family in 1746.[34] Extensive tours of one's house were different. Heller has argued that because granting access to certain rooms indicated the degree of intimacy between host or hostess and guest, 'where a guest was entertained might inadvertently reveal the host's or hostess's opinion of him/her'. When Mary Delany allowed the Chesterfields into what she called 'her apartments' in 1745 (an area which Heller would designate as one of the 'more strictly controlled areas of the home'), as well as the drawing-room, which was the official space for entertaining, she was indicating to them the high level of importance she attached to their friendship.[35]

The quality and cost of entertainments were also loaded with meaning. Musical recitals were pleasant enough, but (assuming the hostess was competent and

1746 (ibid., 241). On the Dublin writer and philanthropist Samuel Madden, see *D.I.B.* (Madden, Samuel Molyneux ('Premium Madden') (1686–1765)). His wife was Jane Magill, of Kirkstown, County Armagh.

32 Pendarves to Granville, 12 June 1732 (*Autobiography and correspondence*, ser. 1, i, 351); same to same, 7 Aug. 1732 (ibid., 369); same to same, 13 Aug. 1732 (ibid., 372–3).

33 Katherine Conolly to Bonnell, 16 Mar. 1728/9, 27 May 1729 (NLI, MS 41, 578/4).

34 Margaret Orrery to Ld Orrery, 25 Aug. 1746 (*Orrery papers*, ii, 241).

35 Delany to Dewes, 22 Oct. 1745 (*Autobiography and correspondence*, ser. 1, ii, 396); Heller, 'Leisure and the use of domestic space', p. 640.

confident enough), they put her to little expense or trouble. Providing meals, on the other hand, showed considerable generosity, particularly if they comprised multiple courses which pushed up the price. Guests were quick to note the size and composition of the spread laid out before them, and Mrs Pendarves felt that the provision of great amounts of food for visitors was a particularly Irish trait.[36] As for beverages, coffee, taken at coffee-houses, where elite women were not welcome, was traditionally seen as a masculine drink, conducive to the perusal of the latest newspapers and the discussion of business matters. However, along with chocolate, women regularly drank it in the home and provided it for guests, suggesting a blurring of gender lines in a domestic social setting.[37] More prestigious than either, though, was tea.

Introduced to England by Charles II's queen, Catherine of Braganza, tea and the ritual of mixing and serving it, had long been associated with refinement, domesticity and, above all, elite femininity.[38] The Irish conduct writer, Wetenhall Wilkes, warned that female overindulgence in tea would have the same results as excessive alcohol consumption in men, and blamed tea for 'a lowness and hurricane of spirits, a tremor of the nerves, a coldness of stomach, many kinds of hysterics, and several distempers peculiar to your sex'.[39] By representing women as unable to 'hold their drink', yet not extending the same warning about tea to men, Wilkes promoted an idea of female physical fragility and reinforced the gender stereotypes associated with tea and alcohol. In doing so, he disguised tea's unisex appeal, for while its purchase and preparation was customarily the sole province of elite women, its consumption was not. The earl of Orrery took it with two aunts of Margaret Hamilton (his intended bride) in 1738 and, shortly afterwards, wrote to a male friend telling him that once the marriage had taken place, he hoped 'to see you at our tea table'. Years later, Margaret, now countess of Orrery, served tea to her male guests at Caledon.[40] Tea was not strictly feminine, then, for men enjoyed it too. They were simply less comfortable taking it in company if it was not served by a woman, again emphasising the importance of women within elite sociability.

Part of the reason tea held such a hallowed place within the visit was because neither it nor its associated accoutrements (which included caddies to store it in, china in which to serve it, sugar, sugar tongs and spoons) came cheap. Bohea tea was selling at the hefty price of ten shillings per pound in Dublin in 1724 (a figure which equates to over £40 in modern terms), and in 1726, Eleanor O'Hara of County Sligo spent £0 11s. 'towards the weight and for the fashion of two spoons

36 Pendarves to Granville, 12 June 1732 (*Autobiography and correspondence*, ser. 1, i, 351–2).

37 Máire Kennedy, 'Dublin's coffee houses of the eighteenth century', *Dublin Historical Record*, lxiii (2010), pp 29–38; Margaret Orrery to Ld Orrery, 20 July 1748 (*Orrery papers*, ii, 252–3).

38 Elizabeth Kowaleski-Wallace, *Consuming subjects: women, shopping, and business in the eighteenth century* (New York, 1997), pp 22–4; eadem, 'Tea, gender and domesticity in eighteenth-century England', *Studies in Eighteenth-century Culture*, xxiii (1994), pp 131–45.

39 Wetenhall Wilkes, *A letter of genteel and moral advice* … (Dublin, 1740), p. 81. Jonathan Swift was also critical of women's tea drinking: see *The journal of a Dublin lady in a letter to a person of quality* (2nd edn, Dublin, 1729), p. 6.

40 Ld Orrery to Margaret Hamilton, 23 May 1738 (*Orrery papers*, ii, 145); same to [Tom?] Southerne, 6 June 1738 (ibid., i, 238–9); Margaret Orrery to Ld Orrery, 20 July 1748 (ibid., ii, 252).

and a pair of tea tongs' and £0 6*s*. 9*d*. 'for changing a tea kettle' in Dublin.[41] This level of expenditure and the provenance of tea and its paraphernalia spoke volumes about a woman's wealth, status and good taste, and gave the beverage a heightened significance when provided in a social setting. The ability of country ladies, such as Eleanor, to purchase what they wanted and needed in Dublin, and keep up with 'the fashion', allowed them to show off to their friends at home, while the decision to share this precious commodity with an individual indicated that a hostess placed a correspondingly high value upon them, rating them as equal, if not superior, to herself. To withhold it would have indicated the opposite.

Another potentially expensive pastime which Irish hostesses enjoyed with their guests was gambling. Whist, quadrille, commerce and basset were particularly popular games among ladies in Ireland, and in many ways, cards were an ideal domestic entertainment, being dependent neither on weather nor daylight and with regular opportunities to withdraw from play provided by the end of individual games. Janet Mullin has stressed the comforting familiarity these games represented to guests, the ways in they could be chosen to complement the numbers of people present (quadrille was a game for four people, for example), and the fact that they could be enjoyed by even comparative strangers by facilitating a certain level of play-based conversation.[42] Some historians have pointed to the arguments and cheating which could arise, especially between married couples, when women were able to compete with and prevail over male family members and friends, but there is little evidence of this in Ireland.[43] If gender tensions existed, they did not prevent men and women, married and unmarried, from playing together. Lady Anne Conolly, with her husband in tow, frequently played cards late into the night among 'great crowds' at the home of his aunt, Katherine Conolly, and several of Mary Pendarves's hosts during her tour of Ireland were married couples who played with her and her travelling companions.[44] Writers such as Jonathan Swift further confirmed (and criticised) the popularity of various card games among the Irish ladies.[45] There were drawbacks for these women, though. The stakes did not always match the purse strings of those present, and the games could advertise wealth or comparative poverty, exclude or push into debt those who had not the means to keep up and establish social cliques. Perhaps bitter because her own financial limitations precluded her from matching her sister Katherine's expenditure, Mary Jones was outraged that what Mrs Conolly had frittered away at basset 'would have made a rich woman of me'. She was not the only one who viewed the amusement with disdain, reporting that Katherine's gambling 'affords the town a great deal of chat',

41 *Dublin Gazette*, 4–7 July 1724; Eleanor O'Hara's personal account book, 1722–33 (NLI, MS 36, 387/7, ff 38, 41); 'National Archives currency converter' (http://apps.nationalarchives.gov.uk/currency/results.asp#mid) (accessed 28 Sept. 2014).
42 Mullin, '"We had carding"', pp 990, 994, 996, 997, 999.
43 Linda Sturtz, 'The ladies and the lottery: elite women's gambling in eighteenth-century Virginia', *The Virginia Magazine of History and Biography: Constructing a Revolution: Women and Gender Roles in Virginia*, civ (1996), pp 171–2.
44 Mary Jones to Bonnell, 11 May [n.d., 1734?] (NLI, MS 41, 577/5); Pendarves to Granville, 25 Nov. 1731 (*Autobiography and correspondence*, ser. 1, i, 315).
45 Swift, *The journal of a Dublin lady*, pp 5–6, 12–16.

before adding with obvious relief that 'at May the act of parliament takes place and then farewell basset'.[46] Even in the face of such opposition, however, it was often elite women who propagated the games. Mrs Conolly had only set up a basset bank at her house in response to the decision of the lord lieutenant, the duke of Dorset, to ban gambling at Dublin Castle because the King did not allow it at the royal court.[47] His decision was especially ironic because up until that point the duchess had been hosting popular quadrille and basset parties.[48] Katherine proved a more effective trend-setter than the viceroy, though, and soon basset parties had 'spread over the whole town', much to Mary Jones's disgust.[49] Peer pressure was a powerful thing, however, and sucked in some who might otherwise have abstained. Playing cards was 'all the fashion and you must do so or nobody will keep you company', declared Ann Brodrick, dowager Viscountess Midleton in 1730. Perhaps this is why she caught even Mrs Jones playing in Lady Rich's drawing room. 'I thought she was wild,' wrote Ann.[50]

Party politics

For those women who were married or closely related to Ireland's prominent politicians, sociability sometimes merged with politics, for the company these ladies kept was often a good indicator of which way the political wind was blowing. Katherine Conolly's husband, William, was Speaker of the Irish House of Commons, a close ally of the duke of Grafton, and the viceroy's main undertaker (an undertaker being an Irish politician who undertook to manage the lord lieutenant's political programme for him and steer it through the Irish parliament).[51] Katherine's visits to Dublin Castle and she and Duchess Henrietta's apparent friendship suggested an air of personal harmony between the two couples, which reinforced the image of political unity their husbands sought to project. For the vicereines in general, sociability likewise provided an opportunity to advertise and hopefully further their spouses' political policies, though approaches varied. Some, like Henrietta Grafton,

46 Jones to Bonnell, 28 Feb. 1733/4 (NLI, MS 41, 577/4). This may be a reference to an act which eventually came to fruition in 1739 entitled 'For the more effectual preventing of excessive and deceitful gaming'. It banned the playing of basset, among other games (13 George II, c. 8; *Country Journal or The Craftsman*, 14 July 1739). There were several other bills passed during this period with similar aims. See, for example, a bill of 1699 entitled 'Against deceitful, disorderly and excessive gaming' and one of 1707 entitled 'For suppressing lotteries and gaming tables' (10 William III, c. 11 (1699); 6 Anne, c. 17 (1707)).

47 Jones to Bonnell, 16 Oct. [1733?] (NLI, MS 41, 577/4).

48 Pendarves to Granville, 26 Sept. 1731 (*Autobiography and correspondence*, ser. 1, i, 290).

49 Jones to Bonnell, 7 Feb. [n.d.] (NLI, MS 41, 577/4).

50 Ann, dowager Viscountess Midleton to same, 18 Mar. 1730 [/1?] (ibid., MS 41, 580/3). It is unclear who the lady was whom Ann was referring to here, although there was an English Lady Rich at this time, married to Sir Robert Rich, 4th Bt (*Oxford D.N.B.* (Rich, Sir Robert, 4th Bt (1685–1768))).

51 D.W. Hayton, 'The beginnings of the "Undertaker System"' in Thomas Bartlett and D.W. Hayton (eds), *Penal era and Golden age: essays in Irish history 1690–1800* (Belfast, 1979), p. 32; *Oxford D.N.B.* (Conolly, William (1662–1729)).

strove for an air of exclusivity at the Castle by socialising with women identified with a particular party or politician, despite the fact that it could irritate those who were not in the inner circle. Others, like Frances, Lady Carteret, who was vicereine between 1724 and 1730, sought to make their residence a neutral ground by attracting and interacting with women whose menfolk came from all political persuasions.[52]

The role and value of a woman as a socio-political consort was even more overt when they hosted with or for their husbands. Lady Midleton was remembered as an excellent hostess who kept the finest table in Dublin during her marriage to Lord Midleton. The monotony of life at Kilkenny Castle was temporarily broken for Mary Butler, duchess of Ormond, in August 1698, when she 'sumptuously entertained' Henri de Massue, earl of Galway and Charles Paulet, marquis of Winchester, while they were making their rounds of Ireland in their capacity as lord justices.[53] By creating an inviting, yet suitably grand, atmosphere at their homes, these women made them attractive social venues which impressed visitors, including their husbands' fellow politicians. This then facilitated the men's political careers, while allowing their wives to show off their abilities as hostesses to maximum advantage and prove their suitability as partners for Ireland's leading politicians. In Mary's case, she also stood for her husband and the entire house of Ormond, reinforcing the Butlers' position as Ireland's premier family, with whom passing dignitaries stopped and stayed and paid their respects (Galway and Winchester obviously not being put off by her rank). More unusual was the widowed Katherine Conolly. Thanks to the wealth and connexions her husband left her with, she continued to attract political visitors to her homes, even after his death in 1729. Despite a comparatively cool relationship with her, probably not helped by her in-house casino, the duke and duchess of Dorset dined with her in Dublin in 1734. Five years later, their successors as lord lieutenant and vicereine, William and Catherine Cavendish, duke and duchess of Devonshire, came to Castletown for Christmas, along with twenty other guests, leading Katherine to report that she had 'had the government and a 100 more at the holidays with me'.[54]

On its own, this evidence would suggest a salon culture similar to that uncovered among eighteenth- and nineteenth-century English women, whose gatherings Irish politicians found especially useful to help them integrate into the English political world.[55] However, similarities notwithstanding, the situation was not replicated in Ireland. The activities of vicereines like Lady Carteret, as described above, were the

52 Wilson, 'The vicereines of Ireland', pp 17–21.

53 William, Baron Castle-Durrow to Swift, 11 Jan. 1736/7 (*The correspondence of Jonathan Swift, D.D.*, ed. David Woolley (4 vols, Dublin, 1999–2007), iv, 383); Charles Smith, *The ancient and present state of the county and city of Cork …* (2 vols, 2nd edn, Dublin, 1774), ii, 226.

54 Katherine Conolly to Bonnell, 30 Apr. 1734 (NLI, MS 41, 578/7); Jones to same, 15 Dec. [1739] (ibid., MS 41, 577/1); Katherine Conolly to same, 15 Jan. 1739/40 (ibid., MS 41, 578/13).

55 Sarah Richardson, '"Well-neighboured houses": the political networks of elite women, 1780–1860' in Kathryn Gleadle and eadem (eds), *Women in British politics, 1760–1860: the power of the petticoat* (London, 2000), pp 56–73; Jupp, 'The roles of royal and aristocratic women', pp 109–10; K.D. Reynolds, *Aristocratic women and political society in Victorian Britain* (Oxford, 1998), pp 170, 176.

closest thing to such salons that the Irish might have seen; however, these were only briefly and very intermittently available, and predominantly run by English women whose position as the wives of the lords lieutenant made them unique in the Irish political system. They did not mimic or inspire a general pattern in Ireland, and in fact it has been argued by Judith Lewis that owing to their time-consuming nature, the duties of being a political patroness and a society hostess made each mutually exclusive.[56] This issue would only have been one of several at play in Ireland, for few among the resident female elite had the money, inclinations or connexions to establish salons, particularly as the focus and attendance of many politicians was split between Ireland and England, creating little demand for them at home. One woman who did have the necessary tools was Katherine Conolly, but she did not make the leap from society to political hostess. Her parties were too irregular and boisterous to allow for serious political discussions, and the guest list was usually too exclusive, with only the viceroy and vicereine in attendance, or not exclusive enough, with hordes of neighbours flooding the house. There is little evidence that she discussed politics with her guests or they with each other. Her husband and the visiting viceroys undoubtedly used the opportunity to discuss business, but Mrs Conolly, despite an obvious interest in politics, did not seem to feel it was the place of wives to discuss such matters with their visitors, or that they would they thank her for so obviously mixing business and pleasure, a view she continued to hold in her widowhood. Socialising was, at best, a way of staying on friendly terms with potential allies.

Having a ball

Along with visits, some of the most popular group activities ladies indulged in were balls, ridottos and assemblies. Balls are the most straightforward to classify, being formal events, attended by invitation only, typically free to the attendees and consisting of dancing and food. They were a favourite way in which to celebrate royal birthdays and state anniversaries, especially at Dublin Castle, though, by the 1720s, the vicereines were ensuring that balls were also held there once a week in an effort to popularise themselves and their husbands.[57] Away from the Castle, they were also held in 'normal' domestic residences (those that did not double as government buildings) and in rural areas, the smaller population meant that organisers were prepared to cast the net a little wider in terms of the type of person they would invite into their homes. Mary Mason wrote from Waterford in early 1738 that 'Mr Bolton gave a very handsome ball a Monday night: 33 ladies, all the officers were invited and were there'.[58] Soldiers, even officers, were not generally found at city balls, where it was easier to muster up the required numbers from among the

[56] Mary O'Dowd agrees that this salon culture did not materialise in Ireland. See *A history of women in Ireland, 1500–1800* (Harlow, 2004), p. 46. For more on the vicereines, see Wilson, 'The vicereines of Ireland', pp 3–28; Lewis, *Sacred to female patriotism*, pp 100–1.

[57] Wilson, 'The vicereines of Ireland', pp 20–7.

[58] Mary Mason to John Mason, 4 Jan. 1737/8 (PRONI, T3131/B/1/47).

elite, but in the provinces they could be accommodated without provoking negative comments. Female attendance was not limited to those of a particular age or marital group, and wives could partake even if their spouses were not with them. Margaret Savage wrote to tell her husband, who was then in Dublin, of the 'very elegant ball' she had recently attended in Portaferry, County Down, organised by the Chancellor (most likely the Chancellor of Down).[59]

The term 'ridotto' described a type of subscription ball. These appeared in England in 1722, and by 1731 had made their way to Dublin, spreading within six years as far afield as Counties Mayo and Londonderry.[60] They were usually held in a theatre or music hall and, like the classic balls described above, they offered dancing and food. The cost of tickets ensured that only the elite could afford to attend, and prices were particularly favourable to ladies. A typical subscription offered tickets for one man and three women at a price of two guineas, while single tickets could be purchased for half a guinea for a man, or a British crown for a lady.[61] This gender distinction was for the sake of politeness, according to Mary Pendarves, and existed from the first ridotto in December 1731.[62] That event ran from nine at night until four the next morning, and drew a great crowd of 'all persons of distinction' who were 'very much delighted with this diversion'.[63] Mary did not attend, but was present at another just two weeks later, though she was not 'much delighted' with it, writing:

> I like it the least of any diversion I have seen here. There was a vast deal of company, two rooms of dancers; above 20 couple in each room. I danced with Mr. Usher 2 dances, and had like to have been torn limb from limb; the Duke of Dorset was there, and [*his daughter*] Lady Caroline Sackville; the Duchess is very ill of a fever. We staid till 12 o'clock.[64]

Mary may have been unimpressed, but ridottos succeeded in attracting a great number of women, including the vicereine and her daughter, and Mrs Pendarves was in the minority in her objections. In their boisterous nature, though, they were better suited to the young, something Mary acknowledged when she said that she and her friend had attended 'with a whole train of young things at our heels'.[65] The duchess was known for her retiring temperament and likely went only to satisfy the demands placed upon her as vicereine by gracing Irish society with her presence.[66]

59 Margaret Savage to Andrew Savage, [n.d., 1738–40] (ibid., D552/A/2/9/13). For a comparison to the balls of the American elite at this time, see Cynthia Kierner, 'Genteel balls and Republican parades: gender and early civic rituals, 1677–1826', *The Virginia magazine of history and biography: Constructing a Revolution: Women and Gender Roles in Virginia*, civ (1996), pp 185–210.
60 *Freeholder's Journal*, 21 Feb. 1722; *Universal Spectator*, 13 Mar. 1731; *Daily Post*, 18 Dec. 1731; *London Daily Post*, 31 Aug. 1736; *Daily Gazetteer*, 22 Jan. 1737.
61 *Faulkner's Dublin Journal*, 11–15 Nov. 1746.
62 Pendarves to Granville, 4 Dec. 1731 (*Autobiography and correspondence*, ser. 1, i, 325–6).
63 *Daily Post*, 18 Dec. 1731.
64 Pendarves to Granville, 14 Dec. 1731 (*Autobiography and correspondence*, ser. 1, i, 332).
65 Ibid.
66 Same to same, 26 Sept. 1731 (ibid., 290).

Assemblies were less formal again. They also had dancing and food, but might mix these with card playing and musical recitals. Some were held in homes, with set guest lists and at the expense of the host or hostess, others took place in the purpose-built assembly rooms which sprang up, even in smaller towns, over the course of the early Hanoverian period. These were publicly owned buildings with a steward to manage the entertainments. Assemblies there were attended by ticket holders and run on a specific schedule, which could be as busy or quiet as the local elite population wanted. By 1738, Belfast had 'a very handsome Town House' with 'a fine room over it' which, when not playing host to the local merchants' meetings, was used for a fortnightly assembly 'where you shall see a fine appearance of ladies and gentlemen, so trade don't always spoil politeness'.[67] Though men attended, all evidence points to assemblies being more readily designed for and associated with women. They were usually arranged by one or two women, and advertisements for the weekly assemblies of Mrs Walker, or the team of Mrs Rice and Mrs Hamilton, became permanent fixtures in the Dublin newspapers of the 1740s. Tickets could be purchased at the door, as opposed to in advance, but, like ridottos, ladies were charged less than men – one shilling per woman for Mrs Rice's assembly, half a crown for a gentleman.[68] Success was judged on how many ladies attended; '29 ladies at the assembly Thursday last', reported Mary Mason from Waterford, but no mention of the number of men.[69] These events were considerably more entertaining and less stuffy than those held in Scotland, where they were managed by lady directresses (further confirmation of their feminine tint) and plagued by 'taciturn stiffness and despondent formality'.[70]

The arrangements surrounding domestic assemblies also suggest a distinctly feminine air (yet another reason why turning them into political salons would have been impractical). Mrs Pendarves often talked of attending an assembly at a lady's house, rather than at a man's and the gender composition of the company was frequently skewed towards women; 'Yesterday Mrs. Clayton had an Assembly', she wrote in 1733, 'a great many ladies, few gentlemen'.[71] The vicereines generally referred to their gatherings in Dublin Castle as 'drawing rooms' rather than assemblies, but while the space and terminology used implies a visit, the regularity with which these gatherings were held, their nighttime slots and the numbers in attendance, indicate an assembly. Comments made by one young woman in the 1720s confirm that they were intended for the young and the female, and were very popular among this demographic: 'Lady Carteret has disappointed the ladies mightily for the chicken pox confined her [*a*] month and last week her ladyship miscarried so that we young folks are threatened with the terrible apprehension of having no more drawing room this winter.'[72] Mary Pendarves's description of one of the duchess of Dorset's drawing rooms in 1731 likewise hints at a predominantly female presence, as well as offering some clues as to how the time was passed:

67 T.G.F. Paterson, 'Belfast in 1738', *Ulster Journal of Archaeology*, ii (1939), p. 112.
68 *Faulkner's Dublin Journal*, 15–19 July 1746.
69 Mary Mason to John Mason, 26 Nov. 1737 (PRONI, T3131/B/1/27).
70 Glover, *Elite women and polite society*, p. 90.
71 Pendarves to Granville, 4 Jan. 1732/3 (*Autobiography and correspondence*, ser. 1, i, 392).
72 Sarah Worth to Bonnell, 11 Dec. [n.d., 1729?] (NLI, MS 41, 580/27).

> there is placed a basset table, at which the Duchess of Dorset sits down after she has received and made her compliments to the company. It is very seldom any ladies sit down to basset, but quadrille parties are made in the other rooms, and such idle ones as I saunter up and down, or pick up some acquaintance to chat with.[73]

There is no explanation given as to why assemblies (and ridottos) were more readily associated with women than men, but several reasons suggest themselves. Women had an edge as organisers and hostesses thanks to the social training they had received as young girls, and it could be argued that their responsibilities for decorating and showing off their homes made them more interested in attending and throwing domestic assemblies in order to research new ideas and display their own good taste and innovations. If gender stereotypes already existed around domestic functions, it would not have been much of a leap for them to become associated with subscription events. On a more practical note, men were more likely to be absent from their local area for extended periods of time, attending business in Dublin or England, or checking on far-flung Irish estates.

Beyond the obvious opportunities to eat, dance and make merry, balls, ridottos and assemblies served several other functions for women. To attend, especially at an invitation-only event, showed a woman's membership of the elite, though some took the opportunity for personal aggrandisement further. At a ball thrown by William Stewart, Viscount Mountjoy, for the duke and duchess of Dorset, Katherine Clayton refrained from dancing, declaring that it was 'beneath the dignity of a Bishop's wife to dance'.[74] By establishing this separate code of behaviour for herself and basing it on her social status, Katherine was making a striking statement about her own perceived self-importance. She was there to preside, not perform. She must have been delighted that the only other woman to abstain and with whom she could therefore be compared, was the duchess herself, who cited a headache (though given the regularity with which illness struck down Elizabeth Dorset at times when she might have been called upon to dance, it seems more likely that she too felt it was beneath her dignity to do so, but did not wish to cause offence by admitting the fact, particularly at a ball thrown in her honour). For others, the opportunity to dance was the main attraction and the best way to garner attention. The same Miss Wesley who had delighted Mary Pendarves with her skills as a hostess likewise impressed her as 'much the best dancer' at a Castle ball in 1731.[75] Dancing could be tiresome and even painful, though, if one's partner was not skilled in the art. At a ball in 1731, Mary complained of being lumbered with 'Captain Folliat, a man six foot odd inches high, black, awkward, ramping, roaring, &c. I thought he would have shook my arms off, and crushed my toes to atoms, every moment he did some blundering thing, and as often asked "my ladyship's pardon".'[76] Five days later she declared that she had lost interest in dancing at the Castle, not out of concern for her toes, or affectations of grandeur, but because it was 'so intolerably crowded'. She was much happier watching and judging the behaviour of the other attendees

73 Pendarves to Granville, 26 Sept. 1731 (*Autobiography and correspondence*, ser. 1, i, 290).
74 Same to same, 25 Nov. 1731 (ibid., 317).
75 Same to same, 16 Nov. 1731 (ibid., 312).
76 Same to same, 4 Dec. 1731 (ibid., 324).

with her friends. On one evening, they got 'a very snug seat in the ball-room, and made ourselves very merry with some good figures that exposed themselves there'.[77] Sometimes it was better to observe the show than to show off (though Mrs Clayton and the duchess of Dorset achieved both simultaneously).

Social events were an opportunity for women to display their clothes, as much as their home or dancing skills, and for women, society and fashion often intersected with politics thanks to intermittent crazes to wear clothing of Irish manufacture only. Officially, these patriotic trends were in objection to the export bans imposed from London, which forbade local manufacturers from selling their wares outside Ireland. Unofficially, some women must have complied simply to fit in with their peers.[78] The wives of lords lieutenant made special efforts to encourage the wearing of Irish dresses at Castle events. Lady Elizabeth Germain, a cousin of the duke of Dorset, was glad to hear from Jonathan Swift of the duchess 'being dressed in your manufacture' at the birthday celebrations for George II in 1731, commenting that 'if your ladies will follow her example in all things, they cannot do amiss'.[79] Given that the vicereines were usually English and in Ireland only temporarily, their reasons for supporting this campaign can hardly be attributed to a strong sense of Irish patriotism. More likely, they sought to increase their own and their husbands' popularity, safe in the knowledge that the brevity of their stay and the fact that their efforts extended only to elite women and to Dublin, meant that their actions had only a minimal effect. Helen Burke has even suggested that they acted this way to undercut genuine Irish patriotism and reduce it to 'a purely benevolent gesture of concern for the poor'.[80] This may have been unnecessary, though. Reinforcing patriotism through clothing away from the Castle and in the vicereines' absence was difficult. Even when 'all Irish' was in vogue, the trend could pass as quickly as it had appeared. As Jane Bonnell's cousin, Jane Bulkeley, wrote, 'the ladies, you may know, are given to change'.[81] Even when the vicereines were available to act as a focal point, there were further problems, for in their rush to suit the fashions, many ladies neglected to pay their clothing bills, completely defeating the point of the exercise by leaving the native manufacturers even worse off than before.[82]

The performance arts

Visits, balls and assemblies relied heavily upon the interaction of the attendees through conversation and dance in order to be successful. Other diversions functioned on the premise that there would be a much clearer distinction between

77 Same to same, 9 Dec. 1731 (ibid., 328).

78 For the export ban, see 10 & 11 Will. III, c. 10 [Eng.] (4 May 1699). See also Helen Burke, 'Putting on Irish "stuff": the politics of Anglo-Irish cross-dressing' in Jessica Munns and Penny Richards (eds), *The clothes that wear us: essays on dressing and transgressing in eighteenth-century culture* (London, 1999), pp 233–49.

79 Lady Elizabeth Germain to Swift, 4 Nov. 1731 (*Correspondence of Jonathan Swift*, iii, 442).

80 Burke, 'Putting on Irish "stuff"', p. 246.

81 Jane Bulkeley to Bonnell, 4 Apr. 1721 (NLI, MS 41, 580/4).

82 Katherine Conolly to same, 3 Nov. 1731 (ibid., MS 41, 578/6).

entertainers and entertained. Some of these were little more than occasional indulgences or passing novelties. There were puppet shows and rope dancing, for instance, the latter being initiated by the performer, Madam Violante, who came to Ireland in 1729 and remained until 1732.[83] Lady Midleton called this 'one of our chief entertainments', and Mary Pendarves made a point of going to see it with her friends.[84] When the novelties had passed though, there were other amusements to fall back on which had much greater longevity.

Private plays had been performed in Ireland for centuries, and in the 1630s, Dublin gained its first theatre in Werburgh Street, on the orders of the then lord deputy of Ireland, Lord Wentworth. This was closed during the Civil War period, never to reopen, but was replaced after the Restoration by the new Theatre Royal in Smock Alley, joined in the 1730s by another theatre in Aungier Street.[85] The repertoires of both venues were repetitive, but the Irish theatres had greater freedom than the English, where licensing laws introduced in the 1730s forbade anti-government plays.[86] They also hosted musical performances, though as time wore on other venues were constructed for these, including Mr Johnston's 'Great Room' in Crow Street, built in 1731 and the Great Hall in Fishamble Street, erected a decade later. There were even open-air performances in parks such as St Stephen's Green.[87] Mary Pendarves hoped for some operatic entertainments in 1731, but these hopes came to nothing and plays and concerts remained more popular.[88] In compiling programmes, managers and organisers often followed the lead set by their London counterparts; however, they also staged shows which were not to be found in England that year, and it was in Dublin that the first performance of Handel's *Messiah* was staged in 1742. Thus, the entertainments on offer to the Irish were similar, but slightly different and at times superior, to those experienced in England and are best described as Anglo-Irish.[89]

The theatre was slower to appear in rural areas, but by the 1730s travelling companies of actors regularly went beyond Dublin, and the elite of Londonderry were delighted in 1737 by a group of comedians visiting from the capital.[90] By the middle of the century, Cork, Waterford and Belfast all had their own playhouses, though this did not stop the practice of staging plays in other venues, and they continued to be available in the homes of the elite, at Dublin Castle and in other

83 Pendarves to Granville, 9 Dec. 1731 (*Autobiography and correspondence*, ser. 1, i, 328); Grainne McArdle, 'Signora Violante and her troupe of dancers 1729–32', *Eighteenth-Century Ireland*, xx (2005), pp 55–78; *Oxford D.N.B.* (Violante [Larini], Signora (1682–1741)).

84 Midleton to Bonnell, 18 Mar. 1730 [/1?] (NLI, MS 41, 580/3); Pendarves to Granville, 4 Nov. 1731 (*Autobiography and correspondence*, ser. 1, i, 309).

85 Christopher Morash, *A history of Irish theatre, 1601–2000* (Cambridge, 2002), pp 3–14, 42.

86 John Greene, 'The repertory of the Dublin theatres, 1720–1745', *Eighteenth-Century Ireland*, ii (1987), p. 147.

87 Brian Boydell, 'Venues for music in 18th century Dublin', *Dublin Historical Record*, xxix (1975), p. 29.

88 Pendarves to Granville, 4 Dec. 1731 (*Autobiography and correspondence*, ser. 1, i, 325).

89 *Faulkner's Dublin Journal*, 31 Dec. 1745–4 Jan. 1746; ibid., 25–28 Jan. 1746; Boydell, 'Venues for music', pp 29–30; Greene, 'The repertory of the Dublin theatres', p. 147.

90 *Daily Gazetteer*, 22 Jan. 1737. See also Lisa Meaney, 'Civic society in eighteenth-century Ulster, c.1740–1780' (Queen's University Belfast, Ph.D. thesis, 2011).

publicly owned buildings.[91] They were often acted by and for a select group of people from among the upper orders, sometimes with the help of servants, while those which took place in homes overlapped and merged with the practice of making visits and blurred the lines between participant and observer. Some were styled as masquerades, and Lord George Sackville, son of the duke of Dorset, delighted onlookers in 1733 when he dressed up in women's clothes as part of the entertainment and 'played his part very archly'.[92] The distraction these self-produced plays provided for women (and men) was particularly welcome in the country, supplying, as they did, a break from the tedium which extended periods of remote rural life could cause. The design and construction of stages and costumes, and the rehearsals needed, could occupy several weeks before the actual performance. When the time came, it could be stretched into an entire day or weekend, with the performance bookended by dinners and dancing.[93]

Elite productions created equal excitement in Dublin, where women were also at the heart of action as performers, ticket sellers and audience members. Mary Pendarves wrote of a performance she was looking forward to in 1733, which was to feature Lord Molesworth's daughter in the leading role and take place in the council chamber. Each of the actors and actresses had twelve tickets to sell, in addition to which 'all the Bishops, Judges, and Privy Counsellors are to be there'. With so many of Dublin's male elite already invited, it was the women among whom the play created the real buzz, for the ability to secure a place at this exclusive event depended upon one's social connexions, and failure would be humiliating. Mary had nothing to worry about, bragging that one of the actors, Lord Mountjoy, with whom she was friendly, 'brought us all tickets last night, so we are happy', but, she added, 'half the girls in town are trembling for fear they should not be admitted'.[94] As Mary's letter hints, though they were open to all who could afford tickets, the performance arts, like ridottos and assemblies, had particularly strong connexions with elite femininity. This is unsurprising given the importance accorded to music within female education and the perceived value of theatrical performances given by touring English companies in honing an Irish lady's accent. At state events in Dublin, plays were also ordered by the viceroy specifically 'for the entertainment of the ladies', as though men's attendance was either non-existent, or at best, an afterthought.[95]

Enjoyment of the performance was only one incentive to attend, and not necessarily the most important if one was seeing a repeat production. The theatre was the perfect space for ladies to broadcast their wealth, importance and politics. The wealthiest could afford to send servants early in the day to save their places, and, thanks to staggered ticket prices and separate doors for differently priced seats,

[91] Raymond Gillespie, 'Music and song in early eighteenth-century Belfast' in idem and R.F. Foster (eds), *Irish provincial cultures in the long eighteenth-century: making the middle sort. Essays for Toby Barnard* (Dublin, 2012), p. 155.

[92] Pendarves to Granville, 4 Jan. 1732/3 (*Autobiography and correspondence*, ser. 1, i, 393–4).

[93] Patricia McCarthy, 'Private theatricals in Irish houses, 1730 to 1815', *Irish Architectural and Decorative Studies: the Journal of the Irish Georgian Society*, xiv (2013), p. 41.

[94] Pendarves to Granville, 4 Jan. 1732/3 (*Autobiography and correspondence*, ser. 1, i, 392).

[95] See, for example, *Dublin Gazette*, 2–6 Mar. 1725.

auditoriums were an 'at a glance' visual representation of Dublin's social hierarchy; where you sat in one, showed where you sat in the other.[96] Just like at balls, female fashion played a part as well. In an incident in Smock Alley in November 1712 (a Williamite anniversary) a Mr Dudley Moore read out a pro-Williamite prologue which had been banned by the Tory government. It immediately led to a violent riot, in which even the elite women in the audience took part, as 'ladies wearing orange ribbons [*in favour of William*] cheered and ladies wearing red roses [*in favour of the Jacobites*] hissed'. As swords were drawn and a brawl began, though, there was 'an indecorous exodus of silk and taffeta from the boxes'.[97]

With such antics going on offstage, watching the audience could be as interesting and informative as watching the play, and both provided topics of conversation for domestic visits and letters as different forms of sociability dovetailed. Ann, Lady Midleton, though not present in the playhouse on any of the relevant occasions, reported to Jane Bonnell that Jane's sister, Mary Jones, had attended three plays in Dublin in 1730, her presence having obviously aroused enough interest for the information to make its way back to Ann each time.[98] Though such anecdotes seem insignificant, they are representative of a more important movement within elite female sociability. The shared experiences of watching and discussing the goings on in the theatre, both on and off the stage, brought elite ladies together, underpinning their personal and social bonds and fostering a sense of group identity and cohesion.

Though the theatre was a diversion for the masses, whatever their rank or gender, it was the elite female clientele who were catered to with the greatest fervour by managers and whose enjoyment and continued patronage was their main preoccupation. When there was a push in the 1740s to keep elite males from the audience off the stage (their presence having previously been a common occurrence), the ladies were still allowed on and special boxes were sometimes constructed there for their use.[99] The actors also did their bit to indulge these women, and Mary Jones was delighted to be mistaken for Lady Rich at one production, 'and attended as such by one of the top players who paid her all the honours he could'.[100] Other measures taken to cater to their whims and comfort included asking audience members to keep their servants outside the 'Great Room' in Smock Alley in 1745, because 'several ladies have complained of the inconvenience of footmen standing in the Great Room with lighted flambeaux'.[101] Even pre-show announcements which criticised wealthy female spectators also confirmed their importance. 'The ladies are requested to be at the house between six and seven for the play will begin exactly at that time', read one newspaper notice, the insinuation being that the ladies were the most likely to be late, but also that the play would not start without them.[102]

96 Swift to Knightley Chetwood, 21 June 1715 (*Correspondence of Jonathan Swift*, ii, 129–30); *Faulkner's Dublin Journal*, 7–11 May 1745.

97 Morash, *A history of Irish theatre*, p. 30.

98 Midleton to Bonnell, 18 Mar. 1730 [/1?] (NLI, MS 41, 580/3).

99 *Faulkner's Dublin Journal*, 5–8 Apr. 1746.

100 Midleton to Bonnell, 18 Mar. 1730 [/1?] (NLI, MS 41, 580/3).

101 *Faulkner's Dublin Journal*, 21–24 Dec. 1745.

102 Ibid., 21–25 Jan. 1746.

This is easily understood for those whose seats were on the stage, but the language used was all-inclusive, covering even those women who were seated in offstage boxes, easily accessible without having to wade through the crowd or the actors. It was their presence within the theatre that mattered, not where they were sitting. If they had not yet arrived, the whole house could be made to wait for them.

A similar fuss was made of such women at musical performances. In 1746, the then vicereine, Lady Chesterfield, held sufficient sway to have a musical production postponed when she was too ill to attend, and some performances were begun and finished early enough to suit 'the ladies who go to the Castle', allowing different amusements to be woven together to create a seemingly non-stop round of entertainments for Irish ladies.[103] It was also standard practice to offer elite women reduced ticket prices or even free entry (especially to open air concerts) to encourage them to attend. This was despite the fact that at indoor performances, more women often meant a smaller audience overall, for the sheer size of their dresses put limits upon audience numbers, and occasionally led to requests that they forbear wearing hoops to free up space for more people at charity performances.[104] Finally, 'Ladies of quality' were frequently allowed to request certain plays or concerts, a fact which organisers were only too happy to advertise, presumably because it also spoke to the calibre of their audiences and the quality of their acting or playing. Appeals were also made for particular productions from 'persons of quality', but 'gentlemen' were rarely mentioned, with the exception of the predominantly English viceroys, whose job it was to promote Irish culture.[105]

A supposed interest in the performance arts on the part of ladies can only partially explain the lengths to which managers and performers went to target elite women for special treatment, especially when it was so often at the expense of men (quite literally in the case of ticket prices). With more leisure time than gentlemen and more money than the lower orders, they could afford to attend plays and musical performances more often, sit in the expensive seats and build up a rapport with the managers, players or musicians. This made them valuable patronesses. Katherine Conolly was rumoured to have given the actress Kitty Clive 'a diamond ring and 10 guineas when she went to one of her plays', and gifted Handel ten guineas in 1742, only to then miss the performance.[106] The demands placed upon elite women by politeness also helped to ensure that they would be a respectful audience and encourage the men around them to be the same, while overlaps between female philanthropy and the performance arts were good for business. Benefit performances for individuals or institutions were an increasingly common occurrence and one with which women were inextricably linked as organisers and attendees, even when their frequency meant they became expensive and tedious. Mary Pendarves wished after one particularly bad performance that 'people would be contented with one's money, and not insist on one's presence it is hard to sacrifice three hours to

[103] Ibid., 25–28 Jan., 8–11 Feb. 1746.
[104] Boydell, 'Venues for music', p. 33.
[105] John Greene and Gladys Clark, *The Dublin stage 1720–1745: a calendar of plays, entertainments, and afterpieces* (London, 1993), *passim*.
[106] Jones to Bonnell, 27 Oct. [n.d., 1734–42] (NLI, MS 41, 577/5); same to same, 28 May [1742?] (ibid.).

nonsense wilfully', while Katherine Conolly complained from the capital in 1745 that 'here is such charity plays to be that I am broke with them'.[107] Even if managers and actors took a smaller cut from the box office takings on these nights, they were still provided with additional opportunities to show off their talents, forge links with wealthy patronesses who might hire them for private productions and attract audiences to future performances.

Conclusion

Ireland had much to offer its female elite by way of entertainment during this period. Visits permeated polite society at all levels and in all areas, forming a complex social web, at the centre of which, as hostesses and guests, were women. As some of the older inhibitions surrounding rank fell by the wayside, ladies broadened their social circle to include those from a wider (though always gentle) range of backgrounds, enjoying domestic entertainments including tea drinking and card playing together. Beyond the domestic, the capital, with its theatres, music halls and Dublin Castle, was the epicentre of the elite's social world, and by the 1730s even the provinces could hold their own as sites of sociability and pleasure, able to provide plays, musical recitals, balls, ridottos and assemblies. Commercialised entertainments were more often than not designed with women in mind, with lower ticket prices and preferential treatment from event organisers to entice them to attend and patronise venues and performers. The common link between all entertainments, though, was not the provision of amusement (for women were often decidedly underwhelmed by the events they hosted or attended), but the opportunities provided to see and be seen. Every visit could be used to forge or strengthen interpersonal connexions and show off wealth, good manners and taste. Every seat in Smock Alley displayed its occupant's status, and every time a lady deigned to dance (or not) she made a statement about her self-image and her place in the world. A dress could be political, a cup of tea a sign of favour, the room it was drunk in an insult or a compliment. From the people she interacted with, to the amusements she partook in and the money she spent on them, a lady's social life told an onlooker much more about her than her interests. It spoke to her wealth, her status, her opinion of herself and her guests and her personality. Most of all, it told them that she was part of that most of exalted of social groups, the elite.

107 Katherine Conolly to Lady Anne Conolly, 20 Apr. 1745 (IAA, MS A/9); Pendarves to Granville, [n.d., c. Mar. 1733] (*Autobiography and correspondence*, ser. 1, i, 402).

6

Political players

On 7 June 1690, three weeks before the Battle of the Boyne (which was fought on 1 July in the Old Style calendar), John Skeffington, 2nd Viscount Massereene, wrote to Ireland from London to report the latest intelligence received concerning the activities of James II, his supporters and the war effort; this information was to be passed on to King William. Sandwiched between news about battle preparations and warnings about possible attempts on William's life, he related the following:

> the Irish have women who daily procure intelligence and bring an account to King James of the state of the Duke of Schomberg's army and its motions, particularly one Mrs Stafford of Dublin wife to Mr Stafford in the county of Antrim and daughter to Sir James MacDonnell [*2nd Bt*], who employs servants daily for that purpose by means of her former residence in the county of Antrim at a place called Portglenone.[1]

The woman named by Lord Massereene was Sarah Stafford, wife of Francis Stafford of Clonwen. As a direct descendant of Hugh O'Neill, earl of Tyrone, she was connected to one of Ireland's most famous families.[2] She was also, as this letter shows, running a ring of pro-Jacobite informants in the midst of one of the most politically tumultuous periods of Irish history. Nor was she alone, being only one among many women doing the same thing. To be in contact with James and spoken of to William, they must have been serious political players, and Massereene's description of Sarah's activities shows why. She was well organised, well enough financed to hire employees to do her bidding and in control of a news network which was growing by the day and feeding her apparently accurate information on the forces and troop movements of the Williamite general, Friedrich Schomberg, duke of Schomberg. She, and other ladies like her, posed a real threat to the Williamite cause and, despite the fact that her natal family were also highly political (Massereene also reported that 'one MacDonnell [*perhaps a brother of Sarah's?*] without all doubt is sent from the late King James to the highlands of Scotland to stir up new trouble in those parts'), there is no hint that she was being used as an unwilling pawn. She and her comrades were credited as dangers to William in their own right.

Of course, one could argue that the events surrounding the Battle of the Boyne constituted exceptional circumstances, a time when the normal rules did not apply and when women found themselves pulled into politics, from which they

1 John, Viscount Massereene to —, 7 June 1690 (NLI, MS 36, 027).

2 John Burke and Sir Bernard Burke, *A genealogical and heraldic history of the extinct and dormant baronetcies of England, Ireland, and Scotland* (2nd edn, London, 1841), p. 610. Sarah Stafford's paternal grandmother, Evelyn Magennis, was the daughter of Lady Sarah O'Neill, who was Tyrone's daughter.

customarily abstained; however, this chapter will show that such was not the case. Even in times of peace, elite women did not stand on the political sidelines. Throughout the period they influenced politics, and politics influenced them. Events like the Glorious Revolution merely gave them greater scope to act and brought their activities into sharper focus.

The historiography of the political participation of elite women in the late seventeenth- and eighteenth-centuries has come a long way in the past twenty years, though work has focused primarily on the English experience. Interest was initially confined to the royal family, particularly queens and princesses of Wales, but now also includes royal favourites, such as Sarah, duchess of Marlborough, and Queen Caroline's confidante, Charlotte Clayton, Viscountess Sundon. Royal mistresses have also proved a popular subject, from the many enjoyed by Charles II, to Melusine von der Schulenburg, paramour and possibly morganatic wife of George I.[3] Female courtiers have also received their fair share of attention, especially the queens' ladies in waiting, for, as one historian has put it, 'women's court places, no less than men's, held a political significance that was widely recognised'.[4]

For those seeking to understand the political roles of ladies not tied to the court, the scholarship for this period is thinner on the ground, although the work of Lois Schowerer and Rachel Weil on women's involvement in the Glorious Revolution and its aftermath makes an excellent starting point.[5] The literature on such women is much stronger for the later eighteenth and the nineteenth centuries, and can only be outlined here. In essence, scholars have shown that there were a number of political outlets available to ladies, outlets which have been grouped together by Elaine Chalus and Fiona Montgomery under the headings of 'social politics, patronage, and electoral politics'.[6] These roles have been explored through

3 The following is merely a sample of this extensive historiography: Hester Chapman, *Mary II, queen of England* (Bath, 1972); Tony Claydon and W.A. Speck, *William and Mary* (Oxford, 2007); Anne Somerset, *Queen Anne: the politics of passion* (London, 2012); Peter Quennell, *Caroline of England: an Augustan portrait* (London, 1939); Christine Gerrard, 'Queens-in-waiting: Caroline of Anspach and Augusta of Saxe-Gotha as Princesses of Wales' in Clarissa Campbell Orr (ed.), *Queenship in Britain 1660–1837: royal patronage, court culture and dynastic politics* (Manchester, 2002), pp 143–61; Frances Harris, *A passion for government: the life of Sarah, duchess of Marlborough* (Oxford, 1991); Sonya Wynne, *The mistresses of Charles II and Restoration court politics, 1660–1685* (Cambridge, 1997).

4 Ingrid Tague, *Women of quality: accepting and contesting ideals of femininity in England, 1690–1760* (Woodbridge, 2002), p. 204. See also Susan Jenkins, 'Lady Burlington at court' in Edward Corp (ed.), *Lord Burlington – the man and his politics: questions of loyalty* (New York, 1998), pp 149–79; Helen Payne, 'Aristocratic women, power, patronage and family networks at the Jacobean court, 1603–1625' in James Daybell (ed.), *Women and politics in early modern England, 1450–1700* (Aldershot, 2004), pp 164–80; Elaine Chalus and Fiona Montgomery, 'Women and politics' in Hannah Barker and Chalus (eds), *Women's history: Britain, 1700–1850* (New York, 2005), pp 223–4.

5 Lois Schwoerer, 'Women and the Glorious Revolution', *Albion*, xviii (1986), pp 195–218; Rachel Weil, *Political passions: gender, the family and political argument in England, 1680–1714* (Manchester, 2009). See also Elaine Chalus, '"Ladies are often very good scaffolding": women and politics in the age of Anne' in Clyve Jones (ed.), *British politics in the age of Holmes: Geoffrey Holmes's* British Politics in the Age of Anne *40 years on* (Oxford, 2009), pp 150–65.

6 Chalus and Montgomery, 'Women and politics', p. 224.

a number of edited volumes, monographs and articles, most notably by Chalus herself, Judith Lewis and Amanda Vickery.[7] Other, more general histories have also helped by including chapters on women's political involvement or threading it through their narratives.[8] Certain individuals, like Georgiana Cavendish, duchess of Devonshire, loom larger than the rest; however, the breadth of the historiography has ensured that a wide cross-section of the English female elite has now been examined.[9] Scotland is catching up too, with an increasing number of scholarly outputs dedicated to, or including studies of, the political machinations of its female elite.[10] Irish historiography still lags behind.

With no royal court to stimulate research and only an intermittent viceregal establishment, there has been little impetus to pursue research into elite women's politicking in Ireland. Nevertheless, pioneering studies have been carried out which provide a solid foundation. Mary O'Dowd has looked at the political avenues open to women of all ranks between 1692 and 1801, while Toby Barnard has used the activities of the Conyngham sisters (who, when married, became Katherine Conolly, Mary Jones and Jane Bonnell) as a case study to show how ladies of the upper orders could operate in the Protestant Ascendancy, including politics. Padhraig Higgins has taken Irish women's consumerism in the eighteenth century and shown how it could intersect with politics. He has also discussed their political exploits with particular reference to their role in electoral politics and in the late eighteenth-century Volunteer movement.[11] What is absent, though, is a study

7 Elaine Chalus, *Elite women in English political life c. 1754–1790* (Oxford, 2005); Judith Lewis, *Sacred to female patriotism: gender, class, and politics in late Georgian Britain* (London, 2003); Elaine Chalus, '"My Minerva at my elbow": the political roles of women in eighteenth-century England' in Stephen Taylor, Richard Connors and Clyve Jones (eds), *Hanoverian Britain and empire: essays in memory of Philip Lawson* (Woodbridge, 1998), pp 210–28; Amanda Vickery (ed.), *Women, privilege, and power: British politics, 1750 to the present* (Stanford, 2001); Kathryn Gleadle and Sarah Richardson (eds), *Women in British politics, 1760–1860: the power of the petticoat* (London, 2000); Hannah Barker and Elaine Chalus (eds), *Gender in eighteenth-century England: roles, representations and responsibilities* (London, 1997); Kathryn Gleadle, *Borderline citizens: women, gender and political culture in Britain 1815–1867* (Oxford, 2009); K.D. Reynolds, *Aristocratic women and political society in Victorian Britain* (Oxford, 1998).

8 See, for example, Linda Colley, *Britons: forging the nation 1707–1837* (3rd edn, London, 2009), ch. 6; Tague, *Women of quality*, ch. 7.

9 Scholarship on Georgiana has exploded over the past twenty-five years, but the most comprehensive item remains Amanda Foreman's biography, *Georgiana, duchess of Devonshire* (London, 1988).

10 Nicola Cowmeadow, '"Your Politick, self designing sister": the role of Katherine, first duchess of Atholl in the Scottish parliamentary elections of 1702', *Parliaments, Estates and Representations*, xxxiii (2013), pp 1–19; Rosalind Carr, 'Female correspondence and early modern Scottish political history: a case study of the Anglo-Scottish Union', *Historical Reflections*, xxxvii (2011), pp 39–75; Katharine Glover, *Elite women and polite society in eighteenth-century Scotland* (Woodbridge, 2012), ch. 5; Sue Innes and Jane Rendall, 'Women, gender and politics' in Lynn Abrams, Eleanor Gordon, Deborah Simonton and Eileen Yeo (eds), *Gender in Scottish history since 1700* (Edinburgh, 2006), pp 43–83.

11 Mary O'Dowd, *A history of women in Ireland, 1500–1800* (Harlow, 2004), ch. 2; Toby Barnard, 'A tale of three sisters: Katherine Conolly of Castletown' in idem, *Irish Protestant ascents and descents, 1641–1770* (Dublin, 2004), pp 266–89; Padhraig Higgins, 'Consumption, gender, and the politics of "Free Trade" in eighteenth-century Ireland', *Eighteenth-Century Studies*, xli (2007),

which combines a focus on elite women's political activities as a group and the time period under consideration here.

In order properly to understand elite women's political activities, it is necessary to first remind ourselves of the political context in which they lived. Ireland at this time was still styled a kingdom, which, although under overall English (after 1707, British) rule, retained its own parliament until the Act of Union in 1801. This parliament, and the political system in general, was managed by a revolving door of lords lieutenant (also known as viceroys), supplemented by two- or three-man teams of lord justices who took over when the lord lieutenant was out of the country, and parliamentary managers, known as undertakers, who assisted the lord lieutenant in getting his legislation through parliament and often acted as lord justices in his absence. Irish men could hold parliamentary seats in the British House of Commons, but they required an English peerage to sit in the House of Lords. Women who held peerages in their own right, however, were not allowed to take up their seats, though their titles could be passed on to their heirs.[12] This gave Ireland more independence than Scotland or Wales, neither of which had their own parliaments (the Scottish parliament having been eradicated by union with England in 1707), but much less than the entirely self-governing English. Elite women in Ireland could not hope to interact on a regular, long-term basis with the English politicians and royal family who held ultimate control over Ireland, though they did have access to the lord justices, viceroys and undertakers, many of whom were related to them. The problem was that many of these men held their posts for short periods of time and, in the case of the lords lieutenant, were absent from Ireland more than they were present.

In England, access to a royal family which was familiar, generally resident and fairly static in its membership (barring births, deaths, marriages and the occasional revolution) provided the consistency needed to allow a pattern of female involvement in court politics to become well established and even normalised by the end of the 1700s. In Ireland, the ground was constantly shifting beneath women's feet, as its political leaders changed, arrived and left. This prevented the acquisition and implementation of the kind of influence wielded at the English court by female favourites or quickly nullified it. Women would have to find other ways to make their political presence felt. They were not helped by their legal position, which left them in a kind of grey area. Like their counterparts in Britain, if they were landowners, it was not illegal for them to vote until the passage of the Reform Act of 1832 and the Municipal Corporations Act of 1835.[13] However, custom mostly overrode law, and in practice, male proxies were usually used to exercise the electoral rights of women who met the appropriate property qualifications.[14] They might still have the final say in who obtained their vote, however, and were courted accordingly. Mary, dowager Lady Shelburne, was petitioned by

pp 87–105; idem, *A nation of politicians: gender, patriotism, and political culture in late eighteenth-century Ireland* (Madison, 2010), esp. ch. 7.

12 Lewis, *Sacred to female patriotism*, pp 15, 127.

13 Chalus, *Elite women in English political life*, p. 31. For a discussion as to why nineteenth-century women did not seek to regain the vote sooner, see Lewis, *Sacred to female patriotism*, p. 63.

14 Chalus and Montgomery, 'Women and politics', p. 220; Gleadle, *Borderline citizens*, pp 28–9.

her brother-in-law, the prominent politician, William Conolly, to lend her support (acquired through jointure lands in County Donegal) to his brother-in-law, Thomas Pearson, at the 1710 election for Killybegs. She agreed and Pearson won the seat, which he held until 1727.[15]

At other times, Irish political customs worked in favour of elite women, particularly when it came to attitudes towards women in parliament. Although ladies in England were permitted to attend debates in Westminster, they were not especially welcome there and were confined to the notoriously uncomfortable and unaccommodating ventilator room, located above the ceiling of the House of Commons (though the space allotted to them in the House of Lords 'behind the red curtains on each side of the throne and in the lord chancellor's room' was slightly more tolerable).[16] It was only after fire destroyed the Commons in 1834 that a ladies' gallery was finally built.[17] The Irish, however, were more progressive. Parliaments became much more frequent after the Glorious Revolution, and female attendance was a common and accepted feature by the early 1700s.[18] When a new House of Commons was opened in November 1731, the English-born Mary Pendarves, then visiting Ireland, described her experience in glowing terms. She and her female friends sat from eleven in the morning until eight o'clock at night in order 'to hear an election determined', and Mary declared that she was 'very well entertained there'. The women were provided with food and drink throughout the day, and during the afternoon break 'were conveyed, by some gentleman of our acquaintance, into the Usher of the Black Rod's room, where he had a good fire, and meat, tea, and bread and butter. Were we not well taken of?' Mary also painted a picture of extensive female attendance, saying that she and her companions 'were the most impartial hearers among all the ladies that were there'.[19] Kathryn Gleadle has pointed to the female solidarity engendered among English women by the discomfort they suffered together at Westminster; on the other hand, Dublin ladies did not attend in defiance of the male political order, but with its blessing and encouragement.[20] For them, parliament was an enjoyable day out and something to be taken for granted, not snatched from the hands of grudging MPs. Their presence

15 Mary, dowager Lady Shelburne to William Conolly, 29 July 1710 (IAA, MS C/48/4); Edith Johnston-Liik, *History of the Irish parliament, 1692–1800: commons, constituencies and statues* (6 vols, Belfast, 2002), vi, 36–7. Lady Shelburne's second husband had been Henry Conyngham, brother to William's wife, Katherine Conolly, while Thomas Pearson was married to William's sister. Shelburne and Pearson were therefore not themselves related. Lady Shelburne's title came from her first marriage and she kept it until her death. See *D.I.B.* (Conolly, William (1662–1729)); ibid. (Conyngham, Henry (1705/6–81)).

16 Peter Jupp, 'The roles of royal and aristocratic women in British politics, c. 1782–1832' in Mary O'Dowd and Sabine Wichert (eds), *Chattel, servant or citizen: women's status in church, state and society. Historical Studies xix* (Belfast, 1995), p. 106.

17 Gleadle, *Borderline citizens*, pp 57–8.

18 Robert Johnson to James, duke of Ormond, 18 Oct. 1707 (NLI, MS 2472).

19 Mary Pendarves to Anne Granville, 25 Nov. 1731 (*The autobiography and correspondence of Mary Granville, Mrs Delany ...*, ed. Lady Llanover (ser. 1, 3 vols, London, 1861), i, 318). See also Mary O'Dowd, 'Women and patriotism in eighteenth-century Ireland', *History Ireland*, xiv (2006), pp 25–30.

20 Gleadle, *Borderline citizens*, pp 57–8.

did not make the same kind of statement about female determination to be a part of the political process as entering the ventilator room did, nor should its importance to them be overstated. Parliamentary attendance was, after all, only available in Dublin on a biennial basis. It was an added bonus to elite women's political involvement, not a key feature.[21]

Conversation and correspondence

The simplest way for women to engage with and learn about politics was through the spoken and written word.[22] Though their conversations are now impossible to reconstruct, much of the content surfaced in correspondence, as the two mediums intertwined to create an intricate web of information exchange. Whether in person or on paper, no political topic was off limits, and women discussed with each other and with men everything from the latest goings-on in the Irish and English parliaments, to changes in the lord lieutenancy, to the activities of mutual relations, friends and acquaintances and the details of local political affairs. For those who were members of highly political families, these issues might overlap, again calling attention to the problems of designating family affairs private and feminine and political issues public and male, when, for so many, politicians and family were one and the same.[23] As if to drive the point home that women were not so easily pigeonholed, even those living a more sedate life took an interest in politics, and it was a staple topic in the general correspondence of most ladies. Writing from Caledon, County Tyrone in 1700 to the countess of Panmure in Scotland, Agnes Hamilton (a paternal aunt of the wealthy Margaret Hamilton, who would later become countess of Orrery), portrayed herself as a 'hermit' who would not have known if 'King James is at London' or King William 'crowned in Spain'. In fact, she was still able to provide details of the earl of Rochester's accession to the lord lieutenancy and the impact this would have on the Dublin court.[24] An absence of political news would have made for a dull correspondence, and some ensured that their letters would be of interest by delaying them in order to be able to send the latest information. Lady Frances Keightley, writing from England, held back a letter to her daughter, Catherine O'Brien, in 1722, because she first wanted to discover 'whether my lord duke of Grafton was continued lord lieutenant or no'. Her patience was rewarded, for she was able to add a postscript several days later reporting that 'I am this

21 C.I. McGrath, *The making of the eighteenth-century Irish constitution: government, parliament and the revenue, 1692–1714* (Dublin, 2000), pp 35, 153–4.

22 On 'correspondence networks' in England, see Chalus, '"That epidemical Madness"', p. 167.

23 Cowmeadow, '"Your Politick, self designing sister"', pp 2–3; S. D. Amussen, *An ordered society: gender and class in early modern England* (New York, 1988), pp 2–3; Anne Laurence, 'Real and imagined communities in the lives of women in seventeenth century Ireland: identity and gender', in Stephanie Tarbin and Susan Broomhall (eds), *Women, identities and communities in early modern Europe* (Aldershot, 2008), pp 13–29.

24 Agnes Hamilton to Margaret, countess of Panmure, 28 Dec. [n.d., 1700] (NRS, GD45/14/238/77). On the Hamilton family's genealogy, see Everard Hamilton, *Hamilton memoirs: being historical and genealogical notices of a branch of that family which settled in Ireland in the reign of King James I* (2nd edn, Dundalk, 1920), pp 5, 8–9.

moment assured by good hands that he certainly does go as soon as the parliament rises', a clear example of conversation transferring to correspondence.[25]

Female networks such as these, incorporating those who lived outside one's own neighbourhood, were crucial for women like Agnes and Catherine, who were living in remote areas (Catherine was in County Clare in 1722), for they relied upon better-placed friends and family members to provide them with political information. Appeals frequently went out to those based in Dublin or London for the latest news.[26] In a letter to her daughter-in-law, Mary, in 1728, Catherine O'Brien, by then living in France, wrote that she was 'pretty impatient to hear of you, and what success your husband has had in his election affair in Ireland'.[27] Four months later, she requested more on the same topic.[28]

Ladies usually provided a context for the information they shared with each other in their correspondence, along with at least a basic analysis of events and opinions on them. In 1719, William Conolly, then Speaker of the Irish House of Commons, was struggling to secure the repeal of the test clause of the 1704 Popery Act, which severely restricted the rights of Dissenters. He discussed the matter with his wife, Katherine, and both spoke to her cousin, Jane Bulkeley, who then talked it over with her local friends and gauged their opinions, before writing to Katherine's sister, Jane Bonnell, to give her a summary of the ongoing events:

> he expected to have the Test taken off but has been so much opposed by the more considerable Whigs that they of his party has thought fit to drop the bill the Tories has left the Whigs to battle it with one another, which they have done very affectly [*sic*]. I meet with very few but what are against the bill.[29]

This letter was followed up by another, six days later, in which Jane Bulkeley surmised that William Conolly was having such trouble with Parliament, because although he had 'carried himself with great civility and good manners to all people', there were 'a great many that has envied his greatness and would fain pull him down if they could'.[30] Katherine herself wrote to her sister, that like William, she suffered great fatigue over the matter.[31] Mrs Bonnell, sitting in London, was thus provided with an overview of the entire situation, her brother-in-law's involvement in it and the impression made on polite Dublin society, all without any communication with William himself. This is not to suggest that men had an aversion to sharing political news with their female friends and relatives, or fulfilling requests for news: as a rule, they did not. Katherine Conolly later obtained much of her information regarding the electoral efforts of her nephew, Colonel Conyngham, from direct correspondence with the colonel himself, and he wrote to her after his defeat in

25 Lady Frances Keightley to Catherine O'Brien, 9 Jan. 1721/2 (NLI, MS 45, 348/5).

26 This was also common practice in England and Scotland and remained so well into the nineteenth century (Richardson, '"Well-neighboured houses"', pp 60, 66; Chalus, '"That epidemical Madness"', p. 167).

27 Catherine O'Brien to Mary, Lady O'Brien, 1 Jan. 1727/8 (NLI, MS 45, 352/1).

28 Same to same, 24 Apr. 1728 (ibid.).

29 Jane Bulkeley to Jane Bonnell, 18 July 1719 (ibid., MS 41, 580/4).

30 Same to same, 25 July 1719 (ibid.).

31 Katherine Conolly to same, 25 July 1719 (ibid., MS 41, 578/3).

1745 to tell her 'of the most villainous treatment he met with in his election'.[32] Alan Brodrick, twice Speaker of the Irish House of Commons and later Viscount Midleton and Lord Chancellor of Ireland, likewise sent his sisters-in-law, Martha and Rachel Courthope, details of recent political events and his part in them.[33] In later years, his brother Thomas wrote to Alan's third wife, Ann, relating the day's events in the Irish parliament and explaining that he wrote her such long political letters, because 'perhaps it may prove some little amusement in a place where you want it'.[34] Such letters were motivated by more than a desire to fill a page or amuse. From a man's point of view, there were distinct advantages to be had from maintaining a political correspondence with women, for they could make ideal political assistants.

Assistants and assistance

Many women were used by their men as political conduits and errand runners. Viscount Midleton often had his English-based daughter, Alice Brodrick, send him London newspapers containing political reports of interest, and sent to her politically loaded letters, which were in fact meant for his brother, Thomas, and contained nothing for Alice beyond a few words of greeting and farewell at the beginning and end. He acted thus because he feared his letters were intercepted by political opponents in the Post Office, but believed that his correspondence with his daughter would be untouched.[35] At first glance, it would appear that it was Alice's youth which he expected to keep her letters safe, for when they were children, Alan used his sons to send information to their uncle as well, telling one that, 'I reckon you are as unsuspected a person to keep a correspondence worth being pried into at the post office as any body [*sic*] in Bond Street; for which reason and to prevent the charge of double postage I will write that to you which might otherwise be as well applied elsewhere.'[36] However, in later years, it seems it was Alice's position as an unmarried woman and a junior member of the family which her father felt was more likely to protect her letters. He was still comfortable using her as a conduit in the 1720s, telling her plainly in 1725 that 'perhaps your correspondence may not be pried into, as I am told by a relation of yours his and mine hath been of late'. For this reason, he decided to send political information to her uncle 'under your cover [*rather*] than in a long letter which I have lately addressed to him directly'.[37]

This suggests one of two things. First, that Alan felt his enemies would not place his daughter under surveillance because they would view a single woman, who had spent most of her life in England, as a political nonentity. Second, that he believed his opponents thought the Brodrick family overlooked Alice in this way. Neither

32 Same to same, 26 Feb. 1744/5 (ibid., MS 41, 578/17).

33 See, for example, Alan Brodrick to Martha Courthope, 7 Nov. 1713 (SHC, MS 1248/3/129–130); same to Rachel Courthope, 27 July 1725 (NLI, MS 41, 675/6).

34 Thomas Brodrick to Ann, Viscountess Midleton, 15 Nov. 1718 (SHC, MS 1248/4/138–141).

35 Alan, Viscount Midleton to the Hon. Alice Brodrick, 4 Sept. 1725 (ibid., MS 1248/6/297–298).

36 Same to Master [Alan] Brodrick, 26 Dec. 1713 (ibid., MS 1248/3/149–150).

37 Same to the Hon. Alice Brodrick, 4 Sept. 1725 (ibid., MS 1248/6/297–298).

option is perfect, for it is hard to see why anyone intent on spying on Alan would not check his daughter's letters, given the well-established culture in Ireland and England of women discussing politics with each other and with men; however, it may simply have been wishful thinking on Lord Midleton's part to believe that Alice's letters were safer. What is more important, and more easily discerned, is her involvement in politics and the trust her father placed in her discretion and ability to ensure that the contents of his letters reached her uncle, but were not made public.[38] In some cases, he even had her pass on oral messages, telling her, when she was only 17, to 'speak to my brother to see Lord Sunderland [*then lord lieutenant of Ireland*] before he goes to Newmarket, and to tell him that if he hath or can make interest in Lord Conway to recommend a member of Parliament for Lisburn, he will keep out a very turbulent one'.[39] Cases such as this make it easy to see how political correspondence and conversation could blend together for women and how they could be pulled into politics without even trying.

More proactive than an involuntary intermediary were those women who acted as informants – gathering and transmitting to absent men information which would keep the latter up to date with political events elsewhere and help them to plan their next move. This activity was common in England, and has been called 'one of the key functions of a political woman'.[40] It demanded trust in a woman's abilities, for she would have to recognise, assemble and, if necessary, properly summarise, the data which was relevant and important to the recipient of her letter. Such data would have been acquired from a lady's own epistolary and conversation networks. When she reported rumours of the fate of the Pretender after his attempted landing in Scotland to her husband in 1708, Rachel, Viscountess Massereene, was pulling together strands of information acquired from other family members' letters and the news passed on to her by neighbours.[41] In this way, written and spoken networks overlapped and intersected, and the woman functioned as a kind of sorting office, acquiring, filtering and relaying news to her male relations. Some could not resist going one step further and taking on an advisory role as well, though their opinions were rarely asked in men's letters. While Jane Bulkeley may have been pressed by William and Katherine Conolly in person for her thoughts on the test clause, when it came to correspondence, which could be saved, produced and shown to any number of people outside the writer's control, even the most astute and well-informed lady was rarely troubled for such advice by the men in her life. Commentary which arrived along with more factual information was an added extra.

Writing to her brother, the MP John Mason, to tell him the outcome of the local Waterford election in early 1738, Mary Mason began by informing him of the basic facts ('we carried the election by 3 votes 20 to 17'), then relayed a request from another gentlemen that John 'not promise your vote again' and gently

38 On those who were rather disinterested in politics, see Glover, *Elite women and polite society*, pp 110, 123.

39 Alan Brodrick to Alice Brodrick, 7 Oct. 1714 (SHC, MS 1248/3/191–192).

40 Chalus, '"Ladies are often very good scaffolding"', pp 158, 161 (quote is from p. 161). On the similar activities of Scottish women, see Glover, *Elite women and polite society*, pp 121–2.

41 Rachel, Viscountess Massereene to Clotworthy, Viscount Massereene, [Mar. 1708?] (PRONI, D562/193).

scolded her brother that he had 'no notion what trouble he has been at about it'. She moved on to make the observation that 'it is happy you were not here to have had your share in it', and concluded by advising him to 'write to Mr Congreve and congratulate him, indeed he deserves it'. In one paragraph, she had married the roles of informant, intermediary and advisor.[42] She obviously felt comfortable and well within her rights to write to her sibling in this manner, and there is no hint on her side of their correspondence that he resented her comments and counsel. Her advice, her use of the word 'we' and the general tone of her letter also betray the degree of her commitment to local politics and to her brother's career, a common feature of the lives of elite women, who often invested much emotional capital in their men's political undertakings, perhaps because their own gender barred them from holding office themselves. Catherine O'Brien told her daughter-in-law Mary that 'Sir Edward's election I take for granted goes as we wish it, but I am a little mortified to hear there will yet be a contest in England, which I flattered myself would have ended with Mr [Wortley's?] life.'[43] She might have been talking about a seat she was standing for herself, had that been possible.

Networks were not infallible. Lady Massereene's story that the Pretender had been captured was untrue, and not all men believed the tales they heard from their female family members. St John Brodrick, son of Alan, was sceptical when Mary Hill, Viscountess Hillsborough (who was his step-brother's wife), told him that she had heard 'that the common talk of Dublin was, that his Grace [*the duke of Grafton, the outgoing lord lieutenant*] was determined not to leave it till the affair of the government was settled to his satisfaction; & that he was assured it should be so as soon as the Parliament here was up'. St John reported that Lady Hillsborough's source was 'old Monmouth', and said that although he was 'not under the least apprehension from this ridiculous piece of boasting', some use might still be made of Lady Hillsborough's story, 'by taking occasion to feel the pulse of the ministers a second time, & making this report the handle for renewing our application to them'.[44] Even the more inept female informants had their uses.

Women could also act as proxies for their men. This could mean something as simple as secretarial work, writing or copying letters on a man's behalf when he

42 Mary Mason to John Mason, 2 Jan. 1737/8 (PRONI, T3131/B/1/46). Mary is referring to Ambrose Congreve, MP for Waterford 1738–9 (Johnston-Liik, *History of the Irish parliament*, iii, 465).

43 Catherine O'Brien to Mary, Lady O'Brien, 4 Mar. 1727/8 (NLI, MS 45, 352/1). Mr Wortley was Sidney Wortley Montagu, MP for Peterborough at the time of his death in November 1727. Sir Edward then ran for this seat and was elected, only to be unseated after a petition in April 1728. Wortley Montagu was then declared elected, despite having died six months earlier. See *H.C. 1690–1715*, ii, 443–6; 'Wortley Montagu (formerly Montagu), Hon. Sidney (1650–1727)' in ibid, iv, 879–9.

44 St John Brodrick to Ld Midleton, 11 Mar. 1723/4 (SHC, MS 1248/6/161–162). 'Old Monmouth' may be a reference to the 3rd earl of Peterborough, who was also the 1st earl of Monmouth by the second creation. However it may also have been Isaac Manley, MP, who was a supporter of William Conolly and Postmaster General. He had been involved in the duke of Monmouth's rising against James II in 1685 (*Oxford D.N.B.* (Mordaunt, Charles, 3rd earl of Peterborough and 1st earl of Monmouth (1658?–1735)); D.W. Hayton, 'Two ballads on the County Westmeath by-election of 1723', *Eighteenth-Century Ireland*, iv (1989), p. 28).

was too busy or ill to do this himself. Many copies or drafts of William Conolly's letters survive that are in Katherine's handwriting (perhaps helping to explain her fatigue when he was especially busy), and Alan Brodrick reported that William Stewart, 2nd Viscount Mountjoy, was having his wife deal with his correspondence and write his letters, because 'his indisposition in his hands makes it impracticable for him to write himself'.[45] At other times, women dealt with politicians on their husbands' behalf. In 1710, Robert Molesworth had his wife, Letitia, approach John Forster, then Speaker of the Irish House of Commons, to ask him to intervene with the lord lieutenant, Lord Wharton, in order to try to secure the Molesworths' son, Walter, a cornetcy of dragoons.[46] To have women carry out these tasks, rather than delegating them to a servant, shows the great trust placed in them by their husbands, who had to allow their wives access to their most private political papers and strategies, and rely upon their discretion not to divulge the information in their own conversations and letters. Even more latitude and trust was afforded to those women who electioneered on a man's behalf by writing letters (in their own name) in order to canvas votes. This divided the workload if more letters needed to be written and more voters needed to be attended to than a candidate could deal with himself, and was especially useful if the woman in question possessed a more charismatic, persuasive personality than he, which would assist her in garnering support on his behalf. Katherine Conolly was just such a woman. She had a strong work ethic and connexions and experience working in politics obtained through years of helping her husband. In 1727 she turned her talents towards electioneering for Francis Burton, her niece's husband, telling her sister that 'we have nothing in this country but hurry and confusion about elections. I have wrote 40 letters about Frank Burton's.' She added that 'how it will go I cannot tell, but most people think well'. She need not have worried. Francis was elected MP for County Clare.[47]

Irish women's electioneering tactics differed from those employed by their English counterparts, for in the later eighteenth century English women would electioneer in person by meeting and canvassing voters on the streets or going into their homes and hosting social events for them.[48] Even these ladies' charitable activities among their husband's tenants had political applications, for 'a reputation as a good landlord was an electoral asset'.[49] Naturally elite women were not expected always to enjoy this socio-political part of their lives, but their activities at such times were 'generally accepted, often expected, and sometimes demanded'.[50]

45 For example, William Conolly to Charles, duke of Grafton, 8 July 1721 (IAA, MS A/3/30); same to [Thomas] Clutterbuck, 18 July 1726 (ibid., MS A/3/37); Ld Midleton to the Hon. Alan Brodrick, 2 Sept. 1727 (SHC, MS 1248/7/102–103).

46 Robert Molesworth to the Hon. Letitia Molesworth, 10 June 1710 (*The Clements archive*, ed. A.P.W. Malcomson (Dublin, 2010), p. 129).

47 Katherine Conolly to Bonnell, 29 Aug. 1727 (NLI, MS 41, 578/4); Johnston-Liik, *History of the Irish parliament*, iii, 322–3.

48 Chalus, '"That epidemical Madness"', pp 155–60; Matthew Cragoe, '"Jenny rules the roost": women and electoral politics, 1832–68' in Gleadle and Richardson (eds), *Women in British politics*, pp 157–65.

49 Lewis, *Sacred to female patriotism*, p. 86. For examples of this in England, see Chalus, '"That epidemical Madness"', p. 156.

50 Chalus, '"That epidemical Madness"', p. 153.

For elite women in Ascendancy Ireland, the personal touch with voters was simply not a part of their political culture. Men may not have felt that they required this type of assistance, but it was also impractical in many instances. If women were members of absentee families there was little to be gained by ferrying them across the Irish Sea at election times to canvass among people to whom they and their husbands were virtual strangers.

Some women took it upon themselves to protect, or try to protect, the interests of their male relations without their knowledge. This is particularly noticeable in those instances where multiple members of a family were involved in politics and were connected through marriage, rather than blood. Nepotism was common, and a husband might reasonably assume that his wife's relations would help to forward his career. The practice had its limits, and for some politics ultimately took priority over family. Men who had been counting on the support of powerful and prominent in-laws to bolster their own careers were often angry when it failed to materialise, and in such situations a wife might enter the fray and try to act as a bridge between the two sides of her family. These unsolicited interventions were not always successful.

In 1713, Mary Jones's husband, Richard, wrote to their brother-in-law, William Conolly, telling him that not only should he 'not oppose me in being elected to serve in the ensuing parliament for Killibegs' (Killybegs, County Donegal), but that he should give Richard his support.[51] William was steadfast in his refusal, and soon Mary was involved. She began, perhaps with her husband's knowledge and approval, by speaking with William and her sister Katherine, and tried 'to prevail on him not to oppose my spouse's election at Killibegs'. Her efforts soon stalled, for 'not withstanding all the arguments I could use, or the concern I was in, it was to no purpose'. She appealed to her sister, believing that Katherine could break William's resolve if she chose to, but Katherine was as devoted to her own husband's cause as Mary was to Richard's, and to her shock, 'my sister Conolly, who I thought would soften matters, told me Mr Jones deserved not to be chose'. Mary was not finished yet, and changed tactics. The following day, of her own accord and without her husband's knowledge, she wrote to her cousin, Captain Stafford, asking him to intercede with William on Richard's behalf. The resulting letter shows her own unshakable belief in political nepotism. She told Stafford that 'Mr Jones thinks, as everybody must, that he being married to me has a right to be elected there' and, using a combination of begging and flattery, asked Stafford to 'interpose and use your friendly endeavours' in order 'to soften brother Conolly, for I am sure nobody has a greater influence on him', even though the previous day she had seemingly been convinced that it was Katherine who held this power. In her view, William was punishing her husband for opposing the lord lieutenant, the earl of Wharton, in several matters, but she protested that 'Mr Jones never voted against brother Conolly and only opposed my Lord Wharton in one or two things'. Mary felt that favouritism towards kinfolk was so expected by society at large, that 'my brother Conolly's opposing him will look very odd in the eye of the world'. This was, after all, the same constituency to which William had nominated his

51 Richard Jones to William Conolly, 3 Dec. 1713 (IAA, MS A/7).

other brother-in-law, Thomas Pearson, in 1710, with Lady Shelburne's help. As there were two seats available, Richard would not have had to displace Thomas. Perhaps not wanting to appear too assertive (though this is exactly what she was), and feeling that emotional blackmail would be a more effective route to take, she insisted that when it came to public opinion, 'I am under no great concern, my chief trouble is for the unhappy breach it probably may make in our families.' The Conollys had little if any of this concern and no difficulty in separating business from family if needs be. Despite Mary's efforts, Richard was not elected.[52] Yet his wife's foray into electoral politics had at least left him no worse off than before. Other men were not so lucky, for some women provided not just unwanted, but unnecessary and even harmful 'assistance' to their male relations, as they strove to control and direct such men's political careers and decisions.

While Francis Burton was happy that his aunt, Katherine Conolly, should write letters on his behalf during his election campaign in 1727, he did not feel the same way about his mother, Alice. Unfortunately, she failed to take the hint, and Katherine complained that 'his good mother is carrying on an interest, as she says, for her son, contrary to his desire and that of all his friends in that country, or at least those that calls themselves so'. Mrs Conolly was prepared to put the blame on such actions for any political mishap suffered by Francis, saying that 'if anything hurt him, it must be his friends all not going one way', and she attempted to intervene with his mother. Despite multiple letters, Mrs Burton failed to respond, preferring to bypass Katherine and write to William Conolly instead, something which his wife found ludicrous, for her husband simply gave her the letters to answer.[53] As this tale shows, elite women in Ireland did not feel constrained by their sex when it came to intervening in political affairs, and when their assistance was rebuffed, it was because it was unwanted or unneeded, not because it came from a woman. Nor was this the only aspect of politics in which gender had a limited role.

Patronage brokers

Patronage brokers typically sought political, military or ecclesiastical favour for their clients, who were usually relations or friends. The best brokers possessed excellent connexions and a forceful personality which incorporated confidence and initiative, but was tempered by enough intelligence to know how best to approach a potential benefactor and frame their requests.[54] As none of these assets were gender-dependent, women with the right combination of character and connexions could be just as useful brokers as men, and several of those who were represented by female brokers were men of a similar social order to their own. More than that, it was fairly

52 Mary Jones to Captain Stafford, 30 Jan. [c. 1714] (ibid.); Johnston-Liik, *History of the Irish parliament*, vi, 36–7.

53 Katherine Conolly to Bonnell, 29 Aug. 1727 (NLI, MS 41, 578/4).

54 A conclusion with which Linda Colley, Gerda Lerner and Katherine Glover agree in their studies of elite British, American and Scottish women (Linda Colley, 'Women and political power', *The Wilson Quarterly*, xvi (1992), pp 51–2; Gerda Lerner, *The majority finds its past: placing women in history* (Oxford, 1979), p. 4; Glover, *Elite women and polite society*, p. 116).

common in any given combination of clients, brokers and patrons, for two or more of those involved to be related to another. Female motivations were twofold. First, they might be able to help a relation or friend politically, itself reason and reward enough for some, especially if seeking to advance the career of a family member. Second, brokering allowed women a prominent role in politics.

The tone and structure of female-authored patronage requests were remarkably similar and consistent.[55] No matter whether they were writing to men or women, family members or strangers, the letters provided information on why the beneficiary should receive the patronage requested and typically focused on a combination of his family connexions, personal merits and, if appropriate, unique qualifications for the job sought. If his circumstances were particularly poor, this could also be used as leverage. The writer would draw attention to her own credentials as a broker, citing her family background and any connexion she had to the patron, and insisting that she rarely petitioned for favour, but had been moved to intervene on this occasion because of the worth of her client. Letters were always couched in terms of the greatest deference, with apologies for bothering the recipient, but ladies sometimes implied that their occasional requests should be granted, specifically because they were so rare. Speed was also of the essence, for even the best-written letter would be of no use if the favour had already been granted elsewhere.

In 1736, perhaps hoping to preserve the honour and position of her family, Katherine Conolly attempted to obtain the post of revenue commissioner, once held by her husband, for her nephew, William Conolly, junior. She was unsure if the previous commissioner was even dead, but sought to mitigate her indecorous haste by explaining that her patronage requests had failed in the past due to hesitation. She invoked the memory of Speaker Conolly by writing, 'I cannot think any of the King's friends can forget the many true and faithful services my dear husband for many years of his life did for the Protestant succession and for the King's service, and it's well known in this kingdom what he suffered in the Queen's reign.' She insisted that her nephew was well qualified for the job and would be of 'the greatest service to the revenue'. As for herself, she was 'no stranger to the affairs of this kingdom', and felt that her request was very reasonable, considering that she had 'never applied for any mark of royal favour for myself, which many thought I had a just right to do, both on my husband and my own family's account'. She closed the letter with a subtle hint of bribery, promising the recipient, that 'if ever you have again any service or friendship for your friends in Ireland, I may assure you of mine and my friends' interest in all your affairs'.[56]

Katherine's letter highlights the fact that female brokers sometimes felt the need to use brokers of their own to obtain patronage. She wrote that 'I have not the assurances to write myself to Sir Robert Walpole, but must entreat your

55 This observation has also been made of mid eighteenth-century English women's patronage letters. See Chalus, '"To serve my friends"', pp 70–1. For further information on the English patronage system in the eighteenth century and women's part in it, see eadem, *Elite women in English political life*, ch. 4.

56 Katherine Conolly to unknown, 2 June 1736 (PRONI, MIC 435/7). Katherine is probably referring to the fact that Speaker Conolly was dismissed from the Irish revenue commission and privy council by the Tory duke of Ormond (*D.I.B.* (Conolly, William (1662–1729))).

making my most humble service acceptable to him'. The use of a further intermediary was just another tactic in her quest for patronage, for her behaviour does not tally with her earlier actions: she admitted she had written to Walpole before, and had his assurance of help when he was able to give it. Rather than showing timidity (a weakness which no broker could afford to have and which Katherine certainly could not have been accused of), Mrs Conolly was demonstrating her shrewdness. Walpole had failed to help her when she had previously approached him directly, and her use of another person was an attempt to ensure that her request came from someone she believed he would be inclined to assist. Had she felt that her chances of success would not have been enhanced by enlisting the help of another, doubtless she would have made the approach herself, as she had done in the past.[57]

A patronage broker was only as good as the man or men she could influence, and as their power rose and fell, so did hers. After the death of her husband in 1729, Katherine Conolly had to admit that her own political influence had waned, and she wrote in 1735 that 'my power is far short of my inclination'.[58] Her attempt to obtain the post of revenue commissioner for her nephew in 1736 ultimately failed, and she wrote with some bitterness on another occasion that 'nothing grates me more than to be denied at that [*the revenue board*]'.[59] However, despite her disappointments, she was not without political connexions in her widowhood. As we saw in Chapter 5, social politics in the form of political salons was not a feature of elite women's lives in Ireland at this time; however, women did still entertain politicians at their homes, and Katherine herself hosted parties attended by numerous politicians.[60] This social networking, combined with pre-existing connexions made during her husband's lifetime, meant that she always knew to whom to send her letters when she wanted a favour and, as well as applying to the Speaker's old colleagues, she used her nephew William and other friends. She wrote to one man in 1735, when she knew a matter of concern to him was to be mentioned in the House of Commons, that she 'was not neglectful of it, I sent to my friends both in town and country for my nephew Conolly, and some more of my friends was out of town but came time enough to do you service – and I am truly glad to tell you, it went as well as you and your friends could wish'. In addition, she was so powerful in ecclesiastical patronage that her nephew William's wife, Lady Anne, reported in 1735 that hopeful candidates rushed to secure her support when a bishopric became vacant.[61]

57 Katherine Conolly to unknown, 2 June 1736 (PRONI, MIC 435/7). Robert Walpole was first lord of the treasury from 1721 until 1742, thus Katherine's attempts to influence him (*Oxford D.N.B.* (Lord treasurers of England (c.1125–1742))).

58 Katherine Conolly to George Bubb Dodington, 16 Dec. 1735 (PRONI, MIC 435/7).

59 *Cal. Treas. bks*, iii, 287; Katherine Conolly to Bonnell, 20 Mar. 1732 [/3?] (NLI, MS 41, 578/7).

60 Katherine Conolly to Bonnell, 15 Jan. 1739/40 (NLI, MS 41, 578/13). Though it was not part of the formal curriculum for girls, Chalus has noted that in most political families, an understanding of how society and politics might be blended together and of the part a woman might play in this 'was part of a young woman's informal education', and could make her 'a valuable member of a political family' (Chalus, '"That epidemical Madness"', p. 160).

61 Katherine Conolly to Dodington, 16 Dec. 1735 (PRONI, MIC 435/7); Lady Anne Conolly to Thomas, earl of Strafford, 27 Nov. 1735 (BL, Add. MS 22228, f. 147).

A mother's prerogative

The limits on ladies' political powers and involvement discussed so far almost all stemmed from the fact that in order to make an impact, they were reliant upon being able to work through the men around them using persuasion or co-operation. There was one group of women however, for whom the normal rules did not apply; the female guardians (usually mothers) of underage landowners. These women dictated who would receive their sons' interest at election times and, as such, possessed electoral and patronage influence which could, for a time at least, equal and in many cases surpass, that of the men around them. What is more, they were generally very good at using these powers to get what they wanted.[62]

When such women spoke of giving their interest to a particular candidate, what they meant was that those qualified tenants of their sons and themselves (for some held jointure lands, which also carried electoral value), would vote as they were instructed. This allegiance was absolutely expected by landowners and guardians, but sometimes needed to be enforced by reminders. In 1707, while managing her son's Irish estates in Counties Waterford and Cork (in addition to his English lands), Juliana Boyle, dowager countess of Cork and Burlington had her secretary, Joseph Waite, write to one of the family's Irish land agents, to tell him that

> My lady commanded me to acquaint you that her honour highly resents the proceeding of your corporation in the last election, for her ladyship expects (as it is but reasonable) that the people of those places belonging to my ladyship or my lord should apply themselves to her honour for her ladyship's concurrence and approbation of such persons as they intend to elect their representatives in parliament.[63]

In theory, obedience should have been easy to impose. The county electorate was comprised of forty-shilling freeholders, but there was no secret ballot and threats could be made, and carried out, against tenants who did not vote as their landlords (or landladies) instructed them to.[64] In practice, however, there was a shortage of tenants (especially those of the Protestant faith) and, with few people to replace them, those already in place sometimes felt that defiance was worth the risk; thus Juliana's problems. Despite her limited options in later years, and perhaps as a reaction against the earlier insubordination, she was not above strong-arming tenants by pressing them for their debts. In 1712 the Irish agents were told that 'as for such ungrateful persons that are tenants to my lord and have had a forbearance in paying their arrears and rent, yet has the impudence to oppose his lordship's interest, your father and yourself are to oblige them to discharge what they owe as speedily as possible'.[65]

62 Chalus and Lewis agree with this assessment of a guardian's power (Chalus, '"That epidemical Madness"', p. 155; Lewis, *Sacred to female patriotism*, pp 104–5).
63 Joseph Waite to Digby Foulke, 5 June 1707 (Chatsworth, Joseph Waite's letter book 1706–8 (Ireland and Yorkshire), Burlington MSS, miscellaneous, box 1).
64 S.J. Connolly, *Divided kingdom: Ireland 1630–1800* (Oxford, 2008), pp 309–10, 439–40.
65 Waite to Foulke and John Walker, 21 Aug. 1712 (NLI, MS 13, 254/3).

The direction in which a mother gave her support at election times could be influenced by requests from her family and others, who could and would approach her for help. In 1709 Sir Richard Pyne, lord chief justice of the King's bench in Ireland, contacted Lady Burlington and requested her help in having his son, Henry, elected as MP for Dungarvan. Juliana agreed, but set conditions. She did not want a Mr Robert Carew standing for the constituency (and had already been taking steps to prevent this from happening), and agreed to support Henry only because his father promised 'that he could prevail with Mr Carew to wave his designs in that affair'.[66] Pyne agreed, and with the countess's support Henry was duly elected.[67] A guardian's powers were not unlimited, however. She could not always help everyone who asked, control everyone she wanted, or deliver on everything she had promised. Lady Burlington assured a Mr Grice Smith that she would support his bid to be elected to Youghal in 1711, but nothing ever came of it.[68] In 1713, she 'had application made to her in favour of Sir John Stanley, who goes for Ireland in quality of secretary to his Grace the duke of Shrewsbury, lord lieutenant of that kingdom, to have him elected on one of my lord's boroughs to serve in the ensuing parliament'. Despite the man's good character and Juliana's desire to be of service, she could not comply, as 'she has already recommended several gentlemen for my lord's boroughs'.[69] More troublesome still were the occasions on which politicians and officials who should have obeyed her commands did not do so, necessitating constant battles to protect her son's rights. In 1707, the JPs suddenly stopped holding sessions at Tallow and Lismore (both in County Waterford) 'to the prejudice of my lord's tenants and without having any regard to my lady's interest'. Juliana had to act quickly. She used 'her best endeavours to prevent their designs by making [interest?] with the lord lieutenant of the county and such other gentlemen as may be serviceable on that account, to break the measures they have taken and bring back the sessions to the accustomed places as they ought to be'.[70] Four years later, the corporation of Youghal, County Cork, insulted her by deliberately holding elections for a new mayor at a time when her candidate, John Wright, was absent, though in this case, there was nothing she could do to repair the damage.[71] These problems were caused in part by Juliana's status as a permanent absentee, which undermined her ability to impose her authority, forced her to rely upon the advice of her son's agents in Ireland to make her decisions and slowed down the decision-making process as letters went back and forth across the Irish Sea.[72] Yet even those mothers who were resident in Ireland had difficulties.

66 Juliana, dowager countess of Cork and Burlington to Richard Musgrave and Thomas Baker, 6 Apr. 1708 (ibid., MS 43, 364/1). Quote from same to same, 19 Feb. 1708/9 (ibid., MS 13, 242/1).
67 Johnston-Liik, *History of the Irish parliament*, vi, 135–6.
68 Waite to Musgrave and Baker, 22 Feb. 1710/11 (NLI, MS 43, 364/5).
69 Same to same, 26 Sept. 1713 (ibid., MS 13, 242/9).
70 Same to same, 19 June 1707 (Chatsworth, Joseph Waite's letter book 1706–8 (Ireland and Yorkshire), Burlington MSS, miscellaneous, box 1). Juliana was referring to the county governor of Waterford, the equivalent of an English county's lord lieutenant.
71 Musgrave and Baker to Burlington, 15 Sept. 1711 (NLI, MS 43, 894/4).
72 For an example of Juliana relying on the Irish agents' political advice, see Waite to Foulke and Walker, 17 Aug. 1714 (ibid., MS 13, 249/3).

Katherine Chichester, dowager countess of Donegall, managed the inheritance of her son, Arthur, the 4th earl, after his father died in 1706 when Arthur was only 11. She took a particular interest in the parliamentary seats for Belfast, for it was with the Chichester family that 'the magistracy and the powers of the corporation always belonged from the first creation of it obtained by their ancestors'.[73] When one of the Belfast MPs, William Cairnes, died in 1707, Katherine put forward to the vacancy Cairnes's brother, Sir Alexander Cairnes. He was then challenged by one Samuel Ogle, supported by the chief magistrate, George McCartney. Despite Katherine appearing personally at the vote, McCartney was able to use the power afforded to him by his position, along with his own political connexions, to see that Ogle was elected.[74] More insulting still was the countess's treatment in the Irish House of Commons. She and some of her friends attempted to remain after the election results had been heard in order to listen to the debates, but were quickly forced to leave after another MP called for the candles to be extinguished, 'at which the ladies fled, very much resenting the affront so openly offered them'. As discussed earlier, the presence of ladies in the visitors' seats in the House of Commons was an accepted custom in Ireland, and the writer of the letter in which this story was told noted that 'it is so usual for everybody here to stay and hear the debates that it was a particular unkindness to refuse them'.[75] Katherine and her friends' poor experience therefore had nothing to do with gender, and a much more likely explanation is that they were Tories faced by a predominantly Whig parliament. If anything, her treatment, which flew in the face of good manners and the dictates of polite society, shows how seriously she was taken as a political player. Even her status as a woman was not enough to protect her from political backbiting.

As well as opposing the interests of female guardians, male politicians also attempted to control or influence their decisions, and it took some strength and determination not to be cowed. Alan Brodrick had little faith in the political abilities of either Lady Burlington or Lady Donegall, and towards Juliana he took a patronising stance. Anticipating trouble because of her absenteeism and unfamiliarity with Irish politics and politicians, he (ironically) expected her to take his advice in order to correct the problem, saying in one letter that he was sure she could be brought around to his way of thinking, for she was 'a woman of good sense', while in another, arguing that she was being led astray by poor advice from her son's agents and that her instructions were not being followed. He believed that the agents were so beyond her control that they were threatening voters on the Burlington estates with distraint or arrest if they did not support a Tory interest, which, Brodrick was sure, would be entirely against what Juliana would wish, for she was a Whig like him.[76] This belief was unfounded, for despite problems with the agents surrounding issues of land management, there is no hint in the Burlington letters that Juliana felt that they were trying to undercut her politically, a move

73 Johnson to Ormond, 18 Oct. 1707 (ibid., MS 2472).

74 Hayton, *Ruling Ireland*, pp 197–9.

75 Johnson to Ormond, 18 Oct. 1707 (NLI, MS 2472).

76 Quote from Alan Brodrick to Thomas Brodrick, 5 Sept. 1712 (SHC, MS 1248/3/83–84). See also same to same, 23 July 1712 (ibid., MS 1248/3/80–81).

which would have been far harder to conceal from her for any length of time and which would have provoked dismissal. Whether misplaced or not, Brodrick used his concern over the political representation of Youghal to justify his interest in the Burlingtons' affairs and attempts to interfere with them, writing that 'I would not interpose in this thing if I did not apprehend it to be of mighty concern how the boroughs and interest of so great a family go: and I hope I shall not be blamed for writing that which I apprehend may prove of public use'.[77] Yet, as it transpired, his anxiety lest the Youghal MPs, John Hayman and Henry Luther, be deposed in 1712 in favour of Tory candidates, proved unwarranted.[78] What is more, despite his constant reservations over Juliana's judgement and abilities, he was never able to challenge her power successfully.[79] In February 1714 he suggested that the underage earl of Cork and Burlington be approached, so that he could prevent his boroughs from being 'a perpetual weight in the scale against what his family have always taken to be the true interest of their country'.[80] Yet the earl was about to embark on his Grand Tour, and seven months later, it was still Juliana whom Brodrick was contending with, writing that 'though Lady Burlington was very well disposed in recommending to her boroughs, yet she had not finally determined in some of them. It is high time she should finally conclude.' In the end, he had to admit that it was she who 'hath absolute power to bring another in that borough' and could only hope that her preferred candidates were also his.[81]

In the case of the countess of Donegall, he had more leverage. As with Lady Burlington, he was unhappy with Katherine's management of her son's political interests, this time because of her own Tory views, rather than those of any agents. Writing to his brother of his concerns, he asked:

> may it not be reasonably expected that the interest of his lordship [*Arthur Forbes, 2nd earl of Granard and Lady Donegall's brother*] in the boroughs of Mullingar and St Johnstown [*County Longford*], and of Lady Donegall at Belfast and Carrickfergus will not be made use of to send up members whose business it will be to distress the government and obstruct the King's affairs in Parliament?[82]

To control Katherine and Lord Granard's actions, he suggested that the pensions they were seeking, 'instead of being put actually on the establishment, were left a little to be considered till my lord lieutenant landed, I cannot see but it would have a good effect'. His intention to force them into managing their family estates in a way he approved of was made even clearer, when he enquired 'may not my lord lieutenant in confidence tell his lordship [*Granard*] that the King's favour entitles him to a better return, then choosing members perfectly disaffected to the present ministry?'[83]

77 Ibid.
78 Johnston-Liik, *History of the Irish parliament*, iv, 389; ibid., v, 140.
79 Alan Brodrick to Thomas Brodrick, 23 July 1712 (SHC, MS 1248/3/80–81).
80 Same to same, 23 Feb. 1713/14 (ibid., MS 1248/3/166–167).
81 Same to same, 4 Nov. 1714 (ibid., MS 1248/3/199–200).
82 Ibid.
83 Ibid.

Given these difficulties, it is understandable that mothers should often have introduced their young sons to the world of politics before their 21st birthdays, both to train them in how to manage their interests alone when the time came, and to ease the burden they themselves faced during their children's minorities. Juliana allowed her 19-year-old son to sit in on her meetings regarding the 1713 elections, though she retained overall control, as Alan Brodrick discovered.[84] Some tried to take matters too far, however. Catherine O'Brien was politely rebuffed in 1723 when she tried to gather support to have her 18-year-old son, Sir Edward, elected.[85] It was pointed out to her that this would be very difficult given his minority, and the recipient of her letter, James Hamilton, replied that he had already promised his support elsewhere, as he hoped Catherine would do.[86] We do not know why she tried to have her son elected at this time, instead of using his interest to support viable candidates and build a network of politicians favourable to the family. Presumably she mistakenly thought the rules could and would be bent for her son, because of his wealth and social position and because minors were occasionally elected (though they were usually closer to their 21st birthdays than Edward was at this point). In the end, it was not until 1727 that Edward was finally chosen an MP, at the age of 22.[87]

For some, such difficulties outweighed the benefits of political involvement. Lady Burlington's experiences appear to have given her a lifelong distaste for politics. The month after her son's 21st birthday, while the earl was still away on his Grand Tour, Joseph Waite wrote that he did not 'perceive that her ladyship intends to concern herself in relation to elections for members of parliament further than to lay before his lordship the several letters sent by gentlemen on that subject, when his lordship returns to London'.[88] Even twelve years later, when writing to her Irish son-in-law, Henry Boyle, she made clear her continuing aversion towards elections, pitying him for having to concern himself with such 'troublesome affairs'.[89]

Conclusion

Influence at the royal court may have been impractical and public office impossible, but with the help of a political culture which embraced and even supported their association with politics by allowing them privileges like easy access to

84 Waite to Foulke and Walker, 18 June 1713 (NLI, MS 13, 254/3). Given the earl's reported Tory sympathies, Brodrick may have been lucky it was Juliana with whom he dealt. See Jane Clark, '"Lord Burlington is here"' in Toby Barnard and Jane Clark (eds), *Lord Burlington: architecture, art and life* (London, 1995), pp 251–310.

85 It is not mentioned which constituency Catherine wanted Edward elected to, but the most likely choice would be County Clare, given his family's land holdings there and the fact that his paternal grandfather, Sir Donat, had held this seat from 1692 to 1714. See Johnston-Liik, *History of the Irish parliament*, v, 367–8.

86 James Hamilton to Catherine O'Brien, 23 Nov. 1723 (NLI, MS 45, 346/4).

87 In England, for example, forty youths between the ages of 16 and 20 were elected between 1690 and 1715 (*H.C. 1690–1715*, i, 276–7). Edward O'Brien held the seat for County Clare until his death in 1765 (Johnston-Liik, *History of the Irish parliament*, v, 368–9).

88 Waite to Foulke and Walker, 9 Apr. 1715 (NLI, MS 13, 249/3).

89 Burlington to Henry Boyle, 27 July 1727 (PRONI, D2707/A/1/11/6).

parliament, elite women in Ascendancy Ireland found many other avenues through which to make a political impact. In an era when conversation and handwritten correspondence were the primary means of communication, they used both to engage with political issues among themselves and with the men in their lives. Some went further and (not always voluntarily) assisted their husbands, fathers, sons, brothers and nephews in advancing their careers by gathering and sending information, acting as conduits, messengers and proxies and electioneering on their men's behalf. Their help may not always have been wanted or even useful, but the fact that they could intervene in politics at all shows the recognised place they held in the political process. Furthermore, the frequent occasions on which men deliberately sought women's help point to the trust the former often placed in the latters' abilities and discretion. There were no age restrictions on female involvement; Alice Brodrick was used by her father as a means to send information to her uncle when she was just a child, and Katherine Conolly was involved in her family's political fortunes well into old age. There were certain women though whose circumstances gave them power which far outstripped that of their contemporaries. The wealthy and the well-connected made the best patronage brokers, and the widows of great landowners, who had charge of their young sons' estates, had electoral influence which placed them on a par with men. In such cases, their talents were given almost free rein to shine, and the men around them could do little but beg and bargain for their help.

The unique social and political position which Ireland and its elite held during this time also played a part in the elite female experience. Absenteeism reduced some widowed mothers' powers and altered the ways in which other women could canvass their family's tenants for votes, setting them apart from English women who campaigned 'on the ground', in person and in voters' homes. Then there was personality. No two women were the same, and some were more interested in politics than others. Not everyone was as independent or strident in their activities as Sarah Stafford and her companions, discussed at the beginning of this chapter, but nor were elite women and politics mutually exclusive. Each affected and informed the other, and the history of both can only be properly understood when they are taken together.

7

Institutional philanthropy

Looking through the wills left behind by elite women in or from Ireland during the Ascendancy period, one of most common features is a tendency to bequeath money for charitable purposes, much of which was to be funnelled through philanthropic institutions. Margaret Boyle, dowager countess of Orrery, who died in 1689, left £21 *p.a.* to erect an almshouse near Castlemartyr in County Cork, which was to care for six poor women. In 1748, Ann Brodrick, dowager Viscountess Midleton, left £700 to be divided among three Dublin hospitals and another £300 for schools. Both left money to be distributed to the poor of various named parishes, indicating that the money was to go through the church. Jane Bonnell, who passed away in 1745, stated this aim more clearly, specifically willing that £200 was to go to 'the Minister, Churchwardens and Vestments of St. John's parish in Dublin to be by them laid out on some convenient purchase the produce of which to be applied towards binding out poor girls of that parish for ever'.[1] Death imitated life, and establishments including, but not limited to, schools, churches and almshouses (which were also known as hospitals) were an attractive means of assisting the poor, as were workhouses. All allowed many people to be helped at once, conformed to a recognisable template which could theoretically be replicated across the country and were a far more structured and controlled method of distributing charity than giving it out to one individual at a time. Elite women's involvement with such places was present from the very beginning of the Ascendancy era, yet relatively little has been written on the subject.

Rosemary Raughter's work provides the best starting point, though she has focused on the later eighteenth century and on women's involvement in associated charity, that is, institutions founded, organised and run by women, for women and catering specifically to women's needs, including childbirth, childcare and the prevention or elimination of prostitution.[2] Within these parameters, she has correctly pointed out that there was a general separation of the sexes when it came to the running of charitable foundations, and that 'within male-run organizations women were almost invariably relegated to a subordinate and supportive role and, where they were not absolutely denied membership, were excluded from the

1 Will of Margaret, dowager countess of Orrery, 8 May 1691 (TNA, Prob. 11/404, f. 295); *London Evening Post*, 23–26 Jan. 1748; quote from the will of Jane Bonnell, 8 June 1745 (TNA, Prob. 11/740, f. 112).

2 Rosemary Raughter, 'A natural tenderness: women's philanthropy in eighteenth-century Ireland' (University College Dublin, M.A. thesis, 1992), pp 26–7; eadem, 'A natural tenderness: the ideal and the reality of eighteenth-century female philanthropy' in M.G. Valiulis and Mary O'Dowd (eds), *Women and Irish history: essays in honour of Margaret MacCurtain* (Dublin, 1997), p. 83.

administrative and policy-making areas of the charity'.[3] It is by using this (perfectly legitimate) approach that she has concluded that the Magdalen Asylum, founded in 1766, was 'one of the earliest examples of organised female philanthropy in Ireland'.[4] However such an approach excludes the input made by many earlier women to institutions like those listed above. When they are taken into account, a greater historiography opens up.[5]

Considerable attention has already been given to the development of eighteenth-century charity schools in Ireland and the education they provided for boys and girls, though the role elite women had in creating and managing these schools has, as yet, received little attention.[6] The donations made to churches by early Irish women have likewise been discussed, but for a timeframe far predating the Glorious Revolution. More useful for a study of Ascendancy period church philanthropy is Rowena Dudley's discussion of how Dublin parishes dealt with the poor between the Restoration and 1740, and the ways in which money was collected, distributed and to whom.[7] The scholarship on Irish almshouses of the non-medical variety is quite limited. However, some work has been done, including a little on the contribution made by elite women. This is further supplemented by the English scholarship, though even this is not as expansive as might be wished.[8] The history

3 Raughter, 'A natural tenderness: women's philanthropy', p. 26. David Hempton and Myrtle Hill agree with this statement when considering Irish Quaker women's involvement in philanthropy in the late eighteenth century (Hempton and Hill, *Evangelical Protestantism in Ulster society, 1740–1890* (London, 1992), p. 132). Donna Andrew also agrees with regard to late eighteenth-century England ('*Noblesse oblige*: female charity in an age of sentiment' in Susan Staves and John Brewer (eds), *Early modern conceptions of property* (London, 1995), p. 278). See also Maria Luddy, 'Women and charitable organisations in nineteenth-century Ireland', *Women's Studies International Forum*, xliv (1989), pp 301–5.

4 Raughter, 'A natural tenderness: women's philanthropy', p. 27.

5 For a basic list of some forty charitable institutions established in County Waterford during the eighteenth and nineteenth centuries, some of which owed their creation to elite women, see Richard Lahert, 'Some charitable institutions of old Waterford', *Decies*, xxvii, xxix (1985), pp 43–54, 24–31. For various discussions of nineteenth-century philanthropy, see Laurence Geary and Oonagh Walsh (eds), *Philanthropy in nineteenth-century Ireland* (Dublin, 2014).

6 D.W. Hayton, 'Did Protestantism fail in early eighteenth-century Ireland? Charity schools and the enterprise of religious and social reformation, c. 1690–1730' in Alan Ford, James McGuire and Kenneth Milne (eds), *As by law established: the Church of Ireland since the Reformation* (Dublin, 1995), pp 166–86; Karen Sonnelitter, '"To unite our temporal and eternal interests": sermons and the charity school movement in Ireland, 1689–1740', *Eighteenth-Century Ireland*, xxv (2010), pp 62–81; Michael Quane, 'Viscount Weymouth grammar school, Carrickmacross', *Journal of the Royal Society of Antiquaries of Ireland*, lxxxvi (1956), pp 27–51; idem, 'Midleton school, Co. Cork' in ibid, lxxxii (1952), pp 1–27; Joseph Robins, *The lost children: a study of charity children in Ireland, 1700–1900* (Dublin, 1980); M.G. Jones, *The charity school movement: a study of eighteenth century Puritanism in action* (Cambridge, 1938). For information on the later charter school movement, which only began in 1734, see Kenneth Milne, *The Irish charter schools 1730–1830* (Dublin, 1997).

7 Lisa Bitel, 'Women's donations to the churches in early Ireland', *Journal of the Royal Society of Antiquaries of Ireland*, cxiv (1984), pp 5–23; Rowena Dudley, 'The Dublin parishes and the poor: 1660–1740', *Archivium Hibernium*, liii (1999), pp 80–94.

8 For a discussion of a later eighteenth-century almshouse founded by an elite Irish woman named Sarah Tighe, see John Dyer, 'The almshouse at Inistioge', *Old Kilkenny Review*, l (1998), pp 43–7. For a more general discussion of some seventeenth- and eighteenth-century Irish almshouses, see Barry Reilly, 'The almshouses of Fethard, County Tipperary' in Conleth Manning

of those institutions which we would now call hospitals is better documented, with volumes dedicated to particular establishments, as well as more general histories of the development of medicine in early modern Ireland. As these hospitals were just beginning to appear during the Ascendancy period and were, in several instances, the result of female philanthropy, this work includes some useful material on certain ladies' efforts.[9] The workhouse system in Ireland originated in the very early eighteenth century, but was slow to develop. Perhaps as a result of this, the current historiography does not favour this time period, being much more concerned with the nineteenth century and the system's failings at the time of the Great Famine.[10] This is a shame, for as we shall see, the original workhouse was in large part, a product of female tenacity.

Recipients and motivations

The practice of elite Irish women aiding those less fortunate than themselves was well established by the eighteenth century, for the curbs which were placed upon their influence in other areas, most notably high politics, were not found here. Contemporary thought, underpinned by biblical teachings, held that they had a special role to play in dispensing philanthropy, as many of the allegedly feminine virtues, including compassion and gentleness, were viewed as necessary components of charity.[11] Combined with women's supposedly inherent maternal instincts and the organisational and care-giving skills they were thought to have acquired through the running of a household, this purportedly made women naturally and uniquely suited to the care of others and even duty bound to provide it.[12]

The people who required help varied hugely: adults and children, male and female, urban and rural. The factors which had reduced them to poverty were

(ed.), *From ringforts to fortified houses: studies on castle and other monuments in honour of David Sweetman* (Wicklow, 2007), pp 217–35. For a sample of the English historiography, see Brian Bailey, *Almshouses* (London, 1988); Brian Howson, *Houses of noble poverty. A history of the English almshouse* (Sunbury-on-Thames, 1993); idem, *Almshouses. A social and architectural history* (Stroud, 2008); Helen Caffrey, *Almshouses in the West Riding of Yorkshire 1600–1900* (King's Lynn, 2006).

9 J.B. Lyons, *The quality of Mercer's: the story of Mercer's Hospital, 1734–1991* (Dublin, 1991); J.D.H. Widdess, *The charitable infirmary, Jervis Street, Dublin, 1718–1968* (Dublin, 1968); Davis Coakley, *Doctor Steevens' Hospital: a brief history* (Dublin, 1992); Helen Burke, *The royal hospital, Donnybrook: a heritage of caring, 1743–1993* (Dublin, 1993); Laurence Geary, *Medicine and charity in Ireland, 1718–1851* (Dublin, 2004), esp. ch. 1. Geary provides a good overview of the development of hospitals in Ireland during this period and a more detailed discussion of the historiography than can be provided here.

10 See, for example, John O'Connor, *The workhouses of Ireland: the fate of Ireland's poor* (Dublin, 1995); Virginia Crossman, 'Workhouse medicine in Ireland: a preliminary analysis 1850–1914' in Jonathan Reinarz and Leonard Schwarz (eds), *Medicine and the workhouse* (Woodbridge, 2013), pp 123–39; Michael Farrell, *The Poor Law and the workhouse in Belfast, 1838–1948* (Belfast, 1978).

11 Raughter, 'A natural tenderness: the ideal and the reality', p. 71; eadem, 'A natural tenderness: women's philanthropy', p. 3; Robert Shoemaker, *Gender in English society, 1650–1850: the emergence of separate spheres?* (London, 1998), pp 225–6.

12 Raughter, 'A natural tenderness: women's philanthropy', pp 28–9, 31, 78–9; eadem, 'A natural tenderness: the ideal and the reality', pp 75–9.

wide-ranging and included, among other things, the effects of Ireland's population boom between 1700 and 1800, multiple famines over the course of the century, unemployment, the loss of a household's main breadwinner, sickness, age and disability.[13] Despite these difficulties, there was still a preconception among the upper orders that some were more deserving than others and that poverty was, in many cases, a choice, brought on by laziness among 'sturdy beggars' who could have worked had they chosen to. These people were differentiated from the 'deserving poor', who were truly destitute and in need of assistance, and the distinction led to even casual almsgiving being condemned, making more organised and controlled institutional philanthropy all the more attractive.[14] The Irish writer Samuel Madden wrote that Ireland was 'a nation of beggars where so many thousands are idle, and lazy enough to be fond of the trade, and an infinite number of people weak enough to encourage them in it by relieving them'.[15] He argued that such behaviour on the part of these so-called beggars was tantamount to 'robbing the honest industrious poor', and lamented the fact that harsher punishments were not used against the culprits.[16] Jonathan Swift was equally unforgiving of the beggars he saw in Dublin and beyond, and recommended badging and even punishing them.[17] Similar mandates were in force in England, where widows were particularly favoured when it came to state poor relief and single women were not because the latter were classed as 'able bodied' (that is, people who could and should find work to support themselves), while a widow might be old, or burdened with children. Of course, this system ignored the severe restrictions upon women's job opportunities and the paradox this created, but still, it persisted.[18] The issue of 'deserving' and 'undeserving poor' induced such strong feelings that it could even filter into seemingly unrelated topics. Susan Staves has shown that those who opposed the naturalisation of foreigners in England were criticised for supposedly defending those English-born citizens who were workshy and did not want their own shortcomings to be highlighted by the industry of others, or deserve to be protected from such competition.[19]

Why elite women chose to spend their time, energy and money on those who seemingly had little to offer in return is a complicated issue, but certain commonly held beliefs are discernible. The most obvious reason was a genuine desire to help those in need, and this was cited as the driving force behind many a helping hand. As Mary Jones said in a letter to her sister, Jane Bonnell, 'happy are those in whose

13 Raughter, 'A natural tenderness: women's philanthropy', pp 8–19.

14 Raughter has also picked up on this point (Raughter, 'A natural tenderness: women's philanthropy', pp 24, 47, 58, 66–7).

15 Samuel Madden, *Reflections and resolutions proper for the gentlemen of Ireland, as to their conduct for the service of their country* ... (Dublin, 1738), pp 154–5.

16 Ibid., p. 156.

17 Jonathan Swift, 'A proposal for giving badges to the beggars in all parishes of Dublin' in *The prose works of Jonathan Swift*, ed. Herbert Davis (14 vols, Oxford, 1939–68), xiii, 127–40. This tract was originally written in 1737. See also Mary Carter, 'Swift and the scheme for badging beggars in Dublin, 1726–1737', *Eighteenth-Century Life*, xxxvii (2013), pp 97–118.

18 Amy Froide, *Never married: singlewomen in early modern England* (Oxford, 2005), pp 34–5.

19 Susan Staves, 'Chattel property rules and the construction of Englishness, 1660–1800', *Law and History Review*, xii (1994), pp 131–2.

power it is to relieve the distressed'.[20] Religious beliefs also demanded and produced a certain level of commitment to the less fortunate, particularly in Ireland with its competing versions of Christianity. Raughter has written that 'religion was certainly the most readily avowed motive for women's philanthropy', and that Protestantism and Catholicism were in philanthropic competition with each other by the end of the eighteenth century, having both experienced something of a revival.[21] This competition is less obvious in the first half of the century, but should not be discounted. Religious motives can often be inferred from elite women's correspondence on charity, and the number of churchmen with whom they co-ordinated their actions confirms that faith played a significant role in the decision-making process. Catholicism in particular promoted salvation through good works, and although its female believers were in some respects hampered by the penal laws, which 'restricted their access to education, their property rights and their freedom of religious practice', the statutes also made it more difficult for the church's male hierarchy to police their activities.[22]

A woman's charity might also be as advantageous to its giver as its receivers, though in very different ways. It could provide her with a sense of purpose, a welcome distraction from the monotony of day-to-day life and, depending on her interests, a more engaging outlet for energy which would otherwise have been directed towards family, household or politics.[23] Some viewed their activities as no more 'than a convention or a duty thoughtlessly fulfilled', but competiveness, social pressure and the status of philanthropy as a fashionable pursuit could also play a role, as ladies strove to emulate, equal or surpass the achievements of other men and women in their position.[24] The geographical spread of ladies' charity and the people they helped is also telling. Lady Midleton's will directed money towards areas in which she had spent a large part of her life and had family connexions, giving money to the poor of parishes in Dublin, where she died, in County Down, where her first husband had held lands which had then passed to her son, and in County Cork, her second husband's power-base and the inspiration behind the Midleton title. Interestingly, she left no money in Wales, her native soil, but she had not lived there since her youth.[25] This type of targeted relief was common among the female elite, and suggests that they felt a particular responsibility to care for those on their own or their husbands' and sons' lands, reinforcing ideas of their maternal role towards family dependants and employees. Focusing on

20 Mary Jones to Jane Bonnell, 14 Mar. [n.d.] (NLI, MS 41, 577/5). See also Raughter, 'A natural tenderness: the ideal and the reality', p. 84.

21 Raughter, 'A natural tenderness: women's philanthropy', pp 46–7. For further examples of later eighteenth-century Irish women who were driven by their religious ideals, see eadem, 'A natural tenderness: the ideal and the reality', pp 82–4.

22 Rosemary Raughter, 'A discreet benevolence: female philanthropy and the Catholic resurgence', *Women's History Review*, vi (1997), p. 466. See also eadem, 'A natural tenderness: women's philanthropy', pp 166–7.

23 Raughter, 'A natural tenderness: women's philanthropy', pp 4, 21; eadem, 'A natural tenderness: the ideal and the reality', pp 87–8.

24 Raughter, 'A natural tenderness: women's philanthropy', p. 39.

25 *D.I.B.* (Brodrick, Alan (c.1655–1728)); *Oxford D.N.B.* (Trevor, Sir John (c.1637–1717)); *London Evening Post*, 23–26 Jan. 1748.

the estate's rent payers also had short- and long-term political benefits, for female philanthropy could be used to boost the public reputation of the benefactress and her family, encouraging a landlord's tenant voters to lend him their support if and when he made a bid for political office.[26] In Ireland, this was particularly important, as finding tenants was difficult, especially if Protestants were wanted. If a show of female munificence helped to keep those already in place on side, it was time and money well spent.[27]

There were also more general social benefits to philanthropy. It could provide a healthier, better-educated and more industrious workforce, and help to prevent social unrest by placating the poor, instilling in them a sense of social hierarchy and teaching them early in life to accept their place in the world, and to respect and obey their social superiors.[28] The charity of elite women was particularly important, as it supplemented the poor governmental responses of this era, which have been characterised as 'sporadic, unplanned and almost invariably inadequate', as well as 'primarily reactive'.[29] As one Irishman wrote in 1732, 'it has been the observation of travellers, as I have been frequently told, that in all the countries they have seen, they have never met with fewer public charitable foundations'.[30] Although the Church of Ireland attempted to fill the breach, it did not represent the faith of most of the population and was, in any case, overwhelmed by the needs of the people. These failings of the state and the state church made private charity (male and female) all the more vital and helped to prevent the 'decay of hospitality' brought on in England in the seventeenth century by its more organised parish poor relief system, which, it has been shown, led to its elite decreasing their philanthropic efforts.[31]

26 Judith Lewis, *Sacred to female patriotism: gender, class, and politics in late Georgian Britain* (London, 2003), p. 86; Elaine Chalus, '"That epidemical Madness": women and electoral politics in the late eighteenth century' in Hannah Barker and Elaine Chalus (eds), *Gender in eighteenth-century England: roles, representations and responsibilities* (London, 1997), p. 156.

27 On landlord paternalism, particularly in the nineteenth century and its political uses, see S.J. Connolly, *Religion, law and power: the making of Protestant Ireland 1660–1760* (Oxford, 1992), p. 138; Conor McNamara '"The monster misery of Ireland": landlord paternalism and the 1822 famine in the West' in Geary and Walsh (eds), *Philanthropy in nineteenth-century Ireland*, pp 82–6; Kevin McKenna, 'Charity, paternalism and power on the Clonbrock estates, County Galway, 1834–44' in ibid., pp 97–114; Joanna McEntee, 'Pecuniary assistance for poverty and emigration: the politics of landed estate management and philanthropy in mid-nineteenth-century Ireland' in ibid., pp 115–32.

28 Hayton, 'Did Protestantism fail', p. 169; Robins, *The lost children*, p. 11; Raughter, 'A natural tenderness: women's philanthropy', pp 21, 84–5; eadem, 'A natural tenderness: the ideal and the reality', pp 47–8, 82. For Scotland, see Mary O'Dowd, 'Politics, patriotism, and women in Ireland, Britain and colonial America, c. 1700–1780', *Journal of Women's History*, xxii (2010), p. 24. O'Dowd also argues that Scottish philanthropy was promoted as a way of 'eradicating idleness and of inculcating a "spirit of industry and diligence" among the poor' (ibid.).

29 Raughter, 'A natural tenderness: women's philanthropy', pp 19, 20.

30 Sir William Fownes to Jonathan Swift, 9 Sept. 1732 (*The correspondence of Jonathan Swift, D.D.*, ed. David Woolley (4 vols, Dublin, 1999–2007), iii, 535).

31 Raughter, 'A natural tenderness: women's philanthropy', pp 20, 57–8; Toby Barnard, 'Public and private uses of wealth in Ireland, c. 1660–1760' in Jacqeline Hill and Colm Lennon (eds), *Luxury and austerity. Historical Studies xxi* (Dublin, 1999), p. 66.

The Dublin Workhouse

> On Thursday, the 12th of October, 1704, the Lord Mayor, Recorder, Alderman, and Sheriffs, waited on her Grace [*Mary, duchess of Ormond*] to the ground enclosed at the West end of St James's-street, where her Grace laid the foundation stone of the City Workhouse; and the Lord Mayor, Francis Stoyt, esq. invited her Grace to a splendid entertainment prepared by him upon this occasion.[32]

This workhouse was the first to be established in Ireland, and remained the only attempt at such an institution for many decades to come.[33] The land on which it was to be built had been purchased in 1703 by the city of Dublin, after which a bill was passed in March 1704 entitled 'For erecting a workhouse in the city of Dublin for employing and maintaining the poor thereof'. Taken out of context, the above sentences describing Mary, duchess of Ormond, laying the foundation stone that October, create the impression that her involvement in its creation was merely ceremonial – a famous name harnessed by the mayor, recorder, alderman and sheriffs to attract attention and donations to a worthy cause. In some ways, this is the truth, however, it was Mary, aware of her power as the matriarch of the Butler family and wife of the then lord lieutenant, who was doing the harnessing, and the full report makes clear that the assistance she rendered went far beyond the foundation ceremony. In fact, she was effectively leading the entire venture. The report paid tribute to her 'singular and unwearied application' in getting the bill passed, and called her efforts 'a bright and eminent pattern' of charity, which, it was to be hoped, others would follow.[34]

No money had been assigned for the construction of the actual building, and so Mary gathered the huge sum of £910 0*s.* 2*d.* herself, having obtained 'subscriptions from several of the nobility and other persons of quality in this kingdom', though the exact amount she personally gave is unclear.[35] A list of subscribers survives, but oddly, given the attachment of the duchess to the scheme, only two other elite women are named, Mary, Lady Dun, a relation of the earls of Cork and the wife of the Scottish born, Dublin-based doctor, Sir Patrick Dun, and Mary, Lady Lanesborough, wife of James Lane, 2nd Viscount Lanesborough, and herself a niece of Bishop Compton of London and granddaughter of the 2nd earl of Northampton.[36] They donated £11 10*s.* and £200 respectively (Lady Lanesborough's £200 being one of the largest personal contributions given). Why there were so few women on the list may be the result of coverture, which gave husbands sole ownership of all marital assets and could lead to contributions from married men, which may well

32 James Ware, *The antiquities and history of Ireland*, ... (London, 1705), p. 196.

33 'The workhouse in Ireland' (http://www.workhouses.org.uk/Ireland/) (accessed 2 Dec. 2014). The next 'workhouse' was in County Cork and opened in 1747. It was only ever a foundling hospital, however.

34 2 Anne, c. 19 [Ire.] (4 Mar. 1704); Ware, *The antiquities and history of Ireland*, p. 196.

35 Ware, *The antiquities and history of Ireland*, p. 196. On Mary's financial contribution, see John Vernon, *Remarks on a paper, entitled, an abstract on the state of the work-house, for maintaining of the poor of the city of Dublin* (Dublin, 1716), p. 12.

36 *D.I.B.* (Dun, Sir Patrick (1642–1713)); Arthur Collins, *Peerage of England* ... (3 vols, London, 1735), iii, 143–50.

have been in concert with, or at the behest of their wives, being listed only under the husband's name. It may also be that many women's contributions were lumped together in the £910 0*s.* 2*d.* covered by 'Her Grace the duchess of Ormond's roll' or conversely, the duchess may have known relatively few Irish women to approach for subscriptions, being better acquainted with their husbands thanks to their political dealings with the duke. What is clear though, is that these three Marys were all English-born, and possibly inspired in their support by the English workhouse system, particularly given the fact that the Dublin workhouse was modelled upon that at Bristol.[37]

The project was certainly popular among the native Irish male elite and received strong support from the likes of Lord Lanesborough, the 3rd earl of Mountrath, the future Speaker, William Conolly, Archbishop William King of Dublin and the bishops of Cork, Kildare and Kilmore.[38] Even with such assistance, however, it remained under constant financial pressure, and the duchess was required to continue her support. She gave it readily, and in June 1705, as she was preparing to return to England, she was 'very desirous to know wherein she might be serviceable to the city – especially to the poorhouse', and was given a memorial relating to the project 'which her Grace received very cheerfully, and promised to take all convenient opportunities therein with her Majesty for our advantage'.[39] With connexions such as these, it is easy to see why those who remained in Ireland and had responsibility for continuing the workhouse were anxious to retain her support. The duchess herself would never return to see the fruits of her labour, but the Irish parliament thanked her for her efforts in bringing it about.[40]

The publication of the list of subscribers shows the publicity afforded to the benefactors of the workhouse, and some of those who supported it were likely to have been motivated by a desire to appear fashionable and magnanimous and to associate themselves with a project so heavily identified with a prominent a figure like the duchess (this was, after all, what Mary was relying upon when she sought their money). One person who is conspicuously absent from the list, though, is the duke of Ormond. As viceroy, he was a member of the newly formed committee entitled The Governor and Guardians of the Poor, which oversaw the institution, but the founding ceremony took place in his absence (he did not return to Ireland until the following month) and it was very much his wife's venture, though other couples, like the Duns and Lanesboroughs, were clearly joint supporters.[41] This would suggest that women were able to distribute institutional philanthropy independently of male relations and lend their support to projects not patronised (or not actively patronised) by their husbands, brothers or fathers. However, the

37 David Hayton, *The Anglo-Irish experience, 1680–1730: religion, identity and patriotism* (Woodbridge, 2012), p. 159.

38 Vernon, *Remarks on a paper*, pp 11–12.

39 Francis Stoyte to William King, 9 June 1705 (TCD, MS 1995–2008, no. 1161).

40 *H.M.C. Ormonde*, n.s., viii, p. xlii. For an image of this workhouse in 1762, which records that it was 170 feet long, see 'The workhouse' (http://www.workhouses.org.uk/DublinSouth/) (accessed 1 Dec. 2014).

41 O'Connor, *The workhouses of Ireland*, pp 31–2; Ware, *The antiquities and history of Ireland*, p. 196; Vernon, *Remarks on a paper*, pp 11–12.

duchess's efforts were far more closely linked to her husband's wellbeing than is initially apparent. It is true that she did make personal gains from such high-profile philanthropy, for it provided her with a distraction to pass the time while her husband was away, and improved her network of friends and contacts in Ireland by giving her an excuse to interact with churchmen and politicians and socialise with them at the 'splendid entertainment' put on after the foundation ceremony.[42] However, it also allowed her to present herself and by extension, the duke, in a highly favourable light to the Irish public, a matter of some importance given the Butler family's prominence in Ireland and the fact that her husband was then lord lieutenant, out of the country and unable to tend to the workhouse personally.

Religion played its part in attracting supporters as well, for as part of its mandate the workhouse was designed 'to preserve the lives of illegitimate children' and educate and instruct them 'in the Protestant religion'; it was 'a pious design', which should appeal to 'the bounty of all good Christians'.[43] Its directive would ultimately be altered by a 1729 act of parliament, which extended the institution's scope to include foundling children and lunatics, and led to it being renamed 'The foundling hospital and workhouse of the city of Dublin', but by this time it was merely one of many Irish hospitals.[44]

Hospitals and almshouses

Hospitals came in many different forms and were known by different names, including infirmaries and almshouses. Some were designed to provide medical care, others were closer to what we now refer to as retirement homes. For simplicity's sake, they will be divided up here, as much as possible, into medical and non-medical institutions, the former being known as hospitals, the latter as almshouses.[45] Physically, the look of both varied considerably, from houses or multiple houses joined together, to courtyard structures.[46] Numbers of residents or patients also changed from place to place. The Charitable Infirmary, a hospital founded in Dublin in 1718, could initially take only four patients. Lady Orrery, as we have seen, intended to help six women in her almshouse, as did the 1st earl of Cork, when he founded an almshouse at Youghal, County Cork, in 1634. Twelve and thirteen were also popular

42 Ware, *The antiquities and history of Ireland*, p. 196.

43 Mandate quoted in Mary Hayden, 'Charity children in 18th-century Dublin', *Dublin Historical Record*, v (1943), p. 94. See also Ware, *The antiquities and history of Ireland*, p. 196.

44 3 Geo. II, c. 17 [Ire.] (15 Apr. 1729); John Warburton, James Whitelaw and Robert Walsh, *History of the city of Dublin, from the earliest accounts to the present time: ...* (2 vols, London, 1818), i, 578.

45 On the many different names given to almshouses and the difficulties of defining their exact functions, see Nigel Goose and Henk Looijesteijn, 'Almshouses in England and the Dutch Republic circa 1350–1800: a comparative perspective', *Journal of Social History*, xlv (2012), p. 1051; Reilly, 'The almshouses of Fethard', pp 217–18.

46 For images of some almshouses of this period (and before and after), see 'National inventory of architectural heritage' (http://www.buildingsofireland.ie) (accessed 28 Nov. 2014). See also Reilly, 'The almshouses of Fethard', pp 218, 220, 231; Goose and Looijesteijn, 'Almshouses in England and the Dutch Republic', pp 1052–3.

numbers in both Ireland and England, used to represent the twelve disciples, plus or minus Jesus Christ (though the disciples could also count as thirteen, if Judas Iscariot's replacement, Matthias, was taken into account). When Lord Cork's son and daughter-in-law, the 2nd earl and countess of Cork (and 1st of Burlington) founded an almshouse in 1680 at Londesborough, on their English estate, it was to serve six men and six women.[47] As these examples show, some houses accepted only one gender, others both. Some were for people of a particular age or marital status, others were for those of a particular profession or from a particular area. The same was true of hospitals. The Royal Hospital of Kilmainham, founded by King Charles II in 1685, was designed only for 'aged and maimed officers and soldiers of the army in Ireland'.[48] Elite women's involvement with such places typically fell into one of three categories; financier, founder, or admissions patroness.

Looking first at hospitals, many women's involvement with them was primarily monetary. In England, Queen Caroline led the way by giving £5,000 to 'the projected foundling hospital', £100 to 'a projected infirmary in Westminster' and another £100 to St George's hospital 'near Hyde Park Corner'.[49] As we have seen, Ann, Viscountess Midleton, left £700 to be split between three Irish hospitals after her death. These were named as Mercer's Hospital, the Charitable Infirmary and the Blue Coat Hospital, though the Blue Coat was actually a school.[50] It was not uncommon for husbands and wives to donate together, but at other times, they gave separately, Robert Fitzgerald, 19th earl of Kildare making a personal contribution to a hospital in 1722 after his wife's recovery from illness.[51] What are less easy to find are examples of married women giving large sums independently of their husbands, though, like the workhouse subscribers, their contributions may have been masked by their husbands. There were ways around this, however. By the 1740s, fundraising activities for hospitals included staging plays and musical recitals for the benefit of a particular establishment, with proceeds from the event going to the institution in question. If women attended, their support for the hospital was broadcast far and wide, while the location of their seat would give away how much they had paid, different seats costing different amounts.[52]

For those women for whom donations or bequests were not enough and who had the money, time and inclination to do more, there was the option of founding their own establishment. It is striking that this was almost always the preserve of unmarried ladies. The building of Dr Steevens's hospital in Dublin, although inspired

47 Geary, *Medicine and charity*, p. 16; Reilly, 'The almshouses of Fethard', p. 218; Goose and Looijesteijn, 'Almshouses in England and the Dutch Republic', p. 1055; earl and countess of Burlington's deed of the foundation of Londesbro' [*sic*] hospital, 29 May 1680 (Chatsworth, MS L/55/40).

48 Guy Miège, *The present state of Great Britain, and Ireland* ... (11th edn, London, 1748), p. 132.

49 R.L. Arkell, *Caroline of Ansbach, George the second's queen* (London, 1939), p. 327. For further information on Caroline's charity, see *Oxford D.N.B.* (Caroline [Princess Caroline of Brandenburg-Ansbach] (1683–1737)).

50 *General Evening Post*, 23–26 Jan. 1748 [n.s.].

51 Henry Maule to Bonnell, 31 Dec. 1722 (NLI, MS 41, 580/30).

52 See, for example, events staged 'for the support of the hospital for incurables'. *Faulkner's Dublin Journal*, 8–12 Apr. 1746. For further information on stage performances and the social and financial implications of seat locations, see above ch. 5.

and initiated by the will of Dr Richard Steevens, who died in the city in 1710, and supported by the likes of Jonathan Swift and William King, was primarily the result of the efforts of his sister, Grizel Steevens.[53] She was not obliged to use her inheritance from her brother to begin work on the hospital during her own lifetime, but chose to do so, and, having been disappointed by Queen Anne's failure to supplement the building fund, gave most of her estate over to trustees in 1717, allowing work to begin in 1719 and the hospital to open in 1733.[54] Mary Mercer, the daughter of a Dublin doctor, founded a school in Dublin in 1724/5 with the intent that it should care for twenty poor girls, but this was later converted into Mercer's Hospital in 1734, for the purpose of accommodating 'such poor persons, as may happen to labour under diseases of tedious and hazardous cure'.[55] It has been argued that elite women did not look on hospitals as a fulfilling way of distributing philanthropy because the barriers to women receiving medical training severely limited their 'scope for practical benevolence in the treatment and care of the sick poor was restricted by the limitations placed on them as a sex'.[56] What made Grizel and Mary so special, and led them to go against the general trend of male domination in this area, was the presence of doctors in their immediate families.[57] Most likely this issue did affect the decisions of some women. However, we should not ignore their predominance in midwifery during this period, nor can we assume that all, or even many of those who supported hospitals, wanted to be involved in the care of their patients.[58] Of the numerous women who were initially involved in reforming the Foundling Hospital in the mid eighteenth century, only Lady Arbella Denny's hands-on commitment stood the test of time. Many were simply happy to restrict themselves to donations.[59]

Financial donations to almshouses were less common, for these institutions typically had lands assigned to them for permanent support. As alienating lands from the family could not be done without the approval of the landowner, married women were at a disadvantage, and this explains why Elizabeth, 2nd countess of Cork and 1st of Burlington founded the Londesborough almshouse only in conjunction with her husband. As a widow, Lady Orrery owned the lands she assigned in her will to support the almshouse she wanted established after her death, and presumably failed to found it during her lifetime, only because she needed the income to support herself.

53 King to Swift, 20 July 1724 (*Correspondence of Jonathan Swift*, ii, 510).

54 *D.I.B.* (Steevens, Richard (c.1654–1710)).

55 *Statutes passed in the parliaments held in Ireland: from the ninth year of George II. A.D. 1735, to the thirty-third year of Geo. II. A.D. 1759, inclusive* (12 vols, Dublin, 1794), iv, 329; Horatio Townshend, *The history of Mercer's charitable hospital in Dublin, to the end of the year 1742 with note and an appendix* (Dublin, 1860), pp 18–26.

56 Raughter, 'A natural tenderness: women's philanthropy', p. 108. For later Irish women in medicine, see Laura Kelly, *Irish women in medicine, c.1880–1920s: origins, education and careers* (Manchester, 2012).

57 Raughter, 'A natural tenderness: women's philanthropy', p. 107.

58 For a recent study of midwifery and of men's gradual incursion into this area during the mid to late eighteenth century in Ireland, see Philomena Gorey, 'Managing midwifery in Dublin: practice and practitioners, 1700–1800' in Margaret Preston and Margaret Ó hÓgartaigh (eds), *Irish Studies: gender and medicine in Ireland, 1700–1950* (New York, 2012), pp 123–37.

59 Raughter, 'A natural tenderness: women's philanthropy', pp 40, 123–4.

In addition to initiating or supporting almshouses, ladies might exert, or be assumed to exert control over whom they assisted. This was for one of two reasons. First, rank and social connexions meant that a lady was unlikely to be refused (as would seem to be the case when Jane Bonnell was asked to help get a woman into an almshouse); second, she or her family had had a hand in founding the establishment in question.[60] This was the situation in which Juliana Boyle, dowager countess of Cork and Burlington, found herself while managing her underage son's estates, and she vetted all admissions to the Burlington almshouses during this period. Her letters, and those of her secretaries and agents do not provide a list of these establishments; however, it seems that there were two in Ireland, both founded by the 1st earl of Cork, one at Youghal, County Cork and another at Lismore, County Waterford. Both were maintained using the income from parcels of land designated for that purpose.[61] There was also the Londesborough establishment, again maintained by the assignation of family lands.[62] It was this arrangement which allowed the almshouses to continue to be supported during the minority of the 3rd earl of Burlington, though his mother could not continue individual annuities and pensions promised by earlier generations of the family.[63] Admission was subject to a waiting list and a set of rules laid down when the institution was created. These documents do not always survive; however, the information given when new residents were being admitted shows that by the early 1700s, the Irish houses took in both widows and widowers (though Youghal had originally been designed for women only), and were designed for those who had previously lived or worked on the Burlington estates or for a branch of the Boyle family. They did not admit the general poor, further evidence of landholders feeling and acting on a sense of moral responsibility for the people living on their lands, over and above the rest of the population.

Requests for assistance were typically sent to ladies via a third party, rather than coming directly from the would-be recipient. Intermediaries might have more sway with the ultimate patroness, and many of those who were so poor that they sought to enter an almshouse must have been illiterate or lacked the means to pay for paper, ink and postage. Like requests for political patronage, the applications would be supported by details of the background of the individual in question, their personal merits and their current condition. In the case of a widow, information would also be given relating to her husband's profession. The following request, sent to Juliana, via her secretary, Joseph Waite, by one of her son's Irish land agents in the early 1710s, is standard:

> Here is one Mrs Sarah Gray an [*sic*] good gentlewoman and widow reduced to poverty from a plentiful living since her husband's decease who had a very considerable

60 E.E. to Bonnell, 24 Aug. [n.d.] (NLI, MS 41, 580/39).

61 Draft of a letter from Roger Power to Juliana, countess dowager of Cork and Burlington 8 [Oct.?] 1705 (ibid., MS 43, 347/3); Joseph Waite to Ralph Thoresby, 12 Apr. 1709 (Chatsworth, Joseph Waite's letter book 1708–10, Burlington MSS, miscellaneous, box 1).

62 Earl and countess of Burlington's deed of the foundation of Londesbro' hospital, 29 May 1680 (Chatsworth, MS L/55/40).

63 Anthony Spurret to Richard Bagge, 28 Mar. 1704 (ibid., Anthony Spurret's letter book 1703–4, Burlington MSS, miscellaneous, box 1).

> employment in the custom house here, and worked both for Mr [...?] to one their honours in town. She was daughter to Captain John Smith that was chief manager of the honourable Mr Robert Boyle's estate in this kingdom, and much esteemed by the late Earl Richard [*Juliana's grandfather-in-law*], she also tells me her sad condition made her presume to send a petition to her Ladyship a considerable time since, she being a constant church woman, appears to everyone that knows to be [*a?*] real object of charity.[64]

The content of the petition Sarah had previously sent to Juliana is unknown, but was probably for general assistance rather than to enter the almshouse, as the agent would hardly have pestered Lady Burlington with a repeat request. Juliana's answer likewise made no mention of a prior attempt to enter the house, when she conveyed that 'from the account you give of Mrs Sarah Grey's circumstances, her ladyship believing her to be a real object of charity is willing she should be admitted into the almshouse at Youghal'.[65]

The case of Sarah Grey, and the countess's response, suggest that Juliana held ultimate control over admissions and most likely, had she demanded anyone be admitted or refused, her word would have been final. However, she was always mindful of the original rules laid down when the almshouses were founded and made efforts to familiarise herself with them and see to it that they were followed. In 1704, she wrote that 'I consent that William Davis of Castlelyons [*County Cork*] may succeed Fran[cis?] Abram in the almshouse, if it be not contrary to the constitutions to take in strangers when there are objects in the neighbourhood.'[66] Four years later, Waite wrote to the land agents regarding the same place (which he referred to as a hospital), and told them that they had her permission to replace the now deceased Davis with a Mr Sherlock, as long as the latter was 'the most proper object of charity according to the rules of the house'.[67] Men and women were treated the same, and in 1712 the countess was 'willing Margaret Thorpe may be admitted into the first vacancy in the almshouse at Youghal, provided that admission be conformable to the constitution and rules of said hospital'.[68] Nor were there any appreciable differences in how the Irish and English almshouses were dealt with. In Yorkshire, demand was also high while places were limited, and Lady Burlington was just as loath to diverge from the strict entrance requirements, which said that Londesborough people were to be admitted first, followed by those from Craven. More than twelve people would be admitted only if the tenants of the local area agreed to pay for the extras.[69]

Despite the fact that these almshouses were for Burlington family tenants and their families (already a limited pool of people in comparison to the entire country), ideas of 'deserving' and 'undeserving' poor still surfaced and guided decisions as to

64 Jeremy Coughlan to Waite, 25 Jan. 1711 (NLI, MS 13, 255/4).

65 Waite to Digby Foulke, 19 Feb. 1711 [/12?] (ibid., MS 13, 249/1).

66 Burlington to Power, Bagge and Thomas Baker, 7 Oct. 1704 (ibid., MS 43, 361/2).

67 Waite to Richard Musgrave and Baker, 2 Oct. 1708 (Chatsworth, Joseph Waite's letter book 1708–10, Burlington MSS, miscellaneous, box 1).

68 Same to same, 21 June 1712 (NLI, MS 13, 242/7).

69 Same to George Myers, 16 Aug. 1707 (Chatsworth, Joseph Waite's letter book 1706–8, Burlington MSS, miscellaneous, box 1).

which individuals were to be helped and which were not. Sarah Grey, for instance, was only admitted because she was 'a real object of charity'. More surprising (and disturbing to modern eyes) is the fact that Juliana used her power for personal gain and allowed charity and estate management to merge. Her English agent, Thomas Brown, was informed by Waite in 1709 that 'upon securing the arrears and rent due from Mrs Tall, I am ready to believe her ladyship will be pleased to admit her into the almshouse'.[70] How a woman who was eligible for the almshouse was supposed to pay up was not explained, but there is no reason to suppose that Juliana would not have repeated this tactic in Ireland, where she was constantly fighting to obtain rents.[71]

Charity schools

Charity schools were one of the few philanthropic institutions designed solely for children. Although they gained popularity in Ireland throughout this period, initial attempts to encourage them in the country progressed only slowly. After the Battle of the Boyne in 1690, Mary II wrote to her husband, William III, to ask that he use some of the confiscated Irish lands 'for public schools, to instruct the poor Irish', but her request went unheeded, and it was not until five years later that the first such school appeared.[72] If a pamphlet from 1706 is to be believed, the Irish institutions in existence by that year sought to emulate their English counterparts. The writer proclaimed that 'there is here published an account of some charity schools set up in the city of Dublin, in imitation, as the account expresseth it, of the charity schools in London, with the method of setting up and governing the same'.[73] This 'method of setting up and governing' meant that such schools were generally funded by subscriptions, catered for the country's poorest children, whether boys or girls, and, using a curriculum built around Anglican teachings, taught them 'such other things as are suitable to their condition'.[74] As a rule, all children, whether English or Irish, male or female, were taught reading in order to enable them to study the Bible. Beyond that, girls focused on household skills, which would prepare them for domestic service, and boys were more likely to learn writing so that they might later add to their income by working as, for example, scribes (a gender bias reminiscent of that applied to elite children).[75] The size of these schools could vary,

70 Same to Thomas Brown, 14 May 1709 (ibid., Joseph Waite's letter book 1708–10, Burlington MSS, miscellaneous, box 1).

71 The problems of bringing in rents are discussed in detail in chapter 4.

72 Mary II to William III, 25 July 1690 (John Dalrymple, *Memoirs of Great Britain and Ireland: from the dissolution of the last Parliament of Charles II, until the sea-battle off La Hogue* (3 vols, Dublin, 1773), iii, 164); Hayton, 'Did Protestantism fail', p. 168.

73 Anon, *An account of charity-schools lately erected in England, Wales and Ireland: ...* (London, 1706), p. 19.

74 Ibid., pp 3–4.

75 Amy Erickson, *Women and property in early modern England* (London, 1993), pp 57–9; Deborah Simonton, 'Women and education' in Hannah Barker and Elaine Chalus (eds), *Women's history: Britain, 1700–1850* (New York, 2005), p. 39; Raughter, 'A natural tenderness: women's philanthropy', pp 79–80.

but enrolment was usually between twenty and eighty, and the children were often clothed at the expense of their school.[76] The author of the 1706 pamphlet listed almost 270 such institutions in England, but could pick out only three in Dublin, though the pamphlet conceded that 'there are many charities of the like nature in several other cities and villages in the country, and endeavours are using for setting up schools in many places where there are none: but of these we can give no certain account'.[77] The situation changed dramatically over the next fifteen years, for by 1719, 230 Irish charity schools had been established.[78] Many factors contributed to this alteration, not least the founding of the Society for the Promotion of Christian Knowledge in England in 1699, but some credit for the sudden boom must also go to those English ladies who, from the 1690s onwards, brought their experience and knowledge of these schools to Ireland and were surely responsible for the English tint these sites of learning reportedly had.[79]

By the 1710s there was already a well-established culture among the English female elite of supporting charity schools. Mary, duchess of Ormond, was one of the many subscribers to the St James, Westminster, charity school for girls.[80] Her sister, Anne, countess of Coventry, supported the writer Mary Astell's school in Chelsea in 1709, as did Lady Elizabeth Hastings, daughter of the 7th earl of Huntington, who gave to many other such institutions besides, as well as having her own girls' school at Ledsham, West Yorkshire.[81] Transferring this culture to Ireland had proved impossible for King William's wife, but his mistress, Elizabeth Hamilton (*née* Villiers), countess of Orkney, fared considerably better. Using the confiscated Irish estates she had been granted by William, in 1696 she founded one of the country's earliest post-Revolution charity schools in Midleton, County Cork, though it was not complete until 1717.[82] Her reasons were highly suspect, however, for she was likely seeking to tighten her hold over the title and lands granted to her by the king, a move which had been deeply unpopular with his sister-in-law (and heiress presumptive), Princess Anne, as the lands had previously belonged to her father, James II.[83] Lady Orkney's practical involvement in the school was limited and although she reserved the right to direct and change how it was managed, she died in 1733 without ever having implemented this power.[84]

She had begun a trend, however, and other English ladies soon followed in her wake. In 1698, Lady Lanesborough also founded a school in Cork, this time in

76 Anon, *An account of charity-schools*, pp 9–18.

77 Ibid., pp 19–20.

78 Robins, *Lost children*, p. 61.

79 *Oxford D.N.B.* (Bray, Thomas (*bap.* 1658, *d.* 1730)). For further information on the S.P.C.K. and its involvement with charity schools, see C.M. Haydon, 'The anti-Catholic activity of the S.P.C.K., c. 1698–1740', *Recusant History*, xviii (1987), pp 418–21; Joan Simon, 'From charity school to workhouse in the 1720s: the S.P.C.K. and Mr. Marriott's solution', *History of Education*, xvii (1988), pp 113–19.

80 Rose, 'Evangelical philanthropy', p. 38.

81 *Oxford D.N.B.* (Coventry [*née* Somerset], Anne, countess of Coventry (1673–1763)); ibid. (Hastings, Lady Elizabeth [Betty] (1682–1739)).

82 Quane, 'Midleton school', pp 8–14.

83 Ibid., p. 8; Edward Gregg, *Queen Anne* (London, 1984), p. 77.

84 Quane, 'Midleton school', p. 17.

Buttevant, while the dowager countess of Cork and Burlington professed herself happy to support the schools on her son's lands between 1704 and 1715, calling them 'a useful charity'.[85] Like the almshouses, there was one each at Lismore and Youghal.[86] Catherine O'Brien went one step further and founded a new school in Corofin, County Clare, in 1719, at the expense of her 14-year-old son, Sir Edward O'Brien, 2nd Bt. His accounts show regular entries of £18 *p.a.* for the maintenance of twenty-four charity boys at Newmarket and to 'Francis Swyny towards his salary for teaching the charity boys in Corofin'. A letter from the O'Briens' agent, James Davoren, confirms that the school was being maintained by using the rents from bogs at Rathfolan on Edward's estate, despite the fact that, as guardian, Catherine should only have been maintaining structures already in place.[87]

The inspiration for these schools may have come from England, but native-born Irish ladies were soon involved as well. Eleanor O'Hara of County Sligo made biannual contributions of £1 10*s*. to an unnamed school in the 1720s, and Jane Bonnell (then living in England) and her cousin, Jane Bulkeley, attempted to establish their own school in 1722, though its intended location is unclear. In order to raise the money to found and support it, they turned to friends and acquaintances for subscriptions and other assistance, but soon encountered difficulties. Mrs Bulkeley disliked asking for money in this way, and many of the people she and Mrs Bonnell approached had charitable commitments of their own and could offer only limited assistance.[88] Jane Bulkeley reported that

> as to my Lady Ram, you cannot demand anything from her. She paid to the time she said she would not pay any more, for she was to pay a school of garle [*recte girls*] in her own parish and Mr Knight said if she would pay to that school for an example to others, he would pay to your school which he does.

The money that had come from Lady Ram and Mr Knight was supplemented by only one other subscription, from a Mr Worth, so that Jane was forced to concede that 'if we keep it I do not find but you and I must pay four pounds apiece every year'. She admitted that this expense would be difficult for her, but told her cousin that 'I would rather stress myself than let it fall, I think it so good a work'. There was some good news at least, for she also wrote that 'Mrs Merser does give them cloth once a year', though this meant 'that I cannot expect that she will pay anything to the mistress'.[89] Mrs Merser is almost certainly the same

85 Warburton, Whitelaw and Walsh, *History of the city of Dublin*, ii, p. xli; Spurret to Sir Richard Cox, 14 Aug. 1704 (Chatsworth, Anthony Spurret's letter book 1703–4, Burlington MSS, miscellaneous, box 1).

86 Spurret to Bagge, 28 Mar. 1704 (Chatsworth, Anthony Spurret's letter book 1703–4, Burlington MSS, miscellaneous, box 1).

87 Account of Catherine O'Brien with her son Sir Edward O'Brien, mainly relating to tenants and workmen, during the minority of the said Sir Edward, 1719–22 (NLI, MS 14, 369); account of Catherine O'Brien with Sir Edward O'Brien, 1723–4 (ibid., MS 45, 350/5); James Davoren to Catherine O'Brien, 21 Dec. 1719 (ibid., MS 45, 347/3).

88 Eleanor O'Hara's personal account book, 1722–33 (ibid., MS 36, 387/7); Jane Bulkeley to Bonnell, 3 Nov. 1722 (ibid., MS 41, 580/4).

89 Bulkeley to Bonnell, [1721/2?] (ibid., MS 41, 580/4). Though it is not clear exactly which Mr

Mary Mercer who founded her own school, later hospital, in Dublin in 1724, and her involvement in so many charitable outlets is further proof of the multi-stranded approach to institutional philanthropy suggested by the wills outlined at the beginning of this chapter. The references to Worth and Knight show that men too had their place in the charity school movement, and others, including Thomas Thynne, Viscount Weymouth, William, 5th Baron Digby (both English) and John Perceval, earl of Egmont (an Irishman), founded their own institutions in Ireland.[90] The support that Mary, Lady Lanesborough, and Sarah, Lady Ram, gave to such ventures, paralleled that of their respective spouses, and in 1733 Jane Bonnell's sister, Katherine Conolly, established a school at Celbridge, County Kildare, according to instructions in her husband's will.[91] Katherine, unlike her sister and cousin, experienced no financial difficulties and was able to grant the school £50 *p.a.* during her life, in addition to the amount William had specified.[92] Once again, it is clear that for elite women, serious involvement with institutional philanthropy was the preserve of the single, the widowed, or wives who were acting jointly with their husbands or whose spouses were, like Lord Lanesborough and Sir Abel Ram, noted philanthropists themselves. Lady Orkney only managed to maintain control over her lands and charity school by transferring her Irish estate to her brother and to Alan Brodrick, future Viscount Midleton, just before her marriage in November 1695.[93]

Aside from financial problems, maintaining a charity school was not as straightforward as many hoped. Lady Burlington felt that it was her right to select new teachers for the schools on her son's estate, but William Jephson, dean of Lismore, chose to dispute this matter with her in 1704, arguing that it was he who should make new appointments and that her choice of a Mr Franklin as a new schoolmaster was inappropriate.[94] The disagreement dragged on for years, but the countess would not give way. Jephson tried to force her hand by refusing to grant Franklin a licence to teach on the grounds that the term 'Master of Arts' had been wrongly inserted on the certificate provided on his behalf by the bishop of Cork, but Juliana countered by having a fresh certificate issued and enlisting to her cause Jephson's superior, Nathaniel Foy, bishop of Waterford and Lismore, while her candidate was promised that he would be 'no sufferer in the meantime, let the Dean be ever so troublesome'.[95] She remained steadfast in her loyalty and, far from being browbeaten by Jephson, over a year later was still telling her son's agents that 'I would have Mr Franklin be easy, for I think myself in some measure obliged to

Worth Jane is referring to here, it is most likely a member of her extended family, as her son-in-law was James Tynte, previously Worth.

90 Hayton, 'Did Protestantism fail', pp 172–3.

91 Mary O'Dowd, *A history of women in Ireland, 1500–1800* (Harlow, 2004), p. 192; *D.I.B.* (Abel Ram (1669–1740)); Lena Boylan, 'The Conollys of Castletown: a family history', *Quarterly Bulletin of the Irish Georgian society*, xi (1968), p. 8.

92 *D.I.B.* (Conolly, Katherine (Catherine) (*c.*1662–1752)).

93 Ibid. (Abel Ram (1669–1740)); Quane, 'Midleton school', pp 4–5.

94 Spurret to William Congreve, 1 Aug. 1704 (Chatsworth, Anthony Spurret's letter book 1703–4, Burlington MSS, miscellaneous, box 1).

95 Same to Mr Franklin, 12 Dec. 1704 (ibid.). Mr Franklin is also sometimes referred to as Mr Frankland.

protect him until I hear better reasons given for refusing to admit him'.[96] Eventually she got her way and Franklin was appointed, though the victory was short-lived, as he died in early 1708.[97] Juliana quickly chose a Mr Wigmore as his replacement, but, anxious to avoid repeating past problems, she made sure that his credentials were unimpeachable before the appointment was made official.[98]

Excepting the very specific set of circumstances which stirred Lady Orkney into action, motivations behind the creation of charity schools were standard. Genuine altruism can be seen in the actions of those like Jane Bonnell and in the donations made by Eleanor O'Hara. Catherine O'Brien and Lady Burlington probably had in mind the good of their sons' estates and the obedience and loyalty of their tenants (whose children they were paying to educate), and Catherine's actions in particular, however much they strayed from the role of a good guardian in their expense to her son, suggest a real feeling of responsibility towards the people on his estate. This is more difficult to safely attribute to Juliana, as the Burlington schools were, like the almshouses, already in existence in 1704 and their maintenance was an unavoidable part of her responsibilities as guardian. Vanity and a desire to show off should not be discounted either, and would explain why the children of charity schools were sometimes made to publicise their benefactors' good works through their conspicuous attendance and participation in church services.[99] Those at St Andrew's school in Dublin had to sing a hymn in 1730, which was designed to commend the actions of the school's subscribers, as much as to glorify God. Its lyrics included the words:

How blessed are they, how greatly blessed?
Whole hands with pious care,
From want to rescue the distressed,
Their kind supplies prepare!
In such, who life so well employ,
Sincere delights abound;
Like providence they feel a joy,
Dispensing blessings round.
…
May all the pleasing pains you share
Be crowned with wished success,
Those living now applaud your care,
And future ages bless.[100]

Religious convictions and the desire to produce a better educated future workforce were important too, and charity schools, both English and Irish, had the dual aims of educating the poor and promoting Protestantism, specifically Anglicanism. Yet

96 Burlington to Foulke, Power, Bagge and Baker, 17 Jan. 1705/6 (NLI, MS 43, 361/3).

97 Waite to Richard Musgrave and Baker, 13 Mar. 1707/8 (Chatsworth, Joseph Waite's letter book 1706–8, Burlington MSS, miscellaneous, box 1).

98 Same to same, 22 Apr. 1708 (ibid.).

99 Hayton, 'Did Protestantism fail', p. 175.

100 'A hymn to be sung by the charity children of St Andrew's Dublin, at the parish-church of St Andrew's, on Sunday the 21 of February, 1730' (PRONI, D562/502).

they hoped to do this by bolstering the faith of those who were already Protestant, rather than converting those who were not. To this end, many actually refused to teach Catholic children unless there was a surplus of places.[101] Not only did these women feel that were they helping to protect the souls of the children concerned, if the words of the St Andrew's charity children were to be believed, by helping the less fortunate 'with pious care', the benefactresses were 'dispensing blessings round' and were themselves 'greatly blessed'. The implication was clear: those who did God's work would 'reap an eternal reward'.[102]

Churches

Churches are perhaps a less obvious philanthropic institution given their primary function as places of worship and use (in that capacity) by people of every rank. However, they played a vital role in doling out support to the poor in their parishes, and the practice observed by some elite women, including Lady Orrery, Lady Midleton and Jane Bonnell, of leaving money to be distributed to the poor of particular parishes, shows that churches were viewed, treated and used as charitable foundations, for the money was obviously to be disseminated via its ministerial hierarchy.[103] Elite women also had a role to play in founding new churches or religious communities, or supporting those already in existence. Religion would seem to be the most obvious motive for such actions. However, other factors included family honour, an obligation to take care of tenants, a desire to obtain their gratitude (particularly in the case of absentee landholders) and self-aggrandisement. Two cases that came before Lady Burlington show all of these issues at work.

Juliana was contacted in 1707 by Mr Beecher, the curate of Tallow, County Waterford, who wrote to her 'at the important request of the inhabitants of this town' because part of the church roof had been blown off in a storm, and what remained was in danger of collapse. Citing the fact that the countess's grandfather-in-law, Richard, 1st earl of Cork, had worshipped in the church and extended it so that it would meet the needs of the townspeople, Beecher begged for the countess's assistance:

> I am very well assured that your ladyship is very sensible of the poverty of our tenants in the town and consequently of their inability [*to*] take down the wall and roof of the south aisle of the church and to raise it up again which will cost a good sum of money and which is indispensably necessary to [be done?] and therefore they have desired me humbly to beg your ladyship's charity for the carrying on [*of*] so pious a work, which without it, is not likely to be effected.[104]

101 Hayton, 'Did Protestantism fail', p. 169; Raughter, 'A natural tenderness: women's philanthropy', pp 80–2. Raughter also notes that the schools were increasingly non-denominational as the eighteenth century wore on.
102 Rose, 'Evangelical philanthropy', p. 43.
103 For a good discussion of the ways in which Dublin Anglican churches collected and distributed money and to whom it went, see Dudley, 'Dublin parishes', pp 80–94.
104 F. Beecher to Burlington, 28 June 1707 (NLI, MS 43, 347/3).

Despite the references to the historical associations of the Boyle family with the church, the piety which her assistance would show and the parishioners' poverty, it took Juliana several months to obtain the relevant reports from her son's agents about the matter and to decide on a course of action. When she did, she agreed only to provide limited help at her son's expense. Instead of paying for the damaged aisle to be taken down and replaced, she agreed to allow it to be removed entirely, or repaired as much as possible without dismantling it.[105] Complete inaction would have been unwise, for Tallow was a parliamentary borough, and Juliana would need the support of its inhabitants at election times, but the countess's sluggish and limited response is indicative of a woman doing only what she felt she had to, rather than what she wanted to.[106] It is in stark contrast to the way in which she dealt with the churches on her son's English estate, for when she received a request to pay for 'beautifying and repairing the chancel of Leeds' old church' the following year, her secretary was soon writing that she was 'very free and willing to gratify the vicar and parishioners in particulars so far as she believes she can safely do it'. She gave orders that her son's agent, George Myers, was to

> pay to the vicar, church wardens etc. fifteen pounds on the account, not as any obligation from his lordship but purely out [*of*] Christian respect and a charitable disposition for and towards keeping the chancel of the said church in good repair and a decent and orderly manner like the other parts of the church (that is to say) £10 to be laid out in the repair of the windows and towards beautifying the chancel and £5 for painting my lord's arms very handsomely in a convenient place in the chancel.[107]

Despite Waite noting that 'her Ladyship is acting for a minor and therefore is in some measure restrained from being so generous as his Lordship might be if of age', when the donation turned out to be insufficient, Juliana granted a further £5 to the church to be placed on Lord Burlington's accounts.[108] These renovations were commendable, but essentially aesthetic and hardly urgent, particularly compared to the need to fix the church at Tallow, which was falling down and certainly not in 'a decent and orderly manner'. Yet it was the Leeds church which received the greatest charity from Juliana, who was obviously biased towards her home country, despite the fact that she was equally responsible for the protection and maintenance of her son's inheritance on both sides of the Irish Sea. A desire to promote her own and her son's name among those living on the estate they actually visited was more important than cost, for she was unwilling to defer having his coat of arms painted in a prominent position in the chancel until he came of age, in case the matter was forgotten.[109] Thus, while charity was a useful way of reminding his tenants and employees of their landlord, and instilling in them a sense of gratefulness and

105 Waite to Musgrave and Baker, 7 Oct. 1707 (Chatsworth, Joseph Waite's letter book 1706–8, Burlington MSS, miscellaneous, box 1).
106 Edith Johnston-Liik, *MPs in Dublin: companion to the history of the Irish parliament, 1692–1800* (Belfast, 2006), p. 184.
107 Waite to Myers, 13 Nov. 1708 (Chatsworth, Joseph Waite's letter book 1708–10, Burlington MSS, miscellaneous, box 1).
108 Ibid. See also same to same, 22 Jan. 1708/9 (ibid.).
109 Same to same, 13 Nov. 1708 (ibid.).

allegiance towards him while he was too young to do so himself, this was less crucial with the tenants he might rarely, or never, meet. Juliana's actions seem at odds with the interest she took in the Irish almshouses and charity schools, but given that she had no choice but to support these establishments, her attitude towards the churches, over which she had sole control, gives a much clearer picture of her feelings.

Not all ladies reacted to the prospect of spending money on Irish churches in the same way as the countess. Catherine O'Brien used her son's money to found a church in Corofin in 1718, despite the reservations of James Davoren about the cost and legality of such a move.[110] Far from being discouraged by this reaction, Catherine saw to it that when the church required maintenance over the next few years, that expense was also put on Sir Edward's accounts.[111] Her actions were tinged with self-importance, for she named the church St Catherine's, at once helping others and creating for herself an enduring reputation as a philanthropist. Her son, whose money financed the project, was not mentioned at all, and intentionally or inadvertently, she missed an opportunity to build and maintain his reputation among his tenants. Other mothers had a more even working relationship with their children, and it was with the help of Arthur Hill, her adult son by her first marriage, that Ann, dowager Lady Midleton, founded and paid for a church to be built at Knockbreda in Belfast in 1733 to replace 'the dilapidated church at Knock'.[112] The process was not an easy one, for Ann had to overcome the objections of Margaret Butler, Viscountess Ikerrin, who felt the site was inconvenient, but, with the assistance of Archbishop Hugh Boulter of Armagh, the church was built and finally consecrated on 7 August 1737.[113] Lady Midleton maintained her links with the parish, and its poorest parishioners were financial beneficiaries of her will.[114] These two churches were Anglican, like their benefactresses and most of the Ascendancy elite; however, there were occasional instances of women establishing Catholic institutions, such as the convent of Poor Clares in Dublin, founded by Frances Talbot, the Jacobite duchess of Tyrconnell, after her return to the city in 1708 (she was the widow of a previous lord lieutenant and had been in the country in the late 1680s, in the midst of the Glorious Revolution).[115]

For some, a church was a way to memorialise themselves, a loved one, or both, for future generations, an idea which must have had particular resonance for those with no children who were facing the end of their direct family line. After the death in 1739 of the unmarried Marmaduke Coghill, chancellor of

110 Davoren to Catherine O'Brien, 23 Oct. 1718 (NLI, MS 45, 347/1).

111 Account of Catherine O'Brien with her son Sir Edward O'Brien, mainly relating to tenants and workmen, during the minority of the said Sir Edward, 1719–22 (ibid., MS 14, 369); account of Catherine O'Brien with her son Sir Edward O'Brien, 1719–23 (ibid., MS 14, 370).

112 Brian MacKey, 'The creation of Knockbreda parish church and Belvoir Park' in Lydia Wilson (ed.), *Knockbreda: its monuments and people* (Belfast, 2009), p. 9.

113 Ibid.

114 *London Evening Post*, 23–26 Jan. 1748. She left 50l. each to the poor of the parish of 'Bradagh', now Knockbreda.

115 *Oxford D.N.B.* (Talbot [*née* Jenyns; *other married name* Hamilton], Frances, duchess of Tyrconnell (1648–1731).

the Exchequer, his sister Mary erected a church in the parish of St John the Baptist, Clonturk, Dublin in which she placed an elaborate statue of her brother complete with melodramatic epitaph. Similarly, in the early 1730s, Katherine Conolly spent vast amounts of money remodelling and extending the church in Celbridge, County Kildare, where her home, Castletown, was located. Like Catherine O'Brien and Mary Coghill, her thoughts were not entirely with God or the congregation, for the alterations were carried out in order to fit a grandiose funerary monument to her husband inside the church. At first she claimed she was motivated partly by the fact that the building was too small for the number of parishioners, but several years later, when the project was nearing completion, she admitted that 'I have erected a handsome monument – and have been obliged to build the church quite new upon that account'.[116] Even after her alterations, it was still too small for the memorial and she was forced to construct a separate building nearby.[117]

Conclusion

The contribution of elite women to institutional philanthropy in eighteenth-century Ireland was considerably greater than has been previously revealed. They donated and raised money, they helped to establish what was then Ireland's only workhouse and they founded and supported charity schools, hospitals and churches, often spreading their support around many different institutions. Though not involved in the kind of female-only associated philanthropy that the next generation would embark upon, and limited in many cases by the rules of coverture, by frequently working in collaboration with each other and with men, their reach extended to young and old, male and female. Their support of charity schools and a workhouse, both concepts imported from England, betrayed their Anglo-Irish connexions and leanings, but there was far more to their activities than that. Their motives were a mix of the honourable, the dutiful and even the selfish and, as such, it is unsurprising that they occasionally succumbed to charitable fatigue when they felt overwhelmed, underappreciated, or simply bored by their commitments. Katherine Conolly, despite her wealth, wrote in 1742 that she was then short of ready money because 'the more one has, the more is expected from them – and I have more demands than I can possibly answer'. She was not exaggerating. Her sister, Mary Jones, admitted that 'I do not wonder she should be scarce of money for she lives at great expense, gives a great deal in charity and to relations of Mr Conolly's'.[118] Even Mary Mercer, who had gone to the trouble of founding a school for girls, allowed it to be turned into a hospital because she had

116 *Letters of Marmaduke Coghill: 1722–1728*, ed. D.W. Hayton (Dublin, 2005), xxii; *D.I.B.* (Coghill, Marmaduke (1673–1739); Katherine Conolly to Bonnell, 27 Nov. 1732 (NLI, MS 41, 478/6); same to same, 14 May 1736 (ibid., MS 41, 578/9).
117 Patrick Walsh, 'The career of William Conolly, 1689–1729' (TCD, Ph.D. thesis, 2007), p. 306. Part of the memorial can now be viewed in Castletown House.
118 Conolly to Bonnell, 9 July 1742 (NLI, MS 41, 578/15); Jones to same, 24 May [n.d.] (ibid., MS 41, 577/5).

grown 'weary of her project'.[119] Despite these wobbles, the good that elite women did should not go unrecognised. Though they were sometimes fussy about who was deemed worthy of their help, doubtless they improved or saved many lives, and many of the institutions they were involved with are still in existence, in one form or another, today.[120]

119 Fownes to Swift, 9 Sept. 1732 (*The correspondence of Jonathan Swift*, iii, 535).

120 For instance, Knockbreda Church in Belfast, founded by Lady Midleton, is still a working church and Dr Steevens's hospital still exists in Dublin, though it now functions as an administrative building for the Irish health service.

Conclusion

Historians of all but the most recent past will always suffer from one insurmountable limitation; the inability to talk to their subjects. Unfortunately we cannot resurrect women like Katherine Conolly, or her sisters, Mary Jones and Jane Bonnell, all of whom were alive in both 1690 and 1745, and ask them to compare what their lives and the lives of their contemporaries had been and had become during this period. However, they, and other women like them, speak to us from beyond the grave in other ways, through the vast collection of letters and papers they have left behind which tell their stories for them. These stories speak of change and continuity, of a Catholic elite which had been forcibly and almost completely replaced by a Protestant Ascendancy and of the challenges which elite women in Ireland faced in this new world, as they negotiated their way through a period marked by great political, social, cultural and religious upheaval and transition. As time went by, they incorporated into their lives elements drawn from across the British elite which would allow them to assimilate more easily with their neighbours and bolster they and their families' positions within Ireland. They adopted a bi-cultural education which would prepare them to move in both the English and Irish elites, the Protestant among them (who formed the bulk of their ranks) decorated their homes in a manner designed to demonstrate their so-called 'right to rule' and they embraced entertainments and philanthropic institutions which had first appeared in England.

Yet the more things changed, the more they stayed the same, and though the lives of these women may have been informed by and in some cases, mirrored that of their English and Scottish counterparts, they were not dictated by the British example. The peculiarly Irish tradition of socially and geographically endogamous marriages remained, as did the high degree of political involvement its ladies were afforded, which extended, through conversation and correspondence, right into the House of Commons itself and was accompanied by a level of acceptance from the male elite which was unmatched elsewhere in the British Isles. The result was a group of women who were a mix of the insular and the cosmopolitan. They looked at the conduct and lifestyle of women in England and Scotland and duplicated only what they liked, making numerous adaptions and filling the gaps with their own beliefs and customs. When neither the past nor their neighbours offered an example they wished to follow, they forged their own path, wearing Irish-made clothing (to give one example) when English imposed trade embargoes threatened the Irish textile industry.

The subjects of this book were never subsumed by the men in their lives, nor by the traditional domestic roles assigned to them. Though the importance of marriage, children and household responsibilities to the existence of many elite women have been looked at and acknowledged here, it is clear that there was much more to them than this, and their presence in Ireland and input into its affairs were indispensable in shaping the country's post-Revolutionary development. They may have been treated as second-class citizens by the law, but the fabric of Irish politics and polite society would have come apart at the seams without them. Their importance was manifested in different ways to that of men, but was no less real, for the creation of a new ruling order, composed of members of the country's minority religion, required a group effort in which these ladies had a key role. They were needed to form interfamilial and sometimes international marriage alliances. They were crucial to the Irish economy, not just in their capacity as household managers, but even in their sartorial choices. Their social and cultural tastes made managers of music halls, assembly rooms and theatres fawn over them, offering them lower ticket prices to attend their events, and their political abilities were so well recognised and often respected that they were badgered on occasion to operate as informants, assistants and patronage brokers by male friends, acquaintances and family members (though many were happy to oblige). Had there not existed a strong and in some ways, very independent female elite, the distribution of philanthropy and the support of the many institutions through which it was channelled would have fallen much more heavily upon men, and Irish estates enduring a minority would have been handled by potentially distant male relatives or the state, neither of whom might have cared as much about their financial health or the fates of their tenants as a mother protecting her son's inheritance.

Thanks to differences in financial, social and personal circumstances, not all women were able to contribute to the creation of the new elite in equal measure, or participate in it. This in turn led to jealous complaints, even within families, when those like Mary Jones, who had once been on a par with her sister Katherine, found herself languishing many rungs beneath her on the social ladder. Overall, though, elite women were exceptionally well integrated into every facet of Ascendancy Ireland. As a group, they held prominent and powerful positions within their families and the country's political, social and cultural structures. Not only were they forces to be reckoned with when they were alive, even now, centuries after their deaths, they cannot be ignored.

Appendix 1: Boyle family tree

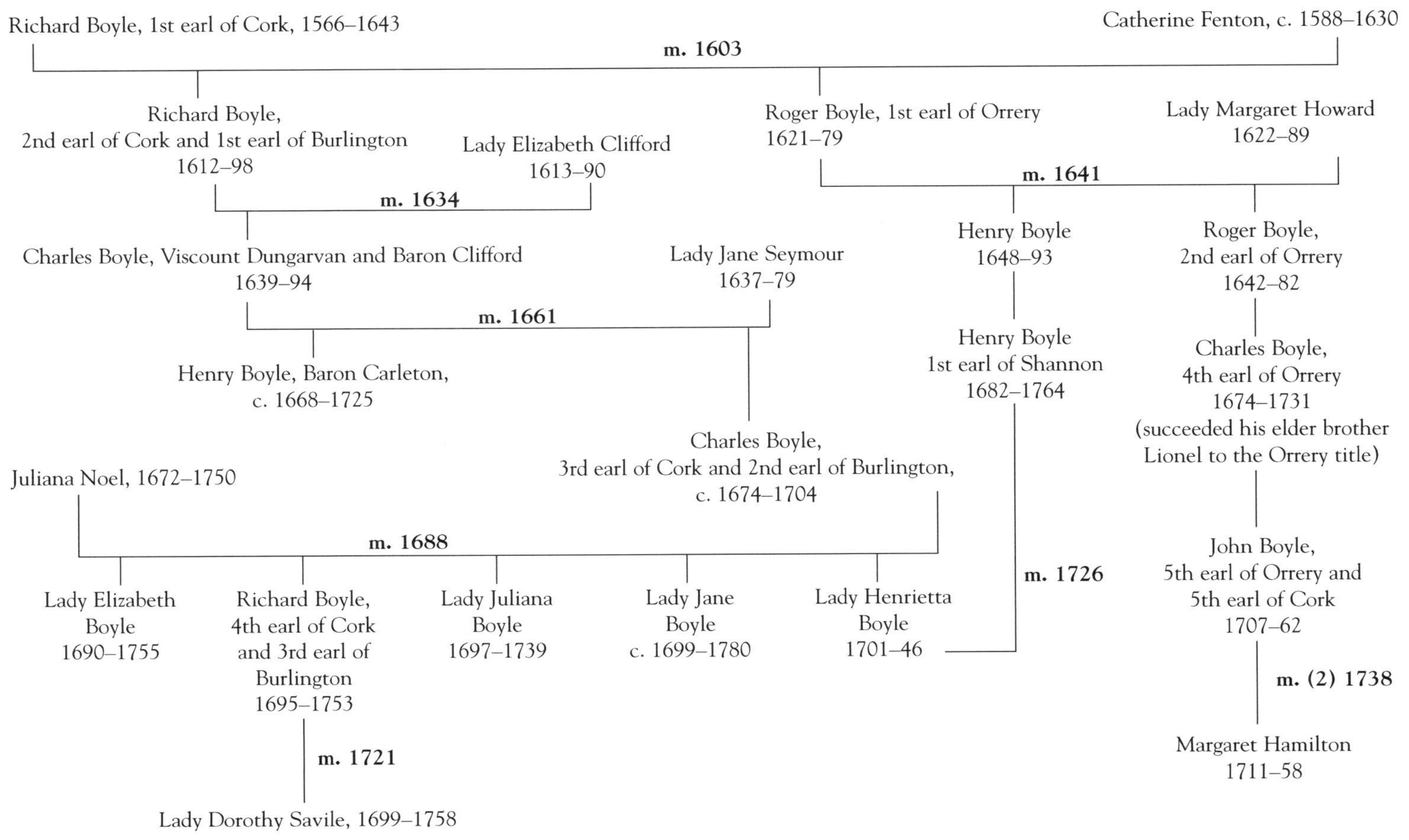

Appendix 2: Brodrick family tree

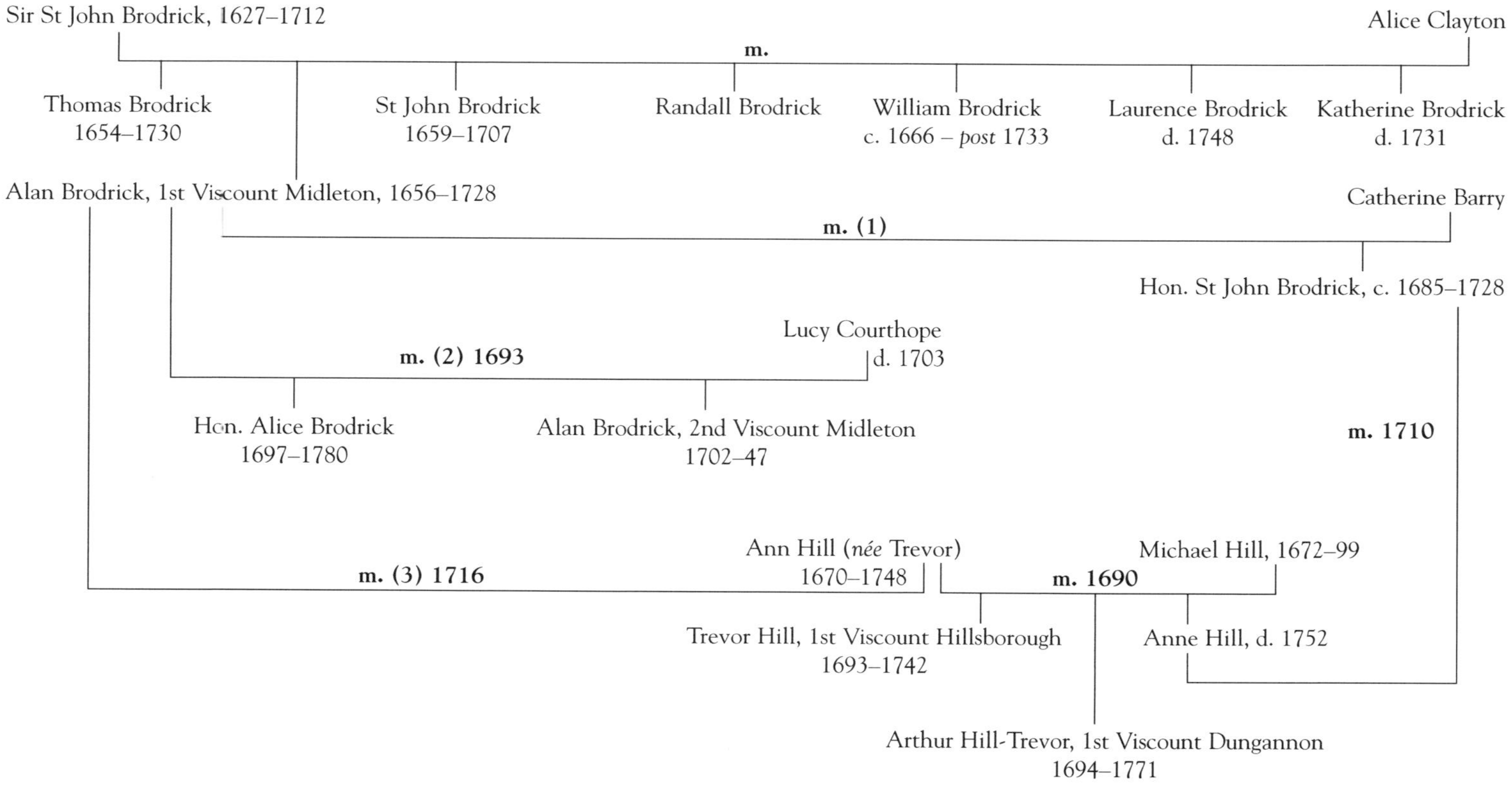

Appendix 3: Butler/Somerset family tree

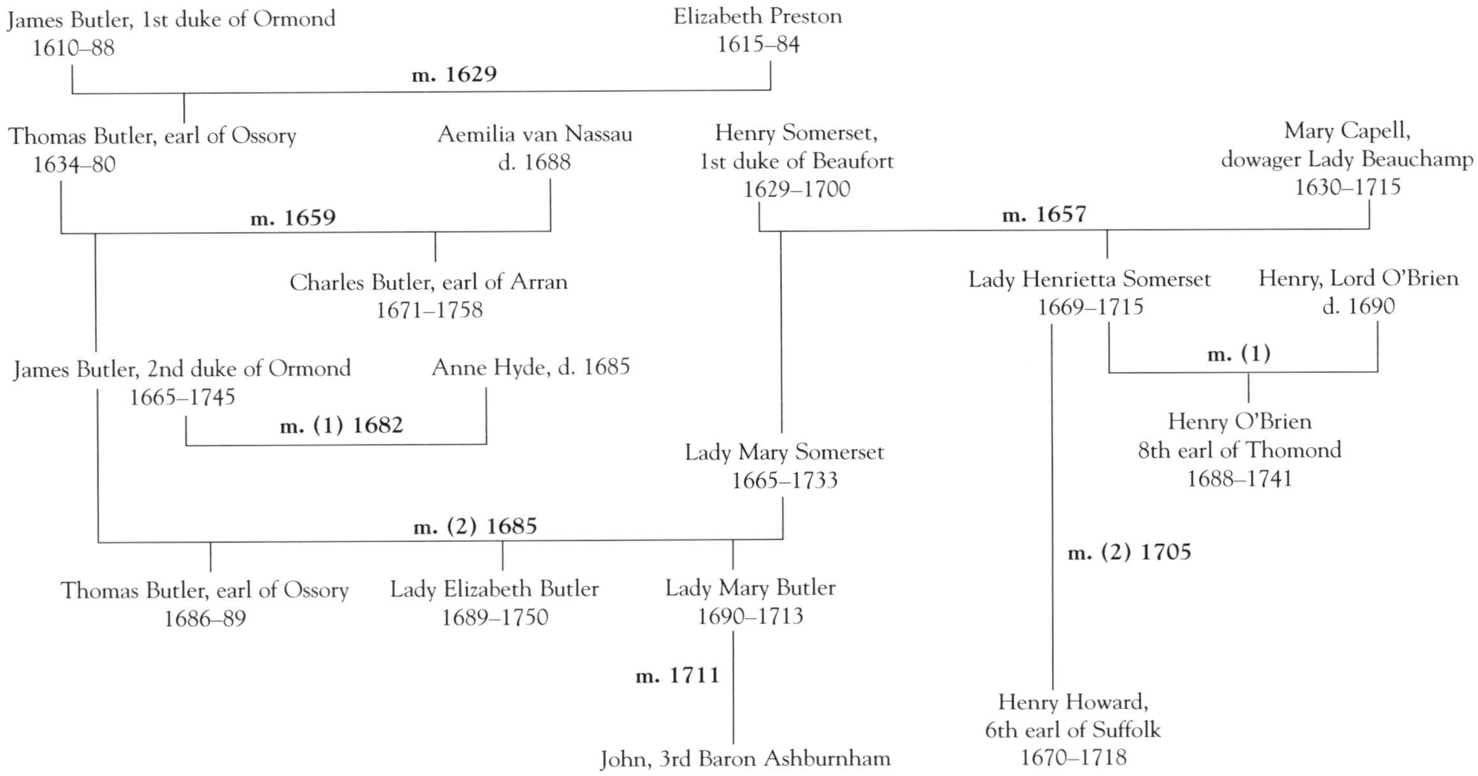

Appendix 4: Conolly/Conyngham family tree

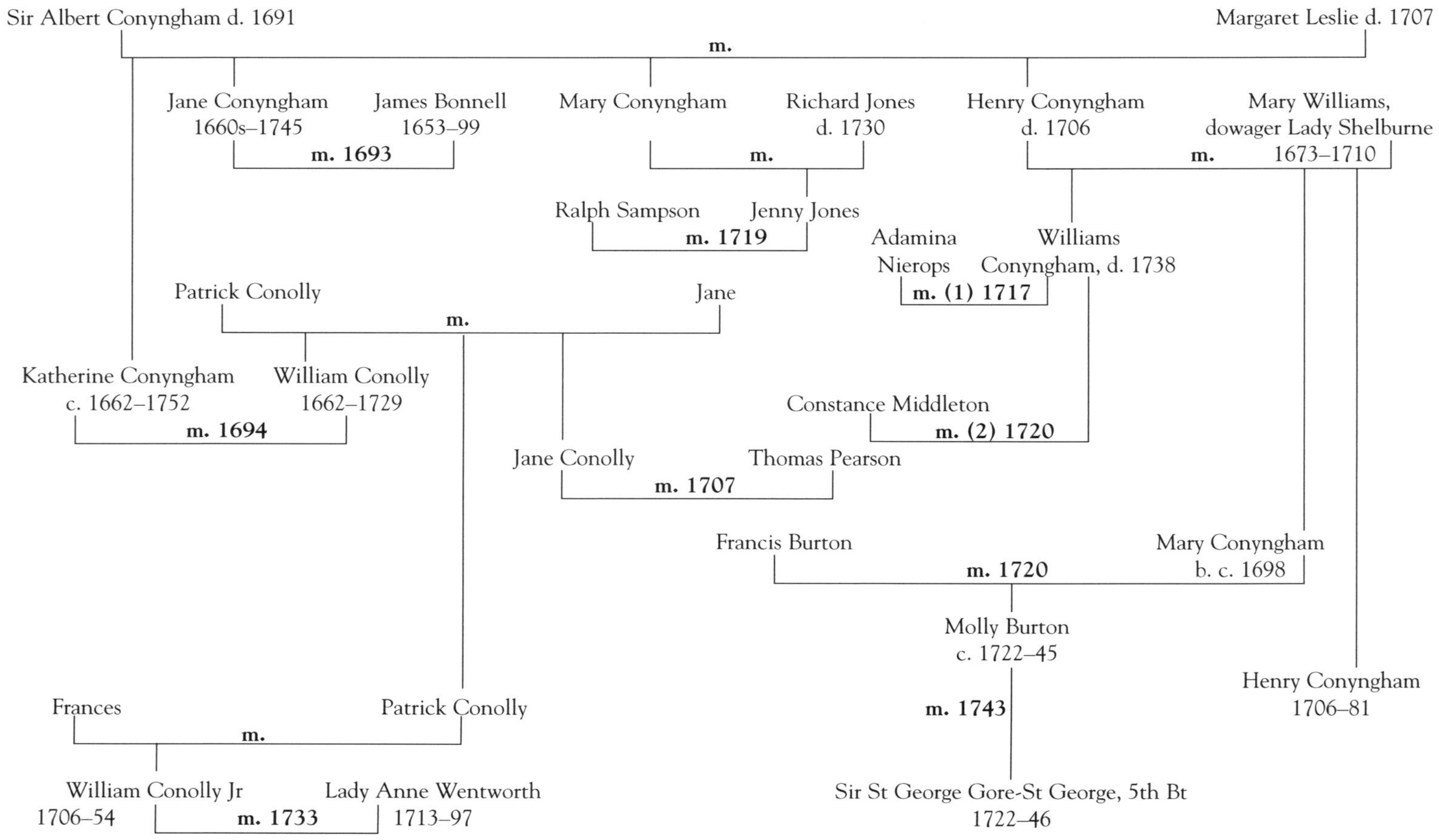

Appendix 5: O'Brien/Keightley family tree

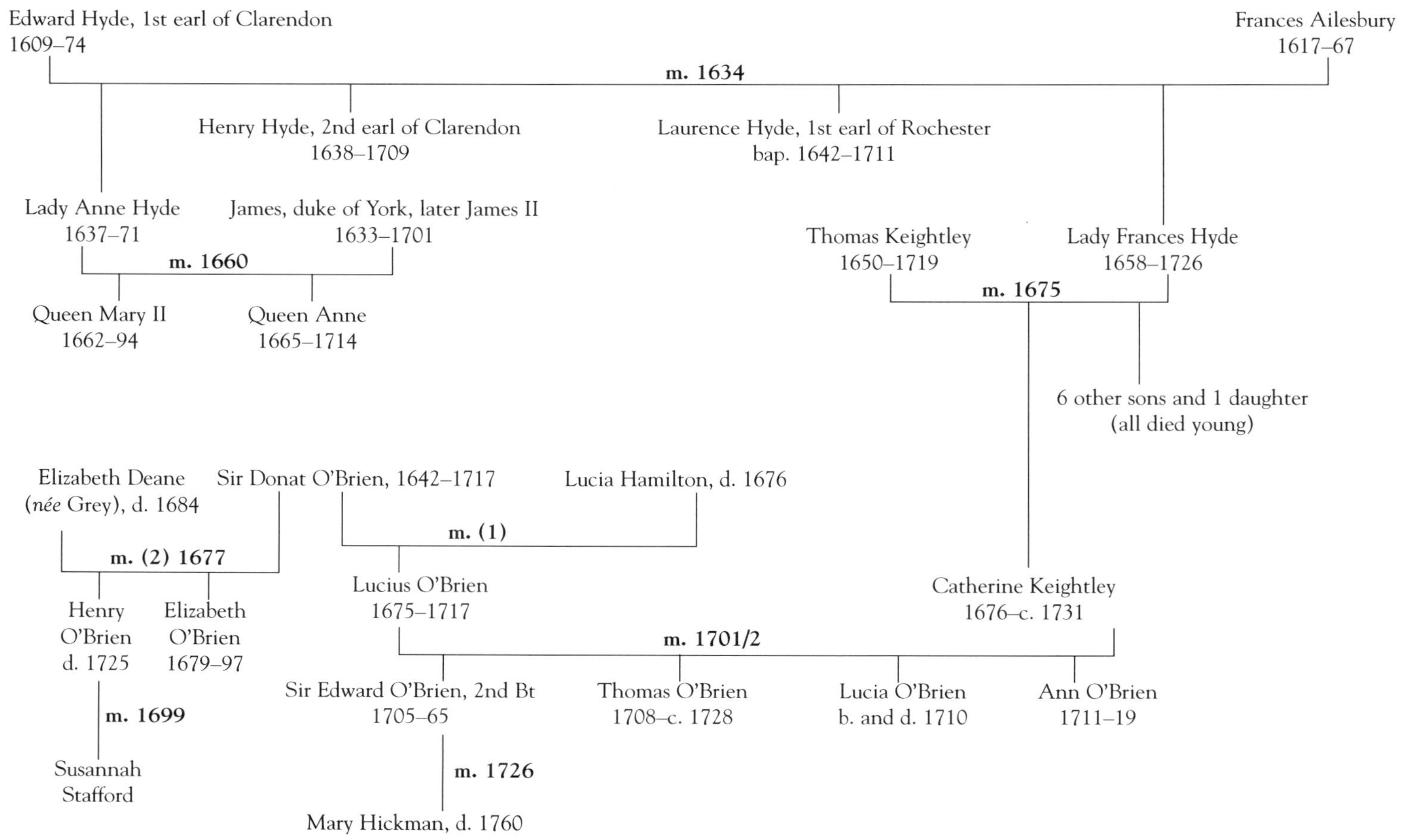

Bibliography

PRIMARY SOURCES

MANUSCRIPTS

British Library

Add. MSS 4804, 4805, 15903, 20102, 20778, 22228, 24023, 28878, 28881, 28882, 28889, 28893, 28926, 28927, 28948, 34195, 47012, 61456, 61474, 61636, 75358.
Sloane Papers, MSS 4052, 4076.

Chatsworth archives

Burlington Papers, miscellaneous, boxes 1, 3.
Cork Papers, miscellaneous, boxes 4, 5.
Cork Papers, vols xxxv, xxxvi.
Devonshire Papers, 1st series, nos 127, 164, 176, 232.
Devonshire Papers, MSS L/1/25, L/4/4, L/4/5, L/6/14, L/9/11, L/17/93, L/24/87, L/24/89, L/28/109, L/30/20, L/46/25, L/46/28, L/46/29, L/55/40, L/88/36, L/88/54, L/88/58.

Irish Architectural Archive

Castletown Papers, MSS A/7, A/8, A/9, C/48/4, F/4, G/2, G/7, G/8, G/9, J/2, J/3, J/11.

National Records of Scotland

Dalhousie papers, GD45/14/238.

National Library of Ireland

Brodrick Papers, MS 8897.
Headfort Papers, MS 25, 430.
Inchiquin Papers, MSS 14, 369–70, 45, 290–722.
Killadoon Papers, MS 36, 027.
Limerick Papers, MS 41, 675.
Lismore Papers, MSS 13, 231–54, 43, 114–894.

Louth Papers, MSS 40, 033, 40, 094.
Ormond Papers, MSS 11, 058–67, 2456–553.
Smythe of Barbavilla Papers, MSS 41, 568–582.
Wicklow Papers, MS 38, 600/7.

Public Record Office of Northern Ireland

Castletown Papers, T2825.
Castle Ward Papers, D2092, viewed on microfilm (MIC 596).
Chancery Papers, T3425/3/8/1.
Chancery Papers: Ridgeway-Pitt estate, T3425/2.
Chatsworth Papers, T3158.
Conolly Papers, D2094, viewed on microfilm (MIC 435).
De Ros Papers, D638, viewed on microfilm (MIC 413).
Foster/Massereene Papers, D562 viewed on microfilm (MIC 500).
Murray of Broughton Papers, D2860.
O'Hara of Sligo Papers, T2812.
Shannon Papers, D2707.
Villiers-Stuart Papers, T3131 viewed on microfilm (MIC 464/3).
Ward (Castleward papers), D2092/1, accessed on microfilm (MIC 596/1 and 596/3).
Wilmot Papers, T3019/278.

Surrey History Centre

Brodrick Papers, 1248/1–7.

The National Archives [of the United Kingdom]

Will of Jane Bonnell, 8 June 1745, Prob. 11/740.
Will of Charles, earl of Burlington, 26 Feb. 1703/4, Prob. 11/475.
Will of Arthur, earl of Donegall, 30 July 1705, Prob. 11/504.
Will of Alice, countess of Drogheda, 14 Jan. 1712 [/13?], Prob. 11/525.
Will of Margaret, dowager countess of Orrery, 8 May 1691, Prob. 11/404.

Trinity College Dublin

Lyons collection of the correspondence of William King, MSS 1995–2008.
Smythe of Barbavilla Papers, MS 11198/3.

NEWSPAPERS AND PERIODICALS

The Craftsman.
Daily Gazetteer.

Daily Journal.
Daily Post.
Dublin Gazette.
Faulkner's Dublin Journal.
Flying Post (London).
Freeholder's Journal.
General Evening Post.
Gentleman's Magazine.
London Daily Post.
London Evening Post.
Mist's Weekly Journal.
Post Man.
Universal Spectator.

PAMPHLETS AND OTHER CONTEMPORARY WORKS

Allestree, Richard, *The ladies calling in two parts by the author of the whole duty of man, the causes of the decay of Christian piety, and the gentleman's calling* (Oxford, 1673).
Allestree, Richard, *The works of the learned and pious author of the whole duty of man* (Dublin, 1723).
— *An account of charity-schools lately erected in England, Wales, and Ireland: with the benefactions thereto; and of the methods whereby they were set up, and are governed. ...* (London, 1706).
— *A short memorial, and character, of that most noble and illustrious princess Mary dutchess of Ormonde* (London?, 1735?).
Astell, Mary, *A serious proposal to the ladies, for the advancement of their true and greatest interest* (London, 1694).
Berkeley, George, *The ladies library* (3 vols, London, 1714).
Boyer, Abel, *The history of the reign of Queen Anne, digested into annals. ...* (11 vols, London, 1703–13).
Burke, John and Sir Bernard Burke, *A genealogical and heraldic history of the extinct and dormant baronetcies of England, Ireland, and Scotland* (2nd edn, London, 1841).
Chetwood, W.R., *The memoirs of most of the principal performers, that have appeared on the Dublin stage, for the last fifty years. ...* (Dublin, 1749).
Collins, Arthur and Brydges, Sir Egerton, *Collins's peerage of England ...* (9 vols, London, 1756).
Dryden, John, *Fables ancient and modern, translated into verse, from Homer, Ovid, Boccace, and Chaucer: with original poems* (London, 1721).
Fénelon, François de Salignac de La Mothe, *Instructions for the education of a daughter, ...* (London, 1708).
Locke, John, *Some thoughts concerning education* (London, 1693).
Lodge, John and Mervyn Archdall, *The peerage of Ireland, ...* (7 vols, Dublin, 1789).
Madden, Samuel, *Reflections and resolutions proper for the gentlemen of Ireland, as to their conduct for the service of their country, as landlords, as masters of families, as protestants, etc.* (Dublin, 1738).
Miège, Guy, *The present state of Great Britain, and Ireland, ...* (11th edn, London, 1748).

Molesworth, Robert, Viscount, *Some considerations for the promoting of agriculture, and employing the poor* (Dublin, 1723).
Prior, Thomas, *A list of the absentees of Ireland, and the yearly value of their estates and incomes spent abroad. …* (London, 1729).
Savile, George, 1st marquess of Halifax, *The lady's new-year's gift: or, advice to a daughter (London, 1688).*
Smith, Charles, *The ancient and present state of the county and city of Cork. …* (2nd edn, 2 vols, Dublin, 1774).
Stebbing, Samuel, *A genealogical history of the kings and queens of England and monarchs of Great Britain, etc. from the Conquest, Anno 1066 to the year 1707* (London, 1707).
Swift, Jonathan, *The journal of a Dublin lady in a letter to a person of quality* (2nd edn, Dublin, 1729).
Vernon, John, *Remarks on a paper, entitled, an abstract on the state of the work-house, for maintaining of the poor of the city of Dublin* (Dublin, 1716).
Ware, James, *The antiquities and history of Ireland, by the Right Honourable Sir James Ware, Knt. …* (London, 1705).
Wilkes, Wetenhall, *A letter of genteel and moral advice to a young lady. …* (Dublin, 1740).

LATER EDITIONS OF CONTEMPORARY SOURCES

The letters of Joseph Addison, ed. Walter Graham (Oxford, 1941).
Cassandra Brydges (1670–1735) first duchess of Chandos life and letters, ed. Rosemary O'Day (Woodbridge, 2007).
Calendar of Treasury books.
Calendar of Treasury books and papers.
The Clements archive, ed. A.P.W. Malcomson (Dublin, 2010).
Letters of Marmaduke Coghill: 1722–1728, ed. D.W. Hayton (Dublin, 2005).
The Conolly archive, eds, Patrick Walsh and A.P.W. Malcomson (Dublin, 2010).
Diary of Mary countess Cowper, lady of the bedchamber to the Princess of Wales, 1714–1720 (London, 1864).
Dalrymple, John, *Memoirs of Great Britain and Ireland …* (3 vols, Dublin, 1773).
Letters from Georgian Ireland: the correspondence of Mary Delany, 1731–68, ed. Angélique Day (Belfast, 1991).
Dunton, John, with introduction and notes Andrew Carpenter, *The Dublin scuffle* (Dublin, 2000).
The autobiography and correspondence of Mary Granville, Mrs Delany: with interesting reminiscences of King George III and Queen Charlotte, ed. Lady Llanover (1st ser., 3 vols, London, 1861).
Historical Manuscripts Commission: Ormonde, n.s., viii.
The correspondence of Henry Hyde, earl of Clarendon, and his brother Laurence Hyde, earl of Rochester: …, ed. S.W. Singer (2 vols, London, 1828).
The Inchiquin manuscripts, ed. John Ainsworth (Dublin, 1961).
Journals of the House of Lords (123 vols, London, 1891).
A great archbishop of Dublin, William King, 1650–1729: his autobiography, family and a selection from his correspondence, ed. C.S. King (London, 1906).
Letters of a grandmother 1732–1735: being the correspondence of Sarah, duchess of

Marlborough with her granddaughter Diana, duchess of Bedford, ed. Gladys Scott Thomson (London, 1943).
Memoirs of Sarah, duchess of Marlborough and the court of Queen Anne, ed. A.T. Thompson (2 vols, London, 1839).
The complete letters of Lady Mary Wortley Montagu, ed. Robert Halsband (3 vols, Oxford, 1965–67).
Memoirs of the life of his grace, James, late duke of Ormond: formerly Captain-General and Commander in Chief of the forces of Great Britain (London, 1738).
The Orrery papers, ed. Emily, countess of Cork and Orrery (2 vols, London, 1903).
Statutes passed in the parliaments held in Ireland: from the ninth year of George II. A.D. 1735, to the thirty-third year of Geo. II. A.D. 1759, inclusive (12 vols, Dublin, 1794).
Letters to and from Henrietta, countess of Suffolk, and her second husband, the Hon. George Berkeley; from 1712 to 1767 ... ed. J.W. Croker (2 vols, London, 1824).
Memoirs of Viscountess Sundon, mistress of the robes to Queen Caroline, consort of King George II; ... ed. A.T. Thompson (2 vols, London, 1848).
Swift, Jonathan, *Irish tracts, 1728–1733*, ed. Herbert Davis (Oxford, 1955).
Swift, Jonathan, *Journal to Stella: letters to Esther Johnson and Rebecca Dingley, 1710–1713*, ed. Abigail Williams (Cambridge, 2013).
The correspondence of Jonathan Swift, D.D., ed. David Woolley (4 vols, Dublin, 1999–2007).
The prose works of Jonathan Swift, ed. Herbert Davis (14 vols, Oxford, 1939–68).
The Synge letters: Bishop Edward Synge to his daughter Alicia, Roscommon to Dublin, 1746–1752, ed. Marie-Louise Legg (Dublin, 1996).
Memoirs of Horatio, lord Walpole ... ed. William Coxe (London, 1802).
Memoirs of the life and administration of Sir Robert Walpole ... ed. William Coxe (3 vols, London, 1798).
The Wentworth papers, 1705–1739 ..., ed. J. J. Cartwright (London, 1883).

SECONDARY SOURCES

BOOKS

Amussen, S.D., *An ordered society: gender and class in early modern England* (New York, 1988).
Arkell, R.L., *Caroline of Ansbach, George the second's queen* (London, 1939).
Bailey, Brian, *Almshouses* (London, 1988).
Barclay, Katie, *Love, intimacy and power: marriage and patriarchy in Scotland, 1650–1850* (Manchester, 2011).
Barnard, Toby, *A new anatomy of Ireland: the Irish Protestants, 1640–1770* (London, 2003).
Barnard, Toby, *Improving Ireland?: projectors, prophets and profiteers, 1641–1786* (Dublin, 2008).
Barnard, Toby, *Making the grand figure: lives and possessions in Ireland, 1641–1770* (London, 2004).
Barnard, Toby, *The abduction of a Limerick heiress: social and political relations in mid-eighteenth century Ireland* (Dublin, 1998).
Beattie, J.M., *The English court in the reign of George I* (Cambridge, 1967).

Beckett, J.V., *The aristocracy in England, 1660–1914* (Oxford, 1986).
Bence-Jones, Mark, *Life in an Irish country house* (London, 1996).
Black, Jeremy, *The British abroad: the Grand Tour in the eighteenth century* (New York, 1992).
Bonfield, Lloyd, *Marriage settlements, 1601–1740: the adoption of the strict settlement* (Cambridge, 1983).
Bucholz, R.O., *The Augustan court: Queen Anne and the decline of court culture* (Stanford, 1993).
Burke, Bernard, *A genealogical and heraldic dictionary of the landed gentry of Great Britain and Ireland* (4th edn, 2 vols, London, 1863).
Burke, Helen, *The royal hospital, Donnybrook: a heritage of caring, 1743–1993* (Dublin, 1993).
Caffrey, Helen, *Almshouses in the West Riding of Yorkshire 1600–1900* (King's Lynn, 2006).
Carter, Philip, *Men and the emergence of polite society, Britain 1660–1800* (Harlow, 2001).
Chalus, Elaine, *Elite women in English political life c. 1754–1790* (Oxford, 2005).
Chapman, Hester, *Mary II, queen of England* (Bath, 1972).
Clark, William, *The early Irish stage: the beginnings to 1720* (Oxford, 1955).
Claydon, Tony and W.A. Speck, *William and Mary* (Oxford, 2007).
Coakley, Davis, *Doctor Steevens's Hospital: a brief history* (Dublin, 1992).
Cohen, Michèle, *Fashioning masculinity: national identity and language in the eighteenth century* (London, 1996).
Cokayne, George *et al.*, *The complete peerage; ...* (13 vols, London, 1910–59).
Colley, Linda, *Britons: forging the nation 1707–1837* (3rd edn, London, 2009).
Connolly, S.J., *Divided kingdom: Ireland 1630–1800* (Oxford, 2008).
Connolly, S.J., *Religion, law and power: the making of Protestant Ireland 1660–1760* (Oxford, 1992).
Conway, Stephen, *Britain, Ireland and continental Europe in the eighteenth century: similarities, connections, identities* (Oxford, 2011).
Craig, Maurice, *Dublin 1660–1860* (Dublin, 1952).
Cruickshanks, Eveline, Stuart Handley and D.W. Hayton (eds), *The history of parliament: the House of Commons 1690–1715* (Cambridge, 2002).
Davidoff, Leonore, *The best circles: society, etiquette and the season* (London, 1973).
Davidoff, Leonore and Catherine Hall, *Family fortunes: men and women of the English middle class, 1780–1850* (London, 1987).
Davidson, L.C., *Catherine of Bragança: infanta of Portugal* (London, 1908)
De Bellaigue, Christina, *Educating women: schooling and identity in England and France, 1800–1867* (Oxford, 2007).
Dickson, David, *Dublin: the making of a capital city* (London, 2014).
Dickson, David, *New foundations: Ireland, 1660–1800* (2nd edn, Dublin, 2000).
Eales, Jacqueline, *Women in early modern England 1500–1700* (London, 1998).
Erickson, Amy, *Women and property in early modern England* (London, 1993).
Farrell, Michael, *The Poor Law and the workhouse in Belfast, 1838–1948* (Belfast, 1978).
Flather, Amanda, *Gender and space in early modern England* (Woodbridge, 2007).
Fleming, D.A., *Politics and provincial people: Sligo and Limerick, 1691–1761* (Manchester, 2010).
Fletcher, Anthony, *Gender, sex and subordination in England 1500–1800* (London, 1995).

Fletcher, Anthony, *Growing up in England: the experience of childhood, 1600–1914* (New Haven, 2008).

Foreman, Amanda, *Georgiana, duchess of Devonshire* (London, 1988).

Froide, Amy, *Never married: singlewomen in early modern England* (Oxford, 2005).

Geary, Laurence, *Medicine and charity in Ireland, 1718–1851* (Dublin, 2004).

Girouard, Mark, *Life in the English country house: a social and architectural history* (London, 1993).

Gittings, Clare, *Death, burial and the individual in early modern England* (London, 1988).

Gleadle, Kathryn, *Borderline citizens: women, gender and political culture in Britain 1815–1867* (Oxford, 2009).

Glover, Katharine, *Elite women and polite society in eighteenth-century Scotland* (Woodbridge, 2011).

Greene, John and Gladys Clark, *The Dublin stage 1720–1745: a calendar of plays, entertainments, and afterpieces* (London, 1993).

Gregg, Edward, *Queen Anne* (London, 1984).

Habakkuk, John, *Marriage, debt and the estates system: English landownership, 1650–1950* (Oxford, 1994).

Habermas, Jürgen, *The structural transformation of the public sphere: an inquiry into a category of bourgeois society* (Darmstadt, 1962).

Hainsworth, D.R., *Stewards, lords and people: the estate steward and his world in later Stuart England* (Cambridge, 1992).

Hamilton, Everard, *Hamilton memoirs: being historical and genealogical notices of a branch of that family which settled in Ireland in the reign of King James I* (2nd edn, Dundalk, 1920).

Harris, Frances, *A passion for government: the life of Sarah, duchess of Marlborough* (Oxford, 1991).

Harris, Tim, *Politics under the later Stuarts: party conflict in a divided society 1660–1715* (London, 1993).

Hatton, Ragnhild, *George I, elector and king* (London, 1978).

Hayton, D.W., *Ruling Ireland, 1685–1742: politics, politicians and parties* (Woodbridge, 2004).

Hayton, D.W., *The Anglo-Irish experience, 1680–1730: religion, identity and patriotism* (Woodbridge, 2012).

Heal, Felicity and Clive Holmes, *The gentry in England and Wales, 1500–1700* (London, 1994).

Hempton, David and Myrtle Hill, *Evangelical Protestantism in Ulster society, 1740–1890* (London, 1992).

Higgins, Padhraig, *A nation of politicians: gender, patriotism, and political culture in late eighteenth-century Ireland* (Madison, 2010).

Hill, Jacqueline, *From patriots to unionists: Dublin civic politics and Irish Protestant patriotism, 1660–1840* (Oxford, 1997).

Holmes, Geoffrey, *British politics in the age of Anne* (London, 1967).

Howson, Brian, *Almshouses. A social and architectural history* (Stroud, 2008).

Howson, Brian, *Houses of noble poverty. A history of the English almshouse* (Sunbury-on-Thames, 1993).

Jenkins, Philip, *The making of a ruling class: the Glamorgan gentry 1640–1790* (Cambridge, 1983).

Johnston-Liik, Edith, *History of the Irish parliament, 1692–1800: commons, constituencies and statues* (6 vols, Belfast, 2002).

Johnston-Liik, Edith, *MPs in Dublin: companion to the history of the Irish parliament, 1692–1800* (Belfast, 2006).
Jones, M.G., *The charity school movement: a study of eighteenth century Puritanism in action* (Cambridge, 1938).
Keeble, N.H. (ed.), *The cultural identity of seventeenth-century women: a reader* (London, 1994).
Kelly, Laura, *Irish women in medicine, c.1880–1920s: origins, education and careers* (Manchester, 2012).
Kowaleski-Wallace, Elizabeth, *Consuming subjects: women, shopping, and business in the eighteenth century* (New York, 1997).
Kugler, Anne, *Errant plagiary: the life and writing of Lady Sarah Cowper, 1644–1720* (Stanford, 2002).
Landes, Joan, *Women and the public sphere in the age of the French Revolution* (London, 1988).
Laurence, Anne, *Women in England 1500–1760: a social history* (New York, 1994).
Lerner, Gerda, *The majority finds its past: placing women in history* (Oxford, 1979).
Lewis, Judith, *Sacred to female patriotism: gender, class, and politics in late Georgian Britain* (London, 2003).
Lyons, J. B., *The quality of Mercer's: the story of Mercer's Hospital, 1734–1991* (Dublin, 1991).
MacLysaght, Edward, *Irish life in the seventeenth century* (2nd edn, Shannon, 1969).
Malcomson, A.P.W., *The pursuit of the heiress: aristocratic marriage in Ireland 1740–1840* (2nd edn, Belfast, 2006).
Marshall, Rosalind, *Virgins and viragos: a history of women in Scotland from 1080 to 1980* (London, 1983).
Maxwell, Constantia, *Country and town in Ireland under the Georges* (2nd edn, Dundalk, 1949).
Maxwell, Constantia, *Dublin under the Georges, 1714–1830* (Dublin, 1979).
McBride, Ian, *Eighteenth-century Ireland: the isle of slaves* (Dublin, 2009).
McClain, Molly, *Beaufort: the duke and his duchess, 1657–1715* (London, 2001).
McGrath, C.I., *The making of the eighteenth-century Irish constitution: government, parliament and the revenue, 1692–1714* (Dublin, 2000).
McNally, Patrick, *Parties, patriots and undertakers: parliamentary politics in early Hanoverian Ireland* (Dublin, 1997).
Meaney, Gerardine, Mary O'Dowd and Bernadette Whelan, *Reading the Irish woman: studies in cultural encounter and exchange, 1714–1960* (Liverpool, 2013).
Milne, Kenneth, *The Irish charter schools 1730–1830* (Dublin, 1997).
Mingay, G.E., *English landed society in the eighteenth century* (London, 1963).
Morash, Christopher, *A history of Irish theatre, 1601–2000* (Cambridge, 2002).
Nenadic, Stana, *Lairds and luxury: the Highland gentry in eighteenth-century Scotland* (Edinburgh, 2007).
O'Brien, Grania, *These my friends and forebears: the O'Briens of Dromoland* (Ballinakella, 1991).
O'Brien, Ivar, *O'Brien of Thomond: the O'Briens in Irish history 1500–1865* (Chichester, 1986).
O'Connor, John, *The workhouses of Ireland: the fate of Ireland's poor* (Dublin, 1995).
O'Dowd, Mary, *A history of women in Ireland, 1500–1800* (Harlow, 2004).
Ohlmeyer, Jane, *Making Ireland English: the Irish aristocracy in the seventeenth century* (London, 2012).
Oman, Carola, *Mary of Modena* (London, 1962).

Outhwaite, R.B., *Clandestine marriage in England, 1500–1850* (London, 1995).
Perry, Ruth, *The celebrated Mary Astell: an early English feminist* (Chicago, 1986).
Pointon, Marcia, *Strategies for showing: women, possession, and representation in English visual culture, 1665–1800* (Oxford, 1997).
Pollock, Linda, *Forgotten children: parent–child relations from 1500 to 1900* (Cambridge, 1983).
Porter, Mark, *Cultural history and postmodernity: disciplinary readings and challenges* (New York, 1997).
Purdue, Olwen, *The big house in the north of Ireland: land, power and social elites, 1878–1960* (Dublin, 2009).
Quennell, Peter, *Caroline of England: an Augustan portrait* (London, 1939).
Raftery, Deirdre and Susan M. Parkes, *Female education in Ireland 1700–1900: Minerva or Madonna* (Dublin, 2007).
Reynolds, K.D., *Aristocratic women and political society in Victorian Britain* (Oxford, 1998).
Robins, Joseph, *Champagne and silver buckles: the viceregal court at Dublin Castle 1700–1922* (Dublin, 2001).
Robins, Joseph, *The lost children: a study of charity children in Ireland, 1700–1900* (Dublin, 1980).
Sawyer, Roger, *We are but women: women in Ireland's history* (London, 1993).
Schwoerer, Lois, *Lady Rachel Russell (1637–1732): 'one of the best of women'* (London, 1988).
Shoemaker, Robert, *Gender in English society, 1650–1850: the emergence of separate spheres?* (London, 1998).
Simms, J.G., *The Williamite confiscation in Ireland, 1690–1703* (London, 1956).
Slater, Miriam, *Family life in the seventeenth century: the Verneys of Claydon House* (London, 1984).
Smith, Hannah, *The Georgian monarchy: politics and culture, 1714–1760* (Cambridge, 2006).
Somerset, Anne, *Queen Anne: the politics of passion* (London, 2012).
Somerville-Large, Peter, *The Irish country house: a social history* (London, 1995).
Southorn, Janet, *Mary of Modena, queen consort of James II and VII* (Royal Stuart Society, 1992).
Spring, Eileen, *Law, land, and family: aristocratic inheritance in England, 1300–1800* (London, 1993).
Staves, Susan, *Married women's separate property in England, 1660–1833* (London, 1990).
Stone, Lawrence, *Broken lives: separation and divorce in England 1660–1857* (Oxford, 1993).
Stone, Lawrence, *Road to divorce: England 1530–1987* (Oxford, 1990).
Stone, Lawrence, *The family, sex and marriage in England, 1500–1800* (London, 1977).
Tague, Ingrid, *Women of quality: accepting and contesting ideals of femininity in England, 1690–1760* (Woodbridge, 2002).
Taylor, Lou, *Mourning dress: a costume and social history* (London, 1983).
Thomas, Gertrude, *Richer than spices: how a royal bride's dowry introduced cane, lacquer, cottons, tea and porcelain to England, and so revolutionized taste, manners, craftsmanship, and history in both England and America* (New York, 1965).
Townshend, Horatio, *The history of Mercer's charitable hospital in Dublin, to the end of the year 1742 with note and an appendix* (Dublin, 1860).

Vickery, Amanda, *Behind closed doors: at home in Georgian England* (London, 2009).
Vickery, Amanda, *The gentleman's daughter: women's lives in Georgian England* (London, 1998).
Walsh, Patrick, *The making of the Irish Protestant ascendancy: the life of William Conolly, 1662–1729* (Woodbrige, 2010).
Warburton, John, James Whitelaw and Robert Walsh, *History of the city of Dublin, from the earliest accounts to the present time: ...* (2 vols, London, 1818).
Weil, Rachel, *Political passions: gender, the family and political argument in England, 1680–1714* (Manchester, 2009).
Whyman, Susan, *Sociability and power in late-Stuart England: the cultural worlds of the Verneys 1660–1720* (Oxford, 1999).
Widdess, J.D.H., *The charitable infirmary, Jervis Street, Dublin, 1718–1968* (Dublin, 1968).
Wilson, Deborah, *Women, marriage and property in wealthy landed families in Ireland, 1750 1850* (Manchester, 2009).
Wolfram, Sybil, *In-laws and outlaws: kinship and marriage in England* (London, 1987).
Wynne, Sonya, *The mistresses of Charles II and Restoration court politics, 1660–1685* (Cambridge, 1997).

ESSAYS IN EDITED VOLUMES

Andrew, Donna, '*Noblesse oblige*: female charity in an age of sentiment' in Susan Staves and John Brewer (eds), *Early modern conceptions of property* (London, 1995), pp 275–300.
Aylmer, Gerald, 'The first duke of Ormond as patron and administrator' in Toby Barnard and Jane Fenlon (eds), *The dukes of Ormond, 1610–1745* (Woodbridge, 2001), pp 115–35.
Bailey, Joanne, 'Reassessing parenting in eighteenth-century England' in Helen Berry and Elizabeth Foyster (eds), *The family in early modern England* (Cambridge, 2007), pp 209–32.
Barclay, Katie, 'Love and courtship in eighteenth-century Scotland' in eadem and Deborah Simonton (eds), *Women in eighteenth-century Scotland: intimate, intellectual and public lives* (Farnham, 2013), pp 37–54.
Barclay, Mary, 'Mary Beatrice of Modena: the "Second Bless'd of Woman-kind"?' in Clarissa Campbell Orr (ed.), *Queenship in Britain 1660–1837: royal patronage, court culture and dynastic politics* (Manchester, 2002), pp 74–93.
Barnard, Toby, 'Aristocratic values in the careers of the dukes of Ormonde' in Toby Barnard and Jane Fenlon (eds), *The dukes of Ormond, 1610–1745* (Woodbridge, 2001), pp 161–75.
Barnard, Toby, 'A tale of three sisters: Katherine Conolly of Castletown' in idem, *Irish Protestant ascents and descents, 1641–1770* (Dublin, 2004), pp 266–89.
Barnard, Toby, 'Considering the inconsiderable: electors, patrons and Irish elections, 1659–1761' in D.W. Hayton (ed.), *The Irish parliament in the eighteenth century: the long apprenticeship* (Edinburgh, 2001), pp 107–27.
Barnard, Toby, '"Grand Metropolis" or "The anus of the world"? The cultural life of eighteenth-century Dublin' in Peter Clark and Raymond Gillespie (eds), *Two capitals: London and Dublin, 1500–1840* (Oxford, 2001), pp 185–210.
Barnard, Toby, 'Hamilton's "Cries of Dublin"; the society and economy of

mid-eighteenth Dublin' in William Laffan (ed.), *The cries of Dublin etc.: drawn from the life of Hugh Douglas Hamilton, 1760* (Dublin, 2003), pp 26–37.

Barnard, Toby, 'Integration or separation? Hospitality and display in Protestant Ireland, c. 1660–1800' in Laurence Brockliss and David Eastwood (eds), *A union of multiple identities: the British Isles, c. 1750–1850* (Manchester, 1997), pp 127–46.

Barnard, Toby, 'Introduction: the dukes of Ormonde' in idem and Jane Fenlon (eds), *The dukes of Ormond, 1610–1745* (Woodbridge, 2001), pp 1–53.

Barnard, Toby, 'Land and the limits of loyalty: the second earl of Cork and the first earl of Burlington' in Toby Barnard and Jane Clark (eds), *Lord Burlington: architecture, art and life* (London, 1995), pp 167–99.

Barnard, Toby, 'Protestantism, ethnicity and Irish identities, 1660–1760' in Tony Claydon and Ian McBride (eds), *Protestantism and national identity: Britain and Ireland, c.1650–c.1850* (Cambridge, 2007), pp 206–35.

Barnard, Toby, 'Public and private uses of wealth in Ireland, c. 1660–1760' in Jacqeline Hill and Colm Lennon (eds), *Luxury and austerity. Historical Studies xxi* (Dublin, 1999), pp 67–83.

Barnard, Toby, 'Scotland and Ireland in the later Stewart monarchy' in S.G. Ellis and Sarah Barber (eds), *Conquest and union: fashioning a British state, 1485–1725* (London, 1995), pp 250–75.

Barnard, Toby, 'The vice-regal court in later seventeenth-century Ireland' in Eveline Cruickshanks (ed.), *The Stuart courts* (Stroud, 2000), pp 256–65.

Beckett, J.C., 'Introduction: eighteenth-century Ireland' in T.W. Moody and W.E. Vaughan (eds), *A new history of Ireland*, iv: *Eighteenth century Ireland, 1691–1800* (Oxford, 1986).

Bergin, John, 'Irish private divorce bills and acts of the eighteenth century' in James Kelly, John McCafferty and Charles Ivar McGrath (eds), *People, politics and power: essays on Irish history 1660-1850, in honour of James I. McGuire* (Dublin, 2009), pp 94–121.

Berry, Helen and Elizabeth Foyster, 'Childless men in early modern England' in eadem (eds), *The family in early modern England* (Cambridge, 2007), pp 158–83.

Bock, Gisela, 'Women's history and gender history: aspects of an international debate' in Robert Shoemaker and Mary Vincent (eds), *Gender and history in western Europe* (London, 1998), pp 25–42.

Bonfield, Lloyd, 'Marriage settlements, 1660–1740: the adoption of the strict settlement in Kent and Northamptonshire' in R.B. Outhwaite (ed.), *Marriage and society: studies in the social history of marriage* (London, 1981), pp 101–16.

Borsay, Peter, 'Children, adolescents and fashionable urban society in eighteenth-century England' in Anja Müller (ed.), *Fashioning childhood in the eighteenth century: age and identity* (Burlington, VT, 2006), pp 53–62.

Brewer, John, 'This, that and the other: public, social and private in the seventeenth and eighteenth centuries' in Dario Castiglione and Lesley Sharpe (eds), *Shifting the boundaries: transformations of the languages of public and private in the eighteenth century* (Exeter, 1995), pp 1–21.

Bucholz, R.O., 'Queen Anne: victim of her virtues?' in Clarissa Campbell Orr (ed.), *Queenship in Britain 1660–1837: royal patronage, court culture and dynastic politics* (Manchester, 2002), pp 94–129.

Burke, Helen, 'Putting on Irish "stuff": the politics of Anglo-Irish cross-dressing' in Jessica Munns and Penny Richards (eds), *The clothes that wear us: essays on dressing and transgressing in eighteenth-century culture* (London, 1999), pp 233–49.

Chalus, Elaine, '"Ladies are often very good scaffolding": women and politics in the age of Anne' in Clyve Jones (ed.), *British politics in the age of Holmes: Geoffrey Holmes's* British Politics in the Age of Anne *40 years on* (Oxford, 2009), pp 150–65.

Chalus, Elaine, '"My Minerva at my elbow": the political roles of women in eighteenth-century England' in Stephen Taylor, Richard Connors and Clyve Jones (eds), *Hanoverian Britain and empire: essays in memory of Philip Lawson* (Woodbridge, 1998), pp 210–28.

Chalus, Elaine, '"That epidemical Madness": women and electoral politics in the late eighteenth century' in Hannah Barker and Elaine Chalus (eds), *Gender in eighteenth-century England: roles, representations and responsibilities* (London, 1997), pp 151–78.

Chalus, Elaine, '"To serve my friends": women and political patronage in eighteenth-century England' in Amanda Vickery (ed.), *Women, privilege, and power: British politics, 1750 to the present* (Stanford, 2001), pp 57–88.

Chalus, Elaine, 'Women, electoral privilege and practice in the eighteenth century' in Kathryn Gleadle and Sarah Richardson (eds), *Women in British politics, 1760–1860: the power of the petticoat* (London, 2000), pp 19–38.

Chalus, Elaine and Fiona Montgomery, 'Women and politics' in Hannah Barker and Elaine Chalus (eds), *Women's history: Britain, 1700–1850* (New York, 2005), pp 217–59.

Clark, Jane, '"Lord Burlington is here"' in Toby Barnard and Jane Clark (eds), *Lord Burlington: architecture, art and life* (London, 1995), pp 251–310.

Clarkson, L.A., 'Hospitality, housekeeping and high living in eighteenth-century Ireland' in J.R. Hill and Colm Lennon (eds), *Luxury and austerity. Historical Studies xxi* (Dublin, 1999), pp 84–105.

Cohen, Michèle, '"Familiar conversation": the role of the "familiar format" in education in eighteenth- and nineteenth-century England' in Mary Hilton and Jill Shefrin (eds), *Educating the child in Enlightenment Britain: beliefs, cultures, practices* (Farnham, 2009), pp 99–116.

Cohen, Michèle, '"To think, to compare, to combine, to methodise": girls' education in Enlightenment Britain' in Sarah Knott and Barbara Taylor (eds), *Women, gender and enlightenment* (New York, 2005), pp 224–42.

Connolly, S.J., 'Family, love and marriage: some evidence from the early eighteenth century' in Margaret MacCurtain and Mary O'Dowd (eds), *Women in early modern Ireland* (Edinburgh, 1991), pp 276–90.

Corp, Edward, 'Catherine of Braganza and cultural politics' in Clarissa Campbell Orr (ed.), *Queenship in Britain 1660–1837: royal patronage, court culture and dynastic politics* (Manchester and New York, 2002), pp 53–73.

Cragoe, Matthew, '"Jenny rules the roost": women and electoral politics, 1832–68' in Kathryn Gleadle and Sarah Richardson (eds), *Women in British politics, 1760–1860: the power of the petticoat* (London, 2000), pp 153–68.

Crawford, W. H., 'Ulster as a mirror of the two societies' in T.M. Devine and David Dickson (eds), *Ireland and Scotland 1600–1850: parallels and contrasts in economic and social development* (Edinburgh, 1983), pp 60–9.

Crossman, Virginia, 'Workhouse medicine in Ireland: a preliminary analysis 1850–1914' in Jonathan Reinarz and Leonard Schwarz (eds), *Medicine and the workhouse* (Woodbridge, 2013), pp 123–39.

Cullen, L.M., 'Patrons, teachers and literacy in Irish: 1700–1850' in Mary Daly and David Dickson (eds), *The origins of popular literacy in Ireland: language change and educational development 1700–1920* (Dublin, 1990), pp 15–44.

Curl, James Stevens, 'The Knockbreda mausolea' in Lydia Wilson (ed.), *Knockbreda: its monuments and people* (Belfast, 2009), pp 36–9.

Davis, Natalie Zemon, 'Women on top' in Robert Shoemaker and Mary Vincent (eds), *Gender and history in western Europe* (London, 1998), pp 285–306.

Dickson, David, 'The place of Dublin in the eighteenth-century Irish economy' in idem and T.M. Devine (eds), *Ireland and Scotland 1600–1850: parallels and contrasts in economic and social development* (Edinburgh, 1983), pp 177–92.

Dixon, Hugh, 'Knockbreda Church' in Lydia Wilson (ed.), *Knockbreda: its monuments and people* (Belfast, 2009), pp 18–21.

Dooley, Terence, '"Till my further orders": rules governing servants at Carton in the mid-eighteenth century' in idem, Patrick J. Cosgrove and Karol Mullaney-Dignam (eds), *Aspects of Irish aristocratic life: essays on the FitzGeralds and Carton House* (Dublin, 2014), pp 106–17.

Ellis, Markman, 'Coffee-women, *The Spectator* and the public in the early eighteenth century' in Elizabeth Eger, Charlotte Grant, Clíona Ó Gallchoir and Penny Warburton (eds), *Women, writing and the public sphere, 1700–1830* (Cambridge, 2001), pp 27–52.

Erickson, Amy, 'Property and widowhood in England 1660–1840' in Sandra Cavallo and Lyndan Warner (eds), *Widowhood in medieval and early modern Europe* (Harlow, 1999), pp 145–63.

Evans, Tanya, 'Women, marriage and the family' in Hannah Barker and Elaine Chalus (eds), *Women's history: Britain, 1700–1850* (New York, 2005), pp 57–77.

Fitzgerald, Alison, 'Taste in high life: dining in the Dublin town house' in Christine Casey (ed.), *The eighteenth-century Dublin town house: form, function and finance* (Dublin, 2010), pp 120–7.

Foreman, Amanda, 'A politician's politician: Georgiana, duchess of Devonshire and the Whig party' in Hannah Barker and Elaine Chalus (eds), *Gender in eighteenth-century England: roles, representations and responsibilities* (London, 1997), pp 179–204.

Froide, Amy, 'Marital status as a category of difference: singlewomen and widows in early modern England' in eadem and Judith Bennett (eds), *Singlewomen in the European past, 1250–1800* (Philadelphia, 1999), pp 236–69.

Gerrard, Christine, 'Queens-in-waiting: Caroline of Anspach and Augusta of Saxe-Gotha as Princesses of Wales' in Clarissa Campbell Orr (ed.), *Queenship in Britain 1660–1837: royal patronage, court culture and dynastic politics* (Manchester, 2002), pp 143–61.

Gillespie, Raymond, 'Music and song in early eighteenth-century Belfast' in idem and R.F. Foster (eds), *Irish provincial cultures in the long eighteenth-century: making the middle sort. Essays for Toby Barnard* (Dublin, 2012), pp 155–69.

Gleadle, Kathryn, 'British women and radical politics in the late nonconformist enlightenment, c. 1780–1830' in Amanda Vickery (ed.), *Women, privilege, and power: British politics, 1750 to the present* (Stanford, 2001), pp 123–51.

Glover, Katharine, '"Polite London Children": educating the daughters of the Scottish elite in mid-eighteenth-century London' in Stana Nenadic (ed.), *Scots in London in the eighteenth-century* (Cranbury, 2010), pp 253–71.

Gonda, Caroline, 'Misses, murderesses and Magdalens: women in the public eye' in Elizabeth Eger, Charlotte Grant, Clíona Ó Gallchoir and Penny Warburton (eds), *Women, writing and the public sphere, 1700–1830* (Cambridge, 2001), pp 53–71.

Gorey, Philomena, 'Managing midwifery in Dublin: practice and practitioners,

1700–1800' in Margaret Preston and Margaret Ó hÓgartaigh (eds), *Irish Studies: gender and medicine in Ireland, 1700–1950* (New York, 2012), pp 123–37.

Harris, Barbara, 'Sisterhood, friendship and the power of English aristocratic women, 1450–1550' in James Daybell (ed.), *Women and politics in early modern England, 1450–1700* (Aldershot, 2004), pp 21–50.

Hayton, D.W., 'British Whig ministers and the Irish question, 1714–25' in Stephen Taylor, Richard Connors and Clyve Jones (eds), *Hanoverian Britain and empire: essays in memory of Philip Lawson* (Woodbridge, 1998), pp 37–64.

Hayton, D.W., 'Constitutional experiments and political expediency, 1689–1725' in S.G. Ellis and Sarah Barber (eds), *Conquest and union: fashioning a British state, 1485–1725* (London, 1995), pp 276–302.

Hayton, D.W., 'Dependence, clientage and affinity: the political following of the second duke of Ormonde' in Toby Barnard and Jane Fenlon (eds), *The dukes of Ormond, 1610–1745* (Woodbridge, 2001), pp 211–41.

Hayton, D.W., 'Did Protestantism fail in early eighteenth-century Ireland? Charity schools and the enterprise of religious and social reformation, c. 1690–1730' in Alan Ford, James McGuire and Kenneth Milne (eds), *As by law established: the Church of Ireland since the Reformation* (Dublin, 1995), pp 166–86.

Hayton, D.W., 'The beginnings of the "Undertaker System"' in Thomas Bartlett and David Hayton (eds), *Penal era and Golden age: essays in Irish history 1690–1800* (Belfast, 1979), pp 32–54.

Hayton, D.W., 'Thomas Prior, Sir John Rawdon, third baronet, and the mentality and ideology of 'improvement': a question of upbringing' in Raymond Gillespie and R.F. Foster (eds), *Irish provincial cultures in the long eighteenth century: making the middle sort: essays for Toby Barnard* (Dublin, 2012), pp 106–33.

Hunter, Jean, 'The 18th-century Englishwoman: according to the *Gentleman's Magazine*' in Paul Fritz and Richard Morton (eds), *Women in the 18th century and other essays* (Toronto, 1976), pp 73–88.

Innes, Sue and Jane Rendall, 'Women, gender and politics' in Lynn Abrams, Eleanor Gordon, Deborah Simonton and Eileen Yeo (eds), *Gender in Scottish history since 1700* (Edinburgh, 2006), pp 43–83.

Jenkins, Susan, 'Lady Burlington at court' in Edward Corp (ed.), *Lord Burlington – the man and his politics: questions of loyalty* (New York, 1998), pp 149–79.

Jupp, Peter, 'The roles of royal and aristocratic women in British politics, c. 1782–1832' in Mary O'Dowd and Sabine Wichert (eds), *Chattel, servant or citizen: women's status in church, state and society. Historical Studies xix* (Belfast, 1995), pp 103–13.

Kelly, James, 'Charitable societies: their genesis and development' in idem and Martyn Powell (eds), *Clubs and societies in eighteenth-century Ireland* (Dublin, 2010), pp 89–108.

Kelly, James, 'Residential and non-residential lords lieutenant – the viceroyalty, 1703–90' in Peter Gray and Olwen Purdue (eds), *The Irish Lord Lieutenancy c. 1541–1922* (Dublin, 2012), pp 66–96.

Landes, Joan, 'The public and the private sphere: a feminist reconsideration' in Johanna Meehan (ed.), *Feminists read Habermas: gendering the subject of discourse* (New York, 1995), pp 91–116.

Laurence, Anne, 'Real and imagined communities in the lives of women in seventeenth century Ireland: identity and gender' in Stephanie Tarbin and Susan Broomhall (eds), *Women, identities and communities in early modern Europe* (Aldershot, 2008), pp 13–27.

Lewis, Judith, '1784 and all that: aristocratic women and electoral politics' in Amanda Vickery (ed.), *Women, power and privilege, and power: British politics, 1750 to the present* (Stanford, 2001), pp 89–122.

Loeber, Rolf and Livia Hurley, 'The architecture of Irish country houses, 1691–1739' in Raymond Gillespie and R.F. Foster (eds), *Irish provincial cultures in the long eighteenth century: making the middle sort* (Dublin, 2012), pp 210–18.

Maccubbin, Robert and Martha Hamilton-Phillips (eds), *The age of William III and Mary II: power, politics and patronage, 1688–1702* (Williamsburg, VA, 1989).

Mackey, Brian, 'The creation of Knockbreda parish church and Belvoir Park' in Lydia Wilson (ed.), *Knockbreda: its monuments and people* (Belfast, 2009), pp 9–17.

Maguire, Nancy, 'The duchess of Portsmouth: English royal consort and French politician, 1670–85' in R. M. Smuts (ed.), *The Stuart courts and Europe. Essays in politics and political culture* (Cambridge, 1996), pp 247–73.

Maguire, W.A., 'A question of arithmetic: Arthur Chichester, fourth earl of Donegall, 1695–1757' in Brenda Collins, Philip Ollerenshaw and Trevor Parkhill (eds), *Industry, trade and people in Ireland 1650–1950, essays in honour of W.H. Crawford* (Belfast, 2005), pp 31–48.

Maguire, W.A., 'The land settlement' in idem, *Kings in conflict: the revolutionary war in Ireland and its aftermath 1689–1750* (Belfast, 1990), pp 139–56.

Malcomson, A.P.W., 'The fall of the house of Conolly 1758–1803' in Allan Blackstock and Eoin Magennis (eds), *Politics and political culture in Britain and Ireland, 1750–1850* (Belfast, 2007), pp 107–56.

McCracken, J.L., 'The political structure, 1714–60' in T.W. Moody and W.E. Vaughan (eds), *A new history of Ireland*, iv: *Eighteenth century Ireland, 1691–1800* (Oxford, 1986), pp 57–83.

McEntee, Joanna, 'Pecuniary assistance for poverty and emigration: the politics of landed estate management and philanthropy in mid-nineteenth-century Ireland' in Laurence Geary and Oonagh Walsh (eds), *Philanthropy in nineteenth-century Ireland* (Dublin, 2014), pp 115–32.

McGrath, C.I., 'Late seventeenth- and early eighteenth-century governance and the viceroyalty' in Peter Gray and Olwen Purdue (eds), *The Irish Lord Lieutenancy c. 1541–1922* (Dublin, 2012), pp 43–65.

McGuire, James, 'The Irish parliament of 1692' in Thomas Bartlett and David Hayton (eds), *Penal era and golden age: essays in Irish history 1690–1800* (Belfast, 1979), pp 1–31.

McKenna, Elizabeth, 'Was there a political role for women in medieval Ireland? Lady Margaret Butler and Lady Eleanor MacCarthy' in Christine Meek and Katharine Simms (eds), *'The fragility of her sex'?: medieval Irishwomen in their European context* (County Dublin, 1996), pp 163–74.

McKenna, Kevin, 'Charity, paternalism and power on the Clonbrock estates, County Galway, 1834–44' in Laurence Geary and Oonagh Walsh (eds), *Philanthropy in nineteenth-century Ireland* (Dublin, 2014), pp 97–114.

McNamara, Conor, '"The monster misery of Ireland": landlord paternalism and the 1822 famine in the West' in Laurence Geary and Oonagh Walsh (eds), *Philanthropy in nineteenth-century Ireland* (Dublin, 2014), pp 82–96.

Mooney, Tighernan and Fiona White, 'The gentry's winter season' in David Dickson (ed.), *The gorgeous mask: Dublin, 1700–1850* (Dublin, 1987), pp 1–16.

Moore, Lindy, 'Education and learning' in Lynn Abrams, Eleanor Gordon, Deborah

Simonton and Eileen Janes Yeo (eds), *Gender in Scottish history since 1700* (Edinburgh, 2006), pp 111–39.

Neely, W.G., 'The Ormond Butlers of county Kilkenny 1515–1715' in William Nolan and Kevin Whelan (eds), *Kilkenny: history and society: interdisciplinary essays on the history of an Irish county* (Dublin, 1990), pp 107–26.

O'Riordan, Maeve, 'Assuming control: elite women as household managers in late nineteenth-century Ireland' in Ciarán O'Neill (ed.), *Irish elites in the nineteenth century* (Dublin, 2013), pp 83–98.

Payne, Helen, 'Aristocratic women, power, patronage and family networks at the Jacobean court, 1603–1625' in James Daybell (ed.), *Women and politics in early modern England, 1450–1700* (Aldershot, 2004), pp 164–80.

Proudfoot, Lindsay, Market fairs and towns in Ireland, c.1600–1853' in eadem and Peter Borsay (eds), *Provincial towns in early modern England and Ireland: change, convergence and divergence* (Oxford, 2002), pp 69–96.

Raughter, Rosemary, 'A natural tenderness: the ideal and the reality of eighteenth-century female philanthropy' in M.G. Valiulis and Mary O'Dowd (eds), *Women and Irish history: essays in honour of Margaret MacCurtain* (Dublin, 1997), pp 71–88.

Reilly, Barry, 'The almshouses of Fethard, County Tipperary' in Conleth Manning (ed.), *From ringforts to fortified houses: studies on castle and other monuments in honour of David Sweetman* (Wicklow, 2007), pp 217–35.

Rendall, Jane, 'Women and the Enlightenment in Britain c. 1690–1800' in Hannah Barker and Elaine Chalus (eds), *Women's history: Britain, 1700–1850* (New York, 2005), pp 9–32.

Richardson, Sarah, '"Well-neighboured houses": the political networks of elite women, 1780–1860' in eadem and Kathryn Gleadle (eds), *Women in British politics, 1760–1860: the power of the petticoat* (London, 2000), pp 56–73.

Ryan, Mary, 'Gender and public access: women's politics in nineteenth-century America' in Craig Calhoun (ed.), *Habermas and the public sphere* (London, 1992), pp 259–88.

Schofield, Roger, 'Did the mothers really die? Three centuries of maternal mortality' in Lloyd Bonfield, R.M. Smith and Keith Wrightson (eds), *The world we have gained: histories of population and social structure: essays presented to Peter Laslett on his seventieth birthday* (Oxford, 1986), pp 131–60.

Scott, Joan, 'Gender: a useful category of historical analysis' in Robert Shoemaker and Mary Vincent (eds), *Gender and history in western Europe* (London, 1998), pp 42–65.

Simms, J. G., 'The Irish parliament of 1713' reprinted in D.W. Hayton and Gerard O'Brien (eds), *War and politics in Ireland 1649–1730* (London, 1986), pp 277–87.

Simms, J. G., 'The Jacobite parliament of 1689' reprinted in D.W. Hayton and Gerard O'Brien (eds), *War and politics in Ireland 1649–1730* (London, 1986), pp 65–90.

Simonton, Deborah, 'Women and education' in Hannah Barker and Elaine Chalus (eds), *Women's history: Britain, 1700–1850* (New York, 2005), pp 33–56.

Staves, Susan, 'Resentment or resignation? Dividing the spoils among daughters and younger sons' in eadem and John Brewer (eds), *Early modern conceptions of property* (London, 1995), pp 194–218.

Tague, Ingrid, 'Aristocratic women and ideas of family in the eighteenth century' in Helen Berry and Elizabeth Foyster (eds), *The family in early modern England* (Cambridge, 2007), pp 184–208.

Victory, Isolde, 'The making of the Declaratory Act of 1720' in Gerard O'Brien (ed.), *Politics, parliament and people: essays in eighteenth-century Irish history* (Dublin, 1989), pp 9–29.

Von Den Steinen, Karl, 'The discovery of women in eighteenth-century English political life' in Barbara Kanner (ed.), *The women of England from Anglo-Saxon times to the present* (Hamden, CT, 1979), pp 229–58.

Walsh, Claire, 'Shops, shopping, and the art of decision marking eighteenth century England' in John Styles and Amanda Vickery (eds), *Gender, taste, and material culture in Britain and North America, 1700–1830* (New Haven, 2006), pp 151–78.

Wynne, Sonya, 'The mistresses of Charles II and Restoration court politics' in Eveline Cruickshanks (ed.), *The Stuart courts* (Stroud, 2000), pp 171–90.

JOURNAL ARTICLES

Arnold, Denis, 'Charity music in eighteenth-century Dublin', *Galpin Society Journal*, xxi (1968), pp 162–74.

Avery, Emmett, 'The Dublin stage, 1736–1737', *Notes and* Queries, cc (1955), pp 61–5.

Barclay, Katie, Rosalind Carr, Rose Elliot and Annmarie Hughes, 'Gender and generations: women and life cycles', *Women's History Review*, xx (2011), pp 175–88.

Bitel, Lisa, 'Women's donations to the churches in early Ireland', *Journal of the Royal Society of Antiquaries of Ireland*, cxiv (1984), pp 5–23.

Boydell, Brian, 'Venues for music in 18th century Dublin', *Dublin Historical Record*, xxix (1975), pp 28–34.

Boylan, Lena, 'The Conollys of Castletown: a family history', *Quarterly Bulletin of the Irish Georgian society*, xi (1968), pp 1–46.

Carr, Rosalind, 'Female correspondence and early modern Scottish political history: a case study of the Anglo-Scottish Union', *Historical Reflections*, xxxvii (2011), pp 39–75

Carter, Mary, 'Swift and the scheme for badging beggars in Dublin, 1726–1737', *Eighteenth-Century Life*, xxxvii (2013), pp 97–118.

Clay, Christopher, 'Property settlements, financial provision for the family, and sale of land by the greater landowners 1660–1790', *Journal of British Studies*, xxi (1981), pp 18–38.

Colley, Linda, 'Women and political power', *The Wilson Quarterly*, xvi (1992), pp 50–8.

Connolly, S.J., 'A woman's life in eighteenth-century Ireland: the case of Letitia Bushe', *Historical Journal*, xliii (2000), pp 433–51.

Cowmeadow, Nicola, '"Your Politick, self designing sister": the role of Katherine, first duchess of Atholl in the Scottish parliamentary elections of 1702', *Parliaments, Estates and Representations*, xxxiii (2013), pp 1–19.

Doyle, Thomas, 'Jacobitism, Catholicism and the Irish Protestant elite, 1700–1710', *Eighteenth-Century Ireland*, xii (1997), pp 28–59.

Dudley, Rowena, 'The Dublin parishes and the poor: 1660–1740', *Archivium Hibernium*, liii (1999), pp 80–94.

Dyer, John, 'The almshouse at Inistioge', *Old Kilkenny Review*, l (1998), pp 43–7.

Fenlon, Jane, 'Moving towards the formal house: room usage in early modern Ireland', *Proceedings of the Royal Irish Academy*, Sect. C, cxi (2010), pp 141–68.

Fleming, David, 'Diversions of the people: sociability among the orders of early eighteenth-century Ireland', *Eighteenth-Century Ireland*, xvii (2002), pp 99–111.

Foster, Sarah, '"Ornaments and splendour": shops and shopping in Georgian Dublin', *Irish Architectural and Decorative Studies*, xv (2002), pp 12–33.

Furlong, E.J. and D. Berman, 'George Berkeley and *The Ladies Library*', *Berkeley Newsletter*, iv (1980), pp 4–7.

Glover, Katharine, 'The female mind: Scottish enlightenment femininity and the world of letters. A case study of the women of the Fletcher of Saltoun family in the mid-eighteenth century', *Journal of Scottish Historical Studies*, xxv (2005), pp 1–20.

Goose, Nigel and Henk Looijesteijn, 'Almshouses in England and the Dutch Republic circa 1350–1800: a comparative perspective', *Journal of Social History*, xlv (2012), pp 1049–73.

Graves, James, 'Extracts from the household expenses of James earl of Ossory', *Transactions of the Kilkenny Archaeological Society*, i (1851), pp 415–19.

Greenberg, Janelle, 'The legal status of the English woman in early eighteenth century common law and equity', *Studies in Eighteenth-Century Culture*, iv (1975), pp 171–81.

Greene, John, 'The repertory of the Dublin theatres, 1720–1745', *Eighteenth-Century Ireland*, ii (1987), pp 133–48.

Habakkuk, John, 'The rise and fall of English landed families, 1600–1800', *Transactions of the Royal Historical Society*, ser. 5, xxix (1979), pp 187–207.

Hayden, Mary, 'Charity children in 18th-century Dublin', *Dublin Historical Record*, v (1943), pp 92–107.

Haydon, C. M., 'The anti-Catholic activity of the S.P.C.K., c. 1698–1740', *Recusant History*, xviii (1987), pp 418–21.

Hayton, D.W., 'The crisis in Ireland and the disintegration of Queen Anne's last ministry', *Irish Historical Studies*, xxii (1981), pp 193–215.

Hayton, D.W., 'Two ballads on the County Westmeath by-election of 1723', *Eighteenth-Century Ireland*, iv (1989), pp 7–30.

Heller, Benjamin, 'Leisure and the use of domestic space in Georgian London', *Historical Journal*, liii (2010), pp 623–45.

Higgins, Padhraig, 'Consumption, gender, and the politics of "Free Trade" in eighteenth-century Ireland', *Eighteenth-Century Studies*, xli (2007), pp 87–105.

Hill, Bridget, 'The marriage age of women and the demographers', *History Workshop Journal*, xxviii (1989), pp 129–47.

Kelly, James, 'The abduction of women of fortune in eighteenth-century Ireland', *Eighteenth-century Ireland*, ix (1994), pp 7–43.

Kennedy, Maire, 'Dublin's coffee houses of the eighteenth century', *Dublin Historical Record*, lxiii (2010), pp 29–38.

Kerber, Linda, 'Separate spheres, female worlds, woman's place: the rhetoric of women's history', *Journal of American History*, lxxv (1988), pp 9–39.

Kierner, Cynthia, 'Genteel balls and Republican parades: gender and early civic rituals, 1677–1826', *The Virginia Magazine of History and Biography: Constructing a Revolution: Women and Gender Roles in Virginia*, civ (1996), pp 185–210.

Klein, Lawrence, 'Politeness and the interpretation of the British eighteenth century', *Historical Journal*, xliv (2002), pp 869–98.

Kowaleski-Wallace, Beth, 'Tea, gender and domesticity in eighteenth-century England', *Studies in Eighteenth-century Culture*, xxiii (1994), pp 131–45.

Lahert, Richard, 'Some charitable institutions of old Waterford', *Decies*, xxvii, xxix (1985), pp 43–54, 24–31.

Lana, Renata, 'Women and the Foxite strategy in the Westminster election of 1784', *Eighteenth-Century Life*, xxvi (2002), pp 49–69.

Langford, Paul, 'The uses of eighteenth century politeness', *Transactions of the Royal Historical Society*, ser. 6, xii (2002), pp 311–31.

Leonard, John, 'Dublin and the duke of Ormonde', *Journal of the Butler Society*, iii (1994), pp 555–60.

Lewis, Judith, '"Tis a misfortune to be a great ladie": maternal mortality in the British aristocracy, 1558–1959', *Journal of British Studies*, xxxvii (1998), pp 26–53.

Lucey, Conor, 'Keeping up appearances: redecorating the domestic interior in late eighteenth-century Dublin', *Proceedings of the Royal Irish Academy*, Sect. C, cxi (2010), pp 169–92.

McArdle, Grainne, 'Signora Violante and her troupe of dancers 1729–32', *Eighteenth-Century Ireland*, xx (2005), pp 55–78.

McCarthy, Patricia, 'Private theatricals in Irish houses, 1730 to 1815', *Irish Architectural and Decorative Studies*, xiv (2013), pp 12–49.

MacCurtain, Margaret, Mary O'Dowd and Maria Luddy, 'An agenda for women's history in Ireland, 1500–1900', *Irish Historical Studies*, xxviii (1992), pp 1–37.

McGrath, C.I., 'English ministers, Irish politicians and the making of a parliamentary settlement in Ireland, 1692–5', *English Historical Review*, cxix (2004), pp 585–613.

McMahon, Michael, 'Lucius and Catherine O'Brien of Corofin', *The Other Clare*, xxv (2001), pp 51–9.

Mullin, Janet, '"We had carding": hospitable card play and polite domestic sociability among the middling sort in eighteenth-century England', *Journal of Social History*, lvii (2009), pp 989–1008.

Nenadic, Stana, 'Experience and expectations in the transformation of the Highland gentlewoman, 1680 to 1820', *Scottish Historical Review*, lxxx (2001), pp 201–20.

O'Dowd, Mary, 'Politics, patriotism, and women in Ireland, Britain and colonial America, c. 1700–1780', *Journal of Women's History*, xxii (2010), pp 15–38.

O'Dowd, Mary, 'Women and Patriotism in eighteenth-century Ireland', *History Ireland*, xiv (2006), pp 25–30.

Ohlmeyer, Jane and Steven Zwicker, 'John Dryden, the house of Ormond, and the politics of Anglo-Irish patronage', *Historical Journal*, xlix (2006), pp 677–706.

O'Kane, Finola, 'Design and rule: women in the Irish countryside 1715–1831', *Eighteenth-Century Ireland*, xix (2004), pp 56–74.

O'Kane, Finola, '"Obliges me to dip my hands in mortar": Catherine O'Brien's influence at Dromoland', *Journal of the Irish Georgian Society*, vii (2004), pp 80–105.

Parks, Stephen, 'George Berkeley, Sir Richard Steele and *The Ladies Library*', *The Scriblerian and the Kit-Cats*, xii (1980), pp 1–2.

Paterson, T.G.F., 'Belfast in 1738', *Ulster Journal of Archaeology*, ii (1939), pp 110–12.

Quane, Michael, 'Midleton school, Co. Cork', *Journal of the Royal Society of Antiquaries of Ireland*, lxxxii (1952), pp 1–27.

Quane, Michael, 'Speaker Conolly', *Dublin Historical Record*, xxv (1971), pp 25–32.

Quane, Michael, 'Viscount Weymouth grammar school, Carrickmacross', *Journal of the Royal Society of Antiquaries of Ireland*, lxxxvi (1956), pp 27–51.

Raughter, Rosemary, 'A discreet benevolence: female philanthropy and the Catholic resurgence', *Women's History Review*, vi (1997), pp 465–87.
Rauser, Amelia, 'The butcher-kissing duchess of Devonshire: between caricature and allegory in 1784', *Eighteenth-Century Studies*, xxxvi (2002), pp 23–46.
Rose, Craig, 'Evangelical philanthropy and Anglican revival: the charity schools of Augustan London, 1698–1740', *London Journal*, xvi (1991), pp 35–63.
Rose, Craig, '"Seminarys in faction and rebellion": Jacobites, Whigs and the London charity schools, 1716–1724', *Historical Journal*, xxxiv (1991), pp 831–55.
Schwoerer, Lois, 'Images of Queen Mary II, 1698–95', *Renaissance Quarterly*, lxii (1989), pp 717–48.
Schwoerer, Lois, 'Women and the Glorious Revolution', *Albion*, xviii (1986), pp 195–218.
Shanahan, Madeline, '"Dining on words": manuscript recipe books, culinary change and elite food culture in Ireland, 1660–1830', *Irish Architectural and Decorative Studies*, xv (2012), pp 82–97.
Simms, J.G., 'County Sligo in the eighteenth century', *Journal of the Royal Society of Antiquaries of Ireland*, xci (1961), pp 153–62.
Simms, J.G., 'The making of a penal law (2 Anne, c.6), 1703–4', *Irish Historical Studies*, xii (1960–1), pp 105–18.
Simon, Joan, 'From charity school to workhouse in the 1720s: the S.P.C.K. and Mr. Marriott's solution', *History of Education*, xvii (1988), pp 113–19.
Smith, E.A., 'The election agent in English politics, 1734–1832', *English Historical Review*, lxxxiv (1969), pp 12–35.
Sonnelitter, Karen, '"To unite our temporal and eternal interests": sermons and the charity school movement in Ireland, 1689–1740', *Eighteenth-Century Ireland*, xxv (2010), pp 62–81.
Staves, Susan, 'Chattel property rules and the construction of Englishness, 1660–1800', *Law and History Review*, xii (1994), pp 123–53.
Stott, Anne, '"Female patriotism": Georgiana, *duchess of Devonshire* and the Westminster election of 1784', *Eighteenth-Century Life*, xvii (1993), pp 60–84.
Sturtz, Linda, 'The ladies and the lottery: elite women's gambling in eighteenth-century Virginia', *The Virginia Magazine of History and Biography: Constructing a Revolution: Women and Gender Roles in Virginia*, civ (1996), pp 165–84.
Tague, Ingrid, 'Love, honor, and obedience: fashionable women and the discourse of marriage in the early eighteenth century', *Journal of British Studies*, xl (2001), pp 76–106.
Urquhart, Diane, 'Irish divorce and domestic violence, 1857–1922', *Women's History Review*, xxii (2013), pp 820–37.
Vickery, Amanda, 'Golden age to separate spheres? A review of the categories and chronology of English women's history', *Historical Journal*, xxxvi (1993), pp 383–414.
Vickery, Amanda, 'His and hers: gender, consumption and household accounting in eighteenth-century England' in *Past and Present*, supplement, i (2006), pp 12–38.
Wilson, Rachel, 'The vicereines of Ireland and the transformation of the Dublin court, c. 1703–1737', *The Court Historian*, xix (2014), pp 3–28.
Wolfram, Sybil, 'Divorce in England 1700–1857', *Oxford Journal of Legal Studies*, v (1985), pp 155–86.

ELECTRONIC RESOURCES

'Castletown house' (http://www.castletownhouse.ie) (accessed 14 Aug. 2013).
'Dictionary of Irish biography' (www.dib.cambridge.org) (accessed 06 Feb. 2015).
'Inchiquin papers' (http://www.nli.ie/pdfs/mss%20lists/143_Inchiquin.pdf) (accessed 3 Aug. 2012).
'Inventing and reinventing the Irish woman'
(http://www.ul.ie/inventing/content/resources) (accessed 09 July 2014).
'Irish Legislation Database'
(http://www.qub.ac.uk/ild/) (accessed 05 Apr. 2011).
'National Archives currency converter' (http://apps.nationalarchives.gov.uk/currency/results.asp#mid) (accessed 28 Sept. 2014).
'National inventory of architectural heritage' (http://www.buildingsofireland.ie) (accessed 28 Nov. 2014).
'Oxford dictionary of national biography' (www.oxforddnb.com) (accessed 06 Feb. 2015).
'The workhouse in Ireland' (http://www.workhouses.org.uk/Ireland/) (accessed 2 Dec. 2014).

THESES

Dain, Angela, 'Assemblies and politeness 1660–1840' (University of East Anglia, Ph.D., 2000).
McNally, Patrick, 'Patronage and politics in Ireland 1714–1727' (Queen's University Belfast, Ph.D., 1993).
Meaney, Lisa 'Civic society in eighteenth-century Ulster, c.1740–1780' (Queen's University Belfast, Ph.D., 2011).
Raughter, Rosemary, 'A natural tenderness: women's philanthropy in eighteenth-century Ireland' (University College Dublin, M.A., 1992).
Walsh, Patrick, 'The career of William Conolly, 1689–1729' (TCD, Ph.D., 2007).
Wilson, Rachel, 'The roles of elite women in Ireland, c. 1690–1745' (Queen's University Belfast, Ph.D., 2013).

Index

All persons are indexed by surname, not title. All women are indexed by their married names, unless known only by their maiden names within the book. In these cases cross references are provided for clarity. Cross references are also provided for women married more than once.